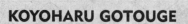

So relaxing!

I got a hot eye mask! →

KOYOHARU GOTOUGE

Hello! I'm Gotouge. Volume 9 is out. Thank you very much to everyone who helps me and cheers me on. If no one read the manga, it would just be a pile of paper, so for people to take it in their hands and open it up is a great honor. I hope for your happiness as I fire the cannon of gratefulness! I always pray for the good fortune of everyone who is kind to this author whose glasses are always askew.

DEMON SLAYER:
KIMETSU NO YAIBA
VOLUME 9
Shonen Jump Edition

Story and Art by
KOYOHARU GOTOUGE

KIMETSU NO YAIBA
© 2016 by Koyoharu Gotouge
All rights reserved. First published in Japan
in 2016 by SHUEISHA Inc., Tokyo. English
translation rights arranged by SHUEISHA Inc.

TRANSLATION John Werry
ENGLISH ADAPTATION Stan!
TOUCH-UP ART & LETTERING John Hunt
DESIGN Adam Grano
EDITOR Mike Montesa

Printed in Italy

Published by VIZ Media, LLC
P.O. Box 77010
San Francisco, CA 94107

10 9
First printing, November 2019
Ninth printing, August 2021

viz.com

DEMON SLAYER
KIMETSU NO YAIBA

9

OPERATION:
ENTERTAINMENT
DISTRICT

KOYOHARU
GOTOUGE

CHARACTERS

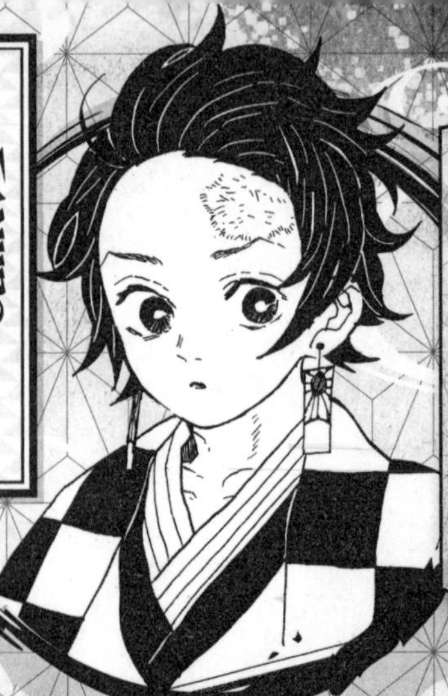

TANJIRO KAMADO

A kind boy who saved his younger sister and now aims to avenge his family. He can smell the scent of demons and an opponent's weakness.

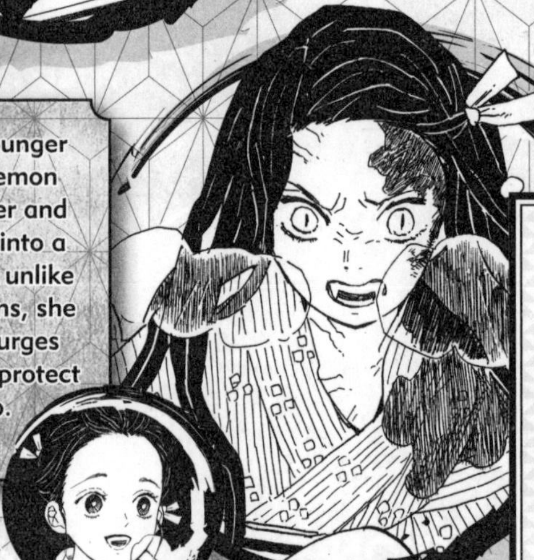

NEZUKO KAMADO

Tanjiro's younger sister. A demon attacked her and turned her into a demon. But unlike other demons, she fights her urges and tries to protect Tanjiro.

STORY

In Taisho-era Japan, young Tanjiro makes a living selling charcoal. One day, demons kill his family and turn his younger sister Nezuko into a demon. Tanjiro and Nezuko set out to find a way to return Nezuko to human form and defeat Kibutsuji, the demon who killed their family!

After joining the Demon Slayer Corps, Tanjiro meets Tamayo and Yushiro—demons who oppose Kibutsuji—who provide a clue to how Nezuko may be turned back into a human. On a new mission, Tanjiro boards a steam train and joins up with Rengoku, the Flame Hashira. A lower-rank demon attacks the train, but they are able to protect the passengers and defeat the demon. However, the upper-rank demon Akaza appears and defeats Rengoku. Tanjiro survives the encounter and embarks on a new mission with the Sound Hashira, Uzui!

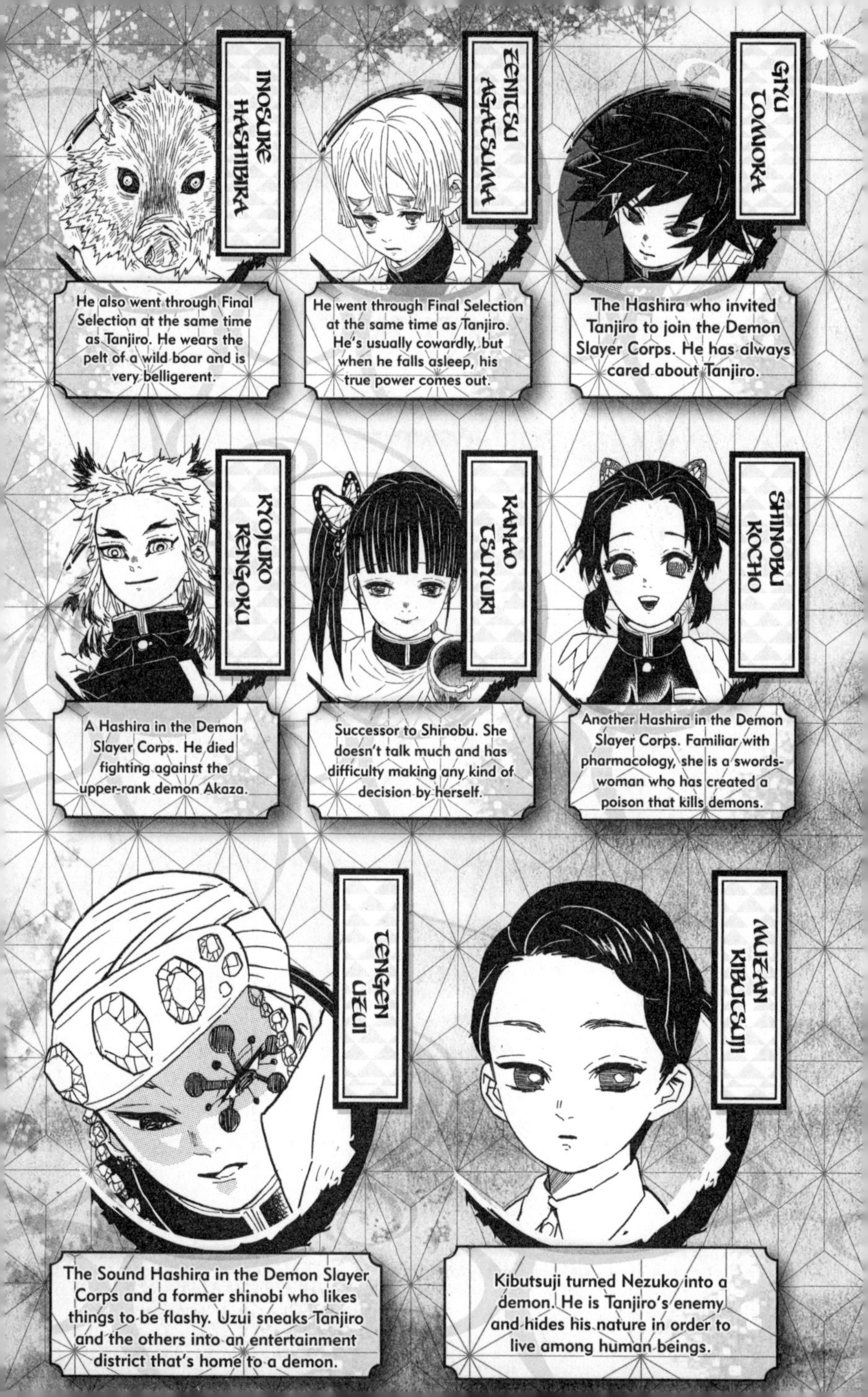
GIYU TOMIOKA
The Hashira who invited Tanjiro to join the Demon Slayer Corps. He has always cared about Tanjiro.
ZENITSU AGATSUMA
He went through Final Selection at the same time as Tanjiro. He's usually cowardly, but when he falls asleep, his true power comes out.
INOSUKE HASHIBIRA
He also went through Final Selection at the same time as Tanjiro. He wears the pelt of a wild boar and is very belligerent.
SHINOBU KOCHO
Another Hashira in the Demon Slayer Corps. Familiar with pharmacology, she is a swords-woman who has created a poison that kills demons.
KANAO TSUYURI
Successor to Shinobu. She doesn't talk much and has difficulty making any kind of decision by herself.
KYOJURO RENGOKU
A Hashira in the Demon Slayer Corps. He died fighting against the upper-rank demon Akaza.
MUZAN KIBUTSUJI
Kibutsuji turned Nezuko into a demon. He is Tanjiro's enemy and hides his nature in order to live among human beings.
TENGEN UZUI
The Sound Hashira in the Demon Slayer Corps and a former shinobi who likes things to be flashy. Uzui sneaks Tanjiro and the others into an entertainment district that's home to a demon.

CONTENTS

DEMON SLAYER
KIMETSU NO YAIBA

9

OPERATION: ENTERTAINMENT DISTRICT

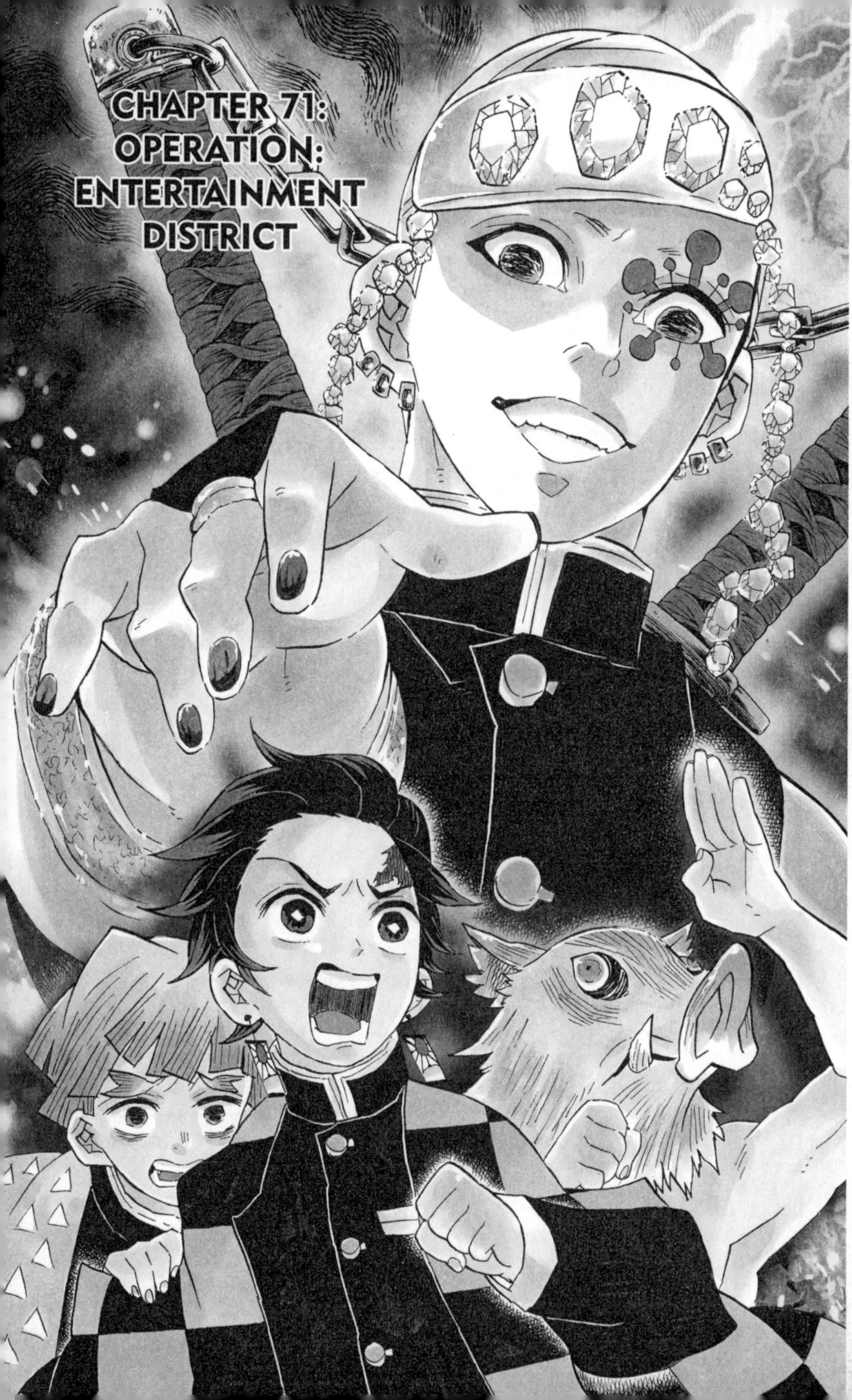
CHAPTER 71:
OPERATION:
ENTERTAINMENT
DISTRICT

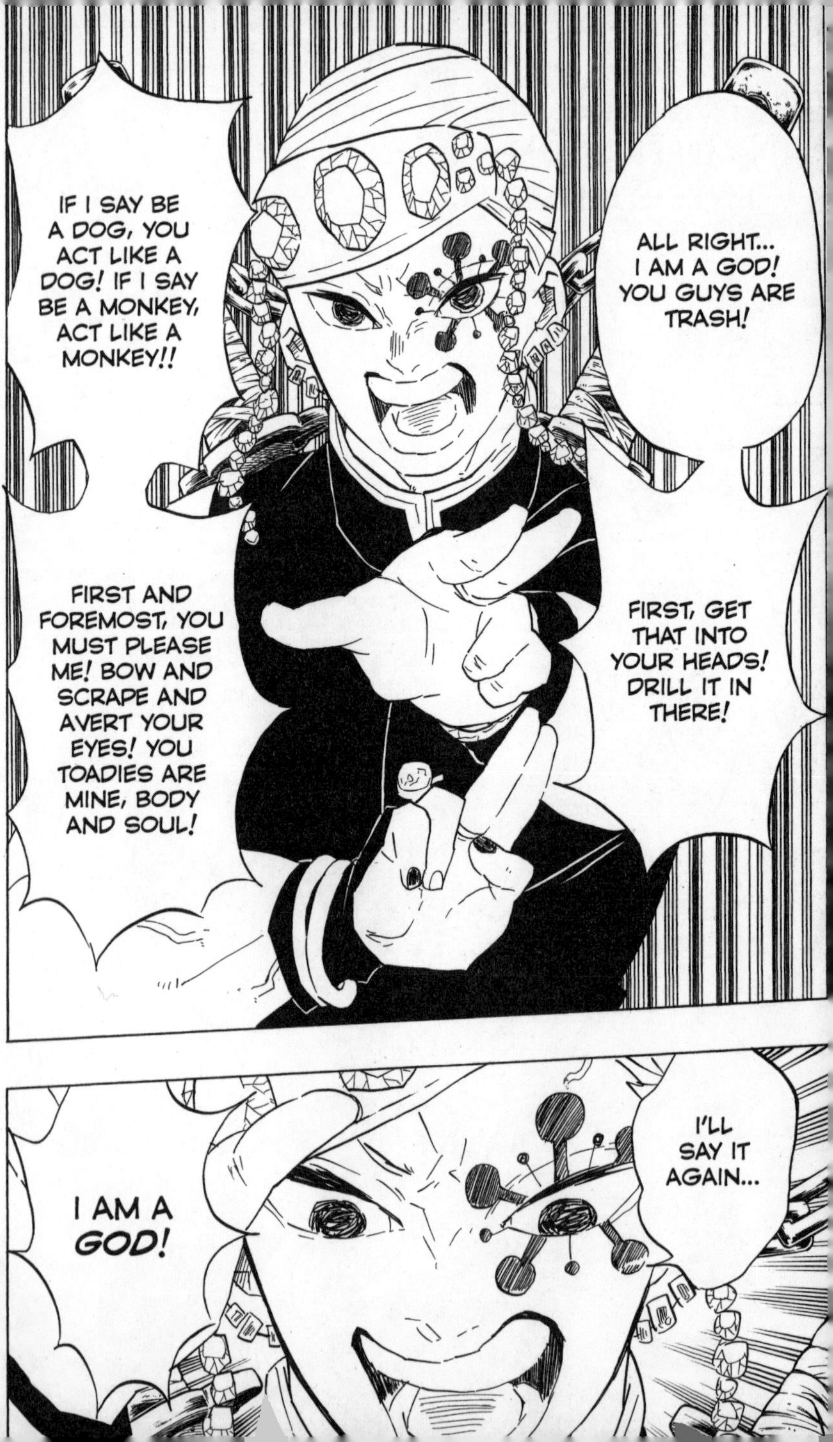
ALL RIGHT... I AM A GOD! YOU GUYS ARE TRASH!
IF I SAY BE A DOG, YOU ACT LIKE A DOG! IF I SAY BE A MONKEY, ACT LIKE A MONKEY!!
FIRST, GET THAT INTO YOUR HEADS! DRILL IT IN THERE!
FIRST AND FOREMOST, YOU MUST PLEASE ME! BOW AND SCRAPE AND AVERT YOUR EYES! YOU TOADIES ARE MINE, BODY AND SOUL!
I'LL SAY IT AGAIN...
I AM A GOD!

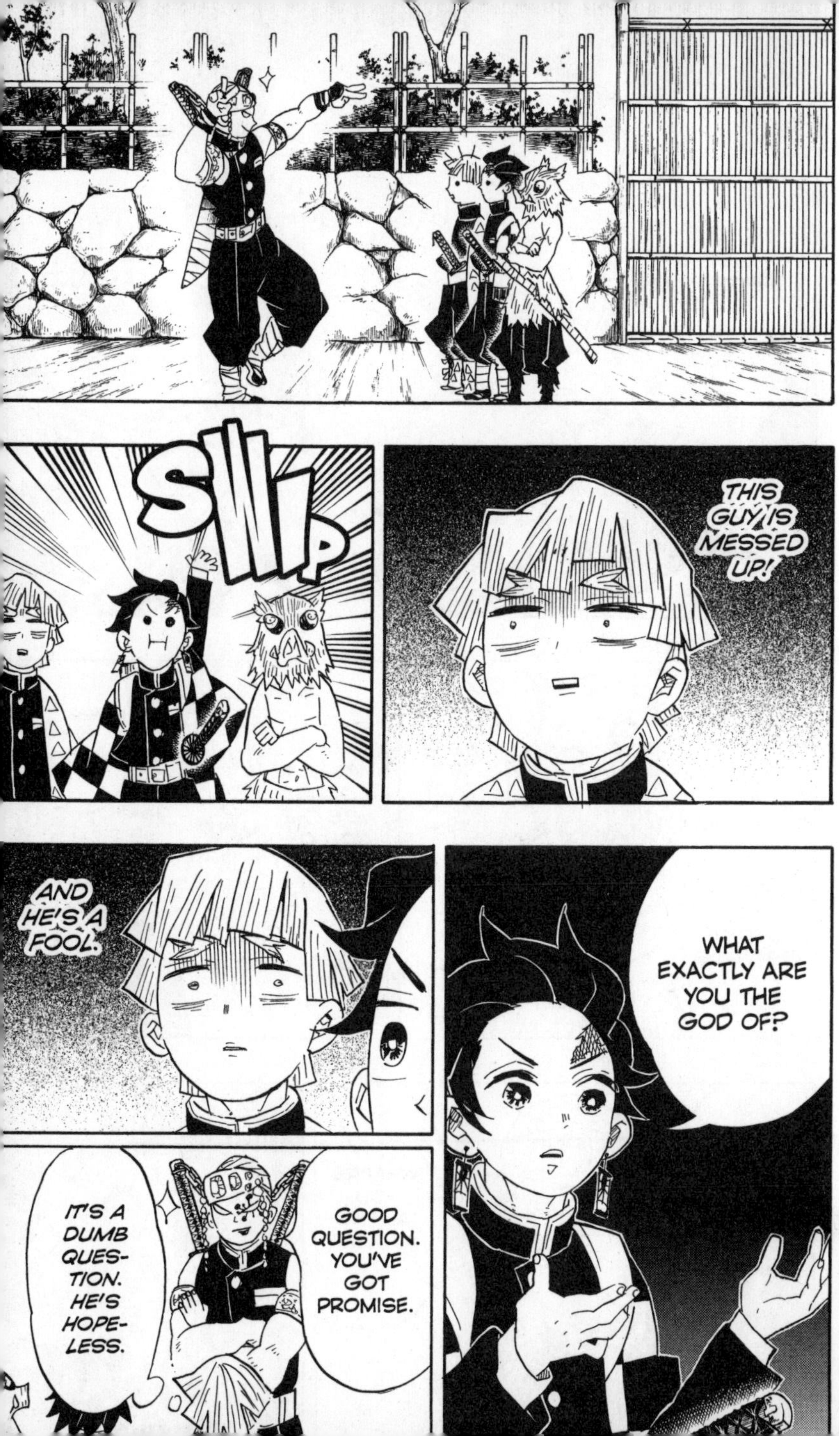
THIS GUY IS MESSED UP!
WHAT EXACTLY ARE YOU THE GOD OF?
AND HE'S A FOOL.
GOOD QUESTION. YOU'VE GOT PROMISE.
IT'S A DUMB QUES-TION. HE'S HOPE-LESS.

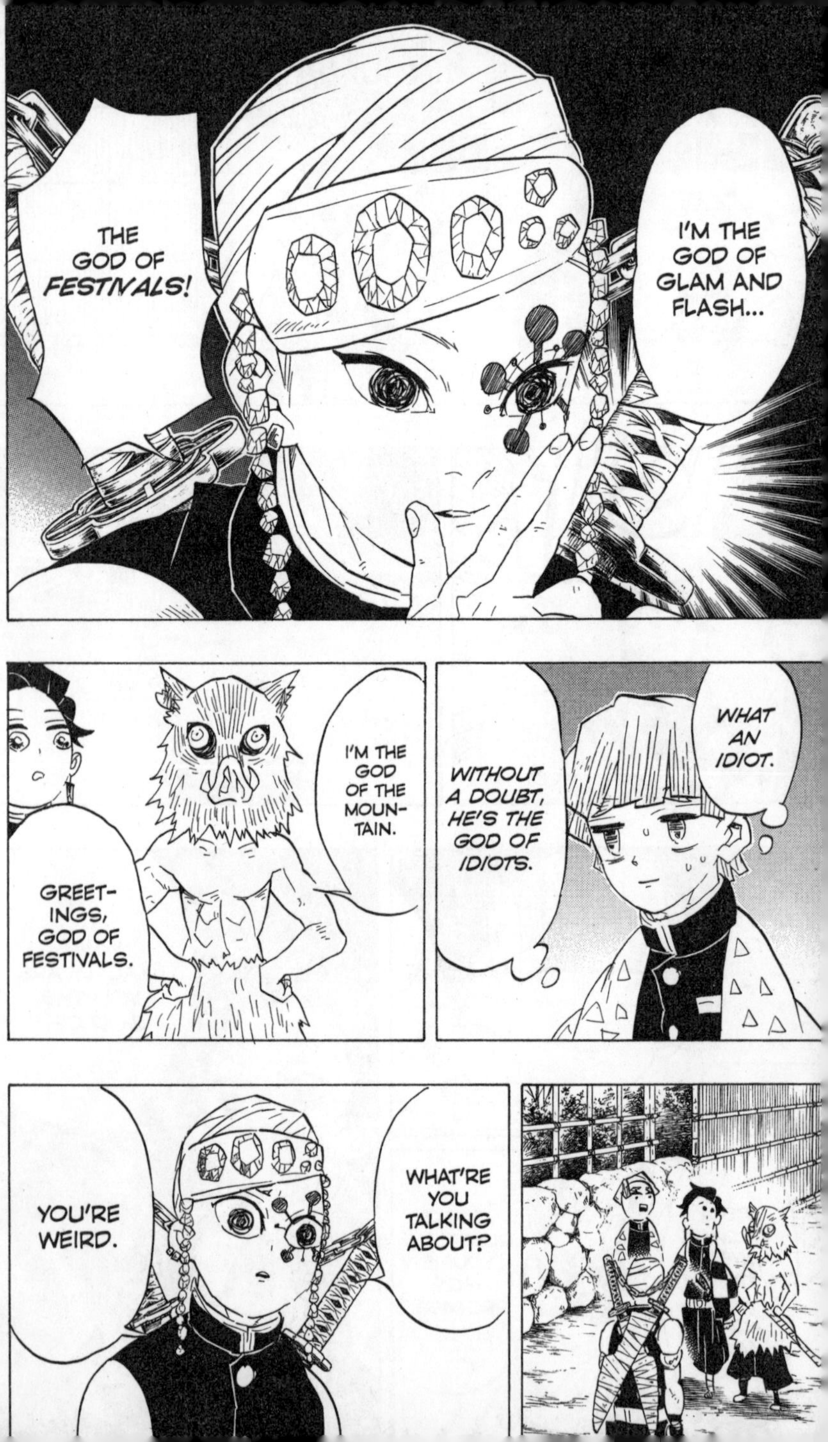
I'M THE GOD OF GLAM AND FLASH...
THE GOD OF *FESTIVALS!*
WHAT AN IDIOT.
WITHOUT A DOUBT, HE'S THE GOD OF IDIOTS.
I'M THE GOD OF THE MOUNTAIN.
GREETINGS, GOD OF FESTIVALS.
WHAT'RE YOU TALKING ABOUT?
YOU'RE WEIRD.

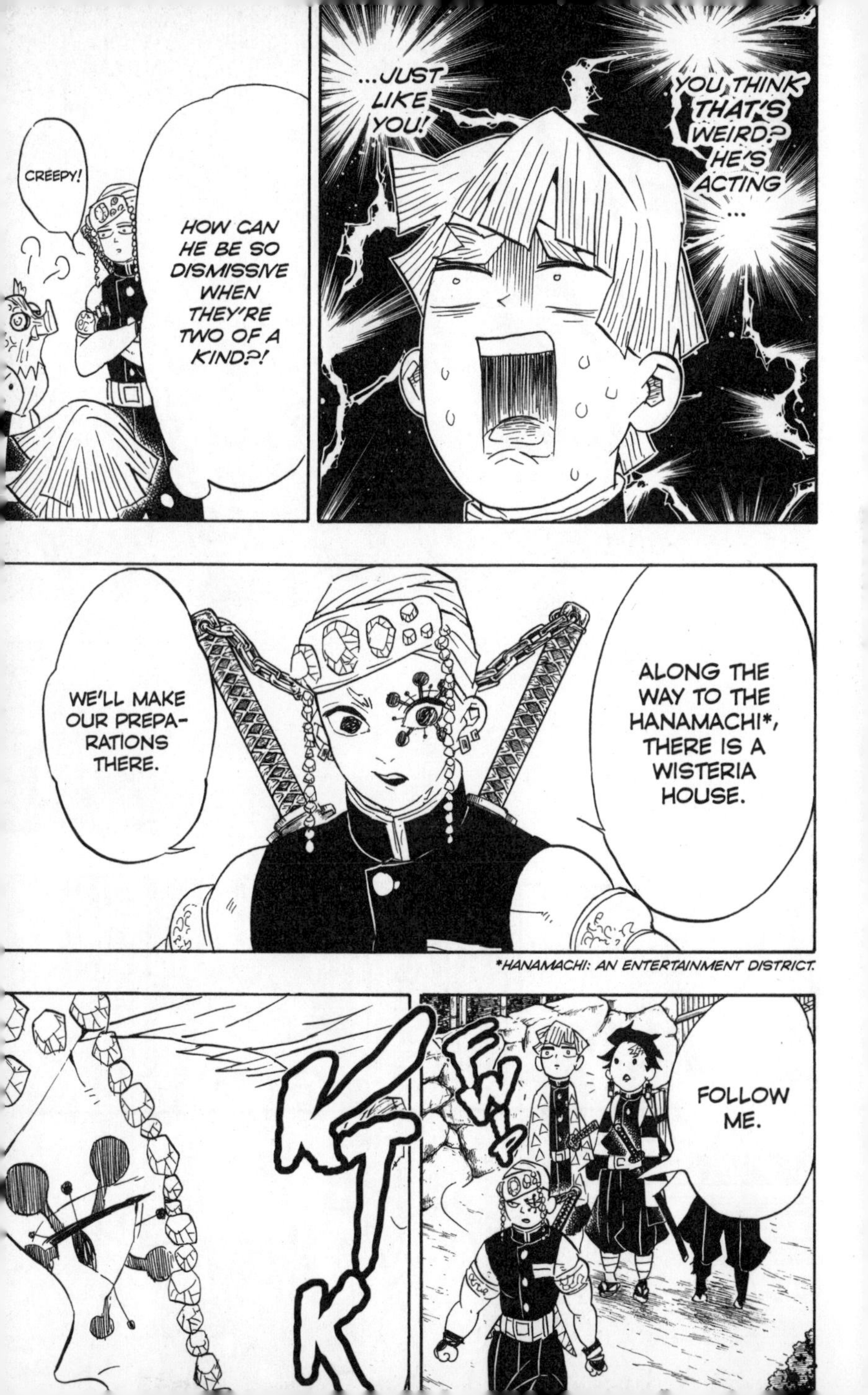
YOU THINK THAT'S WEIRD? HE'S ACTING ...
...JUST LIKE YOU!
HOW CAN HE BE SO DISMISSIVE WHEN THEY'RE TWO OF A KIND?!
CREEPY!
ALONG THE WAY TO THE HANAMACHI*, THERE IS A WISTERIA HOUSE.
WE'LL MAKE OUR PREPA- RATIONS THERE.
FOLLOW ME.
FWIP
KTK

*HANAMACHI: AN ENTERTAINMENT DISTRICT.

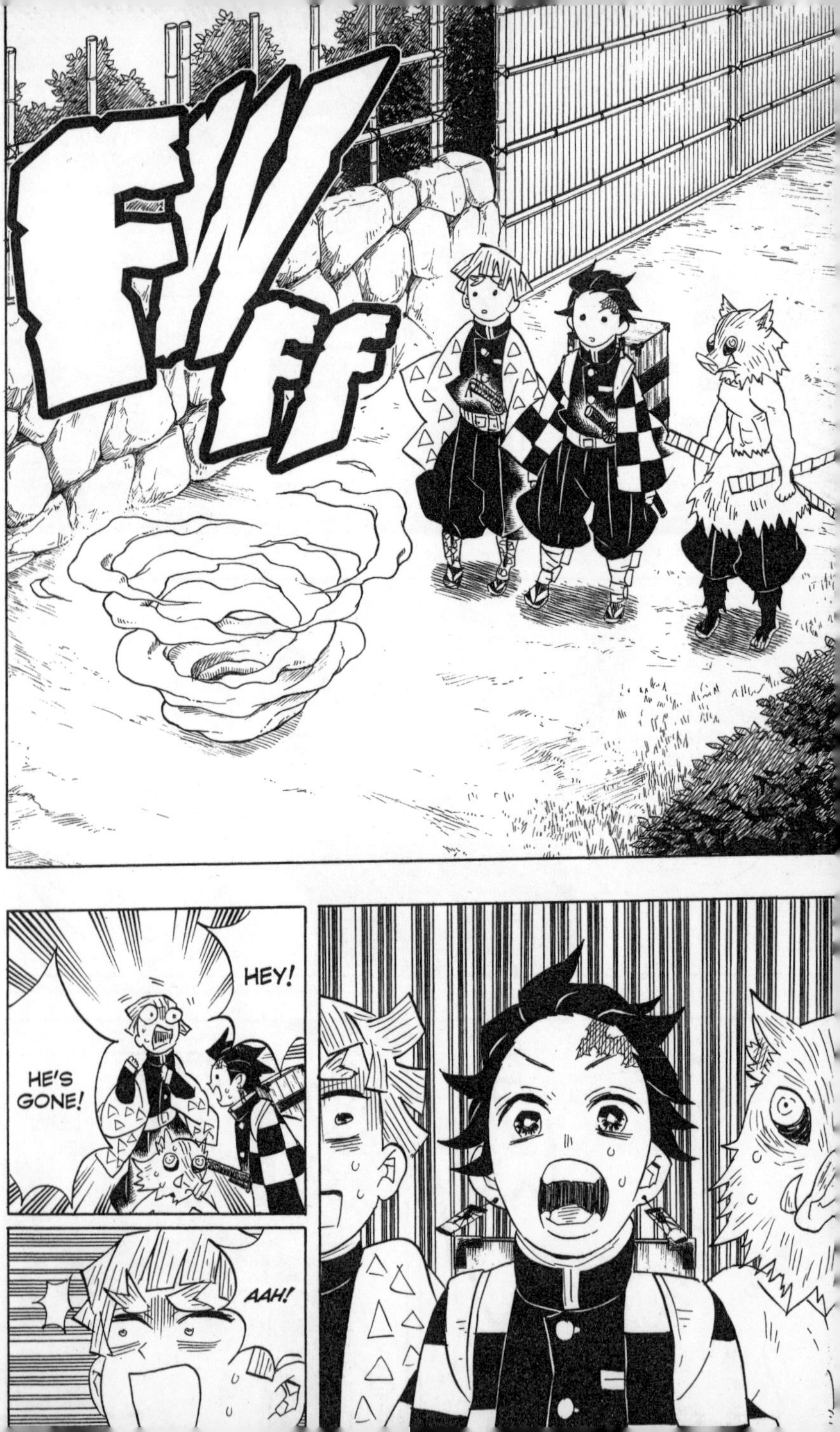
FWFF
HEY!
HE'S GONE!
AAH!

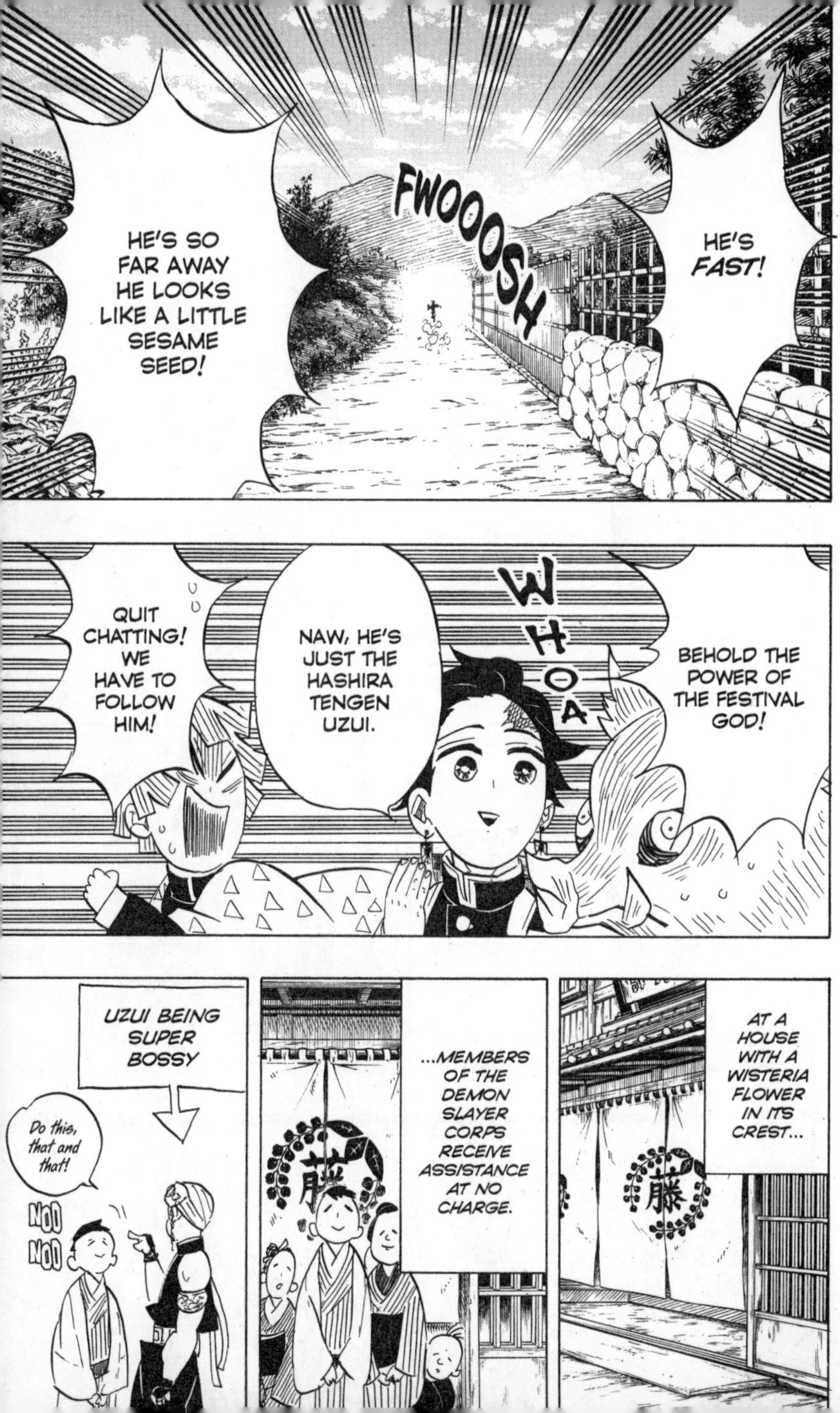
HE'S FAST!
FWOOOSH
HE'S SO FAR AWAY HE LOOKS LIKE A LITTLE SESAME SEED!
BEHOLD THE POWER OF THE FESTIVAL GOD!
WHOA
NAW, HE'S JUST THE HASHIRA TENGEN UZUI.
QUIT CHATTING! WE HAVE TO FOLLOW HIM!
AT A HOUSE WITH A WISTERIA FLOWER IN ITS CREST...
...MEMBERS OF THE DEMON SLAYER CORPS RECEIVE ASSISTANCE AT NO CHARGE.
藤
UZUI BEING SUPER BOSSY
Do this, that and that!
NOD NOD

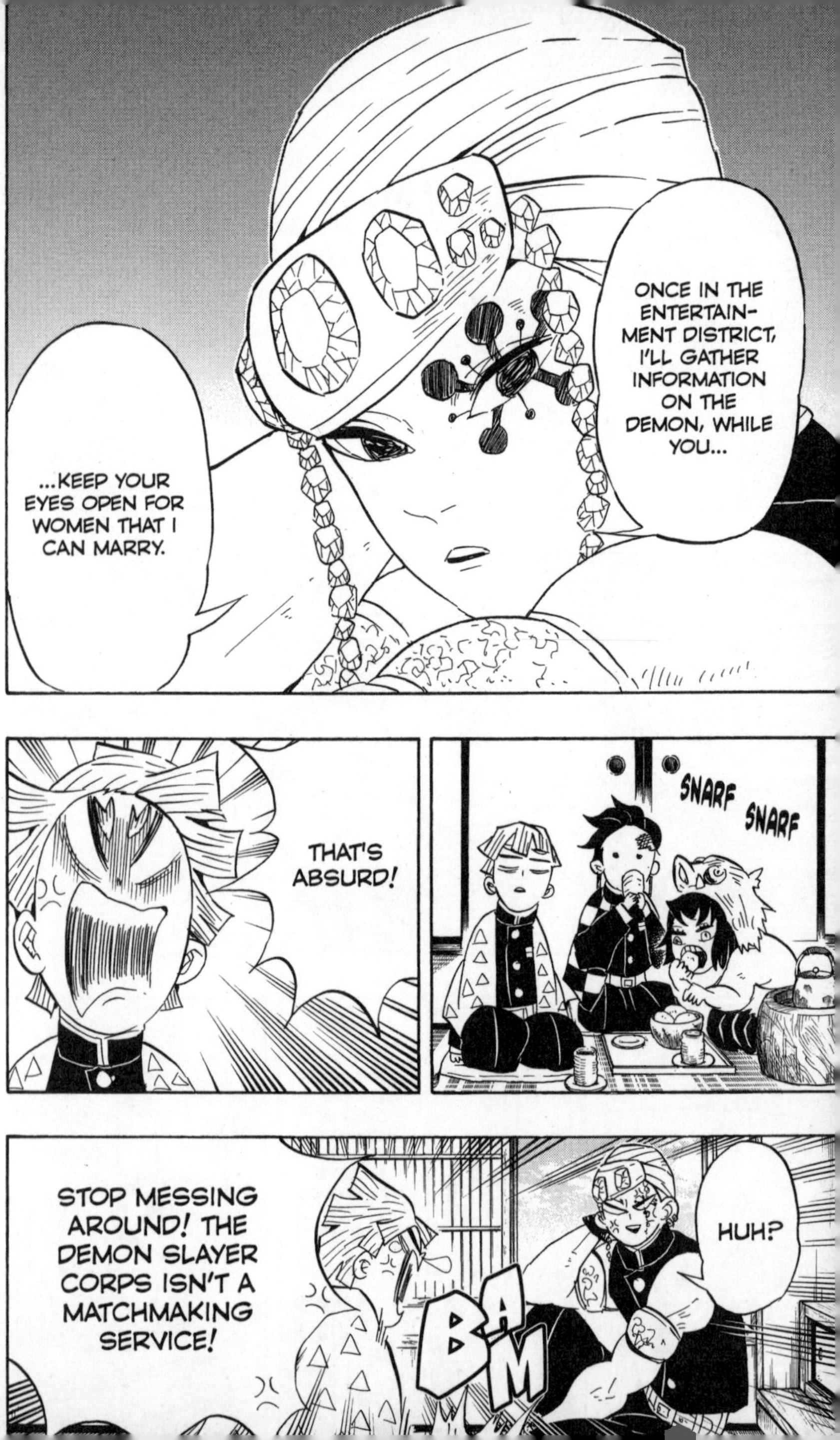
ONCE IN THE ENTERTAIN-MENT DISTRICT, I'LL GATHER INFORMATION ON THE DEMON, WHILE YOU...
...KEEP YOUR EYES OPEN FOR WOMEN THAT I CAN MARRY.
SNARF SNARF
THAT'S ABSURD!
HUH?
STOP MESSING AROUND! THE DEMON SLAYER CORPS ISN'T A MATCHMAKING SERVICE!
BAM

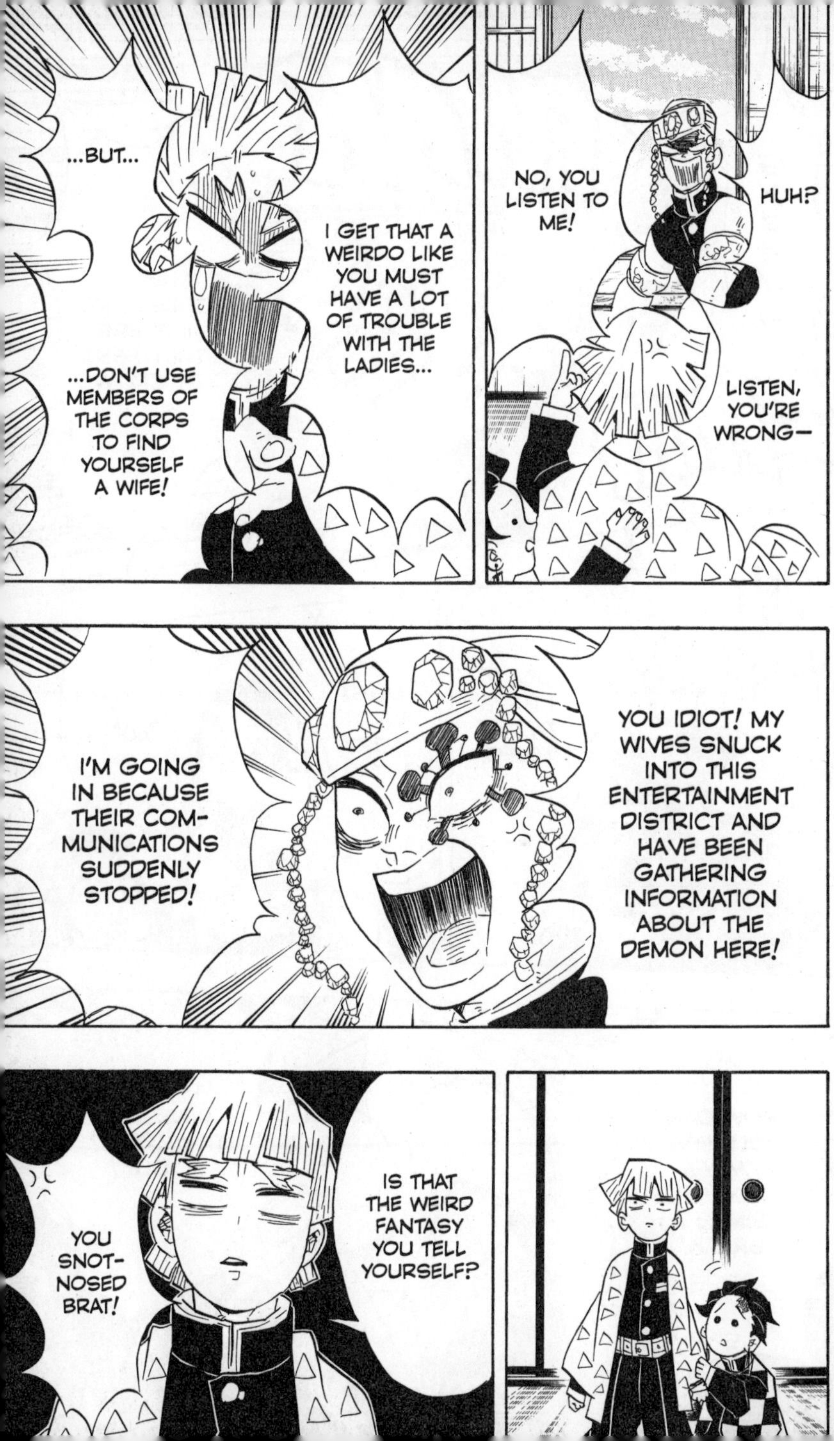
HUH?
LISTEN, YOU'RE WRONG—
NO, YOU LISTEN TO ME!
I GET THAT A WEIRDO LIKE YOU MUST HAVE A LOT OF TROUBLE WITH THE LADIES...
...BUT...
...DON'T USE MEMBERS OF THE CORPS TO FIND YOURSELF A WIFE!
YOU IDIOT! MY WIVES SNUCK INTO THIS ENTERTAINMENT DISTRICT AND HAVE BEEN GATHERING INFORMATION ABOUT THE DEMON HERE!
I'M GOING IN BECAUSE THEIR COM-MUNICATIONS SUDDENLY STOPPED!
IS THAT THE WEIRD FANTASY YOU TELL YOURSELF?
YOU SNOT-NOSED BRAT!

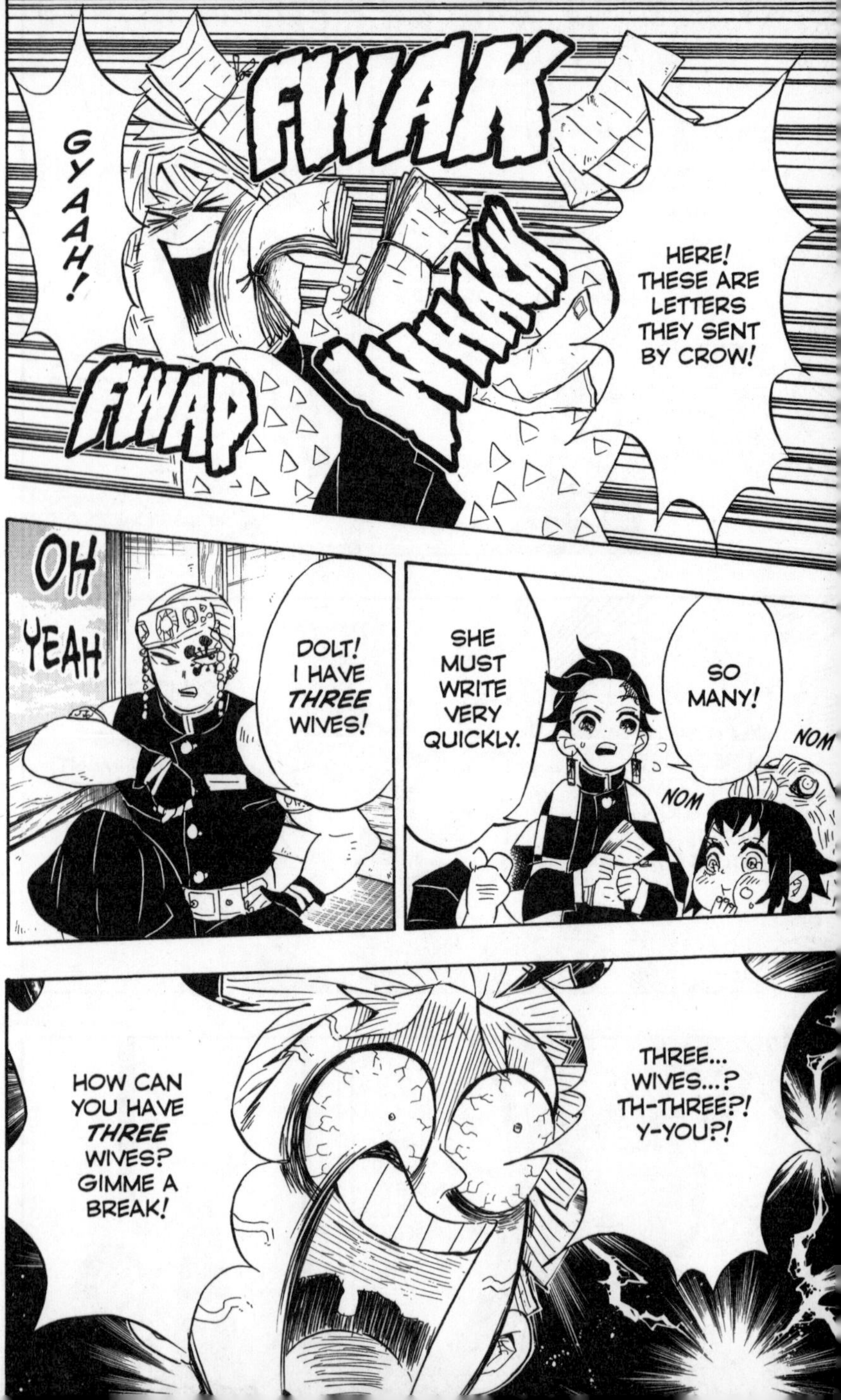
HERE! THESE ARE LETTERS THEY SENT BY CROW!
FWAK
FWAP
GYAAH!
SO MANY!
NOM
NOM
SHE MUST WRITE VERY QUICKLY.
DOLT! I HAVE *THREE* WIVES!
OH YEAH
THREE... WIVES...? TH-THREE?! Y-YOU?!
HOW CAN YOU HAVE *THREE* WIVES? GIMME A BREAK!

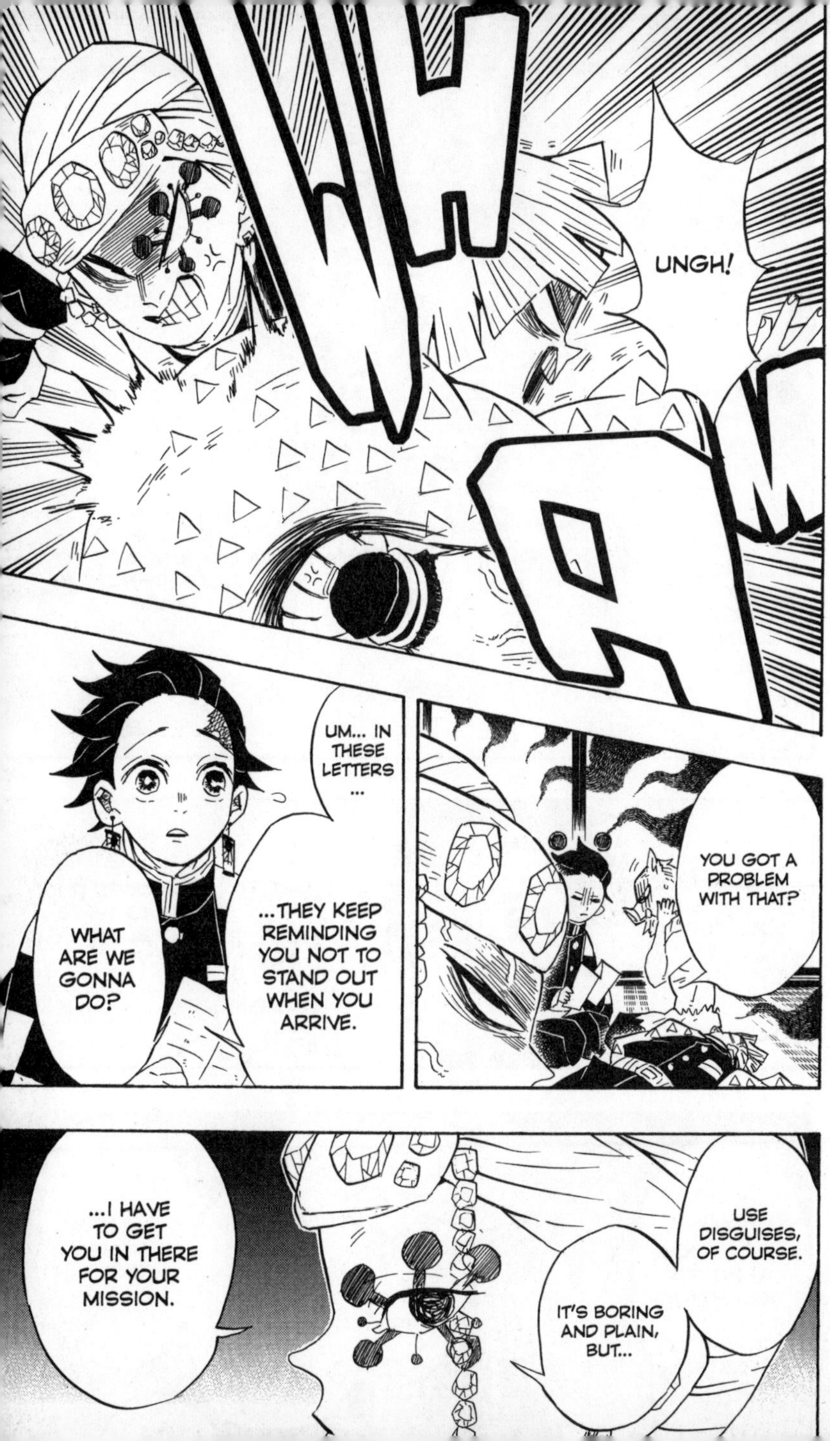
UNGH!
WHAM
YOU GOT A PROBLEM WITH THAT?
UM... IN THESE LETTERS ...
...THEY KEEP REMINDING YOU NOT TO STAND OUT WHEN YOU ARRIVE.
WHAT ARE WE GONNA DO?
USE DISGUISES, OF COURSE.
IT'S BORING AND PLAIN, BUT...
...I HAVE TO GET YOU IN THERE FOR YOUR MISSION.

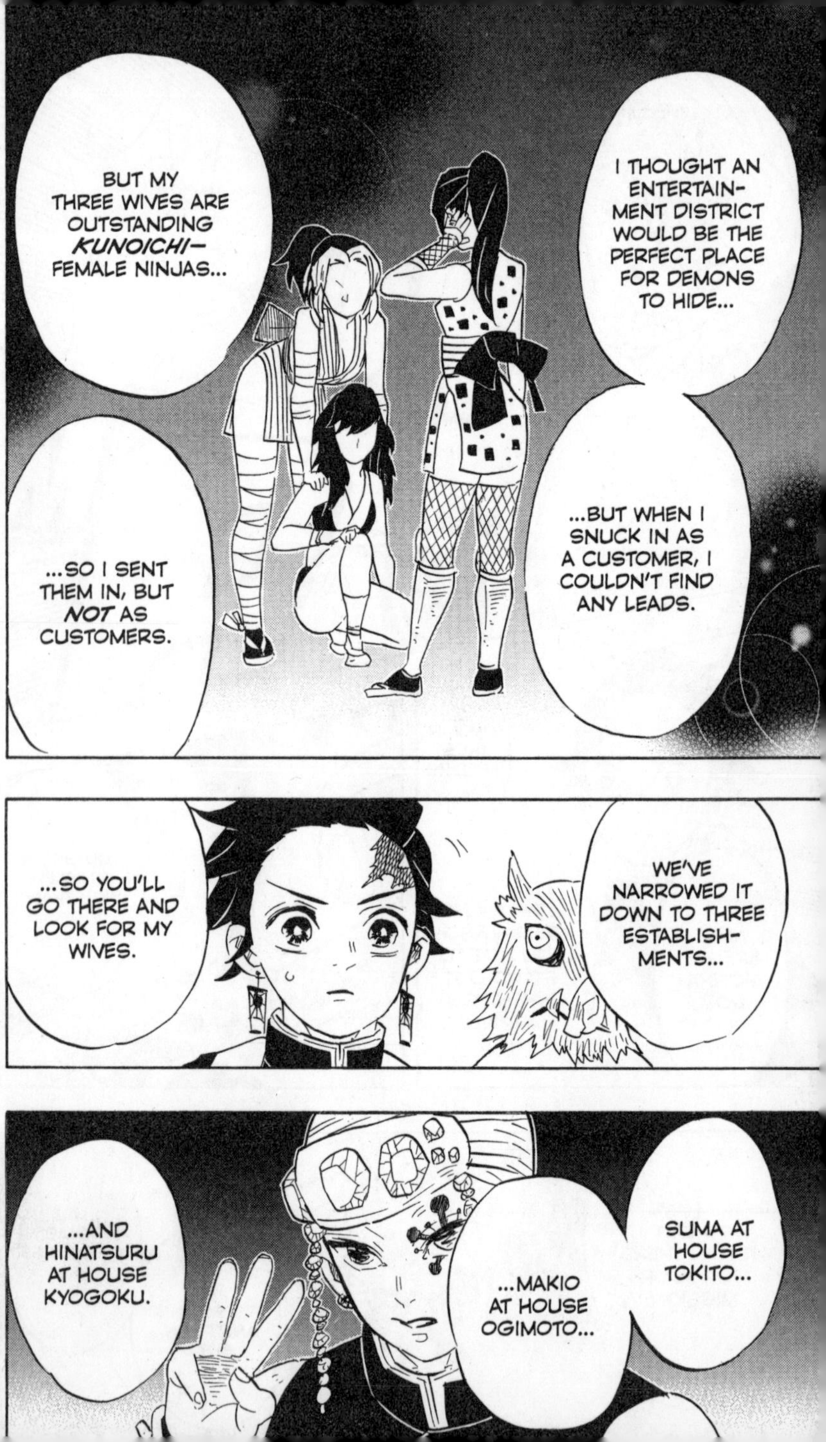
I THOUGHT AN ENTERTAIN-MENT DISTRICT WOULD BE THE PERFECT PLACE FOR DEMONS TO HIDE...
...BUT WHEN I SNUCK IN AS A CUSTOMER, I COULDN'T FIND ANY LEADS.
BUT MY THREE WIVES ARE OUTSTANDING *KUNOICHI*—FEMALE NINJAS...
...SO I SENT THEM IN, BUT *NOT* AS CUSTOMERS.
WE'VE NARROWED IT DOWN TO THREE ESTABLISH-MENTS...
...SO YOU'LL GO THERE AND LOOK FOR MY WIVES.
SUMA AT HOUSE TOKITO...
...MAKIO AT HOUSE OGIMOTO...
...AND HINATSURU AT HOUSE KYOGOKU.

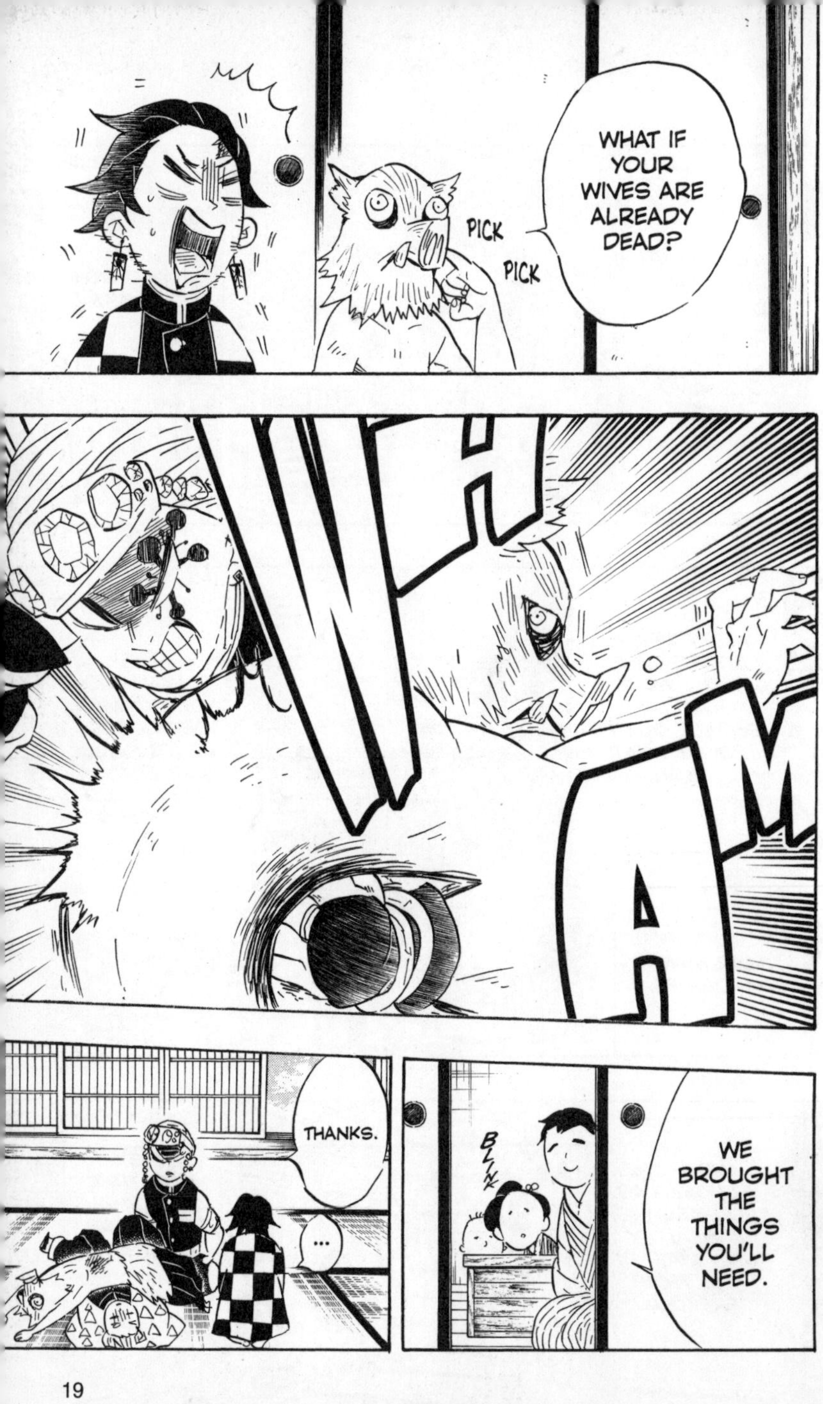
WHAT IF YOUR WIVES ARE ALREADY DEAD?
PICK
PICK
WHAM
WE BROUGHT THE THINGS YOU'LL NEED.
BLINK
THANKS.
...

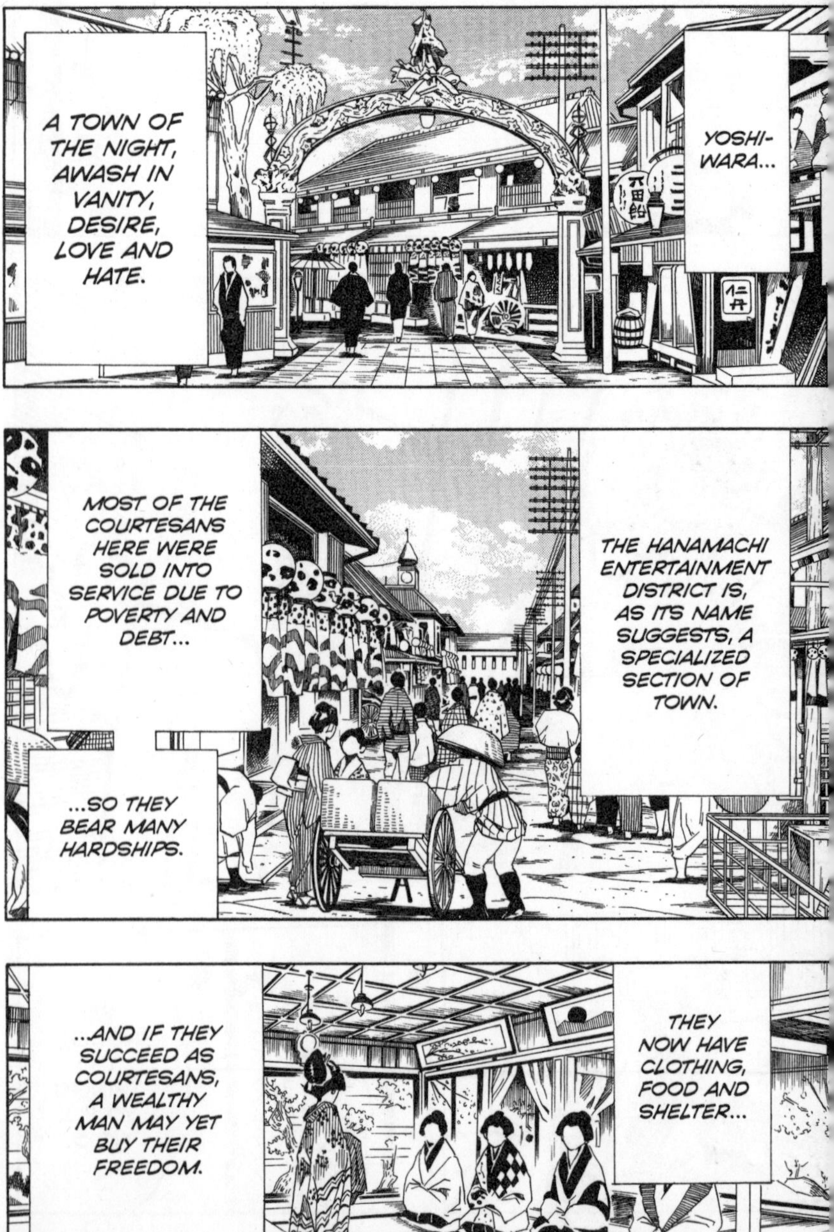
YOSHI-WARA...
A TOWN OF THE NIGHT, AWASH IN VANITY, DESIRE, LOVE AND HATE.
THE HANAMACHI ENTERTAINMENT DISTRICT IS, AS ITS NAME SUGGESTS, A SPECIALIZED SECTION OF TOWN.
MOST OF THE COURTESANS HERE WERE SOLD INTO SERVICE DUE TO POVERTY AND DEBT...
...SO THEY BEAR MANY HARDSHIPS.
THEY NOW HAVE CLOTHING, FOOD AND SHELTER...
...AND IF THEY SUCCEED AS COURTESANS, A WEALTHY MAN MAY YET BUY THEIR FREEDOM.

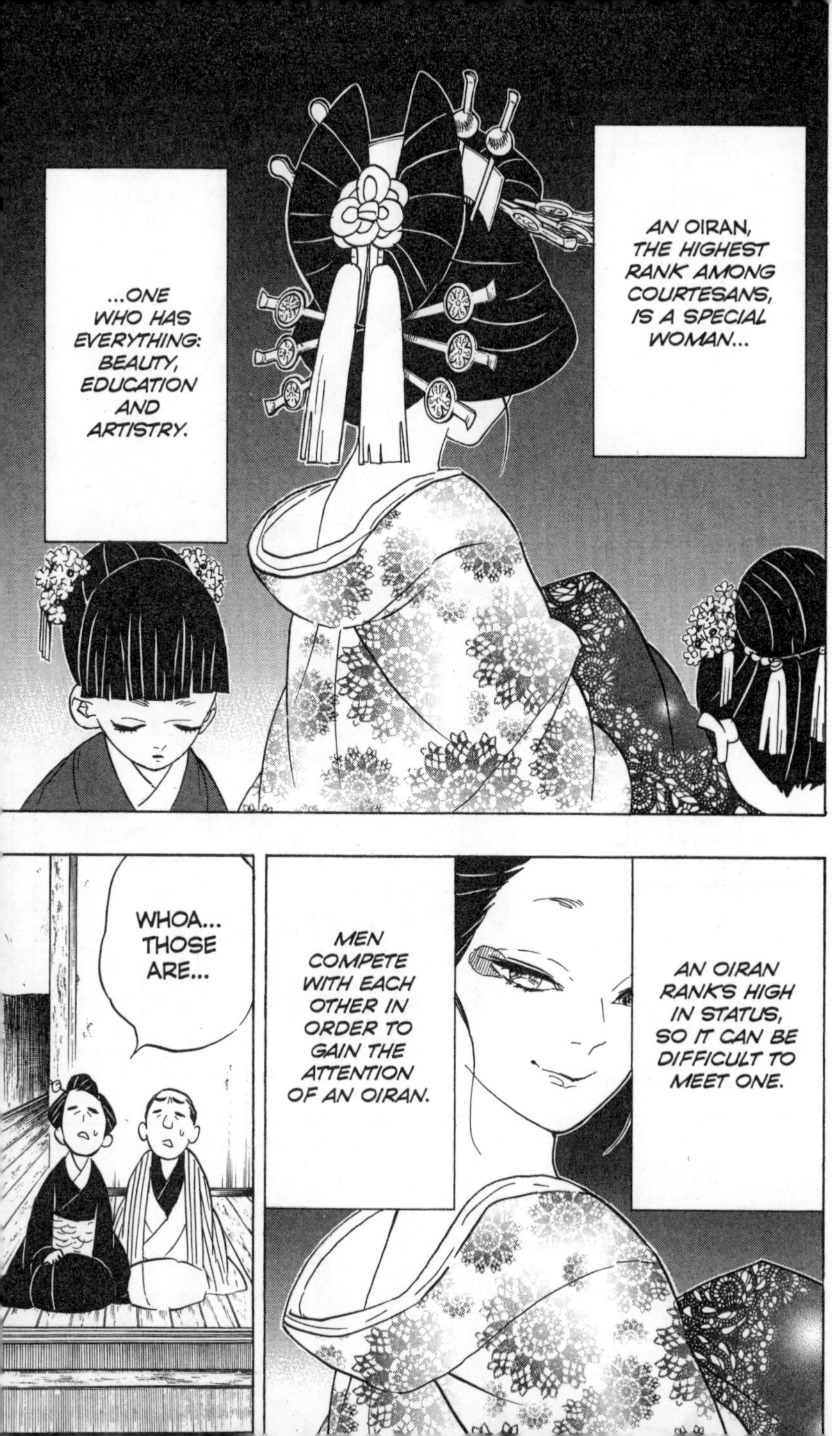
AN OIRAN, THE HIGHEST RANK AMONG COURTESANS, IS A SPECIAL WOMAN...
...ONE WHO HAS EVERYTHING: BEAUTY, EDUCATION AND ARTISTRY.
AN OIRAN RANK'S HIGH IN STATUS, SO IT CAN BE DIFFICULT TO MEET ONE.
MEN COMPETE WITH EACH OTHER IN ORDER TO GAIN THE ATTENTION OF AN OIRAN.
WHOA... THOSE ARE...

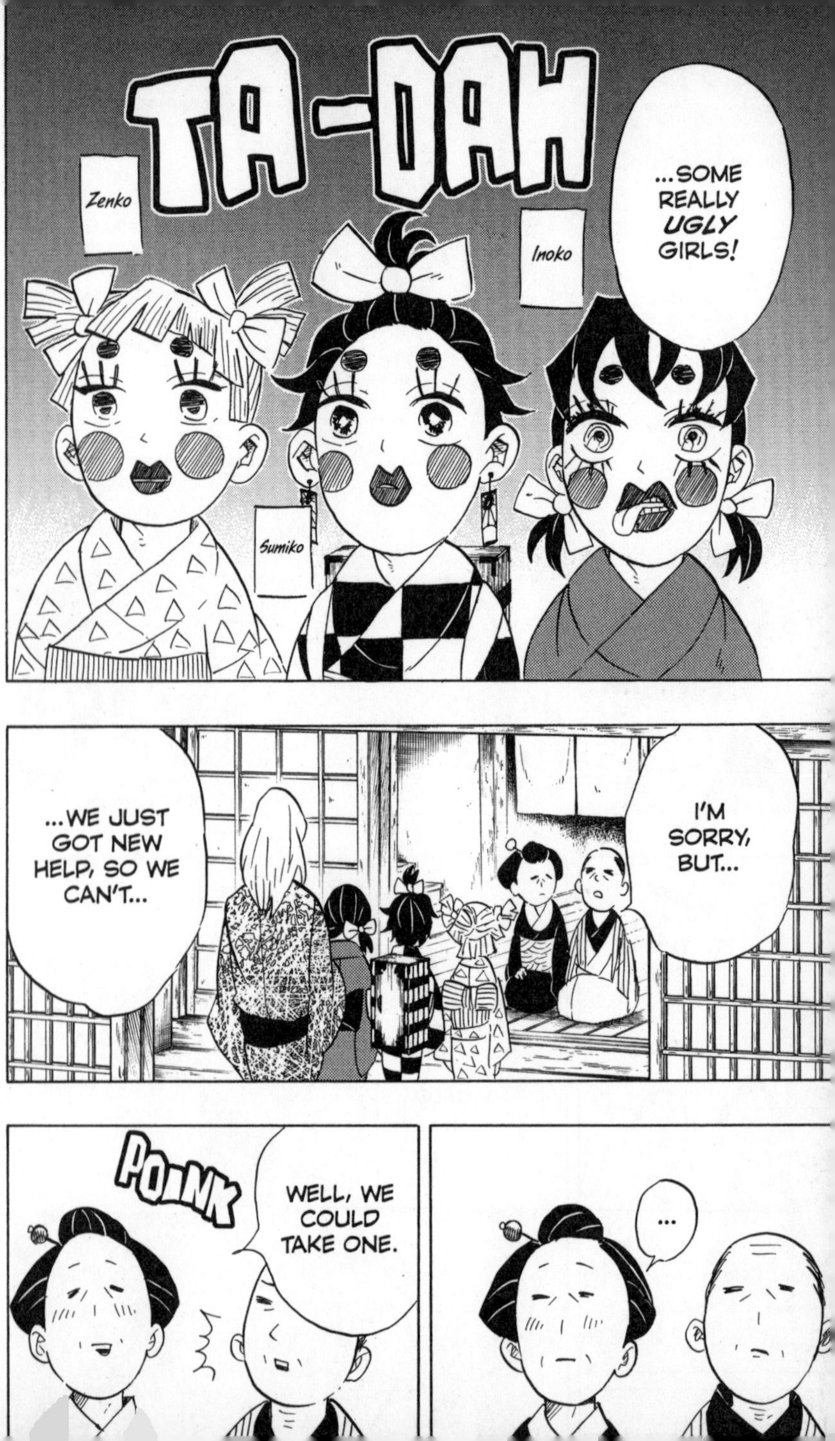

TA-DAH
...SOME REALLY UGLY GIRLS!
Inoko
Zenko
Sumiko
I'M SORRY, BUT...
...WE JUST GOT NEW HELP, SO WE CAN'T...
...
WELL, WE COULD TAKE ONE.
POINK

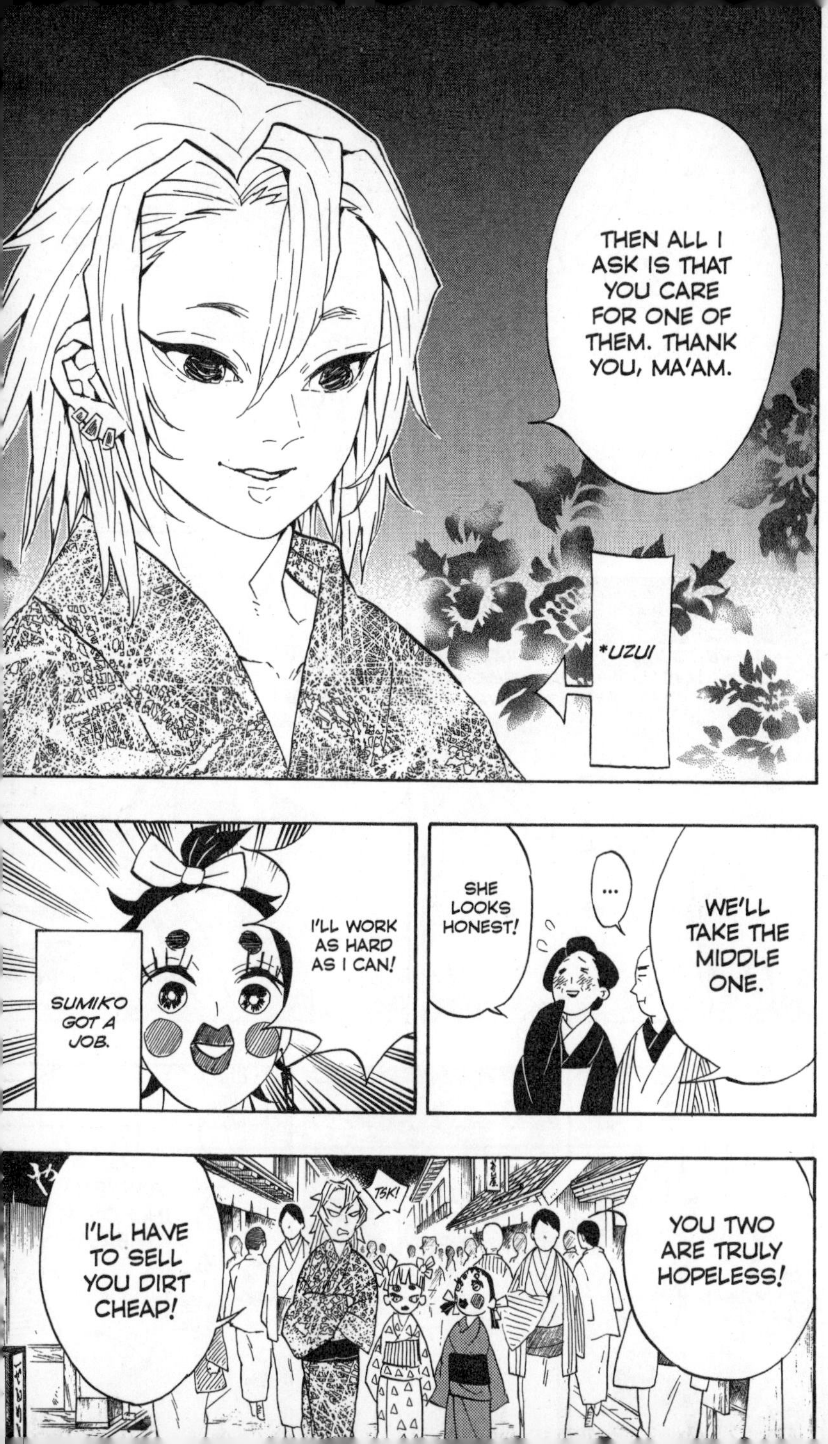
THEN ALL I ASK IS THAT YOU CARE FOR ONE OF THEM. THANK YOU, MA'AM.
*UZUI
WE'LL TAKE THE MIDDLE ONE.
...
SHE LOOKS HONEST!
I'LL WORK AS HARD AS I CAN!
SUMIKO GOT A JOB.
YOU TWO ARE TRULY HOPELESS!
TSK!
I'LL HAVE TO SELL YOU DIRT CHEAP!

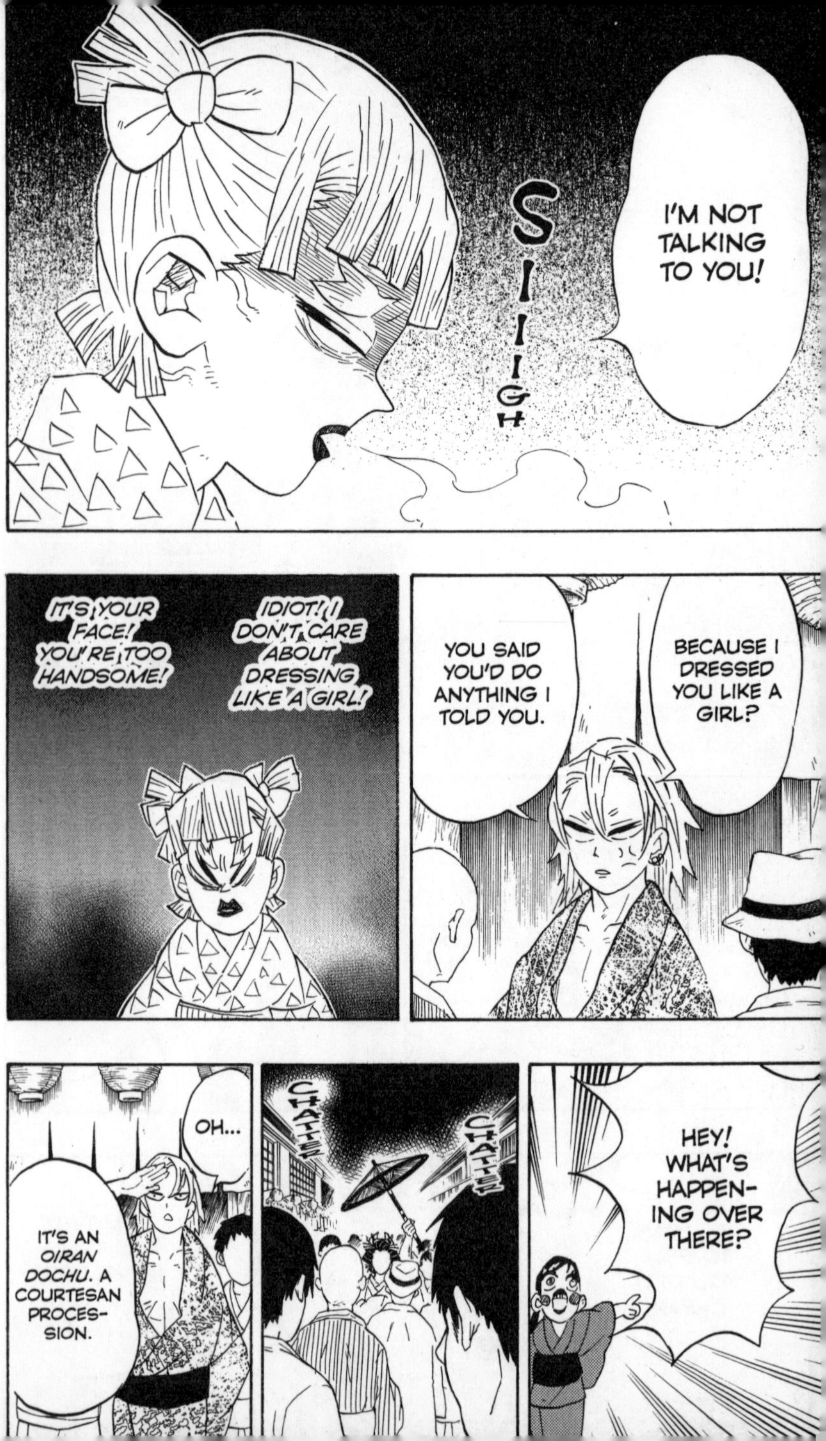
I'M NOT TALKING TO YOU!
SIIIGH
BECAUSE I DRESSED YOU LIKE A GIRL?
YOU SAID YOU'D DO ANYTHING I TOLD YOU.
IDIOT! I DON'T CARE ABOUT DRESSING LIKE A GIRL!
IT'S YOUR FACE! YOU'RE TOO HANDSOME!
HEY! WHAT'S HAPPEN-ING OVER THERE?
CHATTER
CHATTER
OH...
IT'S AN *OIRAN DOCHU*. A COURTESAN PROCES-SION.

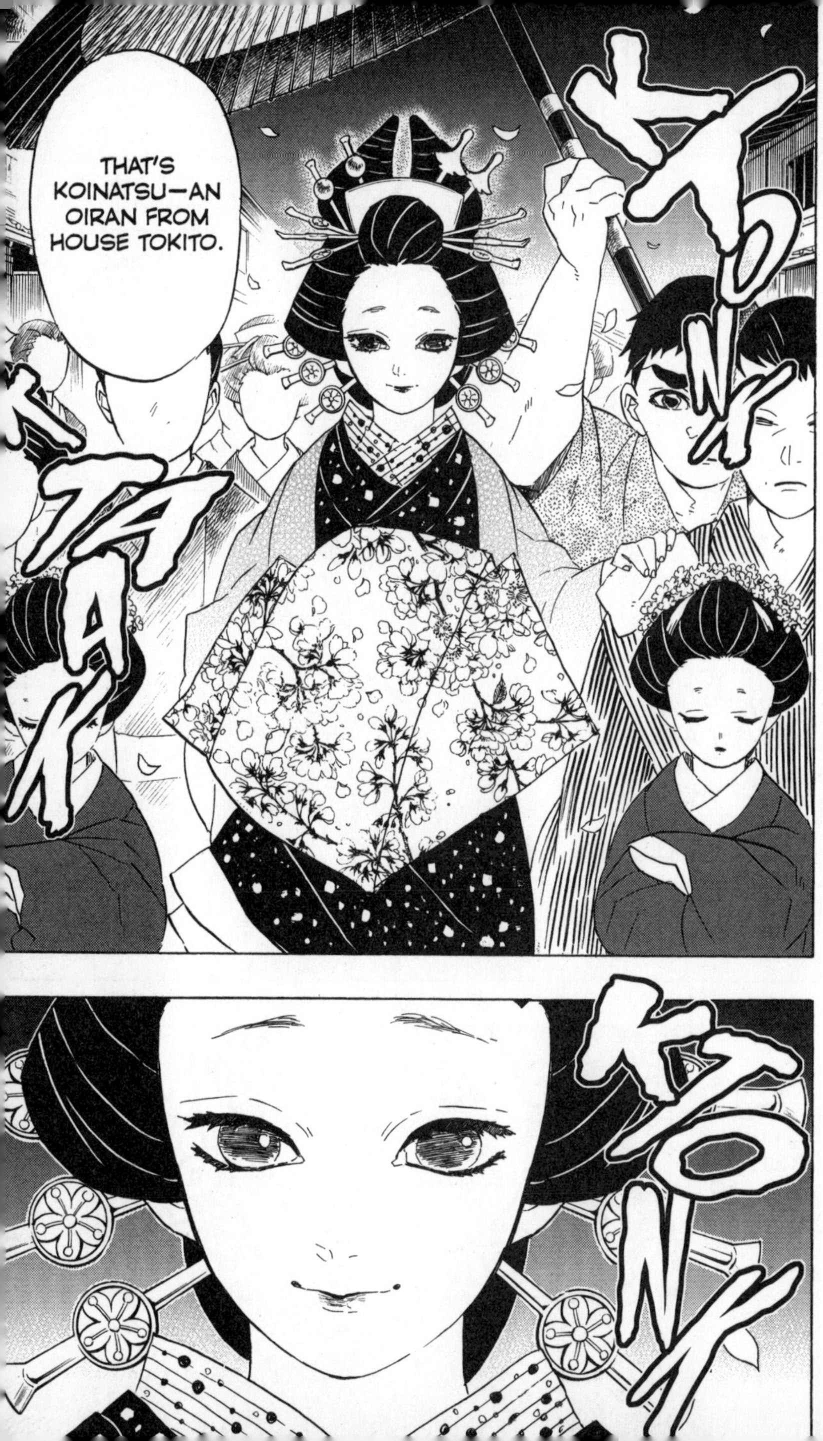
THAT'S KOINATSU—AN OIRAN FROM HOUSE TOKITO.

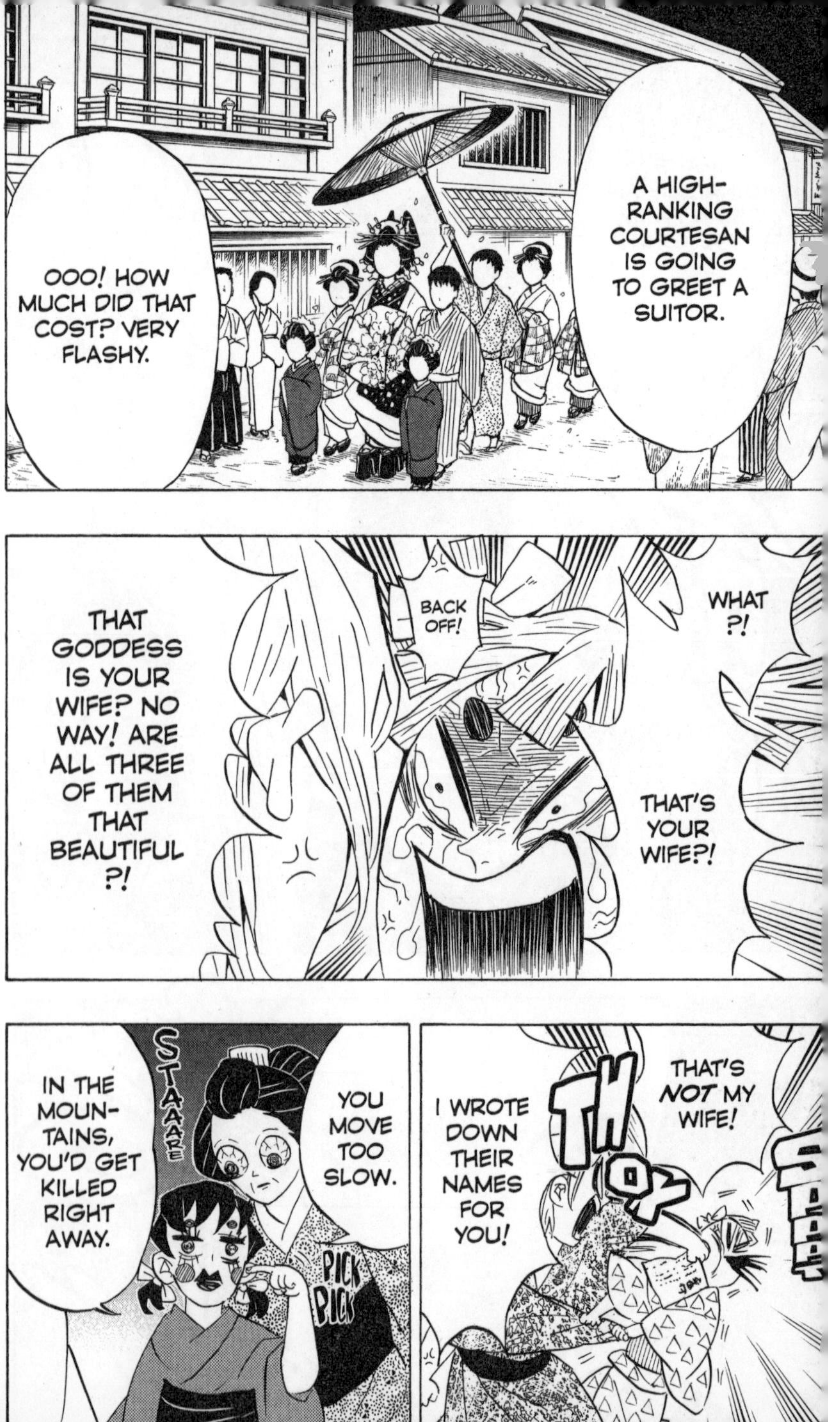
A HIGH-RANKING COURTESAN IS GOING TO GREET A SUITOR.
OOO! HOW MUCH DID THAT COST? VERY FLASHY.
WHAT?!
THAT'S YOUR WIFE?!
BACK OFF!
THAT GODDESS IS YOUR WIFE? NO WAY! ARE ALL THREE OF THEM THAT BEAUTIFUL?!
THAT'S *NOT* MY WIFE!
THOK
I WROTE DOWN THEIR NAMES FOR YOU!
YOU MOVE TOO SLOW.
STAAARE
IN THE MOUNTAINS, YOU'D GET KILLED RIGHT AWAY.
PICK PICK

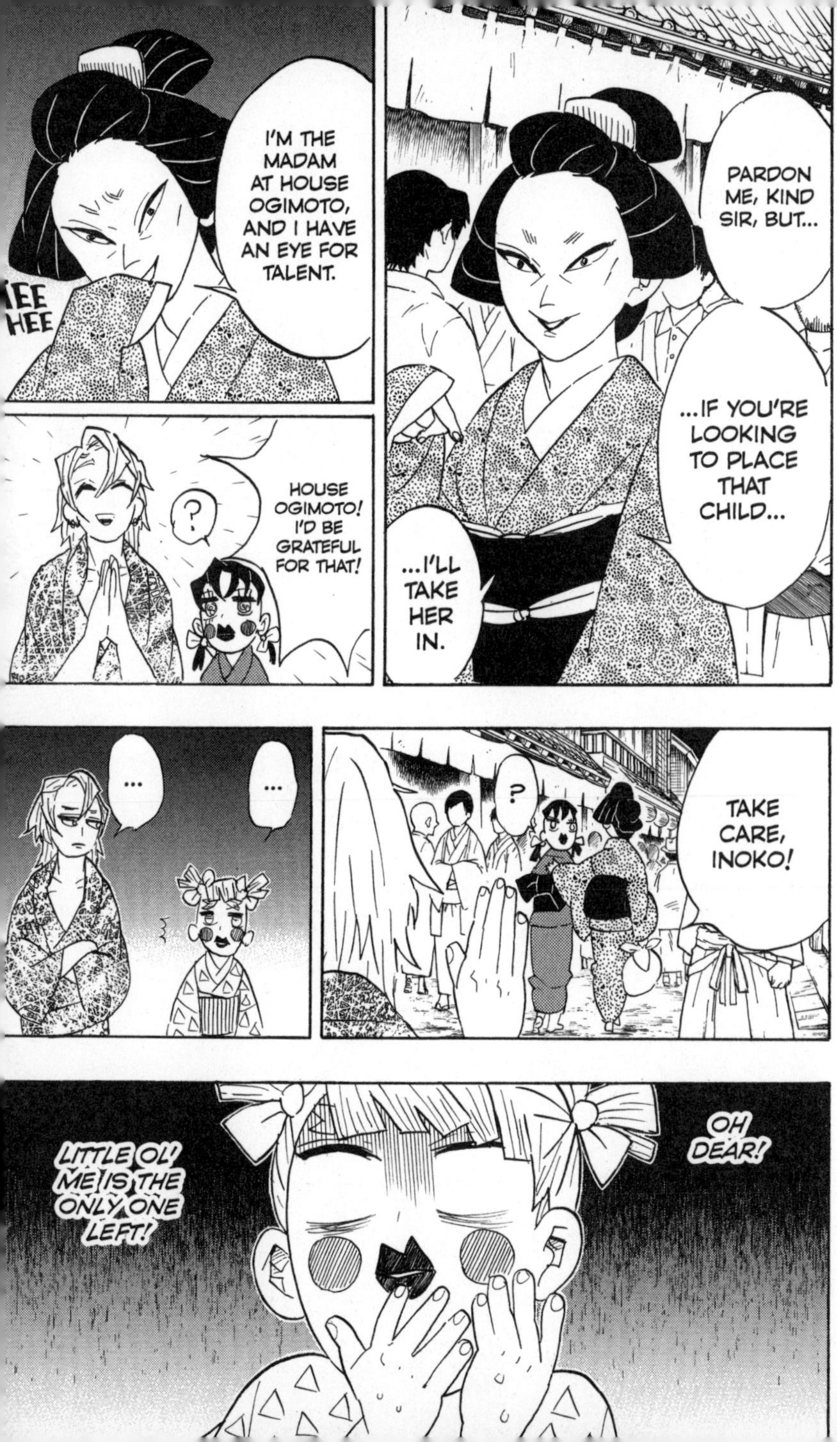
PARDON ME, KIND SIR, BUT...
...IF YOU'RE LOOKING TO PLACE THAT CHILD...
...I'LL TAKE HER IN.
I'M THE MADAM AT HOUSE OGIMOTO, AND I HAVE AN EYE FOR TALENT.
EE HEE
?
HOUSE OGIMOTO! I'D BE GRATEFUL FOR THAT!
TAKE CARE, INOKO!
?
...
...
OH DEAR!
LITTLE OL' ME IS THE ONLY ONE LEFT!

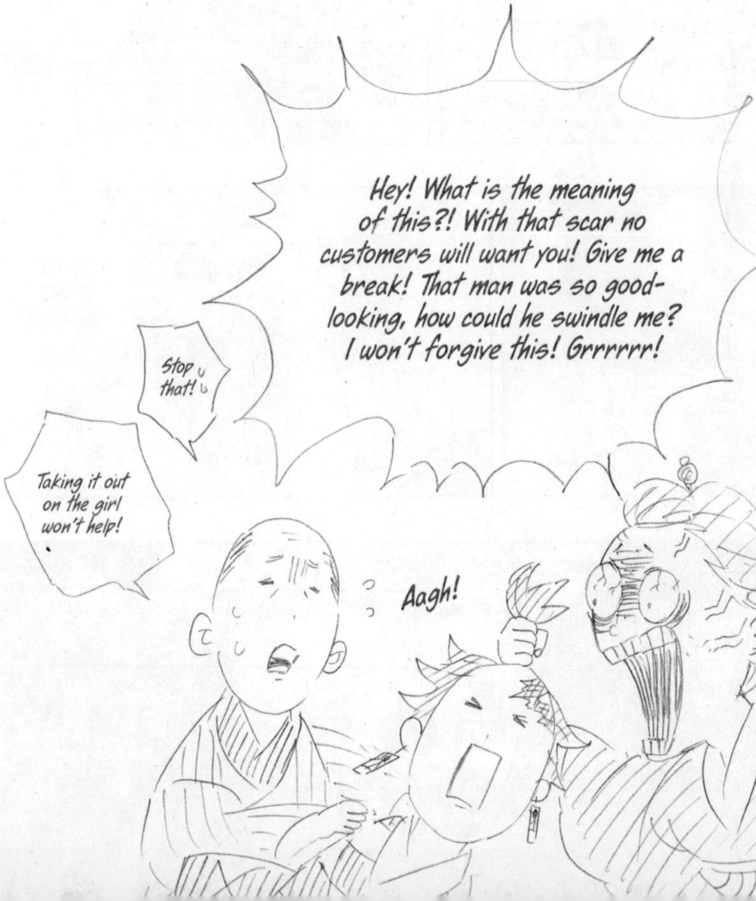
Hey! What is the meaning of this?! With that scar no customers will want you! Give me a break! That man was so good-looking, how could he swindle me? I won't forgive this! Grrrrrr!
Stop that!
Taking it out on the girl won't help!
Aagh!

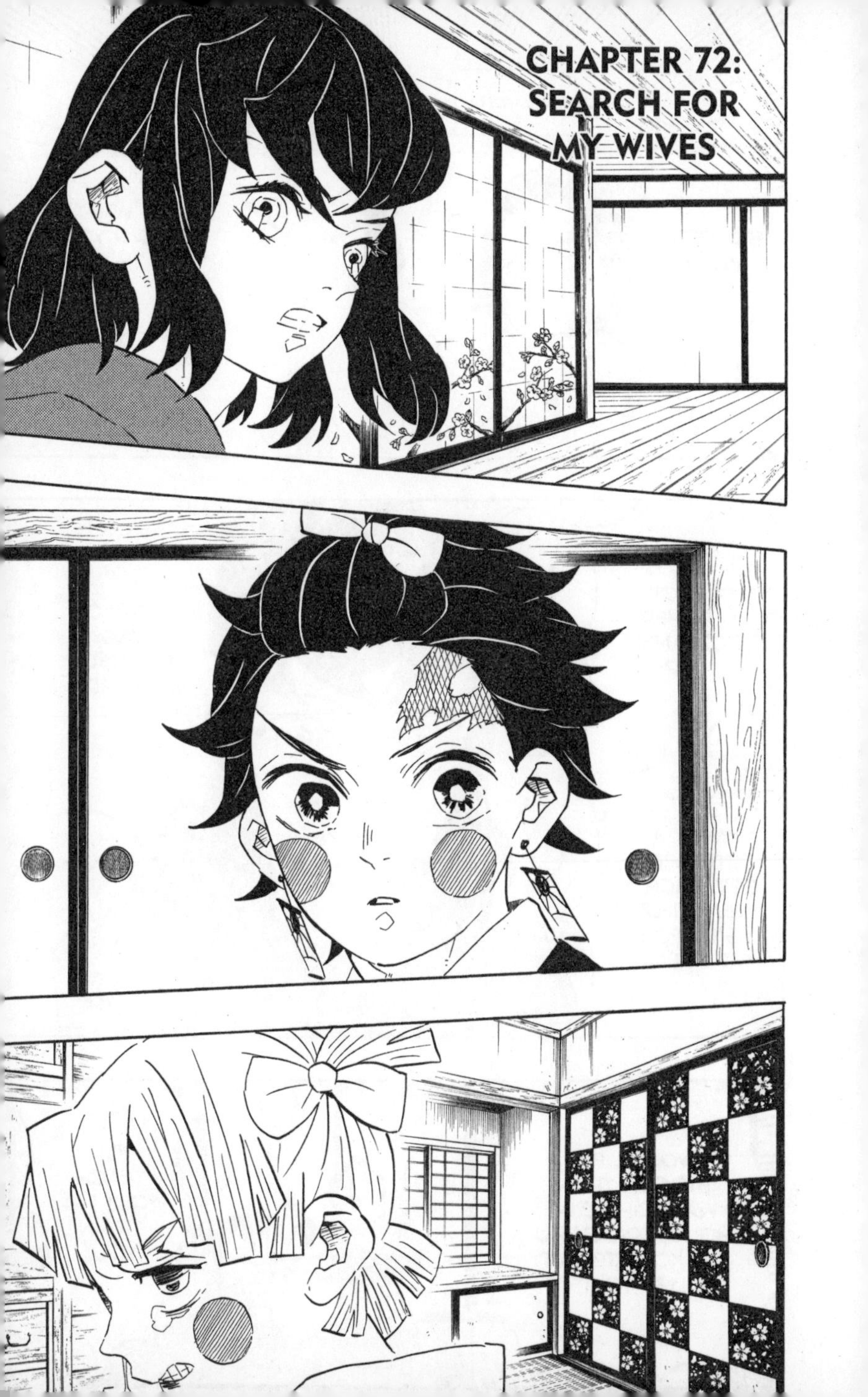
CHAPTER 72:
SEARCH FOR MY WIVES

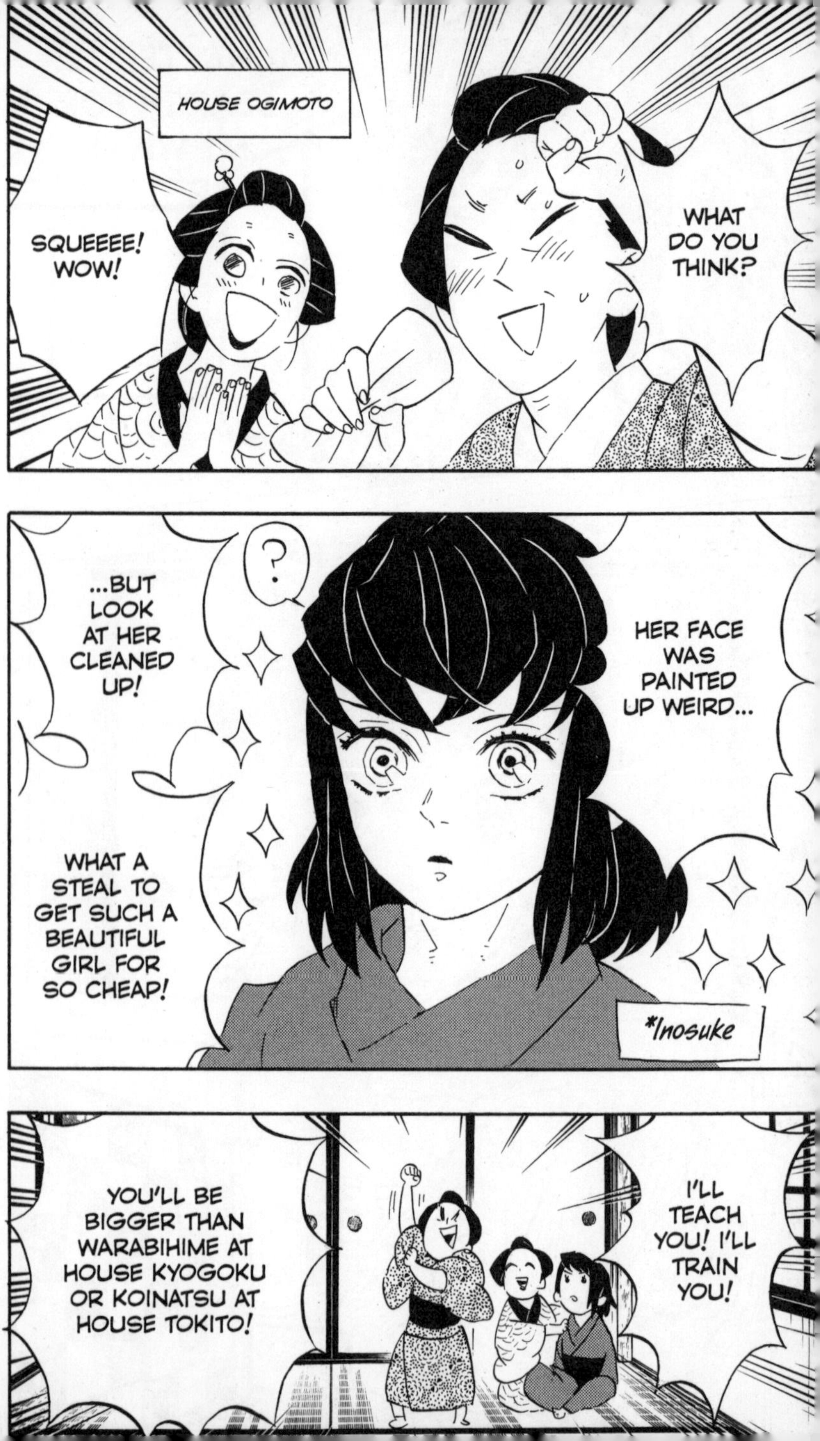
HOUSE OGIMOTO
WHAT DO YOU THINK?
SQUEEEE! WOW!
HER FACE WAS PAINTED UP WEIRD...
...BUT LOOK AT HER CLEANED UP!
?
WHAT A STEAL TO GET SUCH A BEAUTIFUL GIRL FOR SO CHEAP!
*Inosuke
I'LL TEACH YOU! I'LL TRAIN YOU!
YOU'LL BE BIGGER THAN WARABIHIME AT HOUSE KYOGOKU OR KOINATSU AT HOUSE TOKITO!

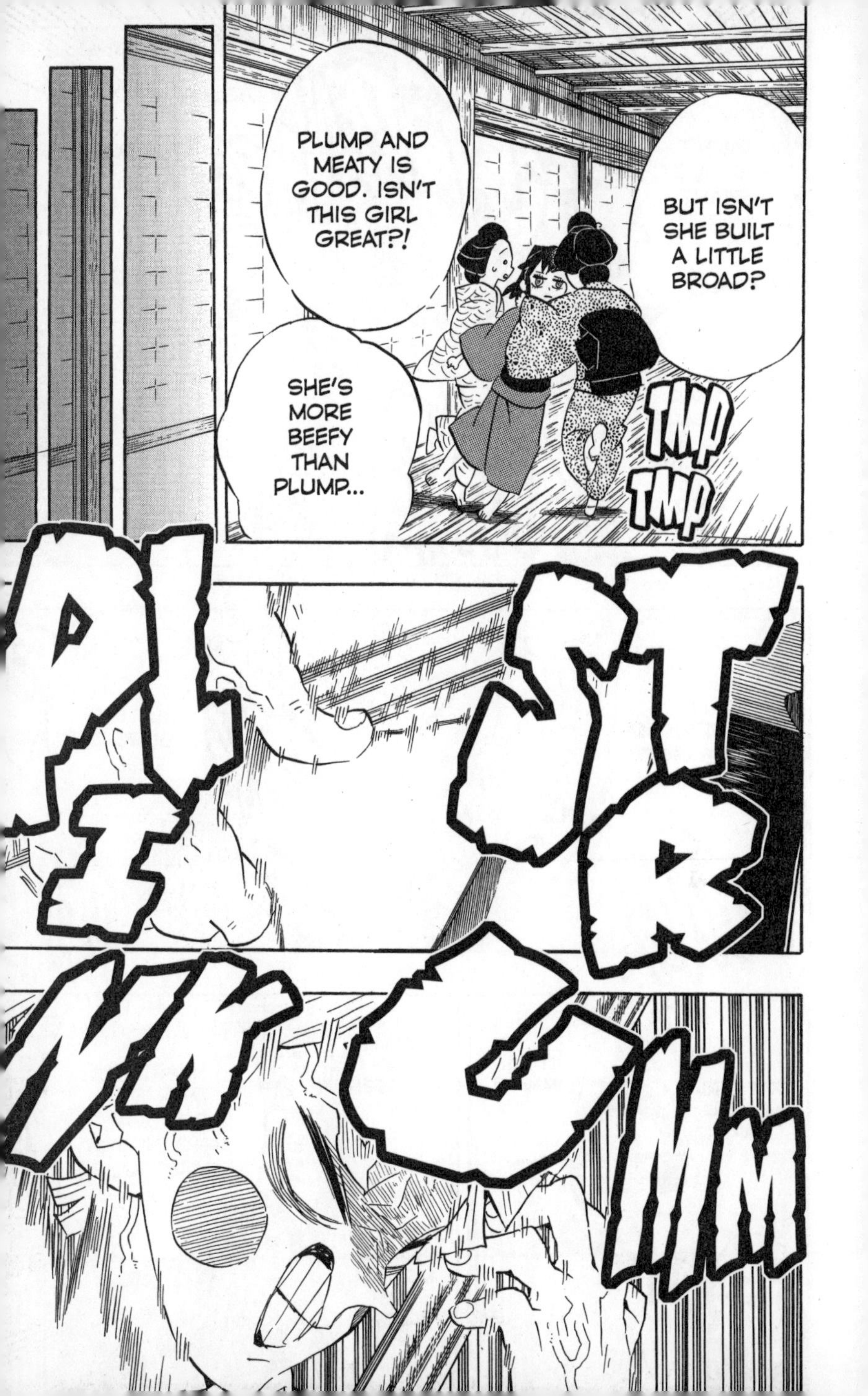
BUT ISN'T SHE BUILT A LITTLE BROAD?
PLUMP AND MEATY IS GOOD. ISN'T THIS GIRL GREAT?!
SHE'S MORE BEEFY THAN PLUMP...
TMP TMP

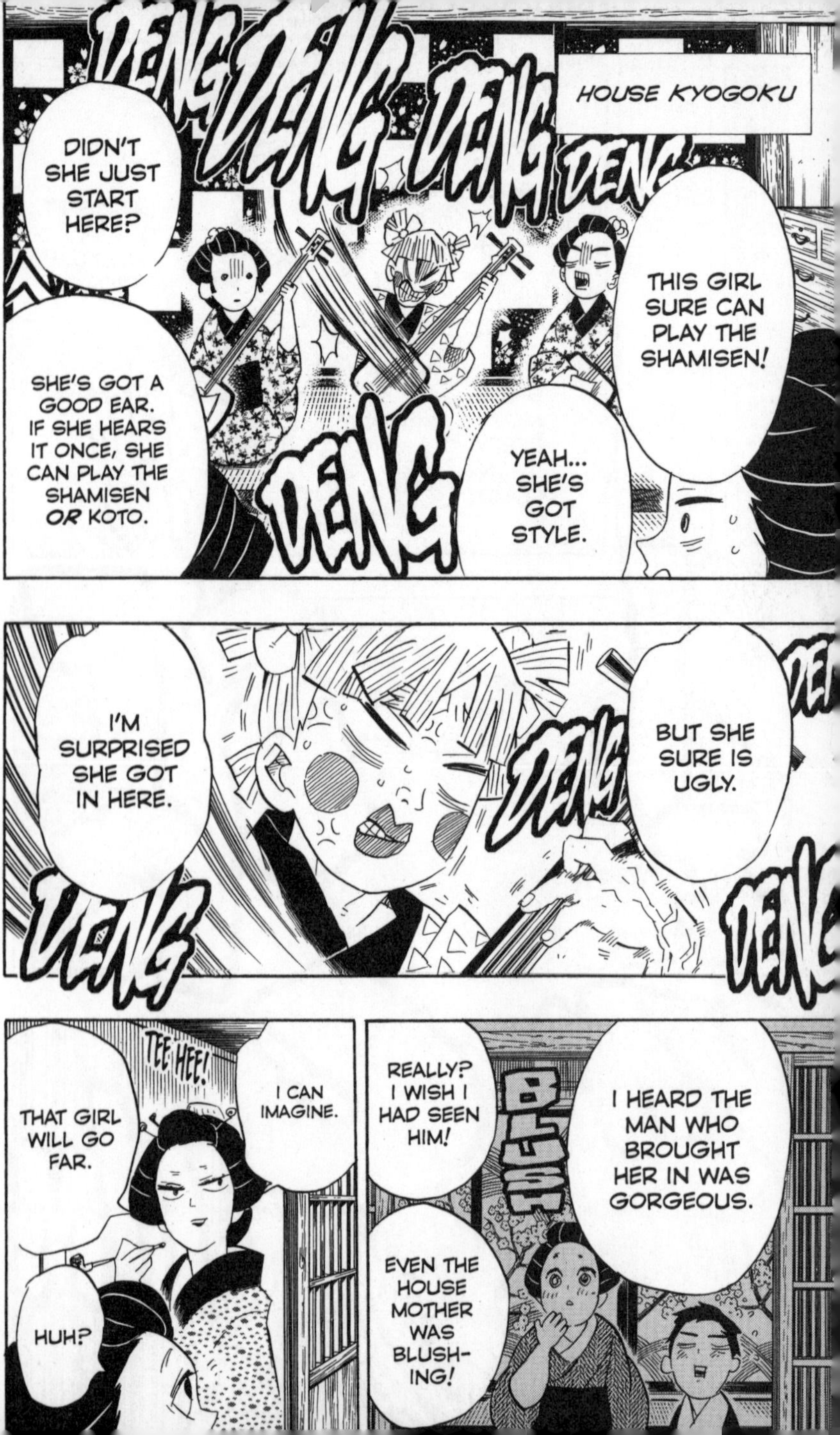
HOUSE KYOGOKU
DENG DENG DENG DENG DENG
THIS GIRL SURE CAN PLAY THE SHAMISEN!
YEAH... SHE'S GOT STYLE.
DIDN'T SHE JUST START HERE?
SHE'S GOT A GOOD EAR. IF SHE HEARS IT ONCE, SHE CAN PLAY THE SHAMISEN *OR* KOTO.
DENG
DENG DENG
BUT SHE SURE IS UGLY.
DENG
I'M SURPRISED SHE GOT IN HERE.
DENG DENG
I HEARD THE MAN WHO BROUGHT HER IN WAS GORGEOUS.
BLUSH
REALLY? I WISH I HAD SEEN HIM!
EVEN THE HOUSE MOTHER WAS BLUSHING!
TEE HEE!
I CAN IMAGINE.
THAT GIRL WILL GO FAR.
HUH?

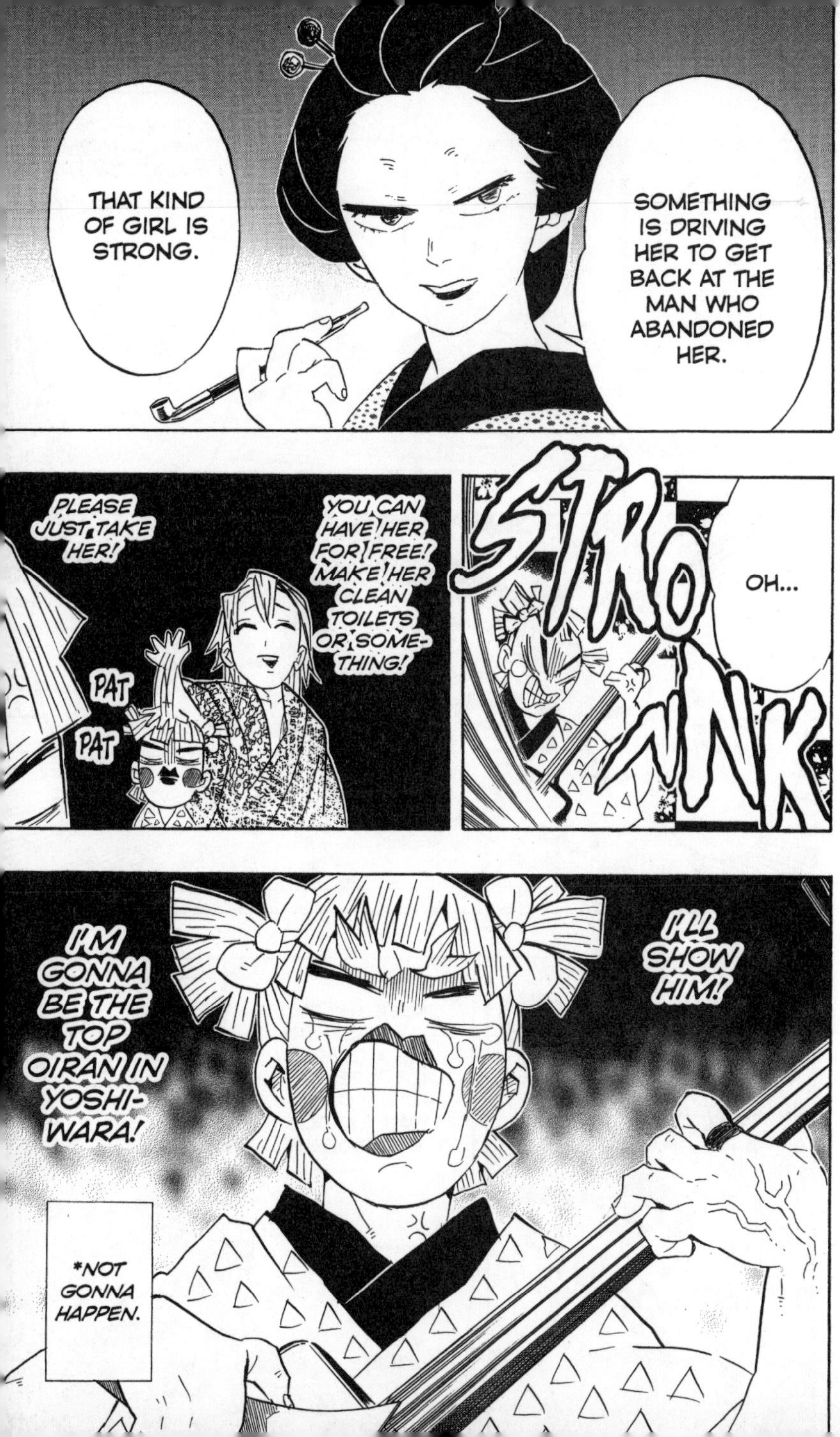
SOMETHING IS DRIVING HER TO GET BACK AT THE MAN WHO ABANDONED HER.
THAT KIND OF GIRL IS STRONG.
OH...
STRONNK
YOU CAN HAVE HER FOR FREE! MAKE HER CLEAN TOILETS OR SOME-THING!
PLEASE JUST TAKE HER!
PAT
PAT
I'LL SHOW HIM!
I'M GONNA BE THE TOP OIRAN IN YOSHI-WARA!
*NOT GONNA HAPPEN.

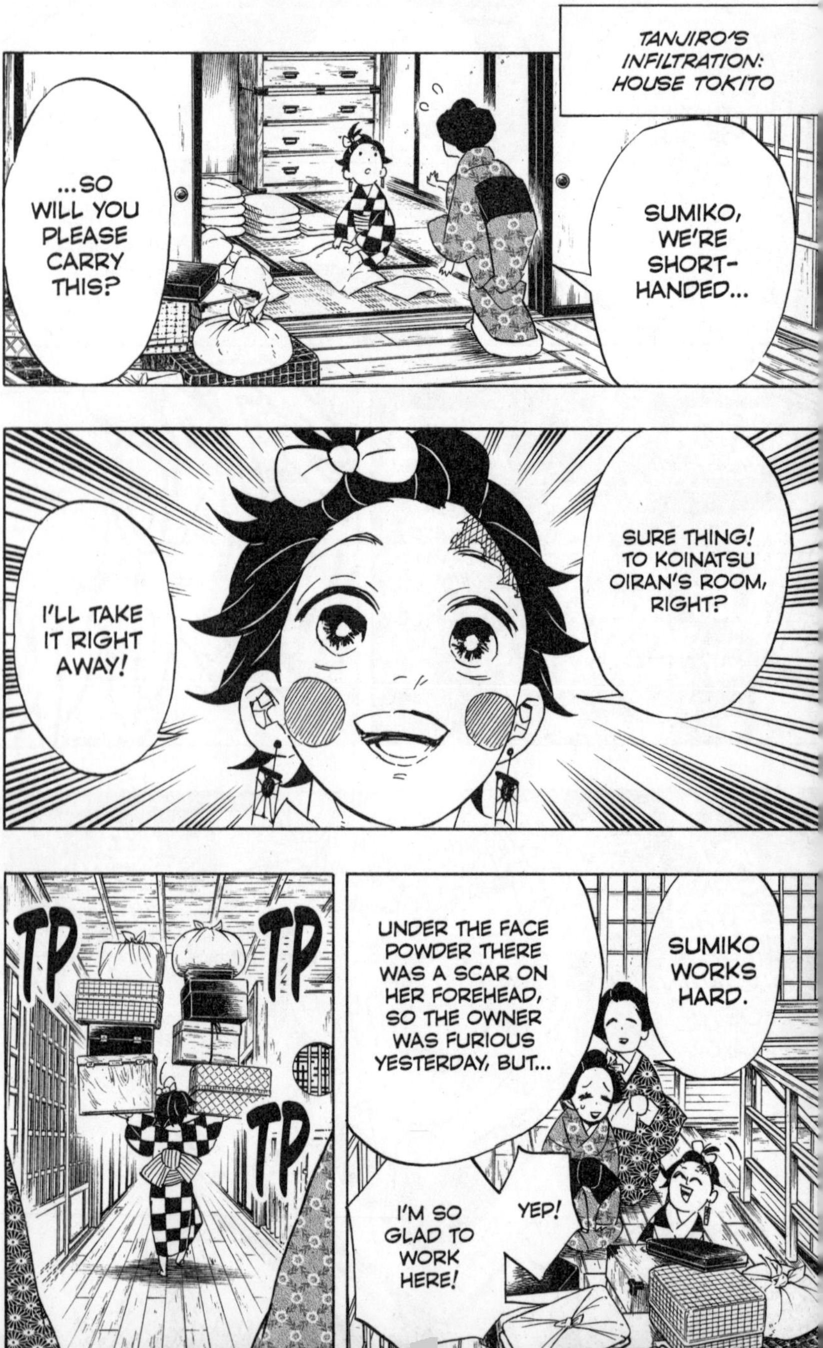
TANJIRO'S INFILTRATION: HOUSE TOKITO
SUMIKO, WE'RE SHORT-HANDED...
...SO WILL YOU PLEASE CARRY THIS?
SURE THING! TO KOINATSU OIRAN'S ROOM, RIGHT?
I'LL TAKE IT RIGHT AWAY!
SUMIKO WORKS HARD.
UNDER THE FACE POWDER THERE WAS A SCAR ON HER FOREHEAD, SO THE OWNER WAS FURIOUS YESTERDAY, BUT...
YEP!
I'M SO GLAD TO WORK HERE!
TP
TP
TP

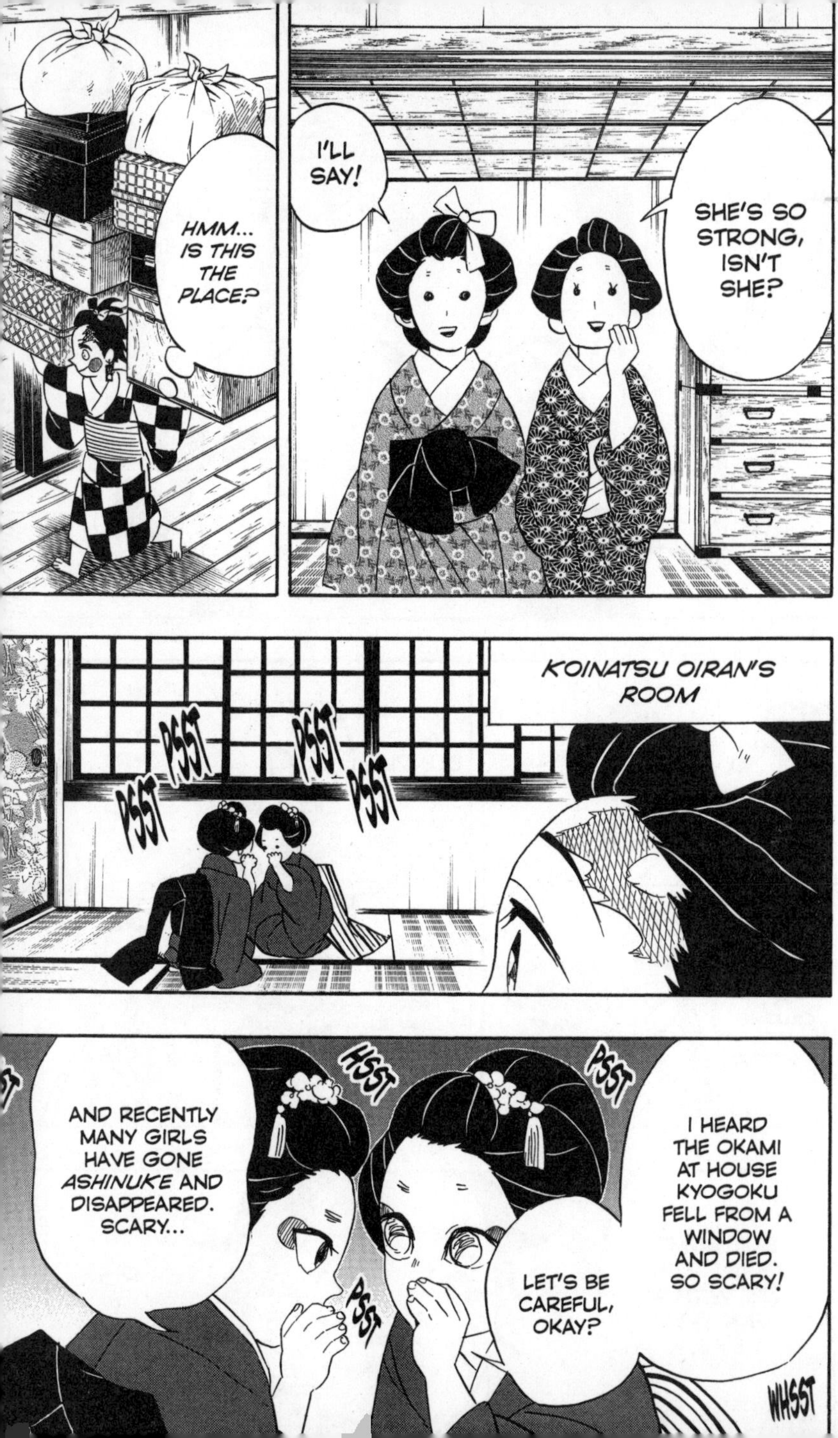
SHE'S SO STRONG, ISN'T SHE?
I'LL SAY!
HMM... IS THIS THE PLACE?
KOINATSU OIRAN'S ROOM
PSST
PSST
PSST
PSST
I HEARD THE OKAMI AT HOUSE KYOGOKU FELL FROM A WINDOW AND DIED. SO SCARY!
PSST
LET'S BE CAREFUL, OKAY?
HSST
AND RECENTLY MANY GIRLS HAVE GONE *ASHINUKE* AND DISAPPEARED. SCARY...
PSST
WHSST

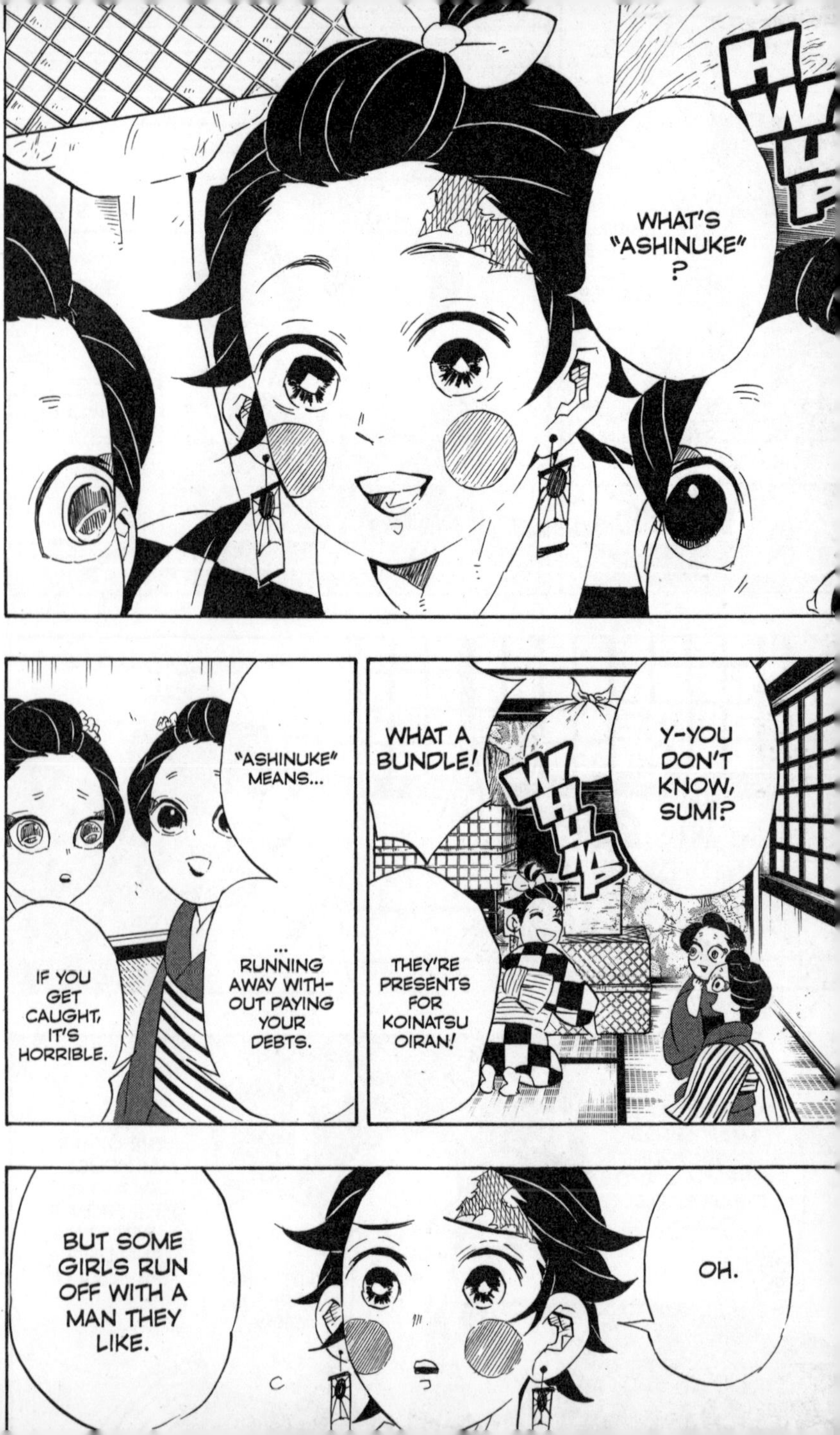
HWUP
WHAT'S "ASHINUKE" ?
Y-YOU DON'T KNOW, SUMI?
WHAT A BUNDLE!
WHUMP
THEY'RE PRESENTS FOR KOINATSU OIRAN!
"ASHINUKE" MEANS...
...RUNNING AWAY WITH-OUT PAYING YOUR DEBTS.
IF YOU GET CAUGHT, IT'S HORRIBLE.
OH.
BUT SOME GIRLS RUN OFF WITH A MAN THEY LIKE.

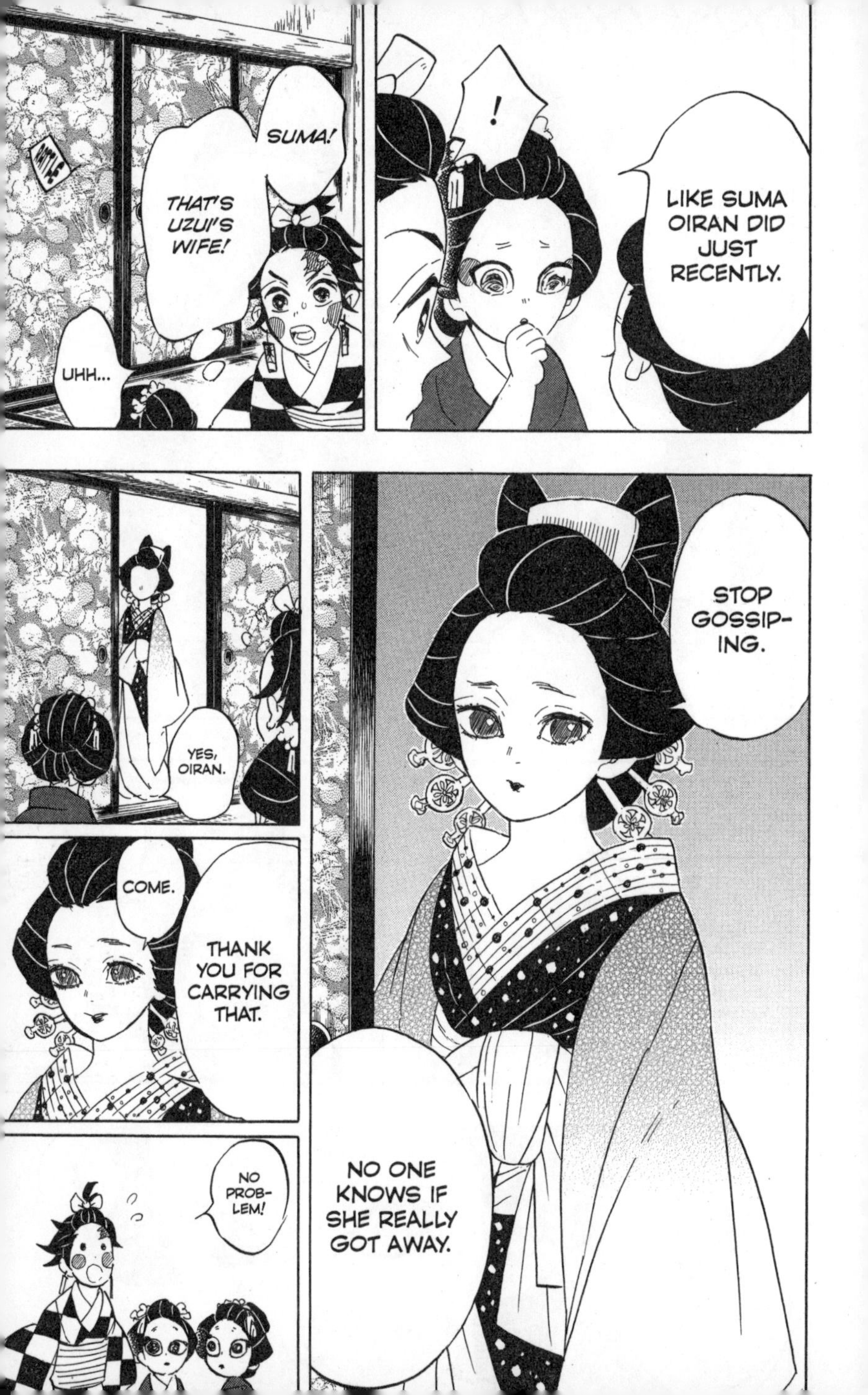
!
LIKE SUMA OIRAN DID JUST RECENTLY.
SUMA!
THAT'S UZUI'S WIFE!
UHH...
STOP GOSSIP-ING.
NO ONE KNOWS IF SHE REALLY GOT AWAY.
YES, OIRAN.
COME.
THANK YOU FOR CARRYING THAT.
NO PROB-LEM!

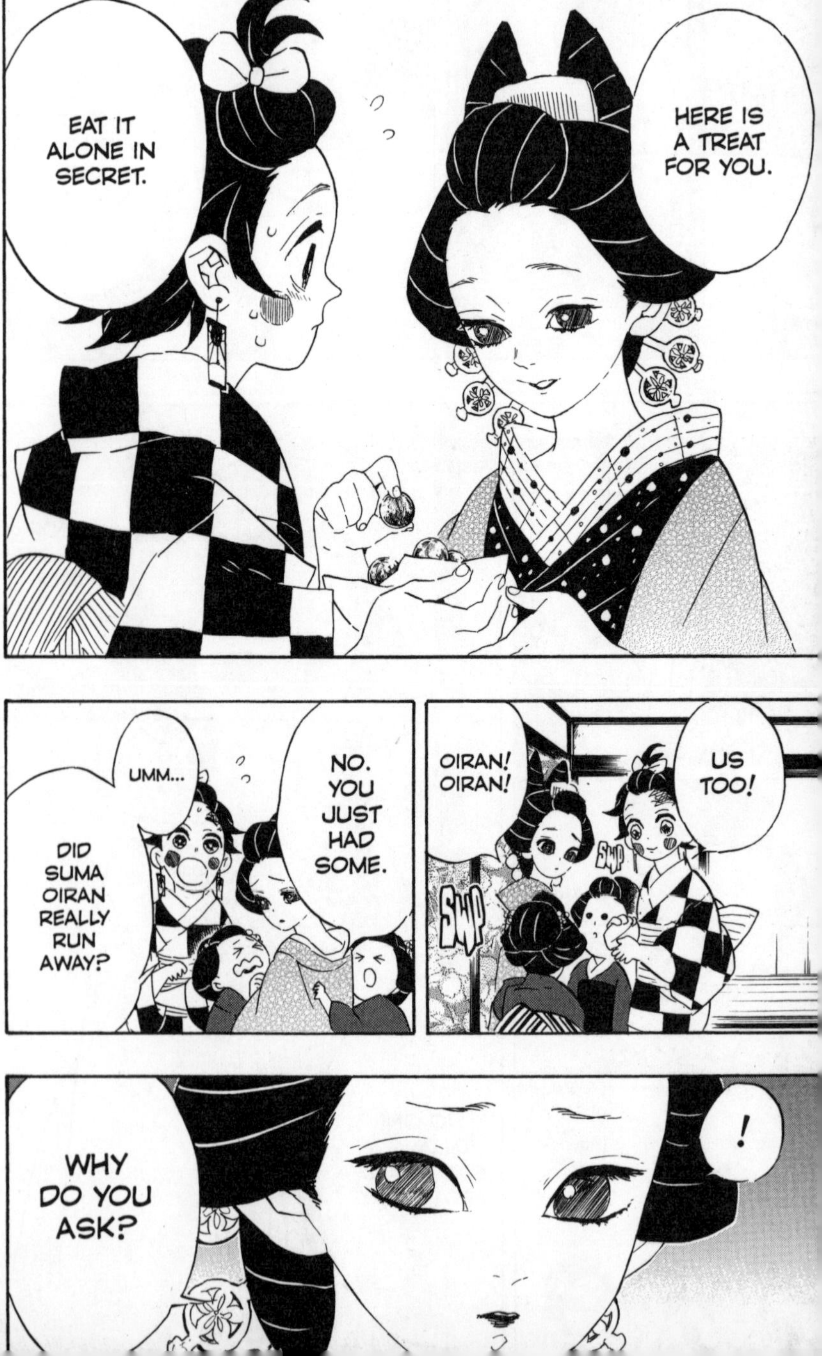
HERE IS A TREAT FOR YOU.
EAT IT ALONE IN SECRET.
US TOO!
OIRAN! OIRAN!
SWP
SWP
NO. YOU JUST HAD SOME.
UMM...
DID SUMA OIRAN REALLY RUN AWAY?
!
WHY DO YOU ASK?

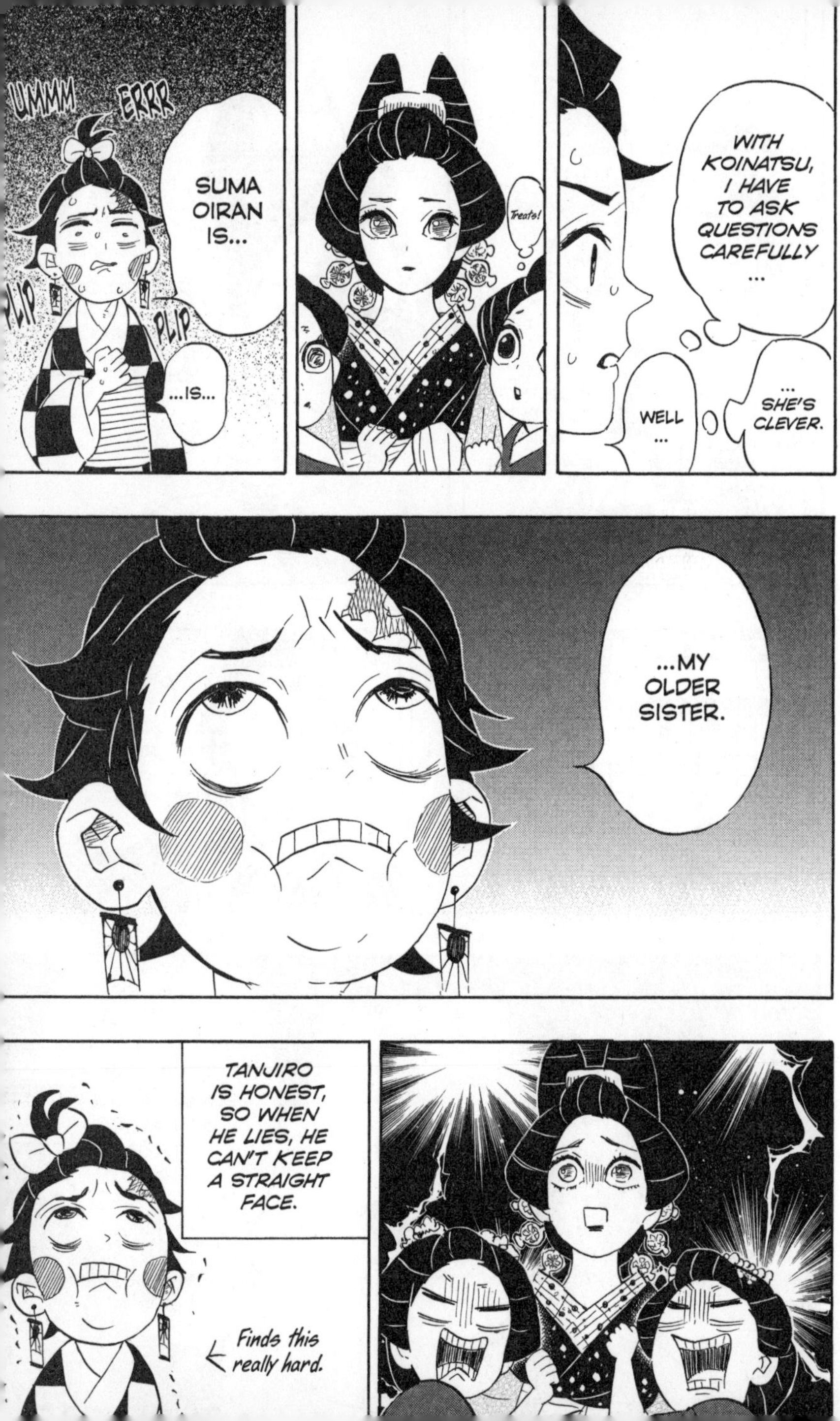
WITH KOINATSU, I HAVE TO ASK QUESTIONS CAREFULLY ...
... SHE'S CLEVER.
WELL ...
Treats!
UMMM
ERRR
SUMA OIRAN IS...
PLIP
PLIP
...IS...
...MY OLDER SISTER.
TANJIRO IS HONEST, SO WHEN HE LIES, HE CAN'T KEEP A STRAIGHT FACE.
← Finds this really hard.

DID YOU GET SOLD TO THE ENTERTAINMENT DISTRICT LIKE YOUR SISTER?
Y-YEAH.
WE EXCHANGED LETTERS FOR A LONG TIME.
SHE'S NOT THE TYPE TO RUN AWAY.
OH... REALLY?
...
I DIDN'T THINK SUMA WOULD RUN AWAY, EITHER.
SHE WAS A DEPENDABLE YOUNG WOMAN.

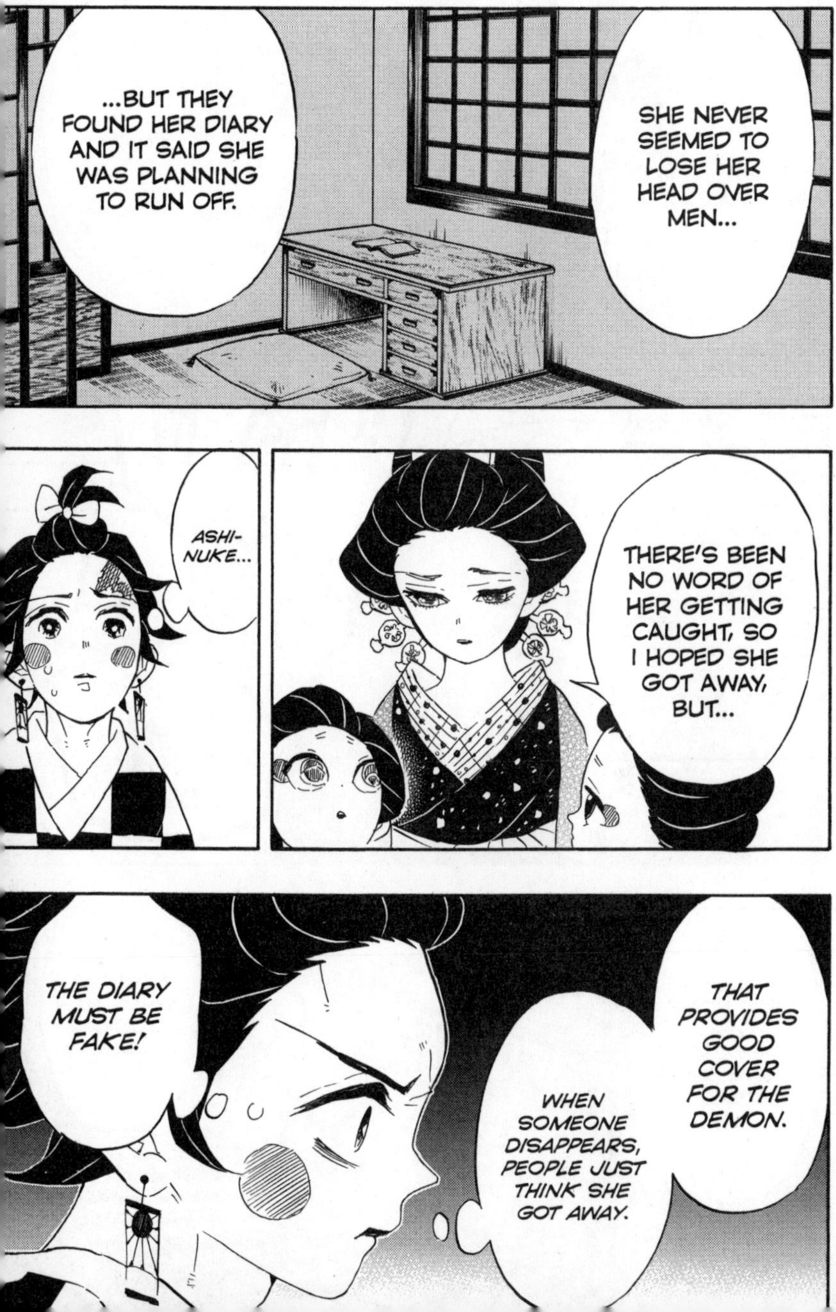
SHE NEVER SEEMED TO LOSE HER HEAD OVER MEN...
...BUT THEY FOUND HER DIARY AND IT SAID SHE WAS PLANNING TO RUN OFF.
THERE'S BEEN NO WORD OF HER GETTING CAUGHT, SO I HOPED SHE GOT AWAY, BUT...
ASHI-NUKE...
THE DIARY MUST BE FAKE!
WHEN SOMEONE DISAPPEARS, PEOPLE JUST THINK SHE GOT AWAY.
THAT PROVIDES GOOD COVER FOR THE DEMON.

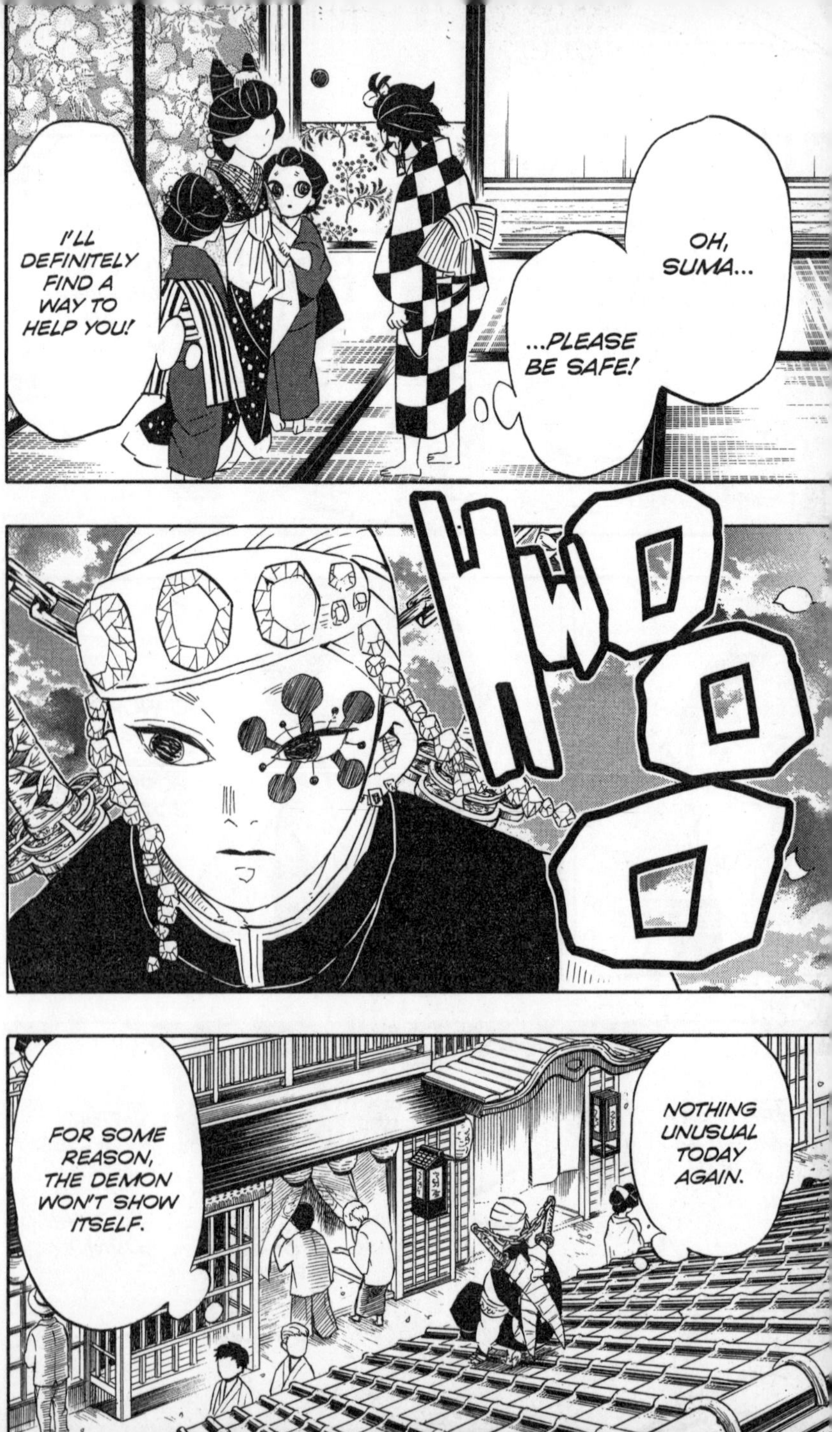
OH, SUMA... ...PLEASE BE SAFE!
I'LL DEFINITELY FIND A WAY TO HELP YOU!
HWOOO
NOTHING UNUSUAL TODAY AGAIN.
FOR SOME REASON, THE DEMON WON'T SHOW ITSELF.

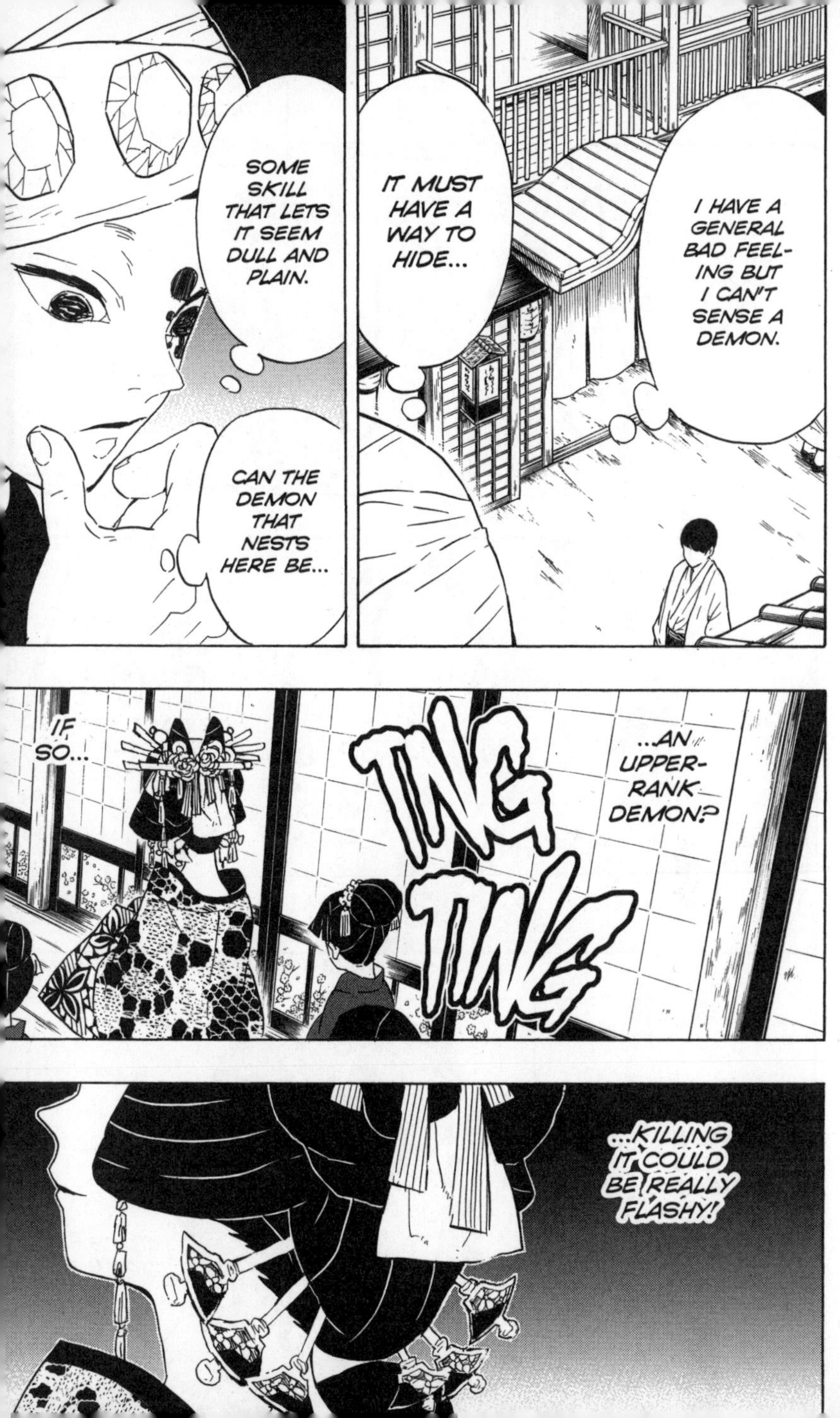
I HAVE A GENERAL BAD FEEL-ING BUT I CAN'T SENSE A DEMON.
IT MUST HAVE A WAY TO HIDE...
SOME SKILL THAT LETS IT SEEM DULL AND PLAIN.
CAN THE DEMON THAT NESTS HERE BE...
...AN UPPER-RANK DEMON?
TING
TING
IF SO...
...KILLING IT COULD BE REALLY FLASHY!

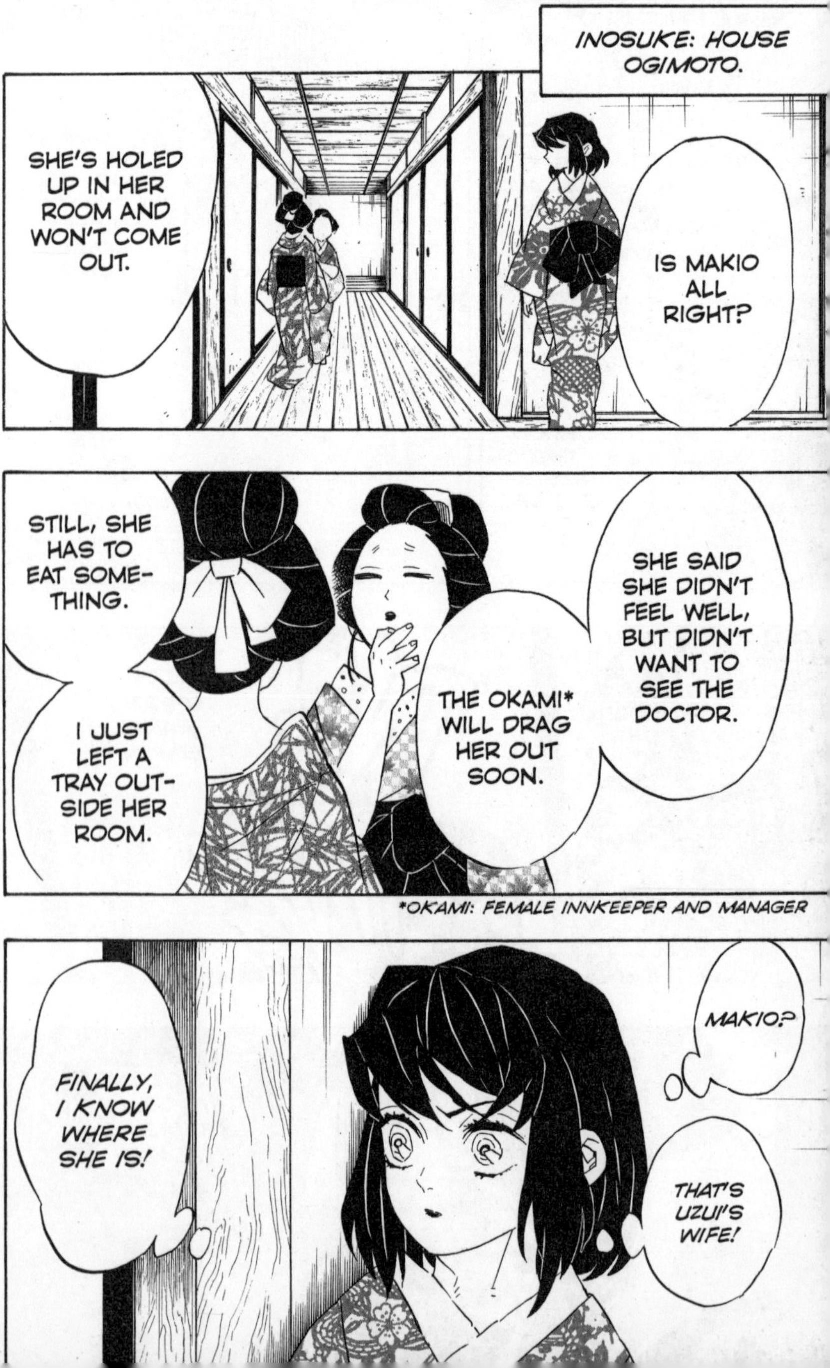
INOSUKE: HOUSE OGIMOTO.
IS MAKIO ALL RIGHT?
SHE'S HOLED UP IN HER ROOM AND WON'T COME OUT.
SHE SAID SHE DIDN'T FEEL WELL, BUT DIDN'T WANT TO SEE THE DOCTOR.
THE OKAMI* WILL DRAG HER OUT SOON.
STILL, SHE HAS TO EAT SOME-THING.
I JUST LEFT A TRAY OUT-SIDE HER ROOM.
MAKIO?
THAT'S UZUI'S WIFE!
FINALLY, I KNOW WHERE SHE IS!

*OKAMI: FEMALE INNKEEPER AND MANAGER

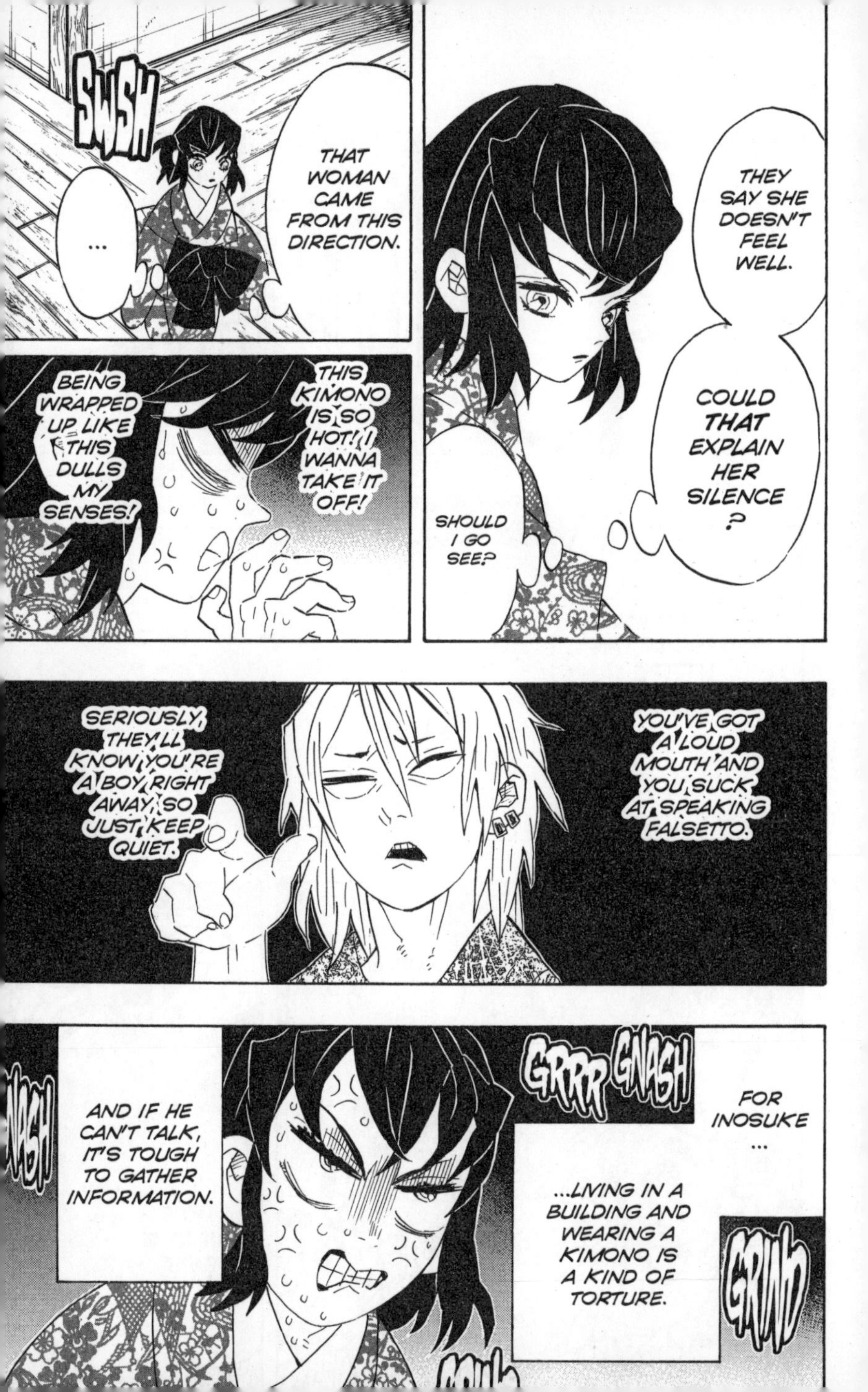
THEY SAY SHE DOESN'T FEEL WELL.
COULD THAT EXPLAIN HER SILENCE?
SHOULD I GO SEE?
THAT WOMAN CAME FROM THIS DIRECTION.
SWSH
...
THIS KIMONO IS SO HOT! I WANNA TAKE IT OFF!
BEING WRAPPED UP LIKE THIS DULLS MY SENSES!
YOU'VE GOT A LOUD MOUTH AND YOU SUCK AT SPEAKING FALSETTO.
SERIOUSLY, THEY'LL KNOW YOU'RE A BOY RIGHT AWAY, SO JUST KEEP QUIET.
FOR INOSUKE...
...LIVING IN A BUILDING AND WEARING A KIMONO IS A KIND OF TORTURE.
GRIND
GNASH
GRRR
AND IF HE CAN'T TALK, IT'S TOUGH TO GATHER INFORMATION.
GNASH

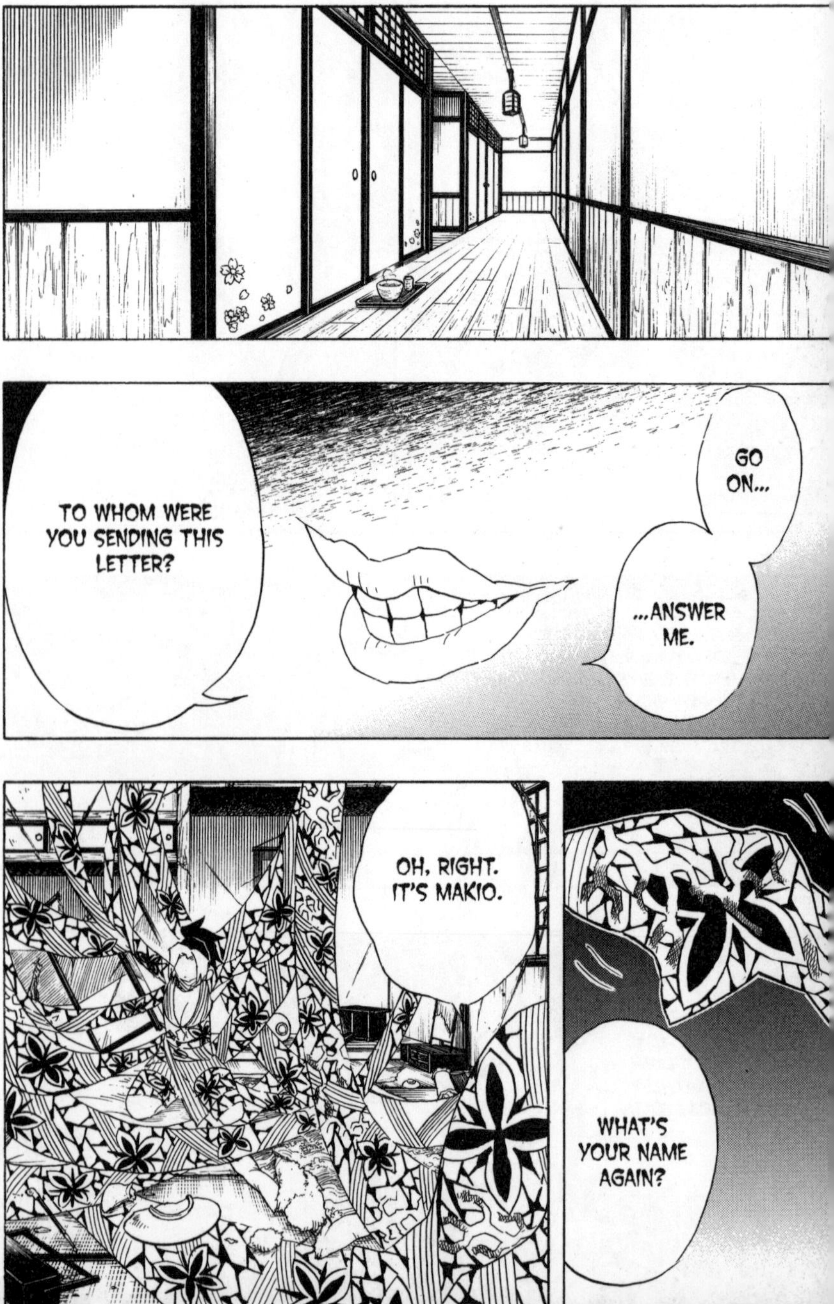
GO ON...
...ANSWER ME.
TO WHOM WERE YOU SENDING THIS LETTER?
WHAT'S YOUR NAME AGAIN?
OH, RIGHT. IT'S MAKIO.

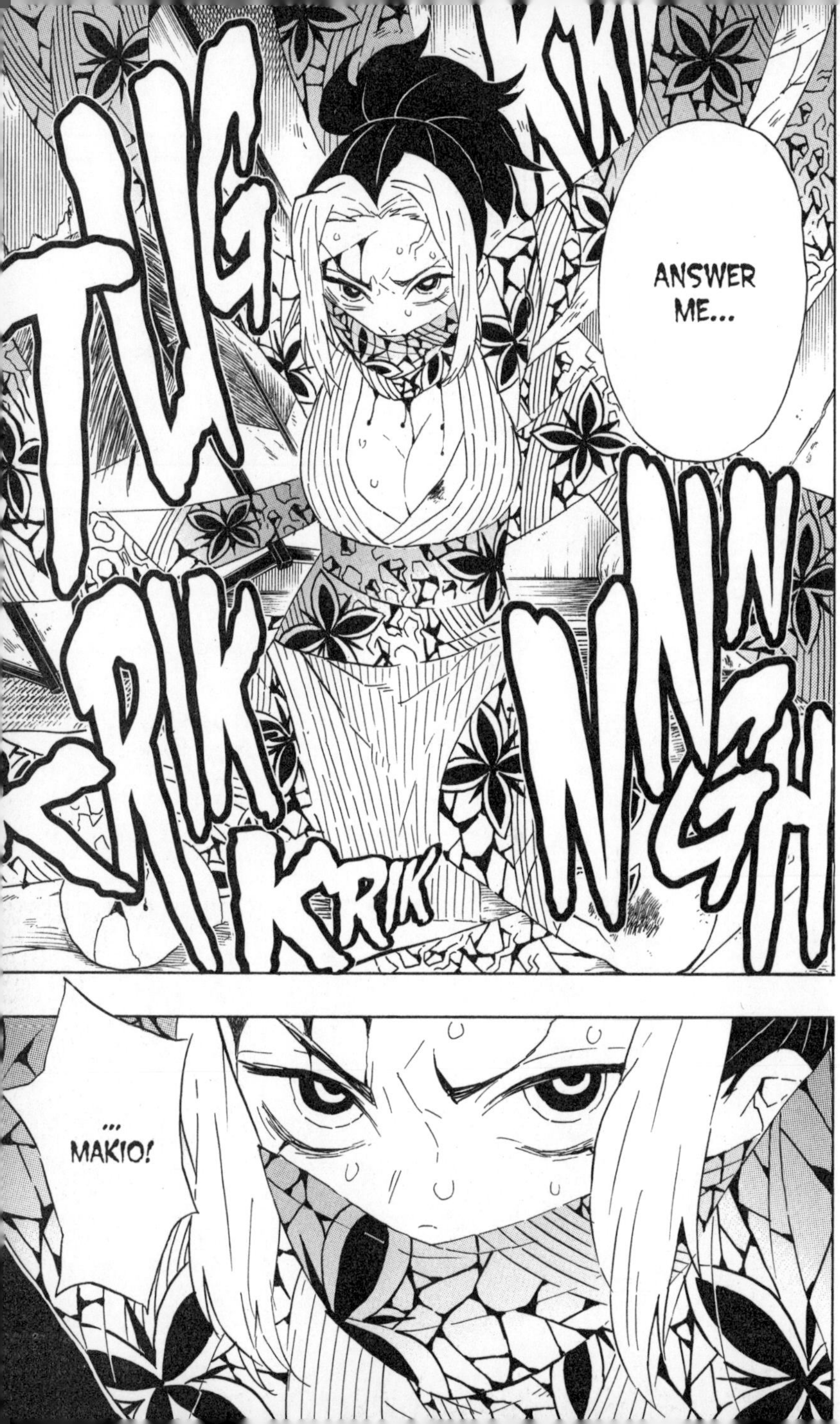
ANSWER ME...
KRIK
...MAKIO!

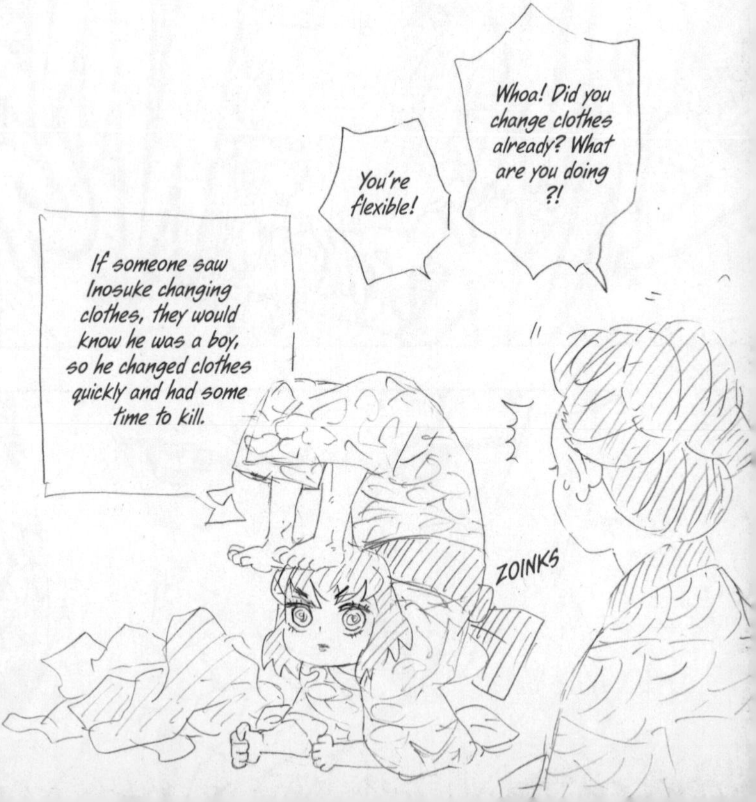
Whoa! Did you change clothes already? What are you doing ?!
You're flexible!
If someone saw Inosuke changing clothes, they would know he was a boy, so he changed clothes quickly and had some time to kill.
ZOINKS

CHAPTER 73: THE CHASE

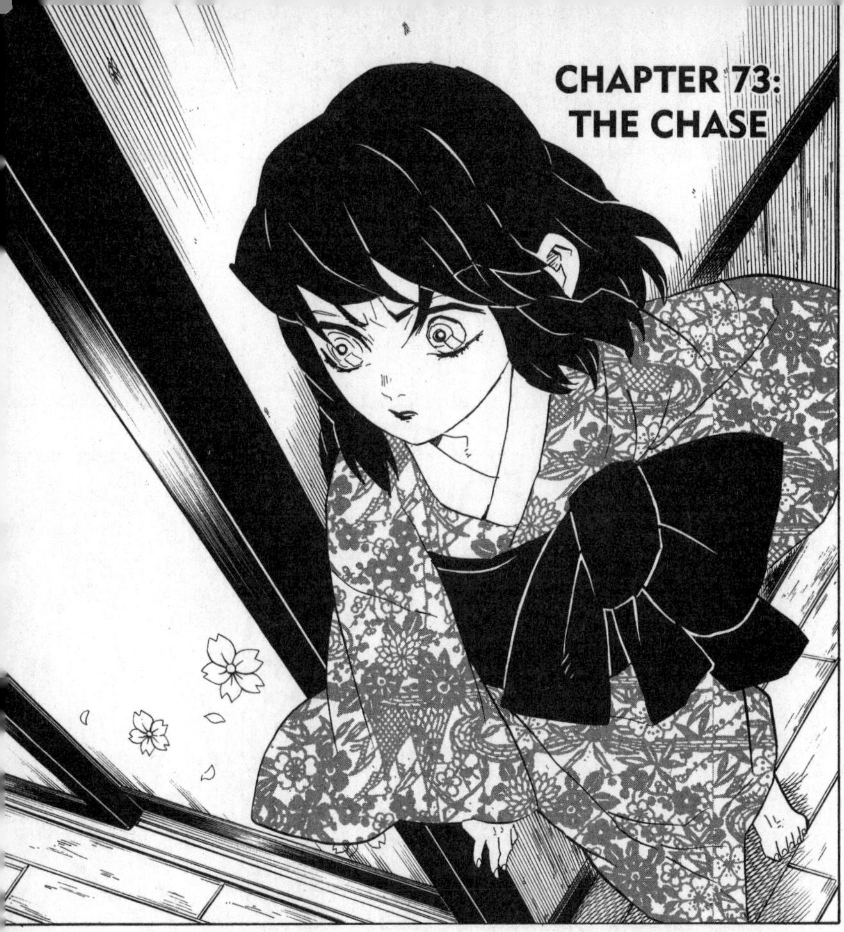

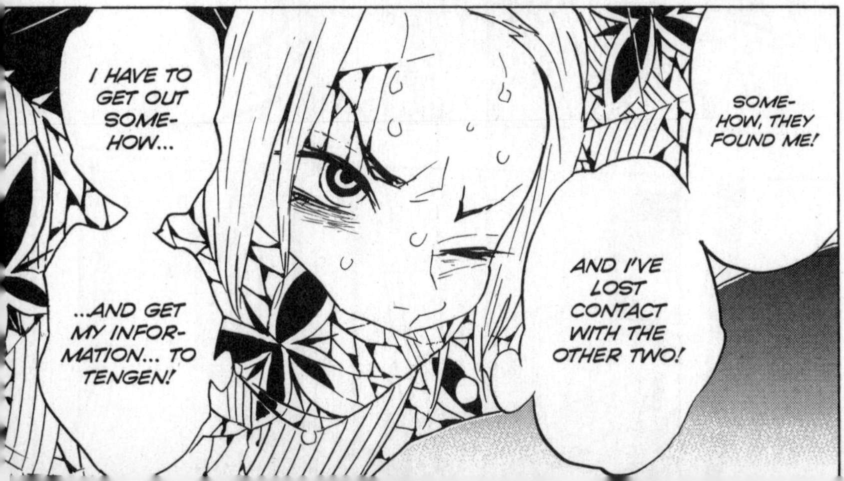
SOME-HOW, THEY FOUND ME!
AND I'VE LOST CONTACT WITH THE OTHER TWO!
I HAVE TO GET OUT SOME-HOW...
...AND GET MY INFOR-MATION... TO TENGEN!

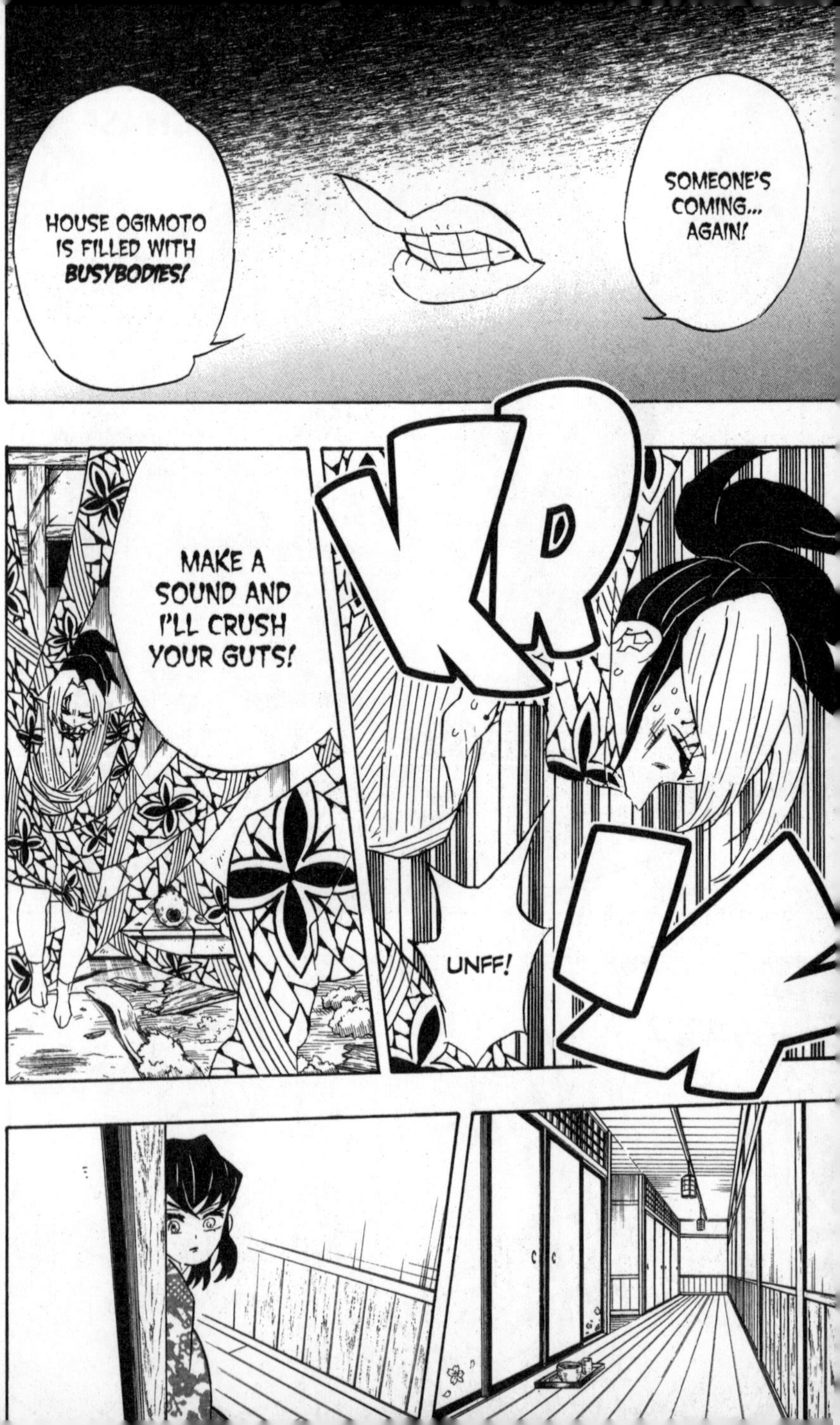
SOMEONE'S COMING... AGAIN!
HOUSE OGIMOTO IS FILLED WITH BUSYBODIES!
KR
UNFF!
MAKE A SOUND AND I'LL CRUSH YOUR GUTS!

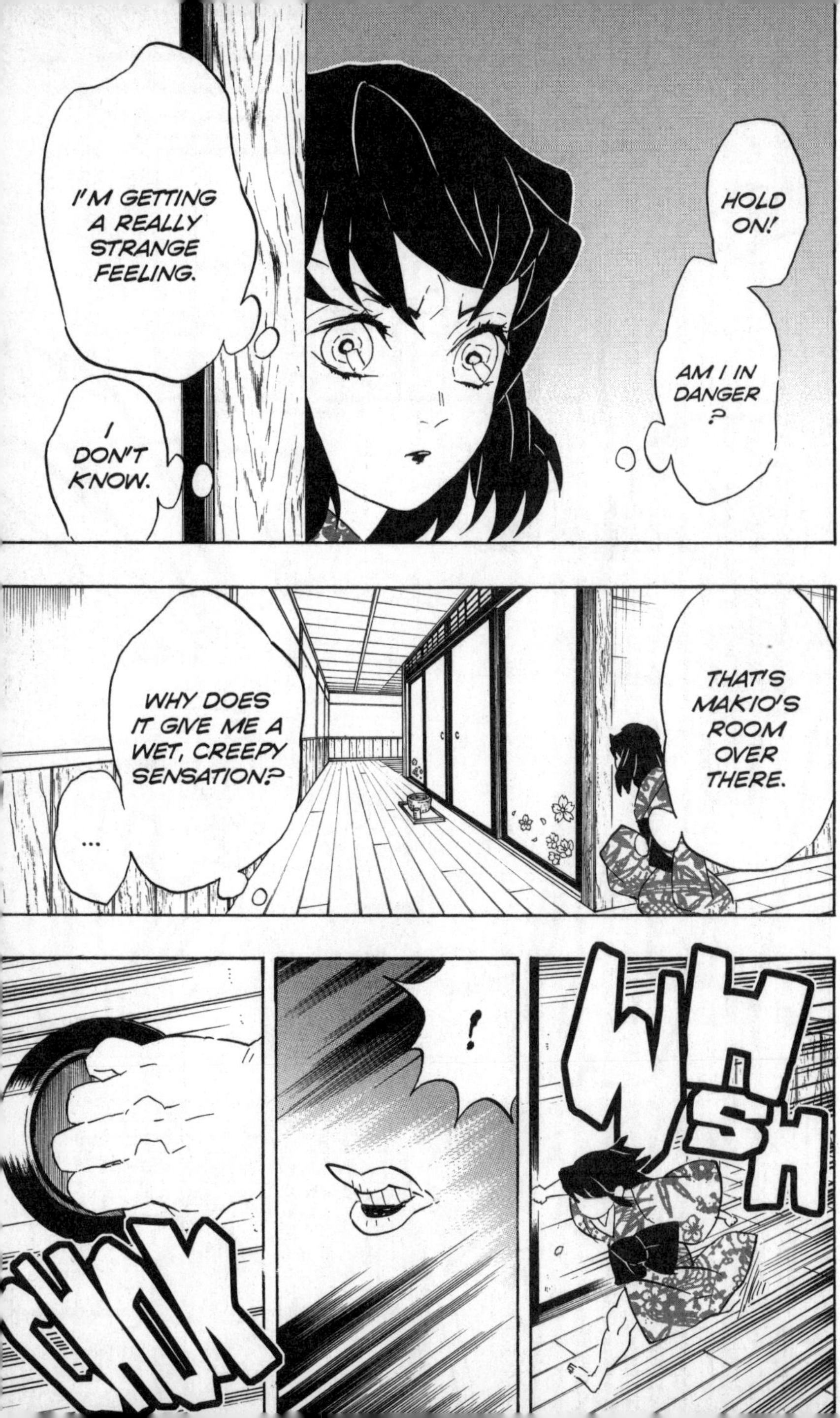
HOLD ON!
AM I IN DANGER?
I'M GETTING A REALLY STRANGE FEELING.
I DON'T KNOW.
THAT'S MAKIO'S ROOM OVER THERE.
WHY DOES IT GIVE ME A WET, CREEPY SENSATION?
...
WHSH
!
CHOK

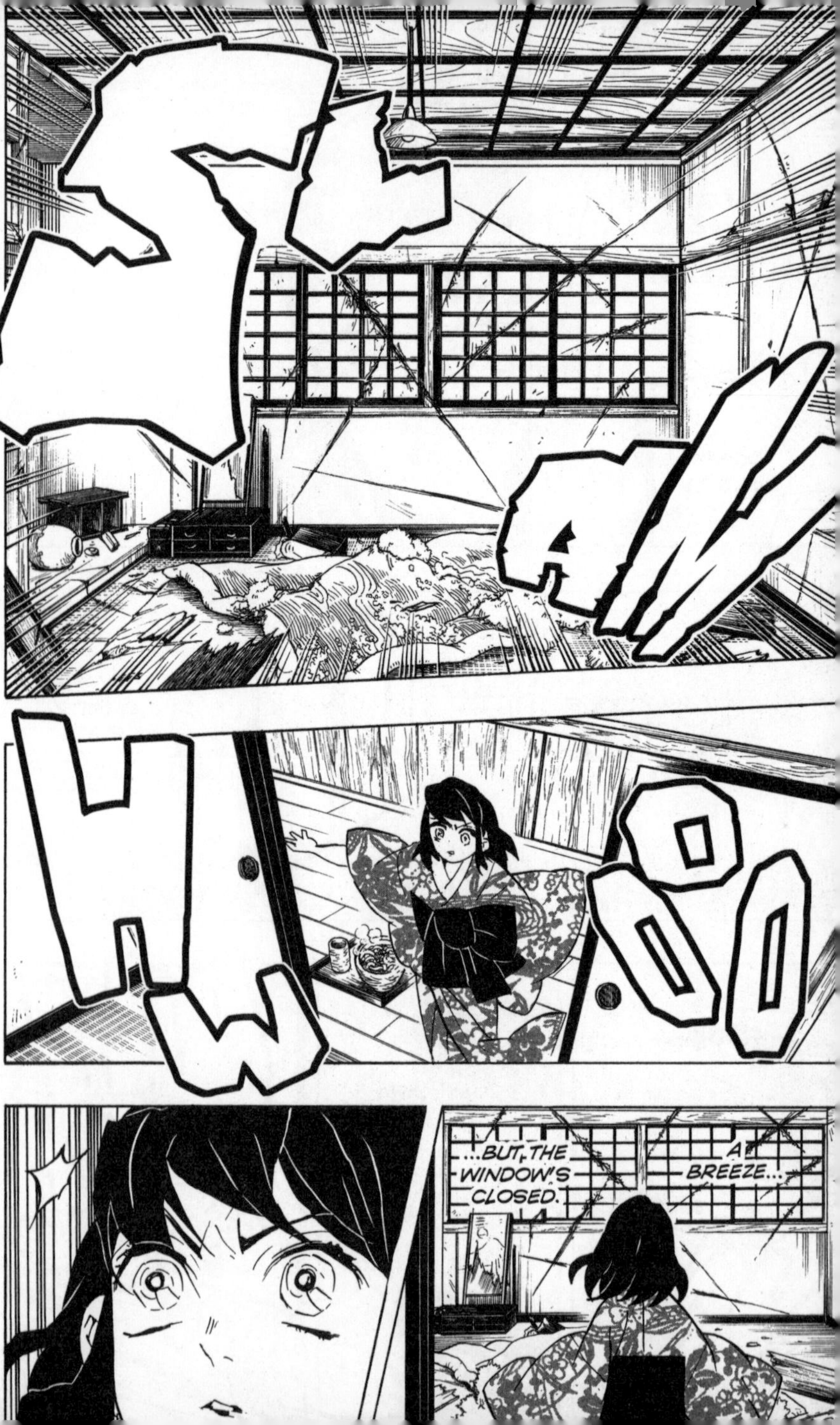
A BREEZE...
...BUT THE WINDOW'S CLOSED.

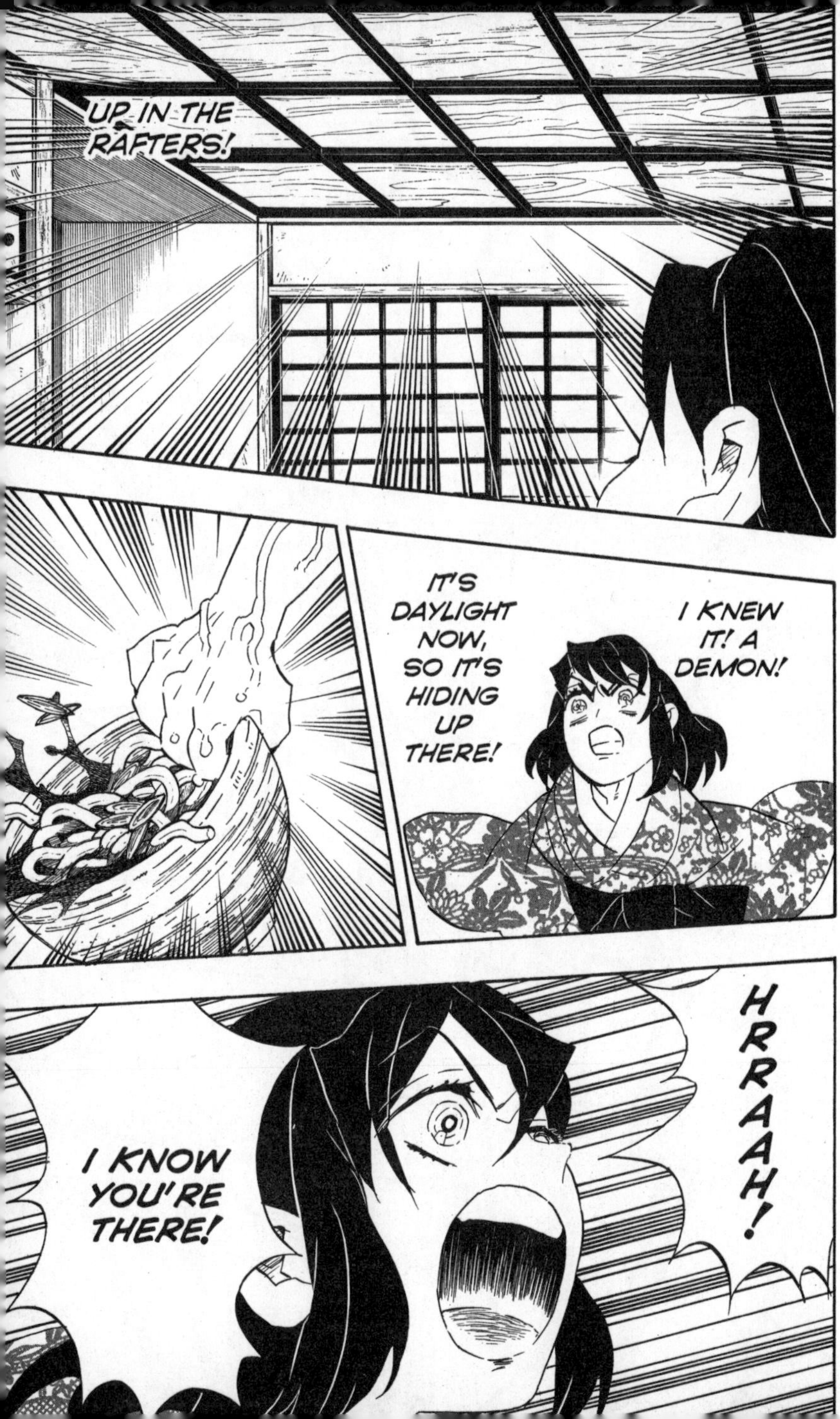
UP IN THE RAFTERS!
I KNEW IT! A DEMON!
IT'S DAYLIGHT NOW, SO IT'S HIDING UP THERE!
HRRAAH!
I KNOW YOU'RE THERE!

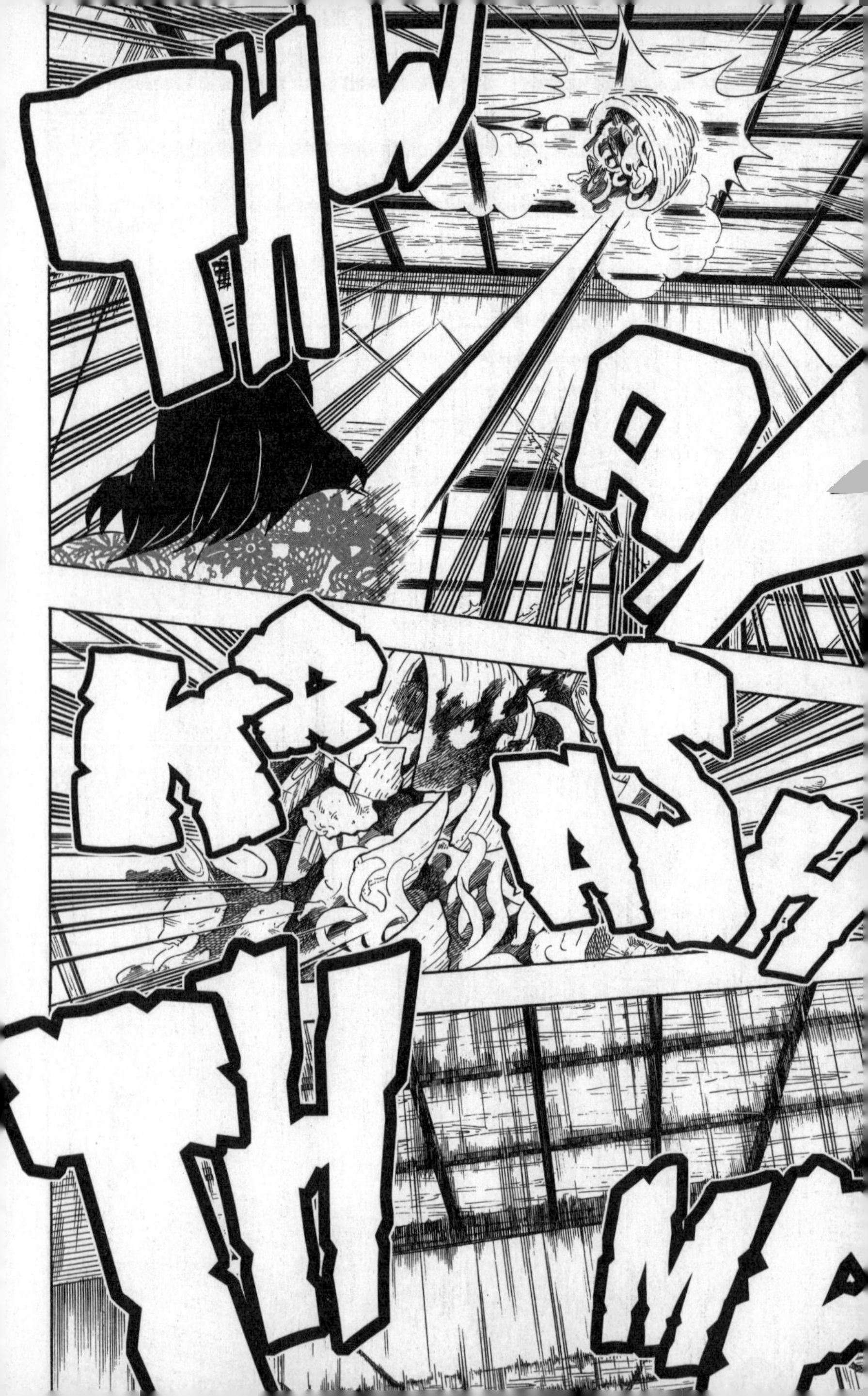

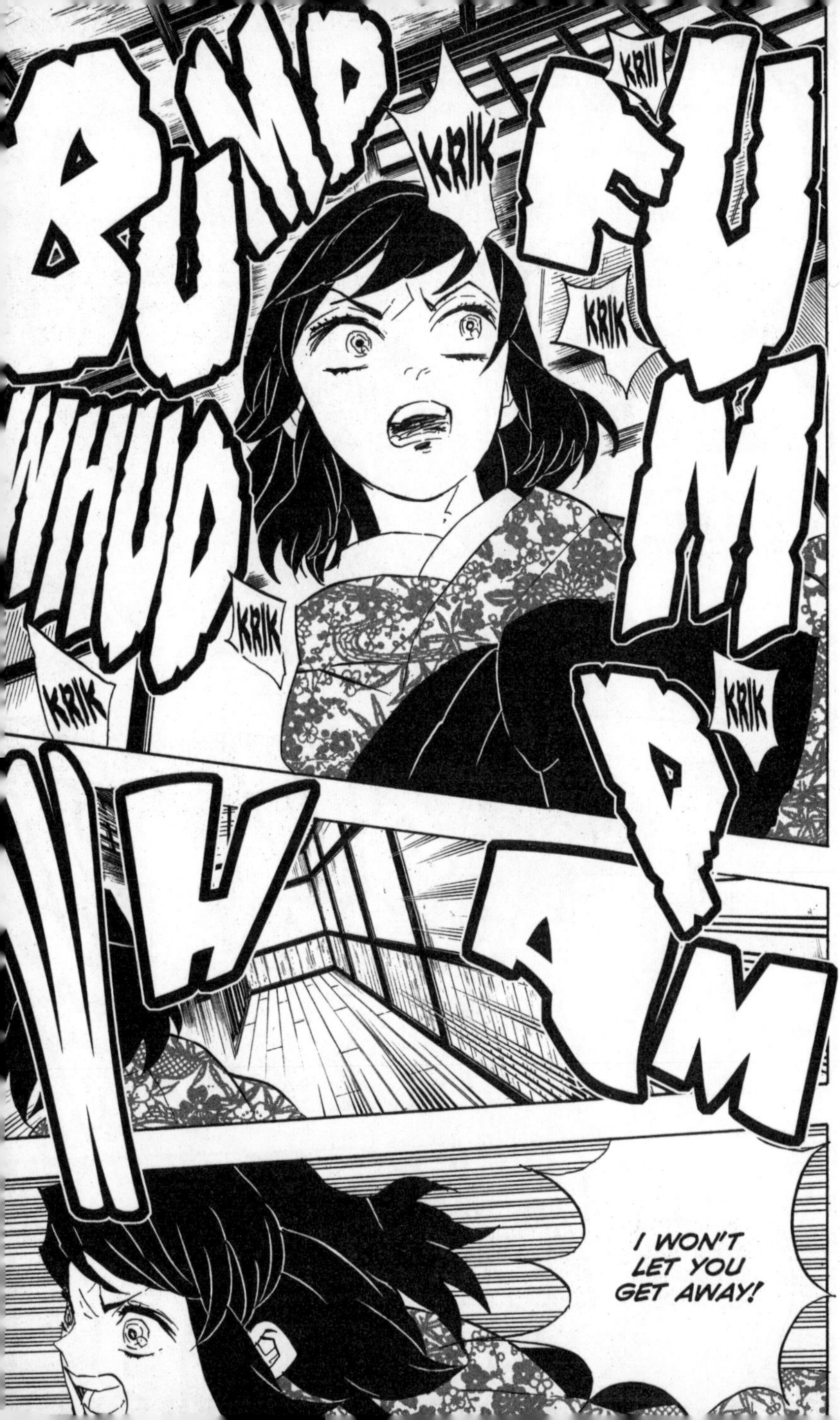
KRII
KRIK
BUMP
KRIK
KRIK
KRIK
KRIK
WHAM
I WON'T LET YOU GET AWAY!

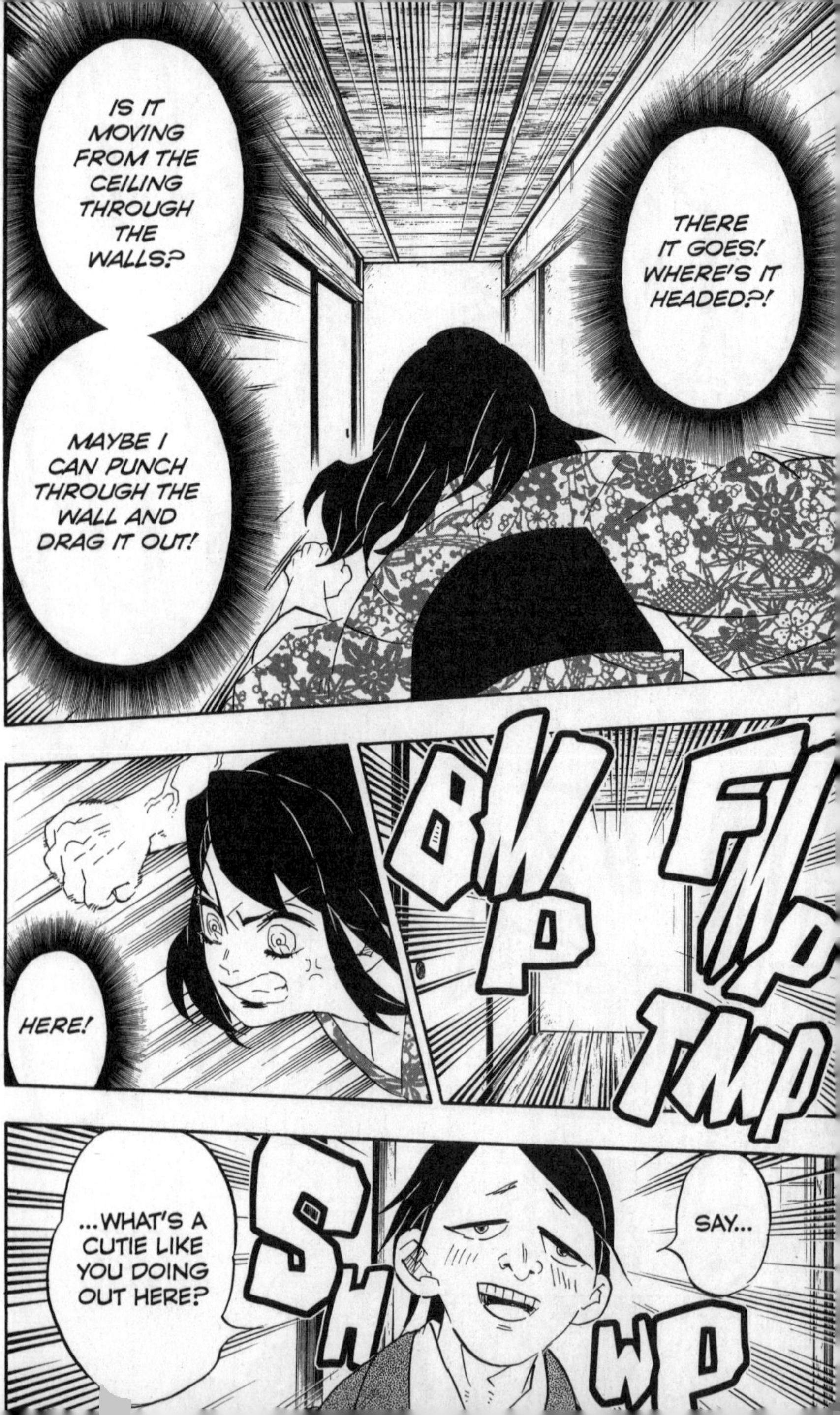
THERE IT GOES! WHERE'S IT HEADED?!
IS IT MOVING FROM THE CEILING THROUGH THE WALLS?
MAYBE I CAN PUNCH THROUGH THE WALL AND DRAG IT OUT!
FWP
TMP
BWP
HERE!
SAY...
...WHAT'S A CUTIE LIKE YOU DOING OUT HERE?
SHWP

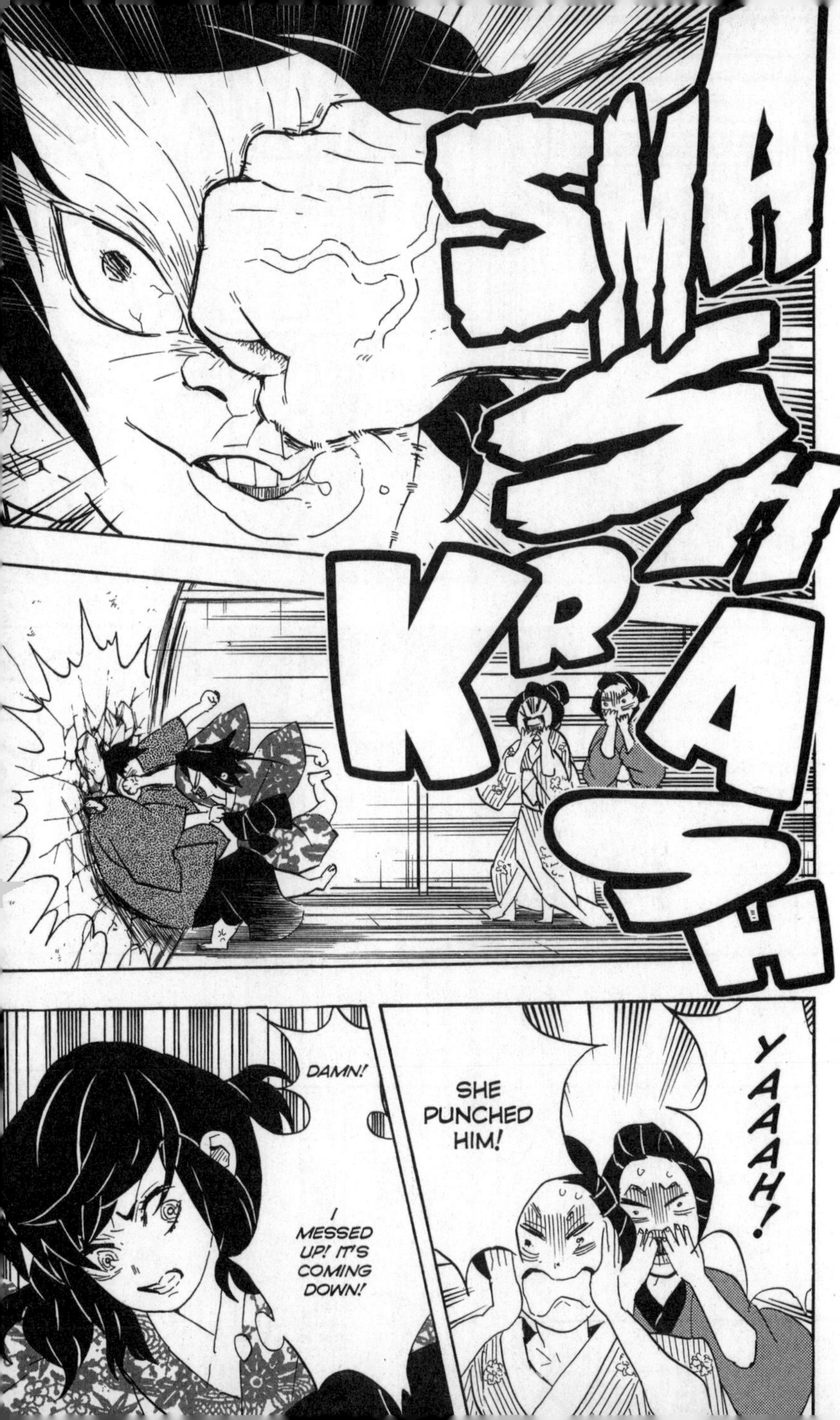
SMASH
KRASH
YAAAAH!
SHE PUNCHED HIM!
DAMN!
I MESSED UP! IT'S COMING DOWN!

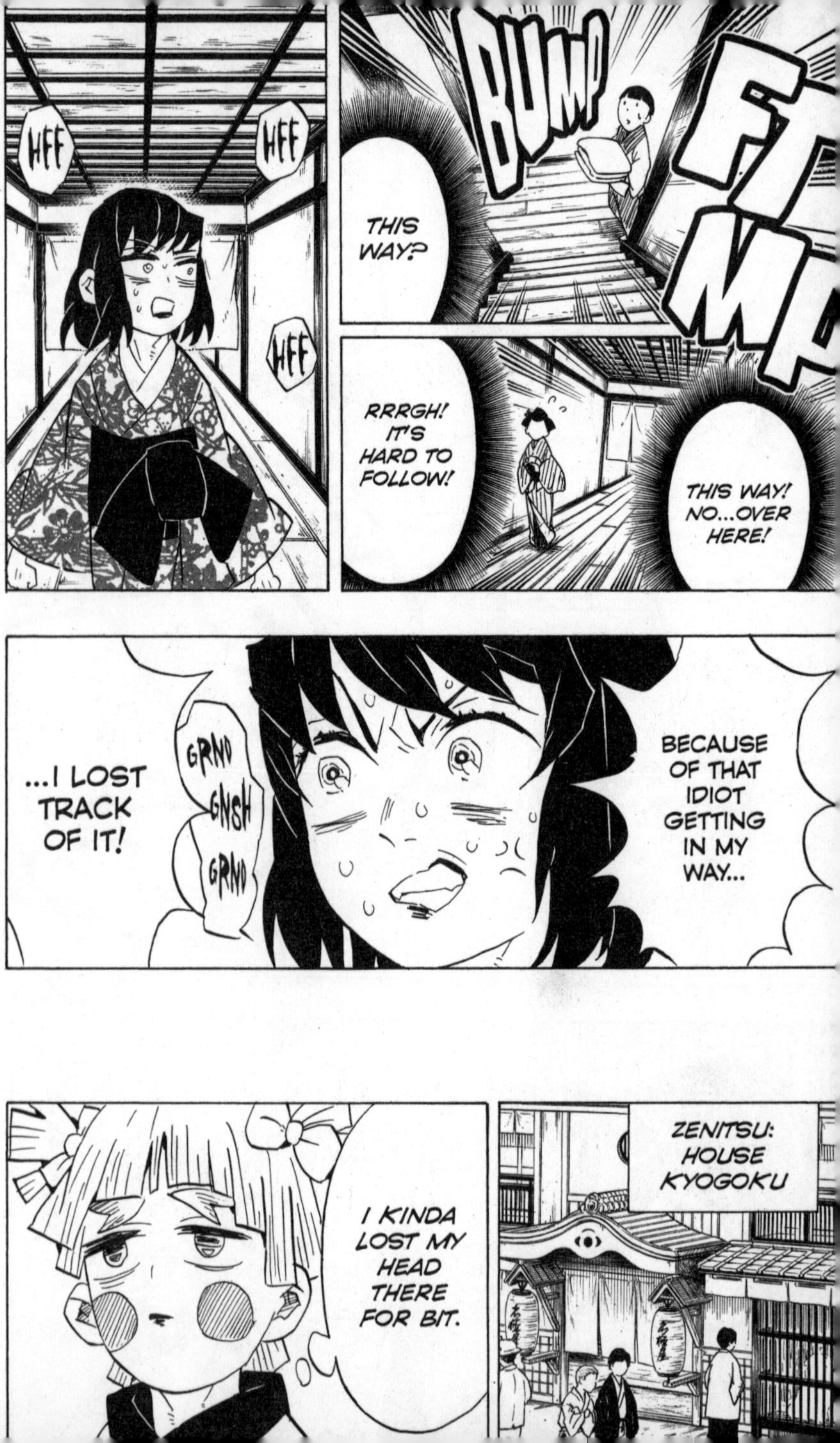
FTMP
BUMP
THIS WAY?
THIS WAY! NO...OVER HERE!
RRRGH! IT'S HARD TO FOLLOW!
HFF
HFF
HFF
BECAUSE OF THAT IDIOT GETTING IN MY WAY...
GRND
GNSH
GRND
...I LOST TRACK OF IT!
ZENITSU: HOUSE KYOGOKU
I KINDA LOST MY HEAD THERE FOR BIT.

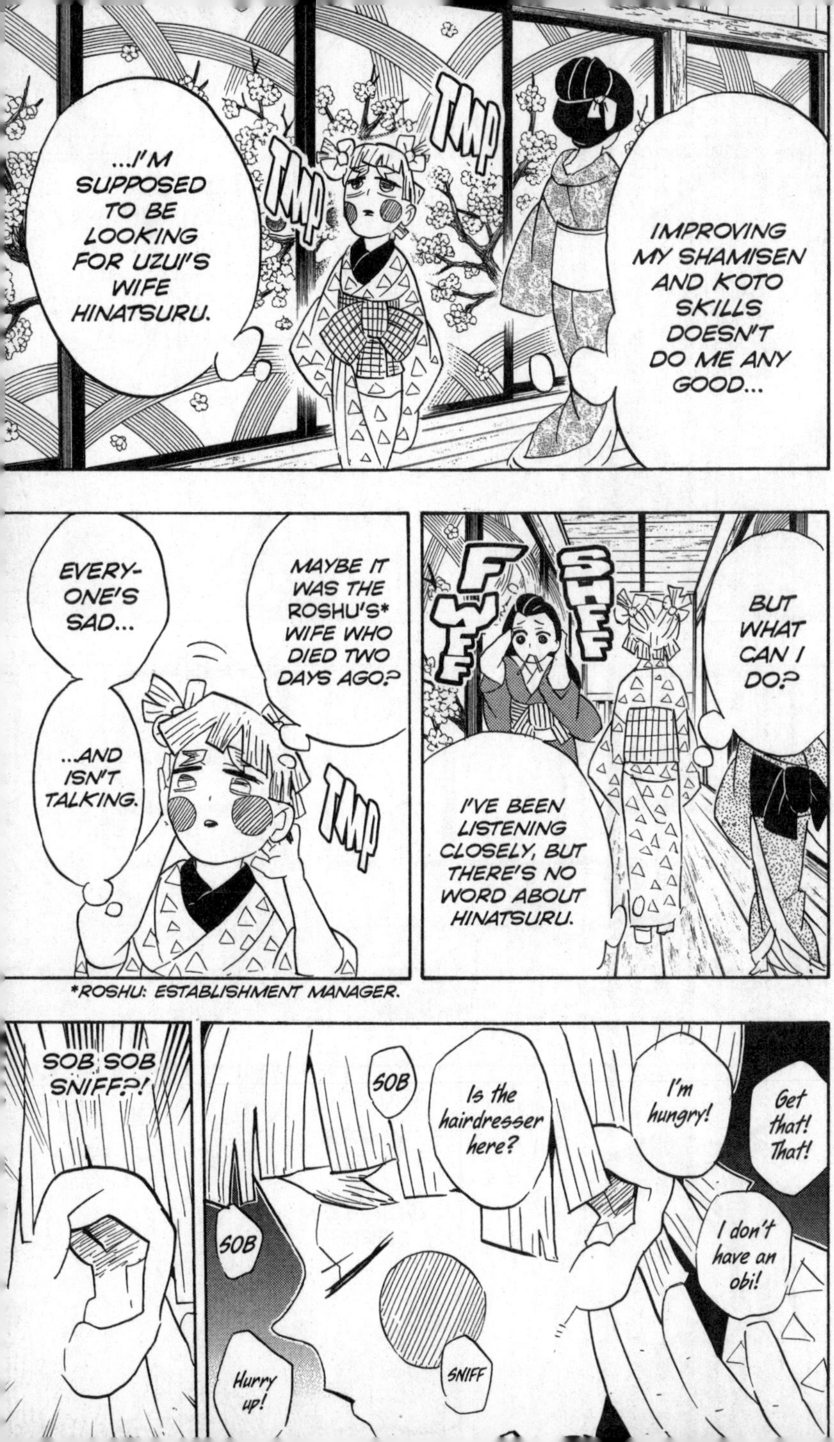
IMPROVING MY SHAMISEN AND KOTO SKILLS DOESN'T DO ME ANY GOOD...
TMP
TMP
...I'M SUPPOSED TO BE LOOKING FOR UZUI'S WIFE HINATSURU.
BUT WHAT CAN I DO?
SHFF
FWF
I'VE BEEN LISTENING CLOSELY, BUT THERE'S NO WORD ABOUT HINATSURU.
MAYBE IT WAS THE ROSHU'S* WIFE WHO DIED TWO DAYS AGO?
EVERY-ONE'S SAD...
...AND ISN'T TALKING.
TMP
Get that! That!
I'm hungry!
Is the hairdresser here?
SOB
I don't have an obi!
SOB
SNIFF
Hurry up!
SOB SOB SNIFF?!

*ROSHU: ESTABLISHMENT MANAGER.

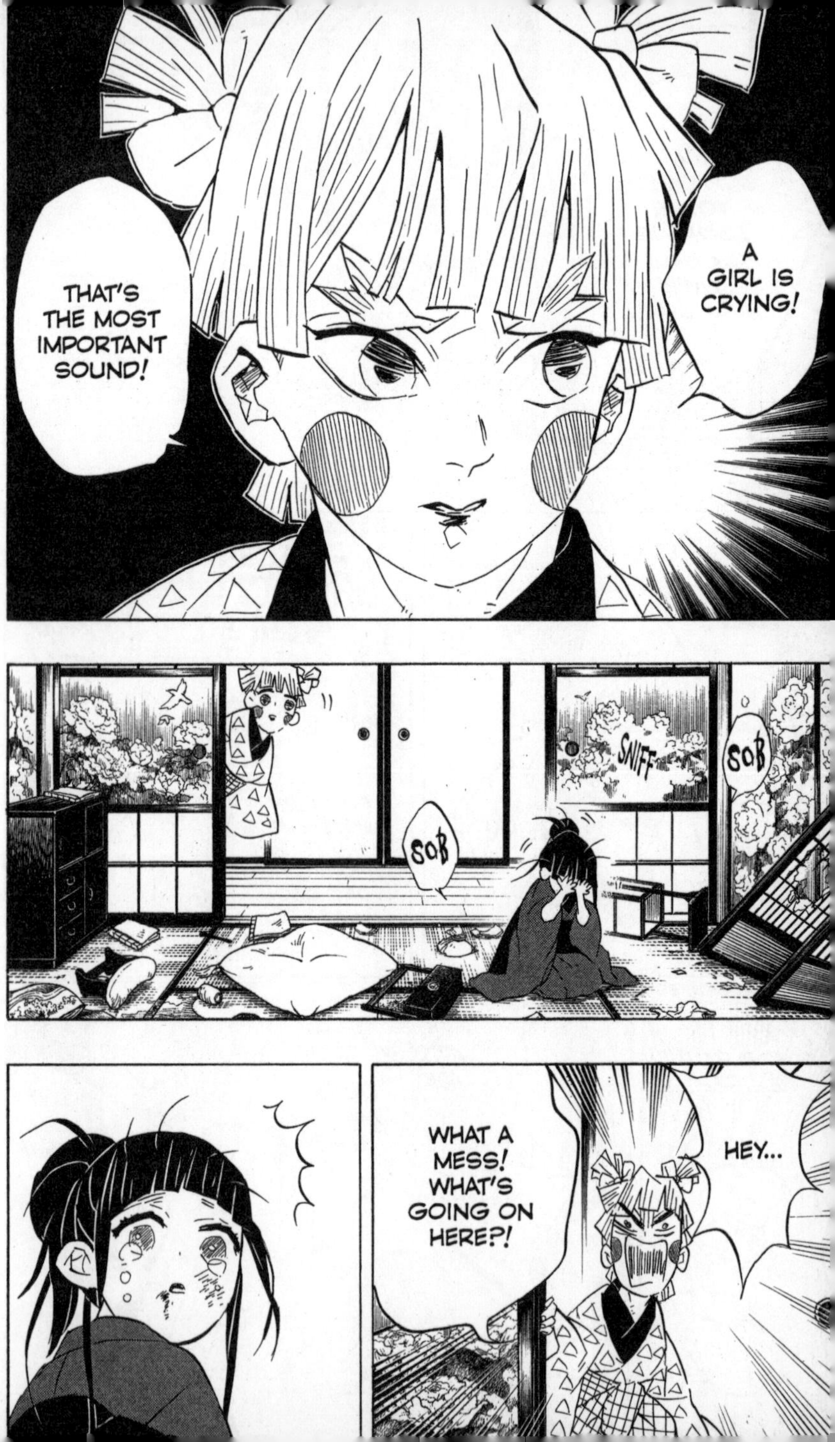
A GIRL IS CRYING!
THAT'S THE MOST IMPORTANT SOUND!
SOB
SNIFF
SOB
HEY...
WHAT A MESS! WHAT'S GOING ON HERE?!

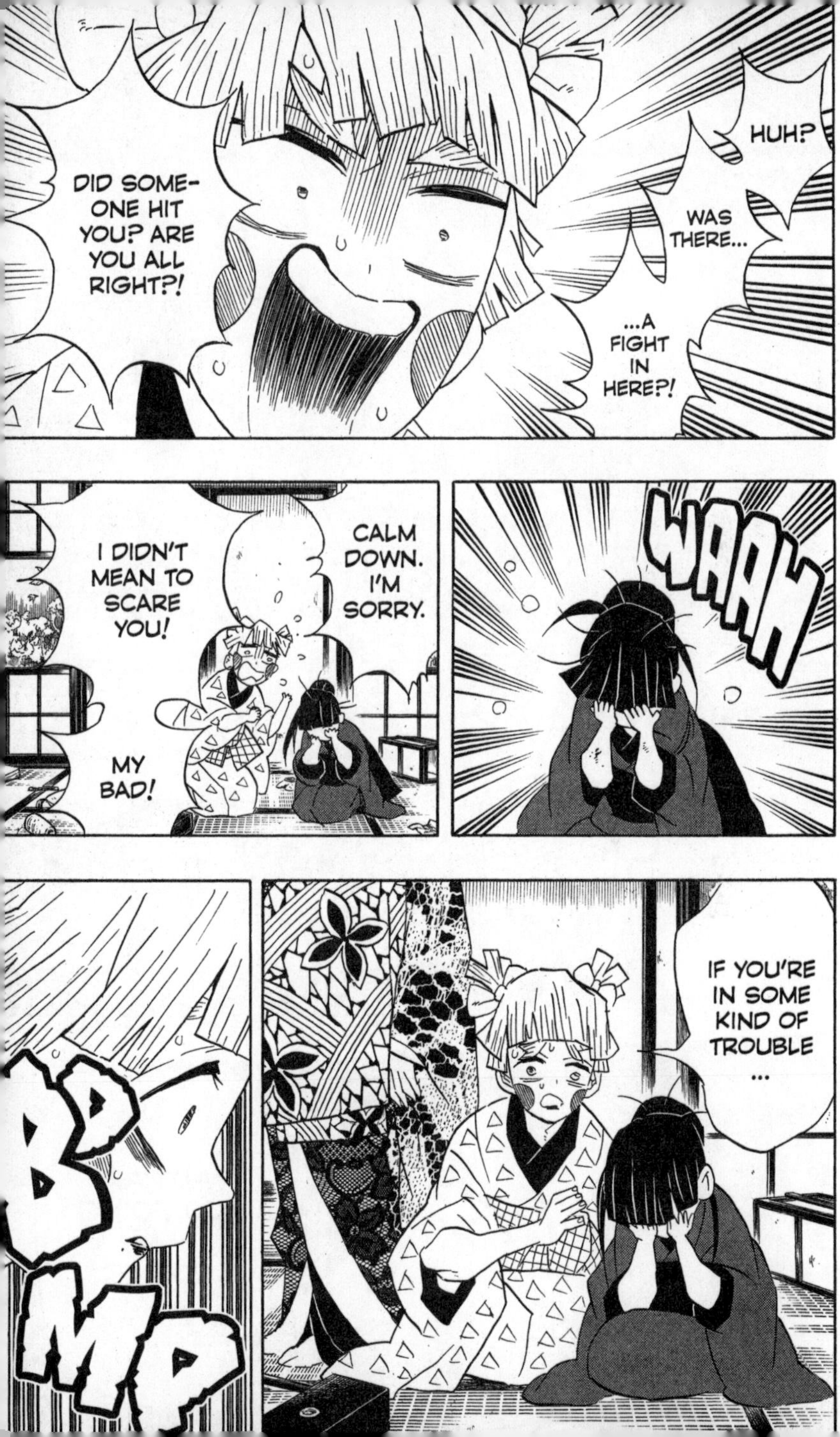
HUH?
WAS THERE...
...A FIGHT IN HERE?!
DID SOME-ONE HIT YOU? ARE YOU ALL RIGHT?!
WAAH
CALM DOWN. I'M SORRY.
I DIDN'T MEAN TO SCARE YOU!
MY BAD!
IF YOU'RE IN SOME KIND OF TROUBLE ...
BOMP

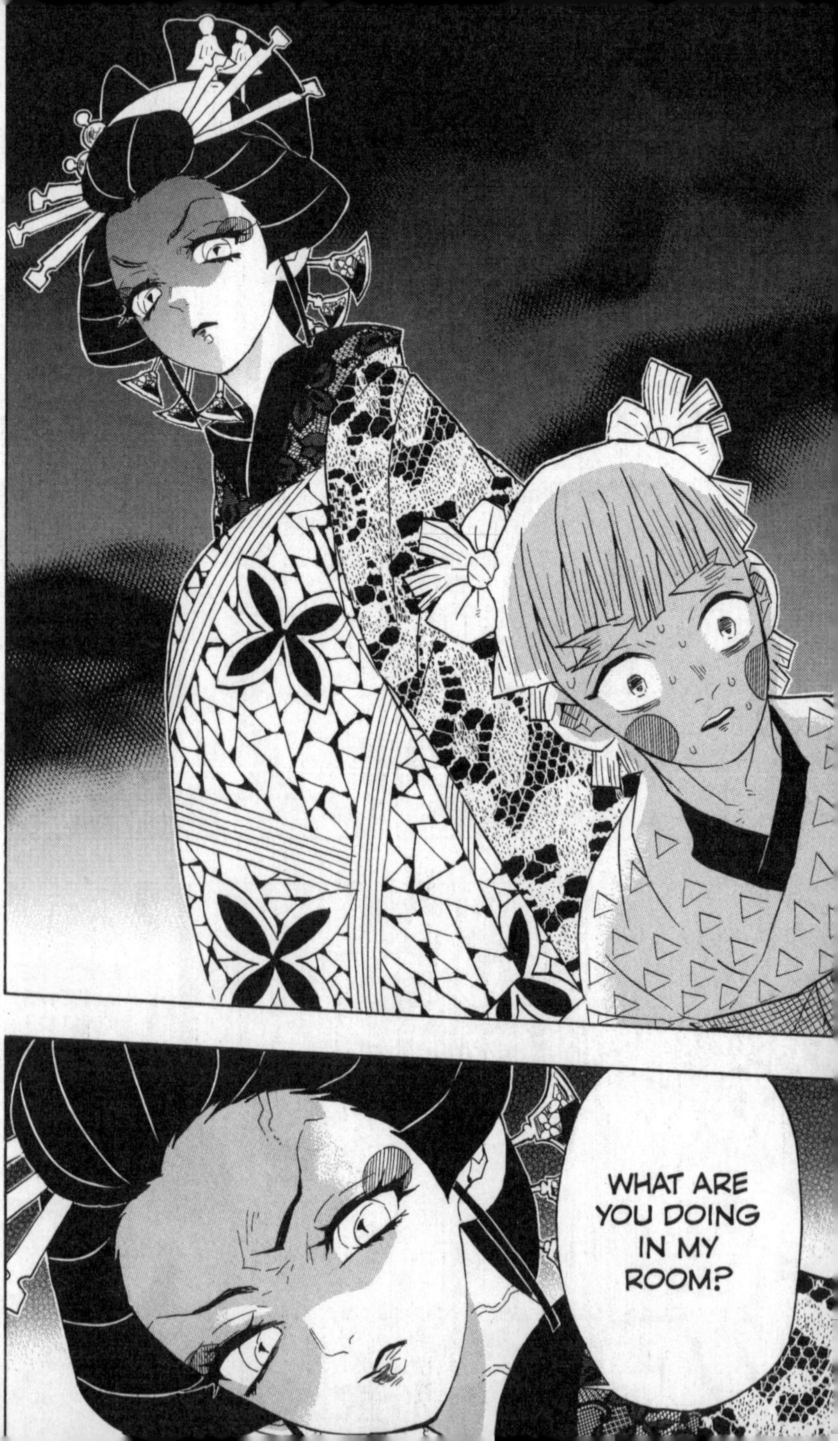
WHAT ARE YOU DOING IN MY ROOM?

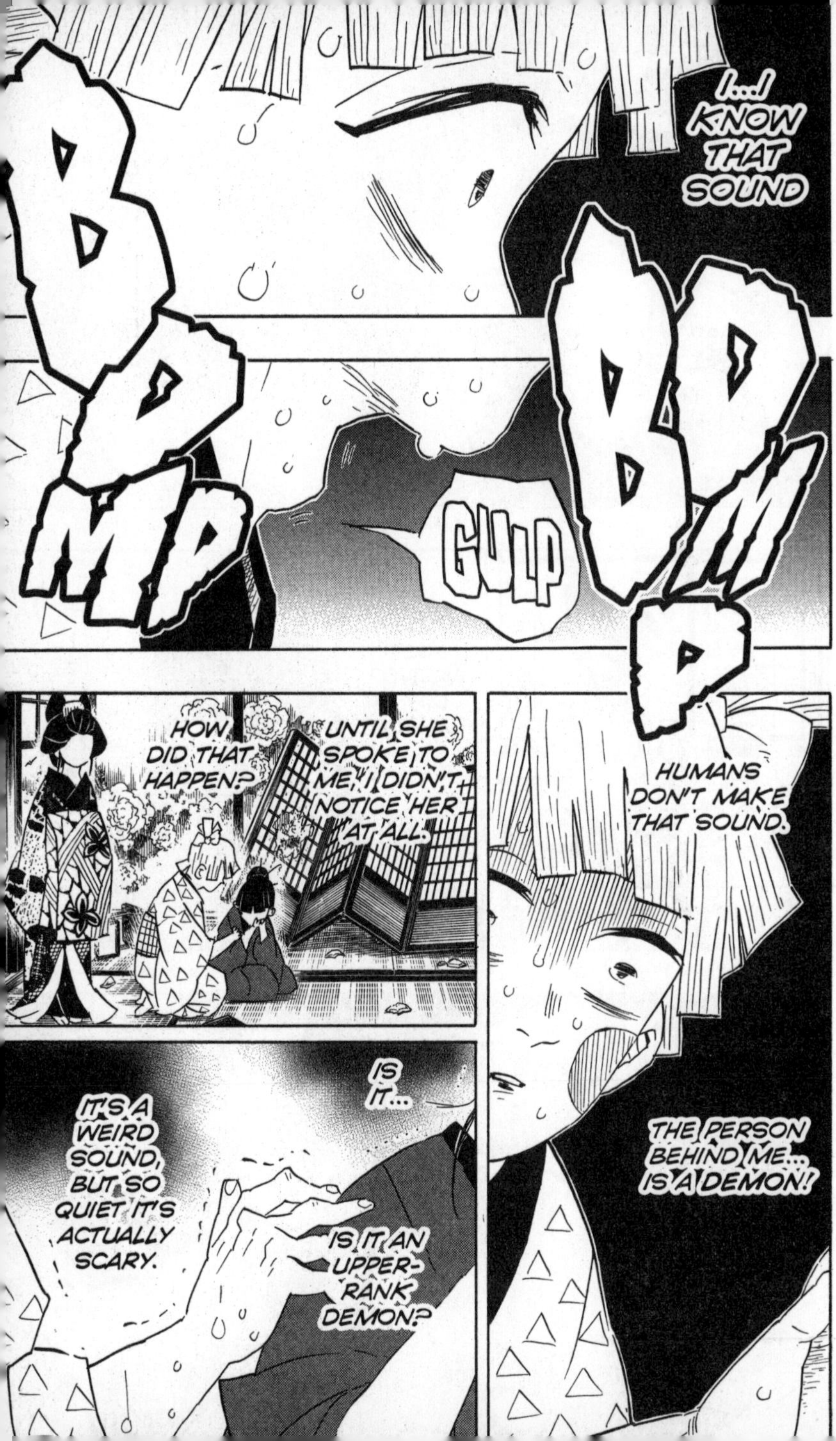
I...I KNOW THAT SOUND
BDMP
GULP
BDMP
HUMANS DON'T MAKE THAT SOUND.
THE PERSON BEHIND ME... IS A DEMON!
UNTIL SHE SPOKE TO ME, I DIDN'T NOTICE HER AT ALL.
HOW DID THAT HAPPEN?
IS IT...
IT'S A WEIRD SOUND, BUT SO QUIET IT'S ACTUALLY SCARY.
IS IT AN UPPER-RANK DEMON?

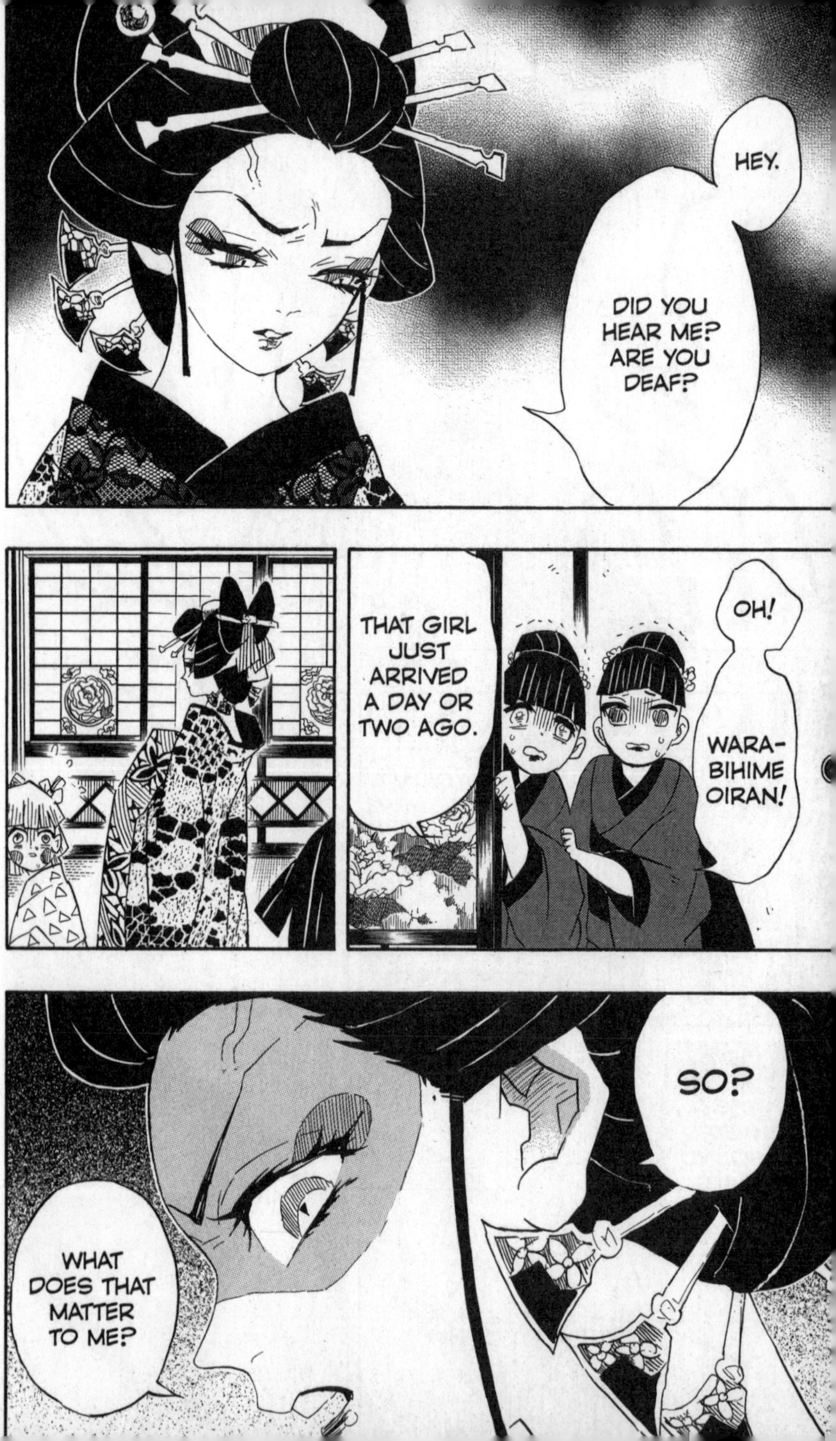
HEY.
DID YOU HEAR ME? ARE YOU DEAF?
OH!
WARA-BIHIME OIRAN!
THAT GIRL JUST ARRIVED A DAY OR TWO AGO.
SO?
WHAT DOES THAT MATTER TO ME?

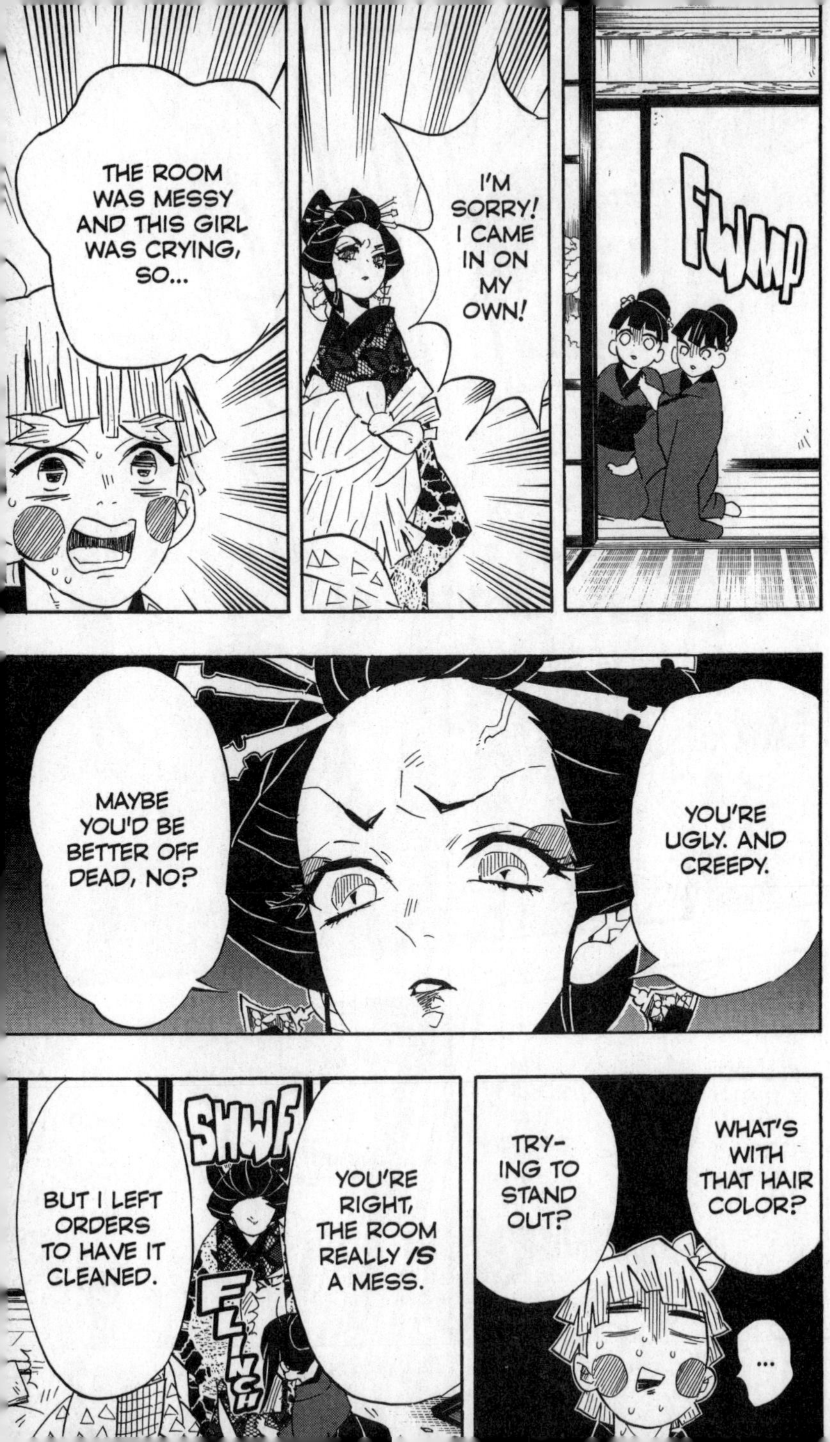
FWMP
I'M SORRY! I CAME IN ON MY OWN!
THE ROOM WAS MESSY AND THIS GIRL WAS CRYING, SO...
YOU'RE UGLY. AND CREEPY.
MAYBE YOU'D BE BETTER OFF DEAD, NO?
WHAT'S WITH THAT HAIR COLOR?
TRY-ING TO STAND OUT?
...
YOU'RE RIGHT, THE ROOM REALLY IS A MESS.
SHWF
BUT I LEFT ORDERS TO HAVE IT CLEANED.
FLINCH

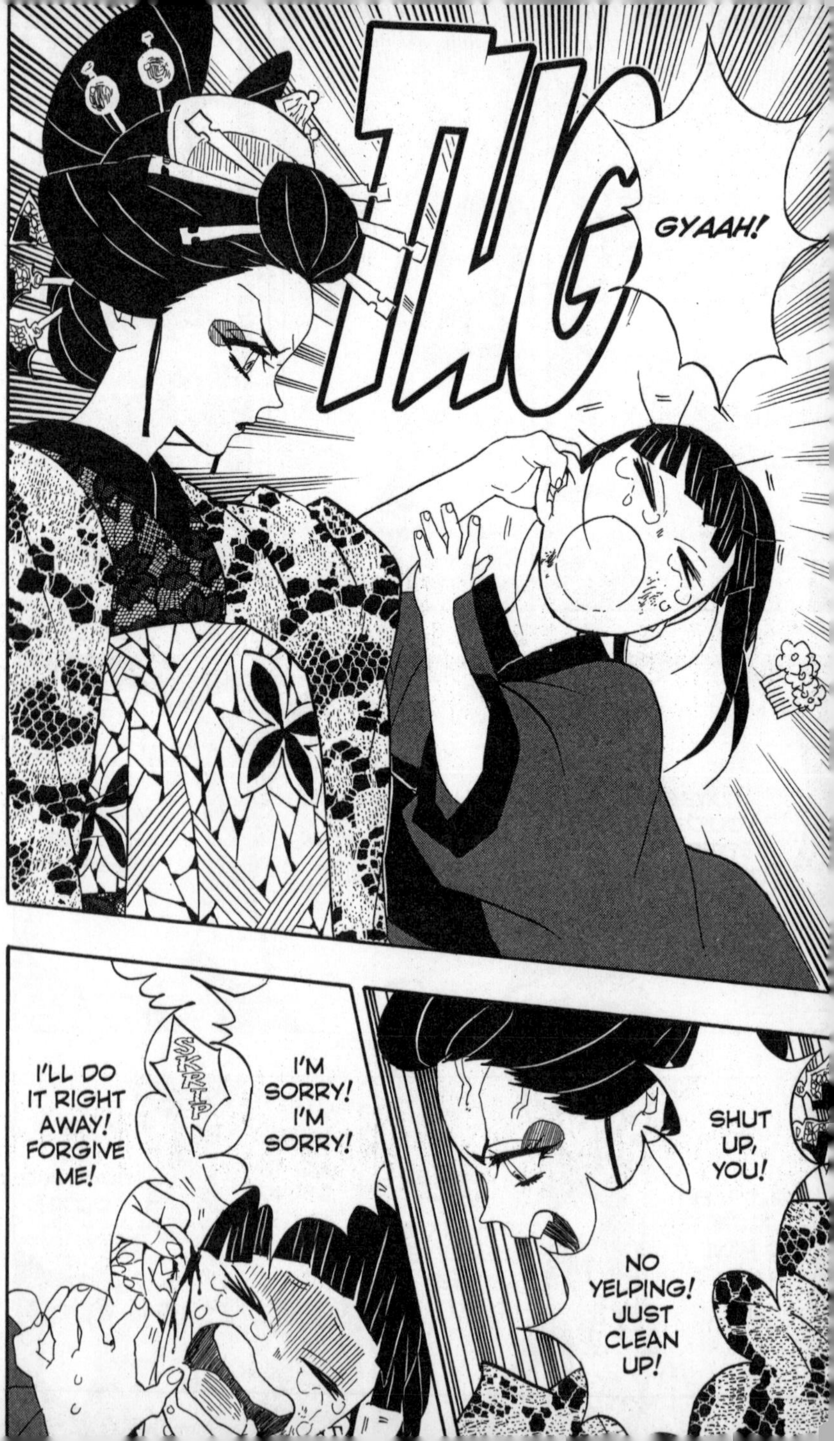
THG
GYAAH!
SHUT UP, YOU!
NO YELPING! JUST CLEAN UP!
I'M SORRY! I'M SORRY!
SKRIP
I'LL DO IT RIGHT AWAY! FORGIVE ME!

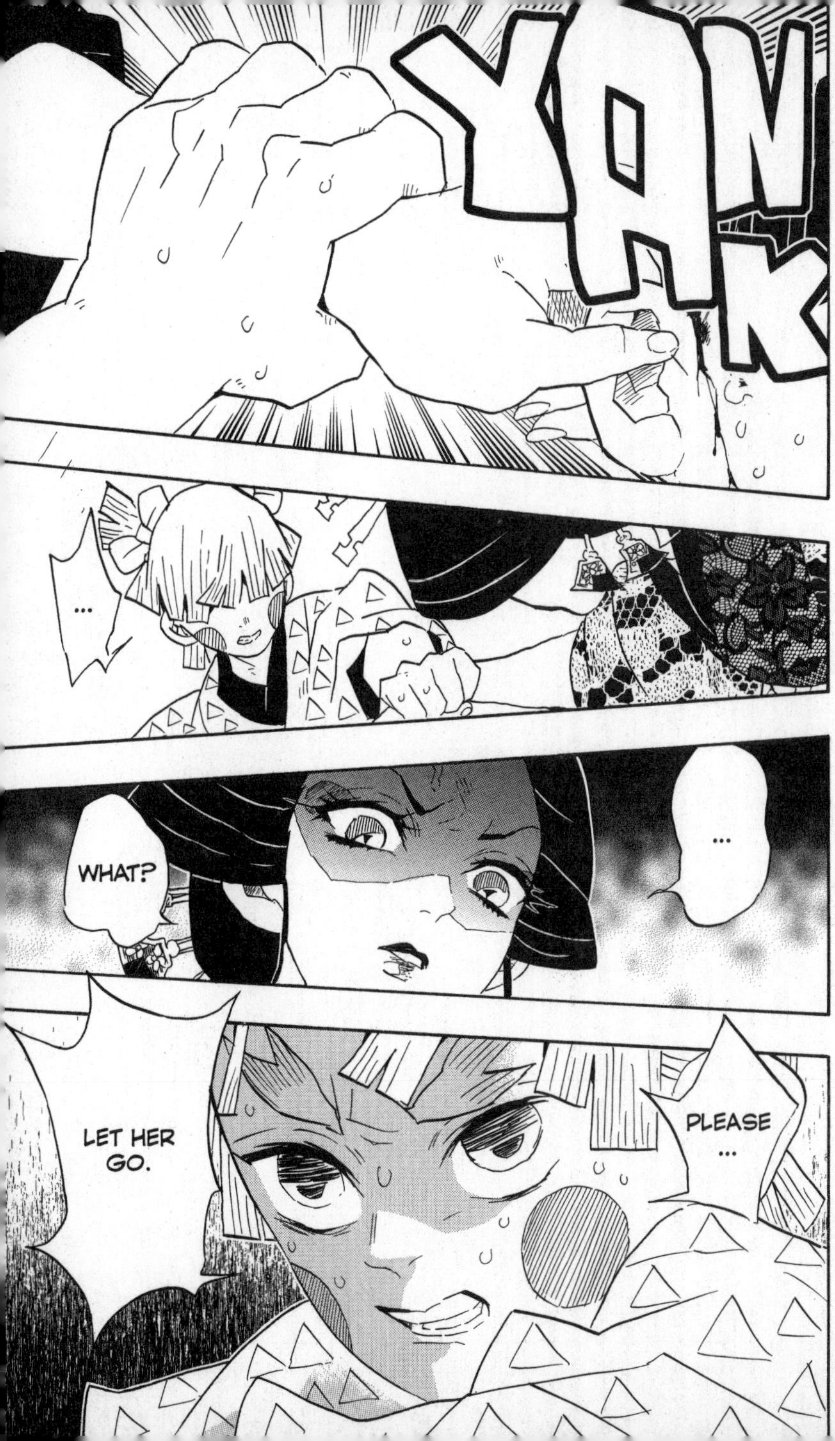
YANK
...
...
WHAT?
PLEASE ...
LET HER GO.

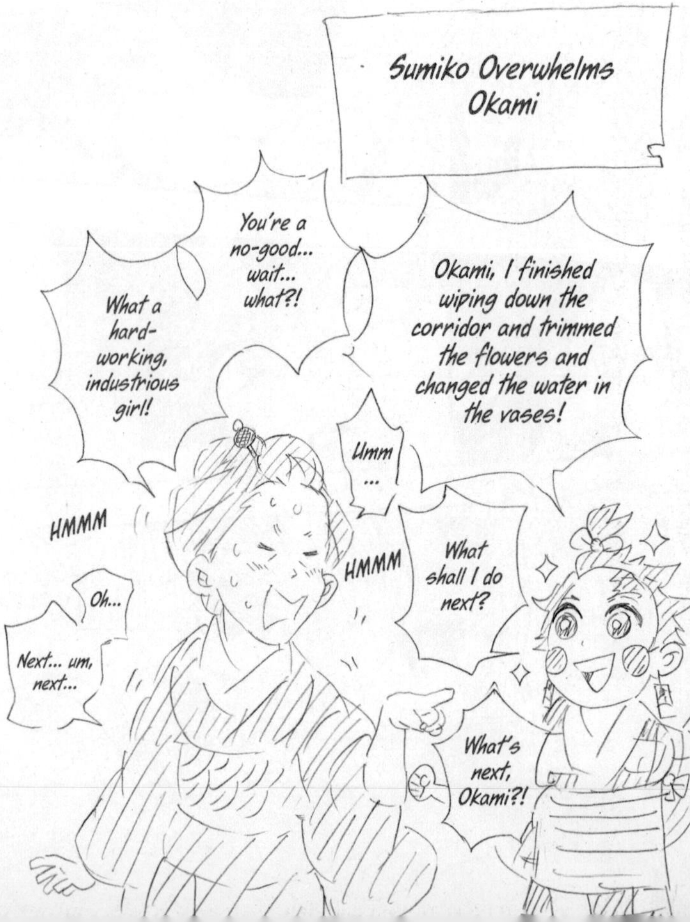
Sumiko Overwhelms Okami
Okami, I finished wiping down the corridor and trimmed the flowers and changed the water in the vases!
You're a no-good... wait... what?!
What a hard-working, industrious girl!
Umm ...
What shall I do next?
HMMM
HMMM
What's next, Okami?!
Oh...
Next... um, next...

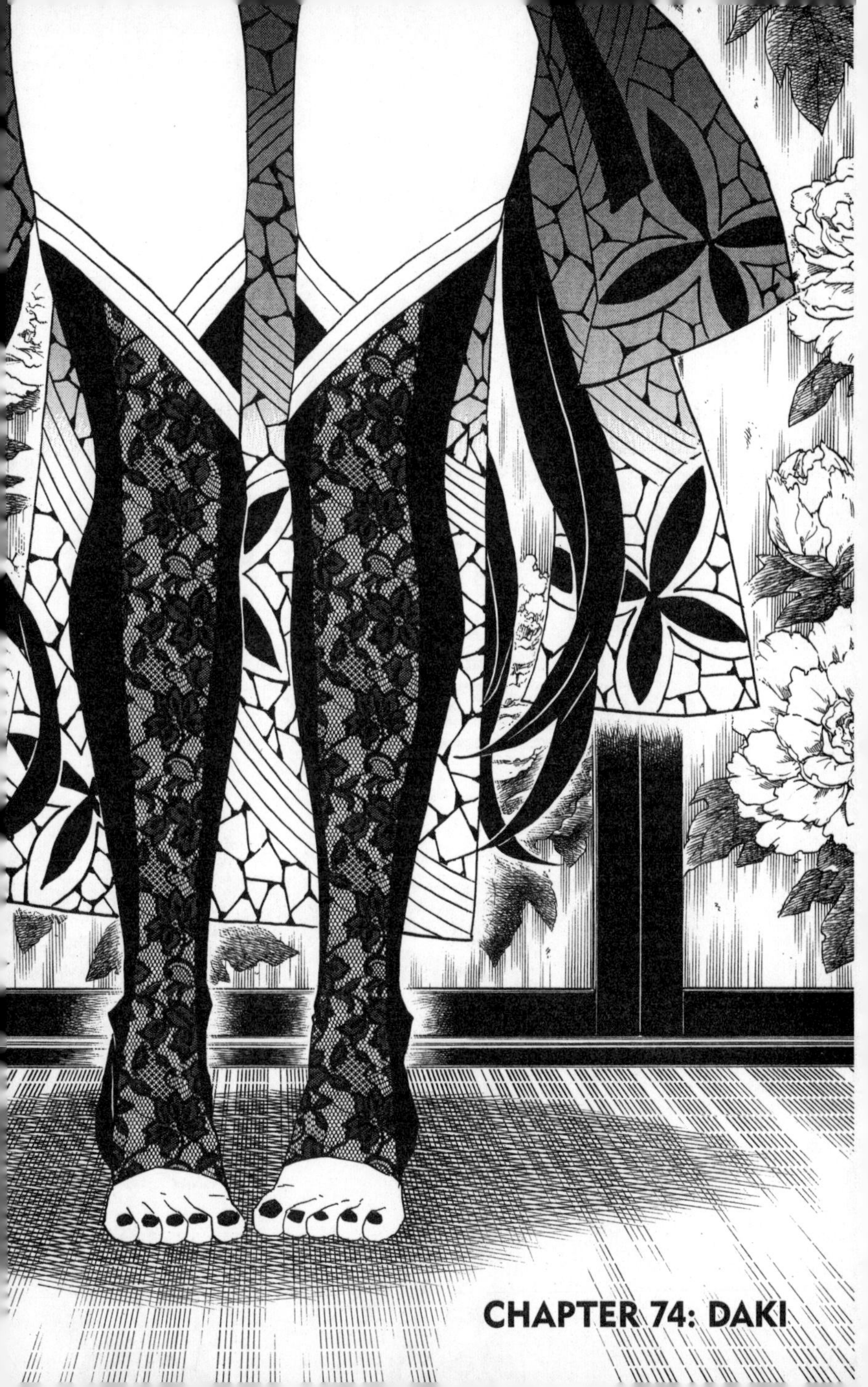

CHAPTER 74: DAKI

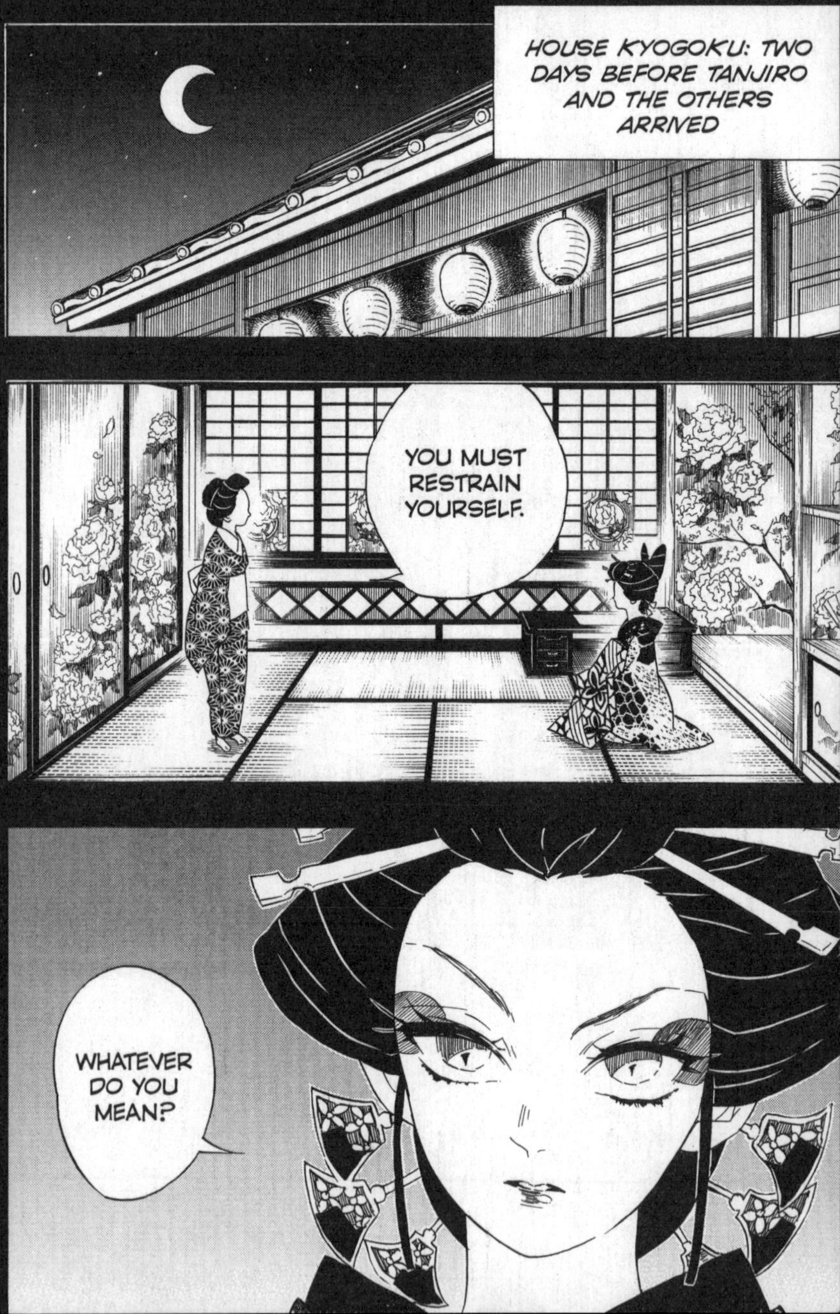
HOUSE KYOGOKU: TWO DAYS BEFORE TANJIRO AND THE OTHERS ARRIVED
YOU MUST RESTRAIN YOURSELF.
WHATEVER DO YOU MEAN?

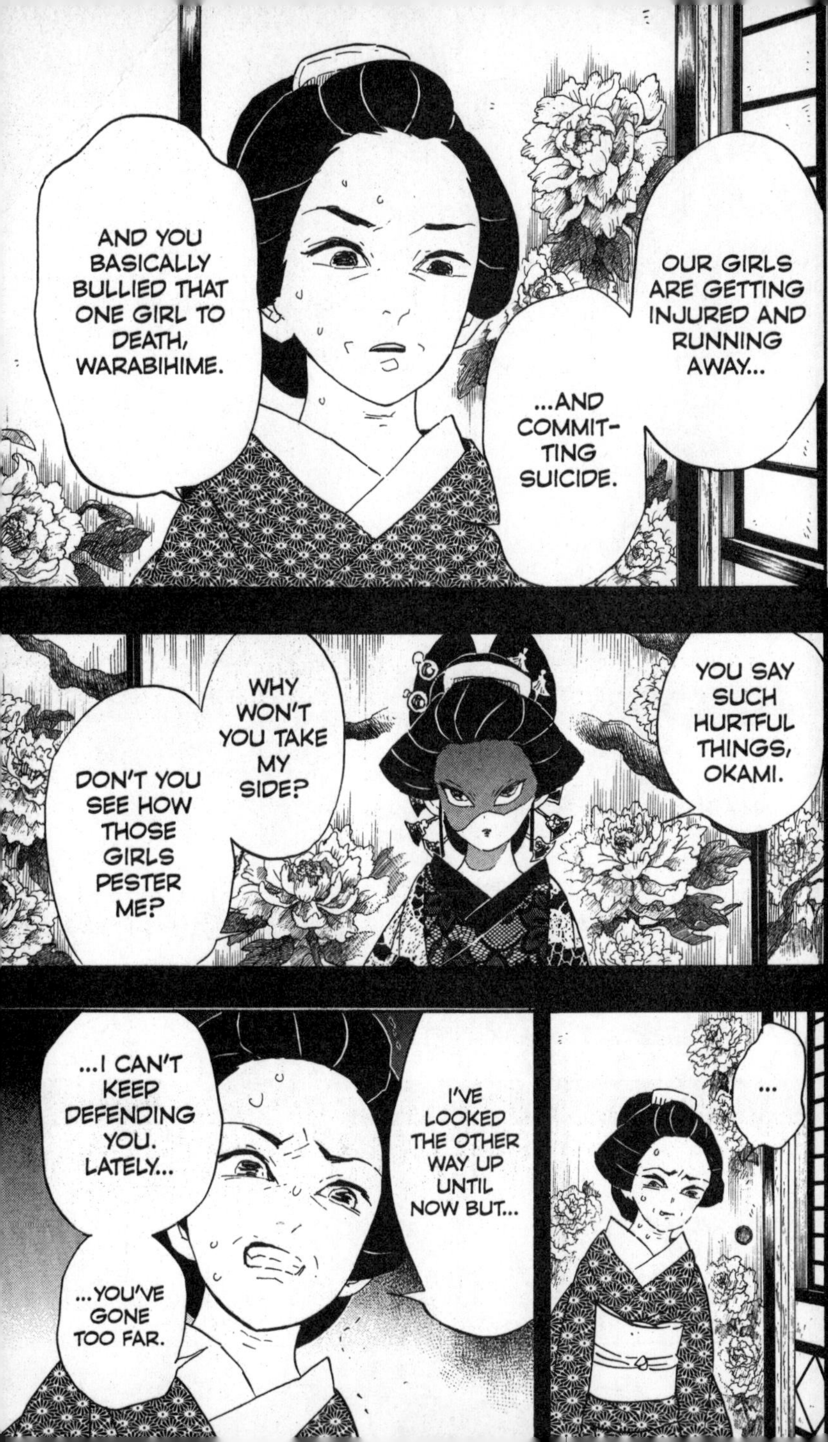
OUR GIRLS ARE GETTING INJURED AND RUNNING AWAY...
...AND COMMIT-TING SUICIDE.
AND YOU BASICALLY BULLIED THAT ONE GIRL TO DEATH, WARABIHIME.
YOU SAY SUCH HURTFUL THINGS, OKAMI.
WHY WON'T YOU TAKE MY SIDE?
DON'T YOU SEE HOW THOSE GIRLS PESTER ME?
...
I'VE LOOKED THE OTHER WAY UP UNTIL NOW BUT...
...I CAN'T KEEP DEFENDING YOU. LATELY...
...YOU'VE GONE TOO FAR.

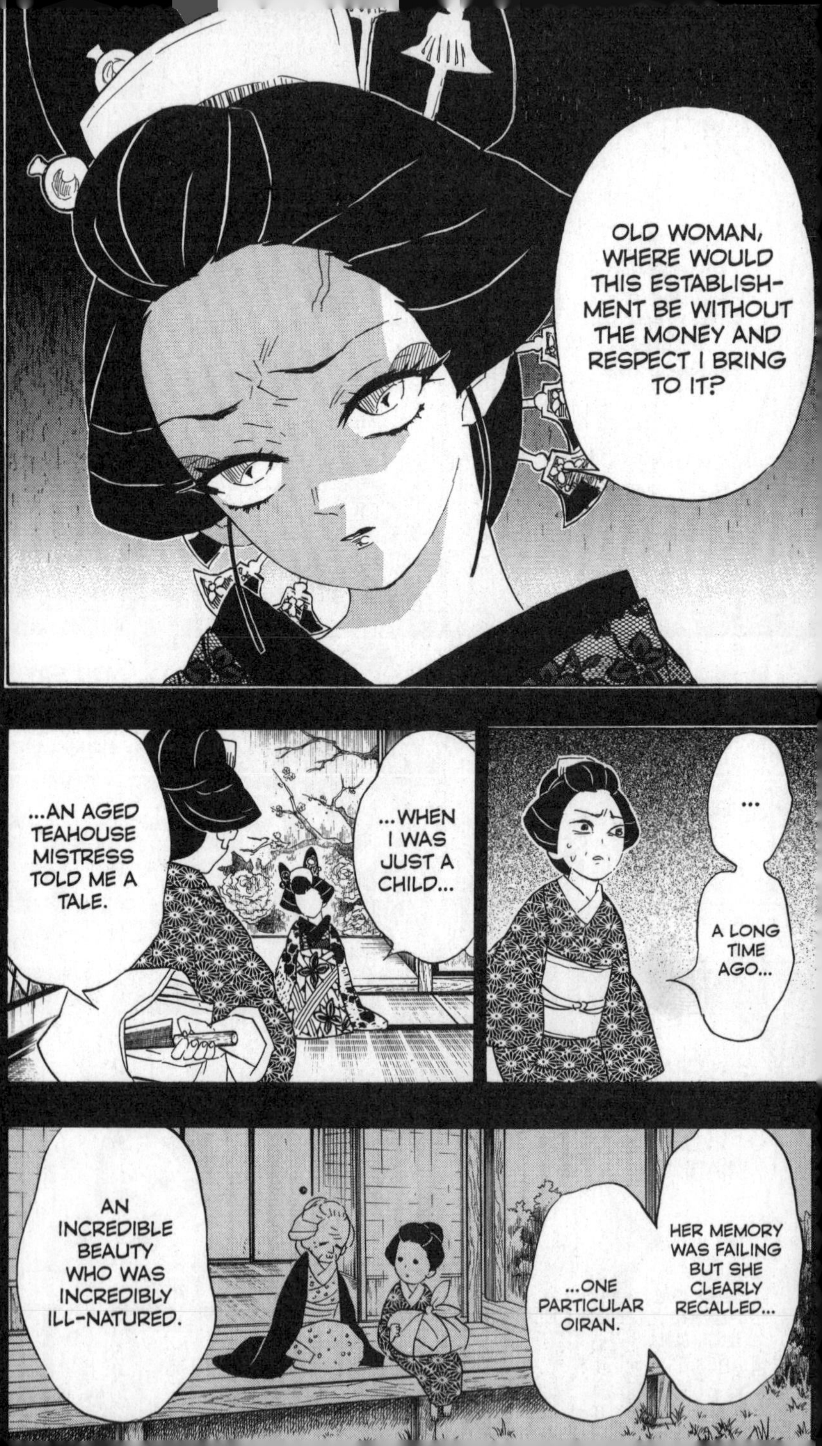
OLD WOMAN, WHERE WOULD THIS ESTABLISHMENT BE WITHOUT THE MONEY AND RESPECT I BRING TO IT?
...
A LONG TIME AGO...
...WHEN I WAS JUST A CHILD...
...AN AGED TEAHOUSE MISTRESS TOLD ME A TALE.
HER MEMORY WAS FAILING BUT SHE CLEARLY RECALLED...
...ONE PARTICULAR OIRAN.
AN INCREDIBLE BEAUTY WHO WAS INCREDIBLY ILL-NATURED.

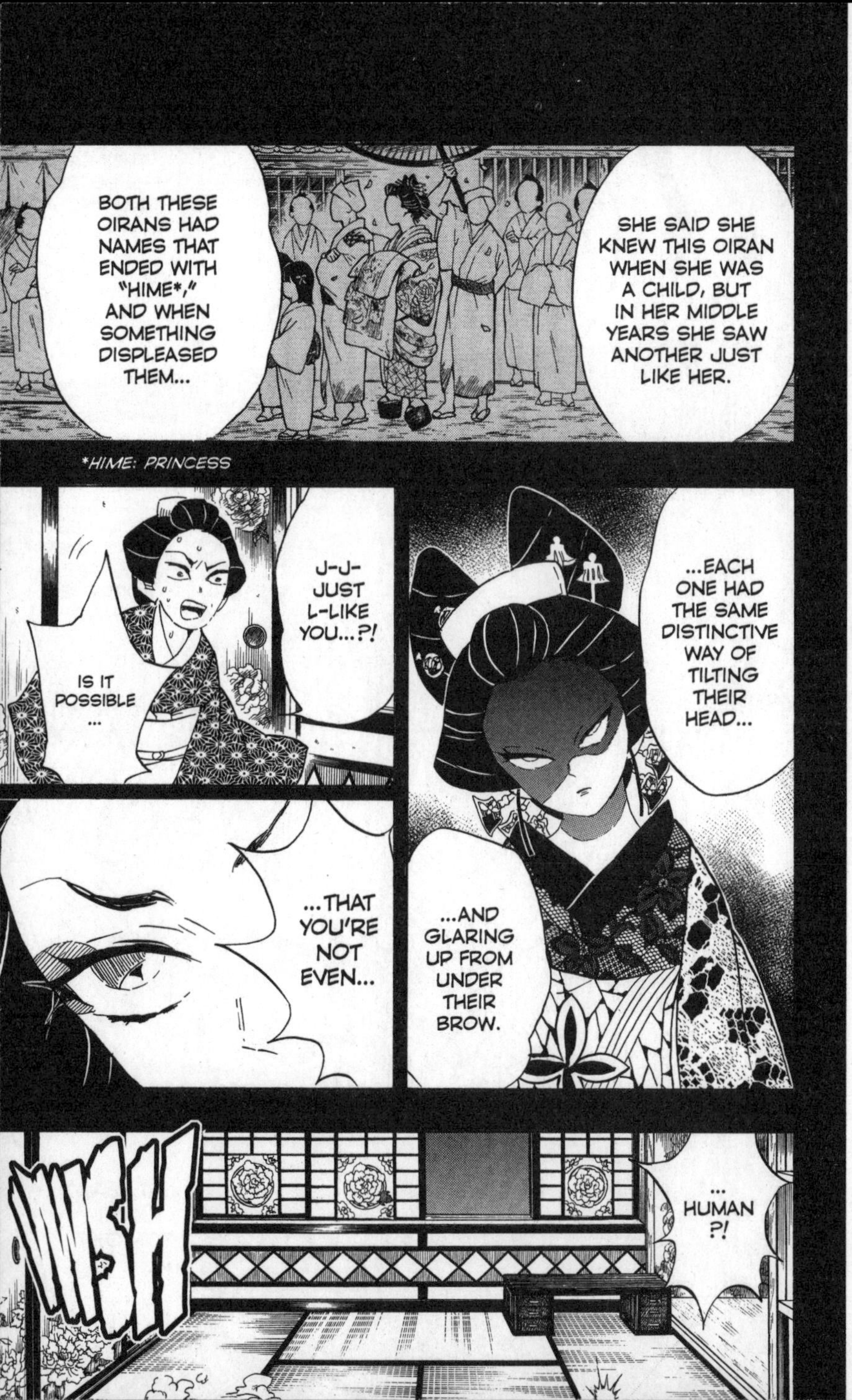
SHE SAID SHE KNEW THIS OIRAN WHEN SHE WAS A CHILD, BUT IN HER MIDDLE YEARS SHE SAW ANOTHER JUST LIKE HER.
BOTH THESE OIRANS HAD NAMES THAT ENDED WITH "HIME*," AND WHEN SOMETHING DISPLEASED THEM...
*HIME: PRINCESS
...EACH ONE HAD THE SAME DISTINCTIVE WAY OF TILTING THEIR HEAD...
...AND GLARING UP FROM UNDER THEIR BROW.
J-J-JUST L-LIKE YOU...?!
IS IT POSSIBLE ...
...THAT YOU'RE NOT EVEN...
...HUMAN?!

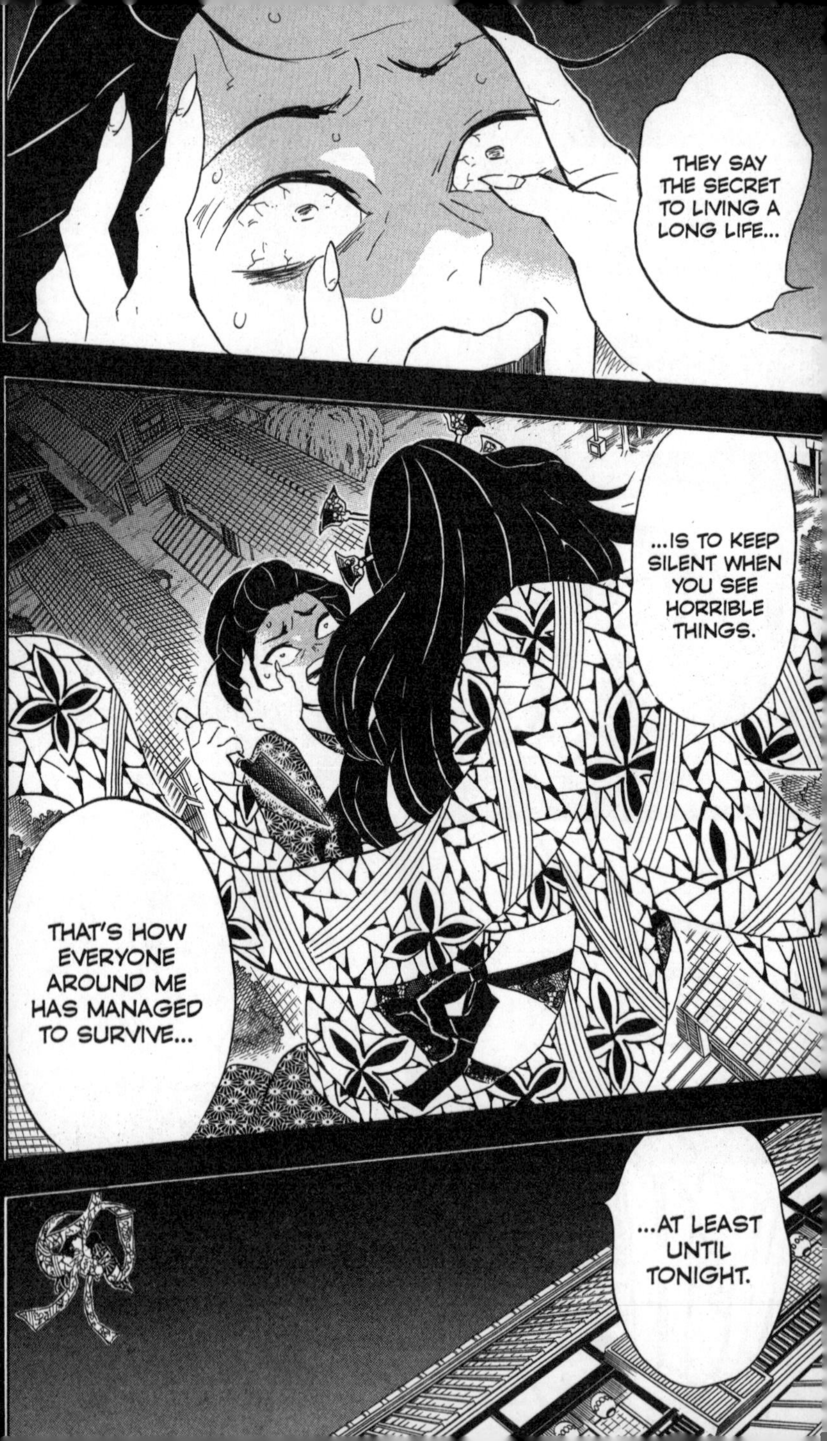
THEY SAY THE SECRET TO LIVING A LONG LIFE...
...IS TO KEEP SILENT WHEN YOU SEE HORRIBLE THINGS.
THAT'S HOW EVERYONE AROUND ME HAS MANAGED TO SURVIVE...
...AT LEAST UNTIL TONIGHT.

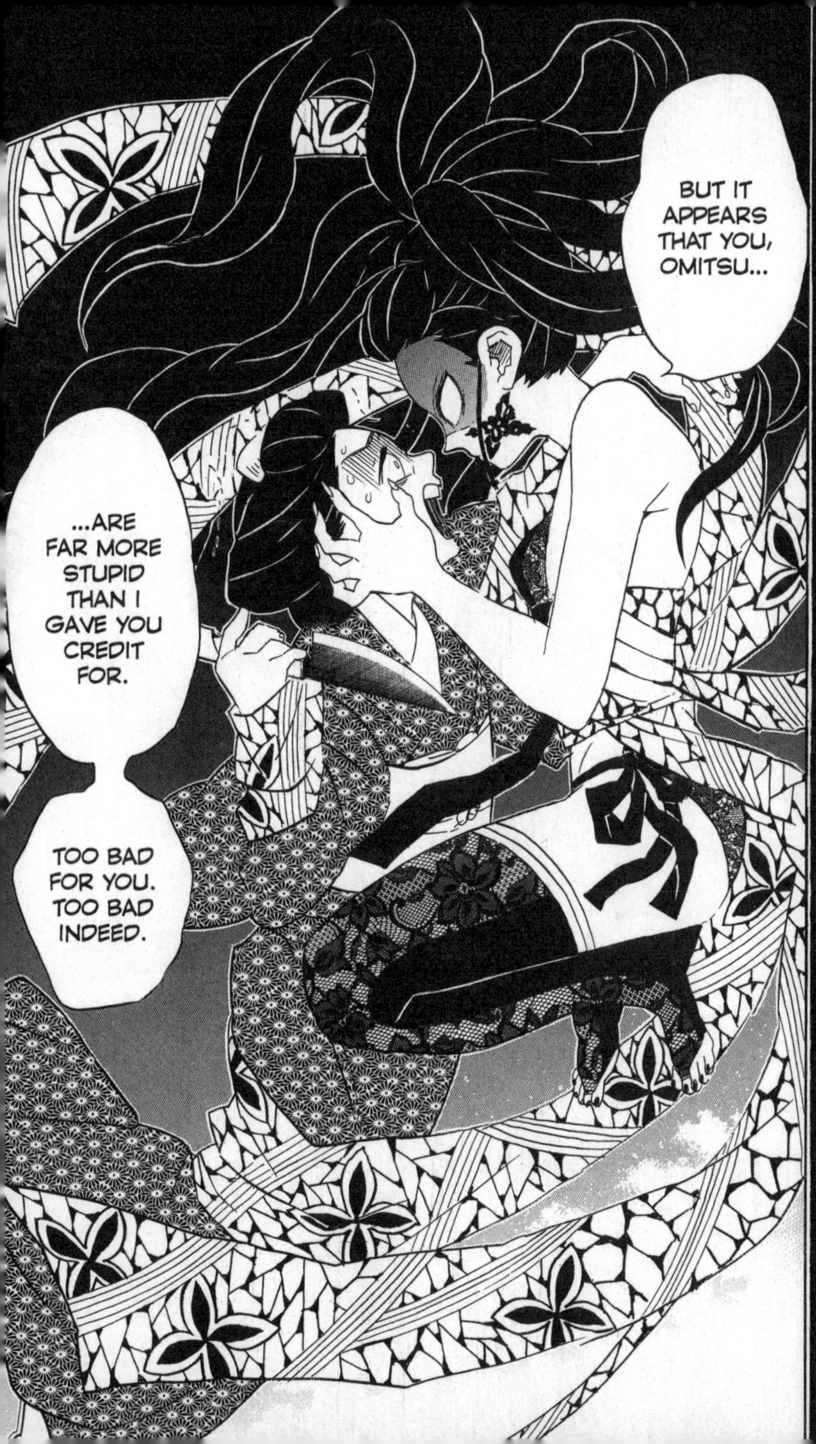
BUT IT APPEARS THAT YOU, OMITSU...
...ARE FAR MORE STUPID THAN I GAVE YOU CREDIT FOR.
TOO BAD FOR YOU. TOO BAD INDEED.

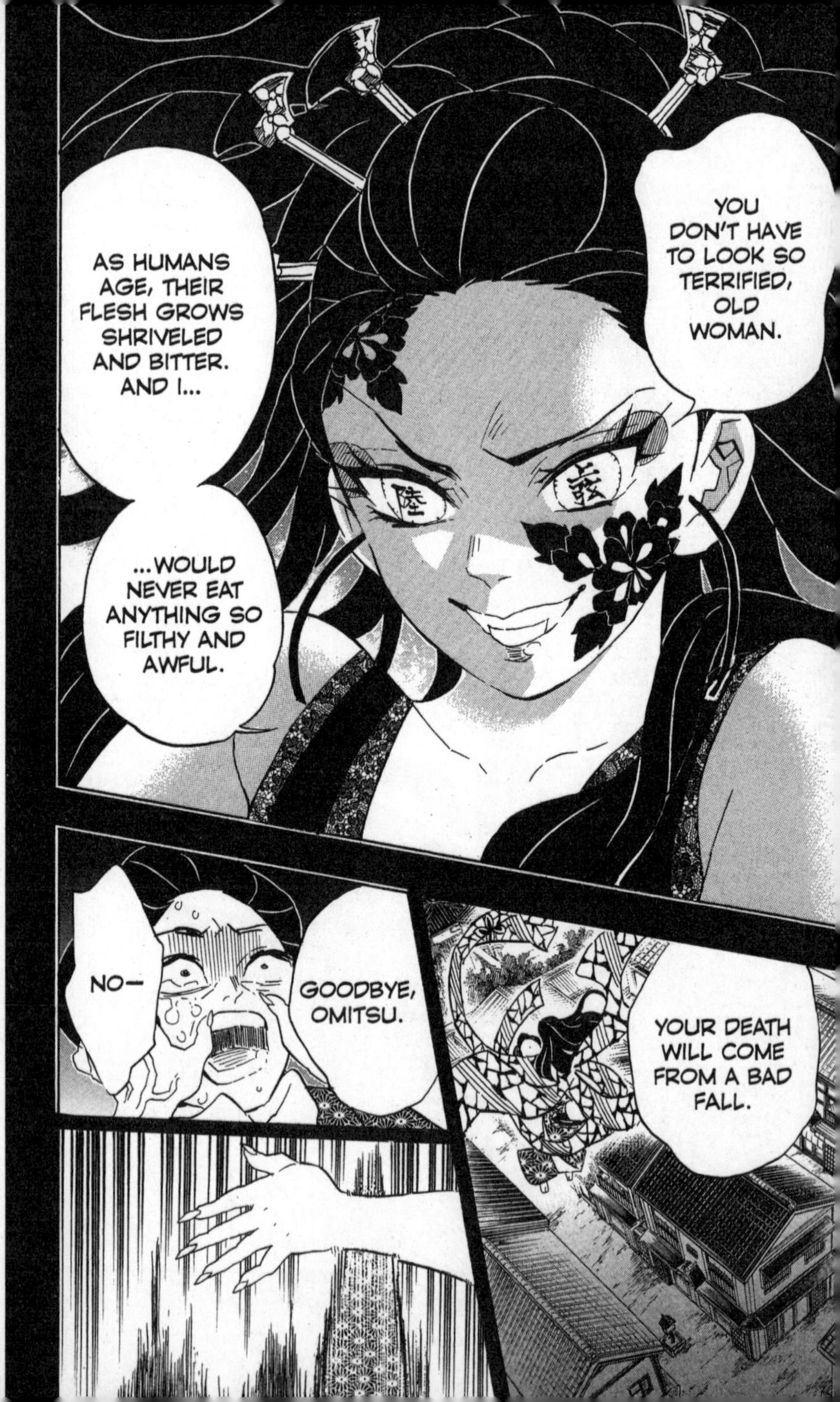
YOU DON'T HAVE TO LOOK SO TERRIFIED, OLD WOMAN.
AS HUMANS AGE, THEIR FLESH GROWS SHRIVELED AND BITTER. AND I...
...WOULD NEVER EAT ANYTHING SO FILTHY AND AWFUL.
YOUR DEATH WILL COME FROM A BAD FALL.
GOODBYE, OMITSU.
NO—

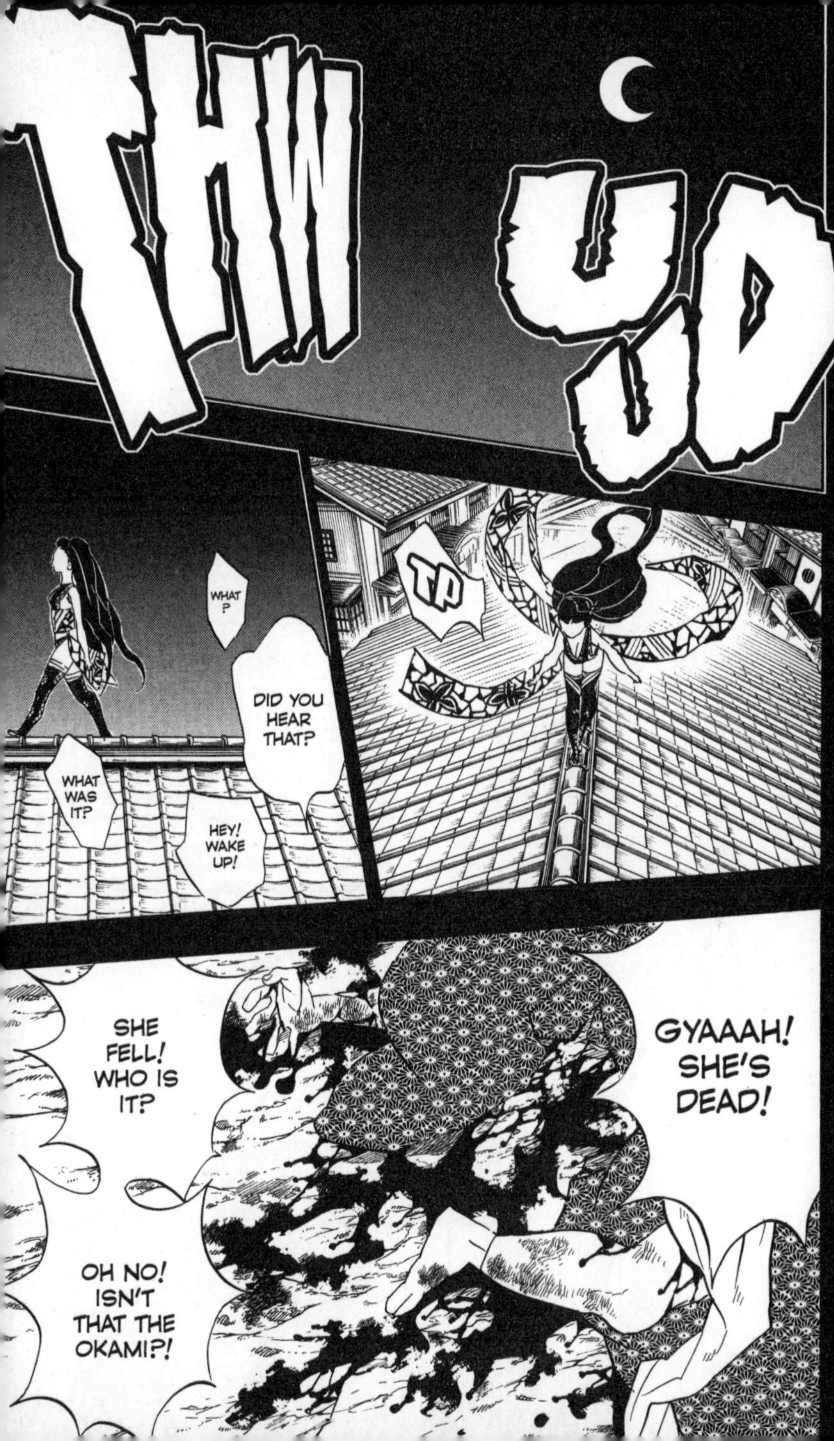
THW
UD
TP
WHAT?
DID YOU HEAR THAT?
WHAT WAS IT?
HEY! WAKE UP!
GYAAAH! SHE'S DEAD!
SHE FELL! WHO IS IT?
OH NO! ISN'T THAT THE OKAMI?!

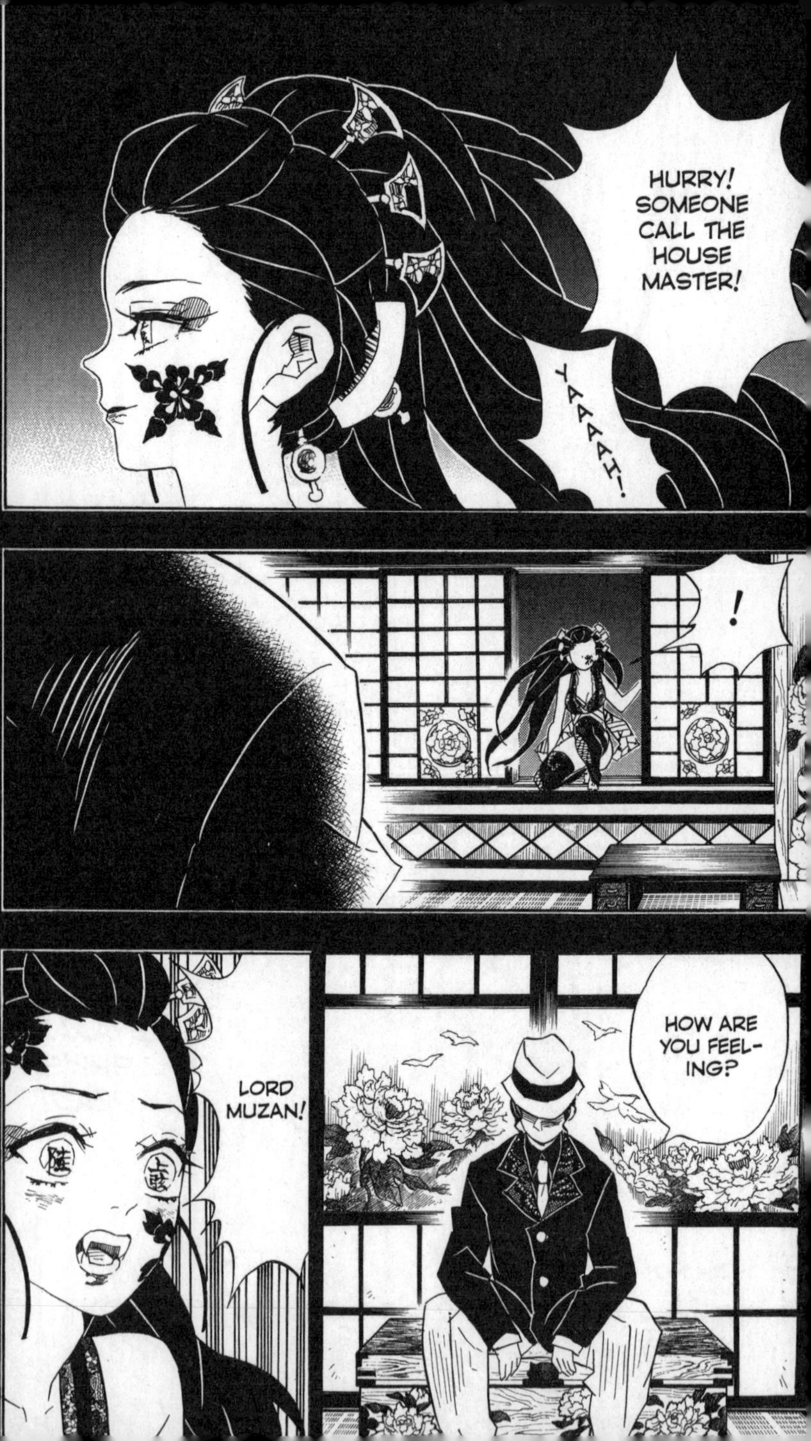
HURRY! SOMEONE CALL THE HOUSE MASTER!
YAAAAH!
!
HOW ARE YOU FEEL-ING?
LORD MUZAN!

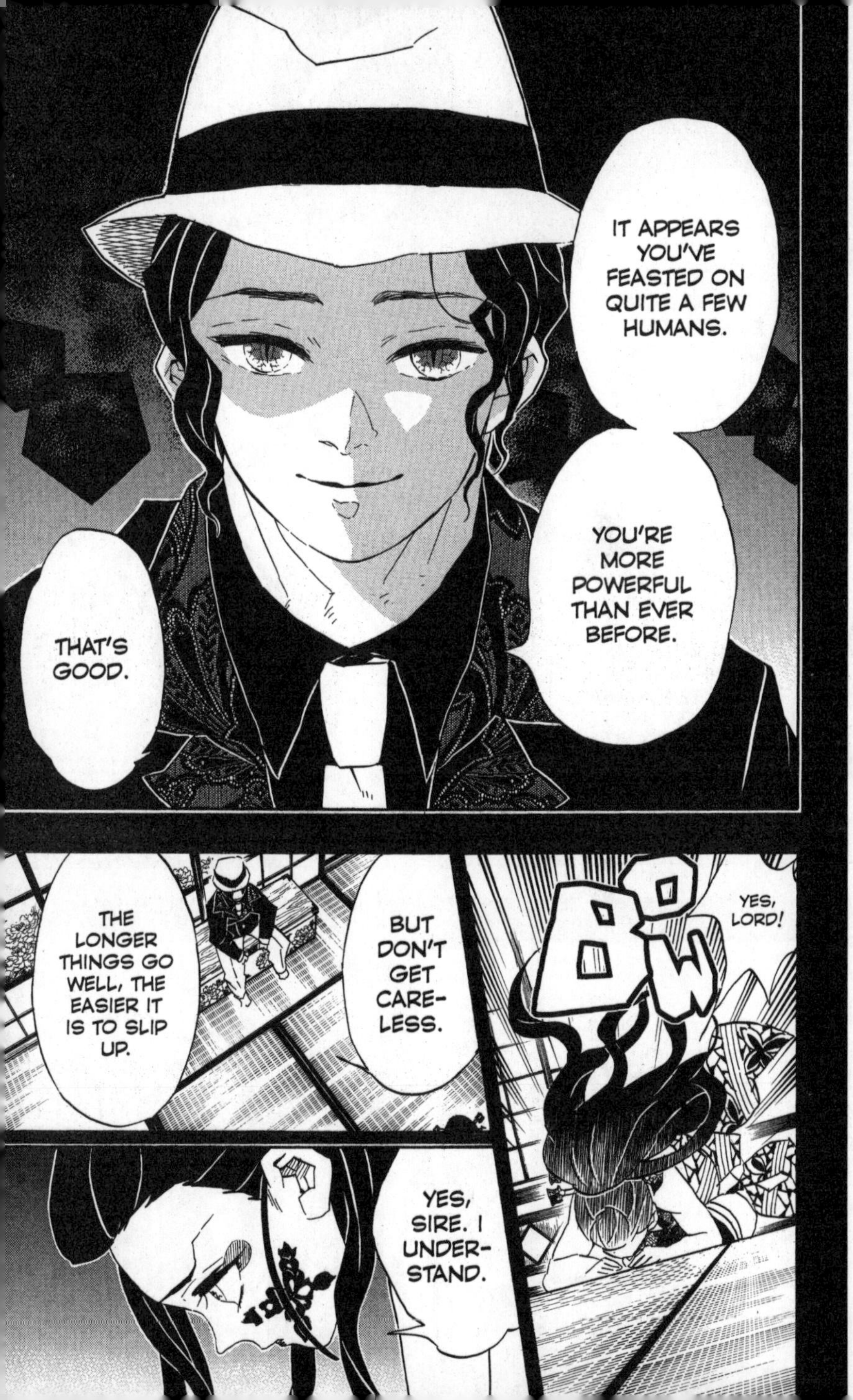
IT APPEARS YOU'VE FEASTED ON QUITE A FEW HUMANS.
YOU'RE MORE POWERFUL THAN EVER BEFORE.
THAT'S GOOD.
BOW
YES, LORD!
BUT DON'T GET CARE-LESS.
THE LONGER THINGS GO WELL, THE EASIER IT IS TO SLIP UP.
YES, SIRE. I UNDER-STAND.

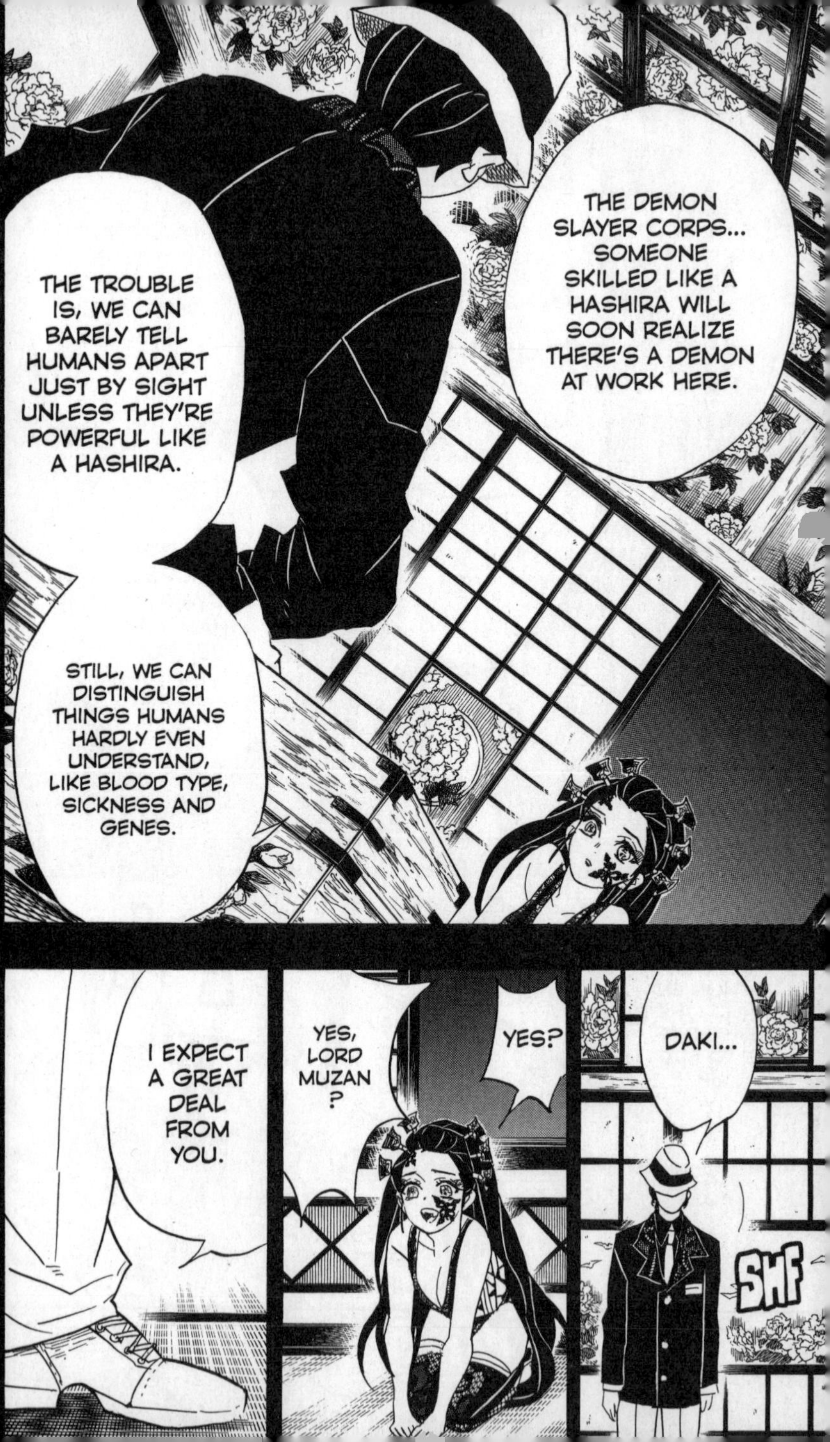
THE DEMON SLAYER CORPS... SOMEONE SKILLED LIKE A HASHIRA WILL SOON REALIZE THERE'S A DEMON AT WORK HERE.
THE TROUBLE IS, WE CAN BARELY TELL HUMANS APART JUST BY SIGHT UNLESS THEY'RE POWERFUL LIKE A HASHIRA.
STILL, WE CAN DISTINGUISH THINGS HUMANS HARDLY EVEN UNDERSTAND, LIKE BLOOD TYPE, SICKNESS AND GENES.
DAKI...
SHF
YES?
YES, LORD MUZAN?
I EXPECT A GREAT DEAL FROM YOU.

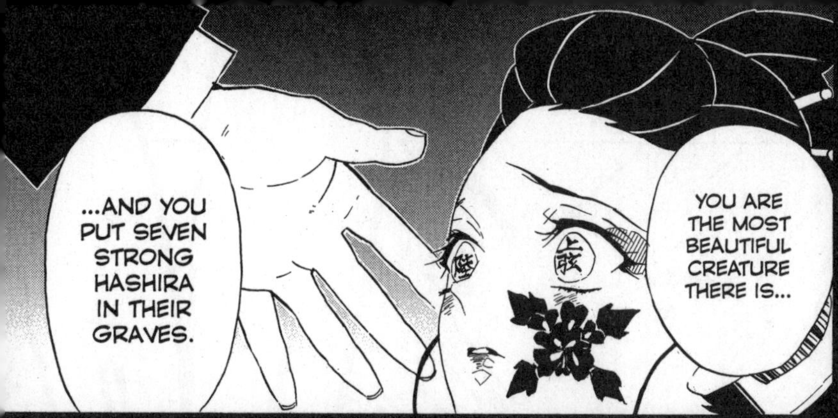
YOU ARE THE MOST BEAUTIFUL CREATURE THERE IS...
...AND YOU PUT SEVEN STRONG HASHIRA IN THEIR GRAVES.
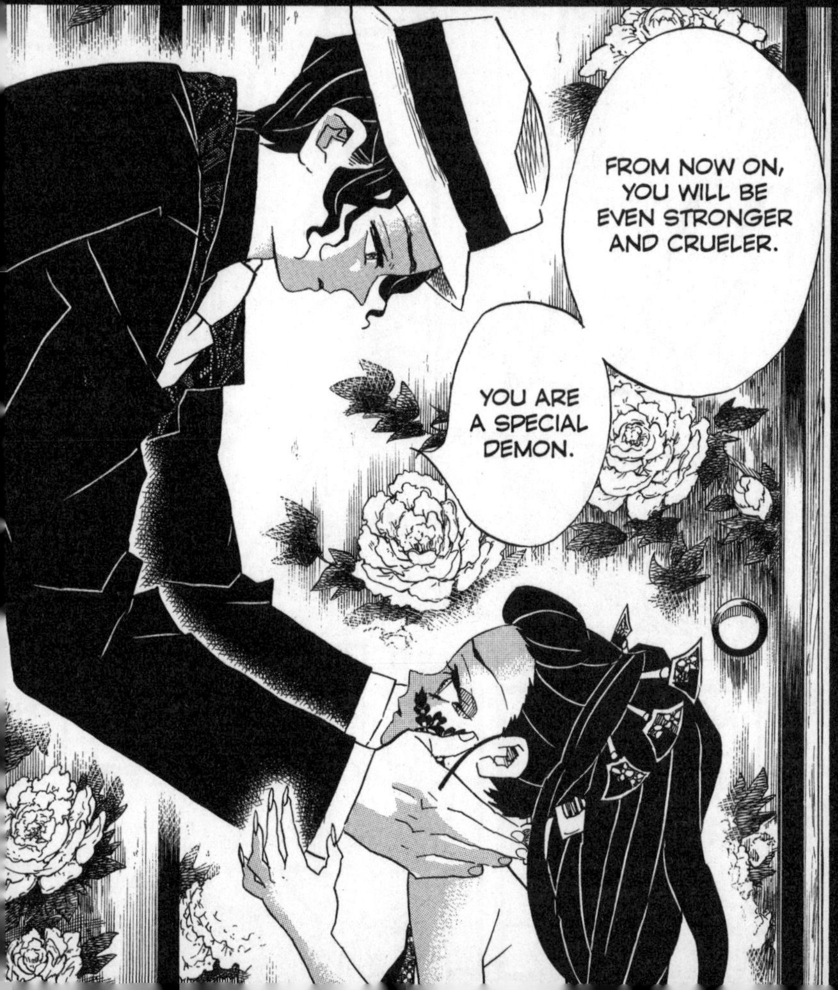
FROM NOW ON, YOU WILL BE EVEN STRONGER AND CRUELER.
YOU ARE A SPECIAL DEMON.

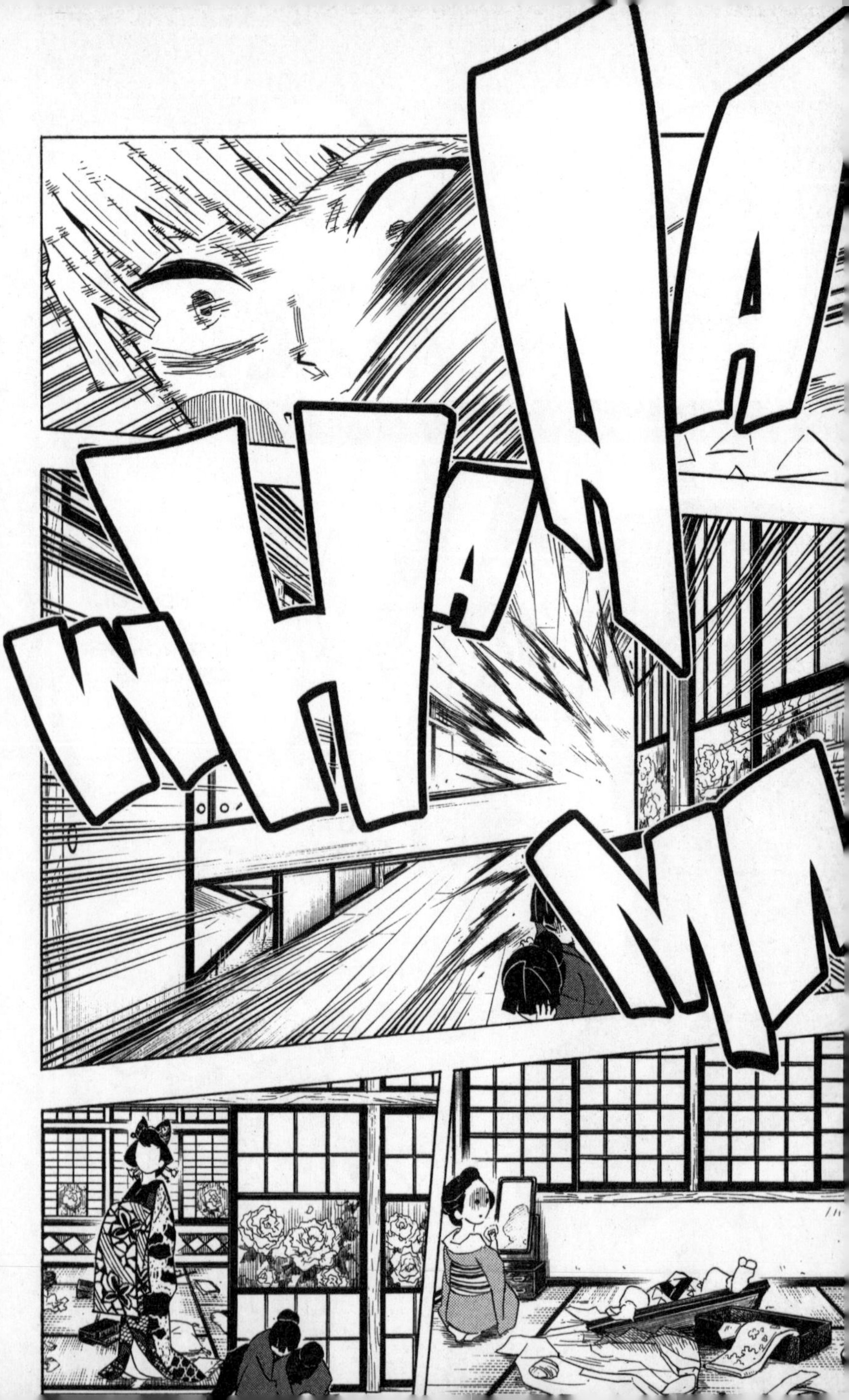
WHAM

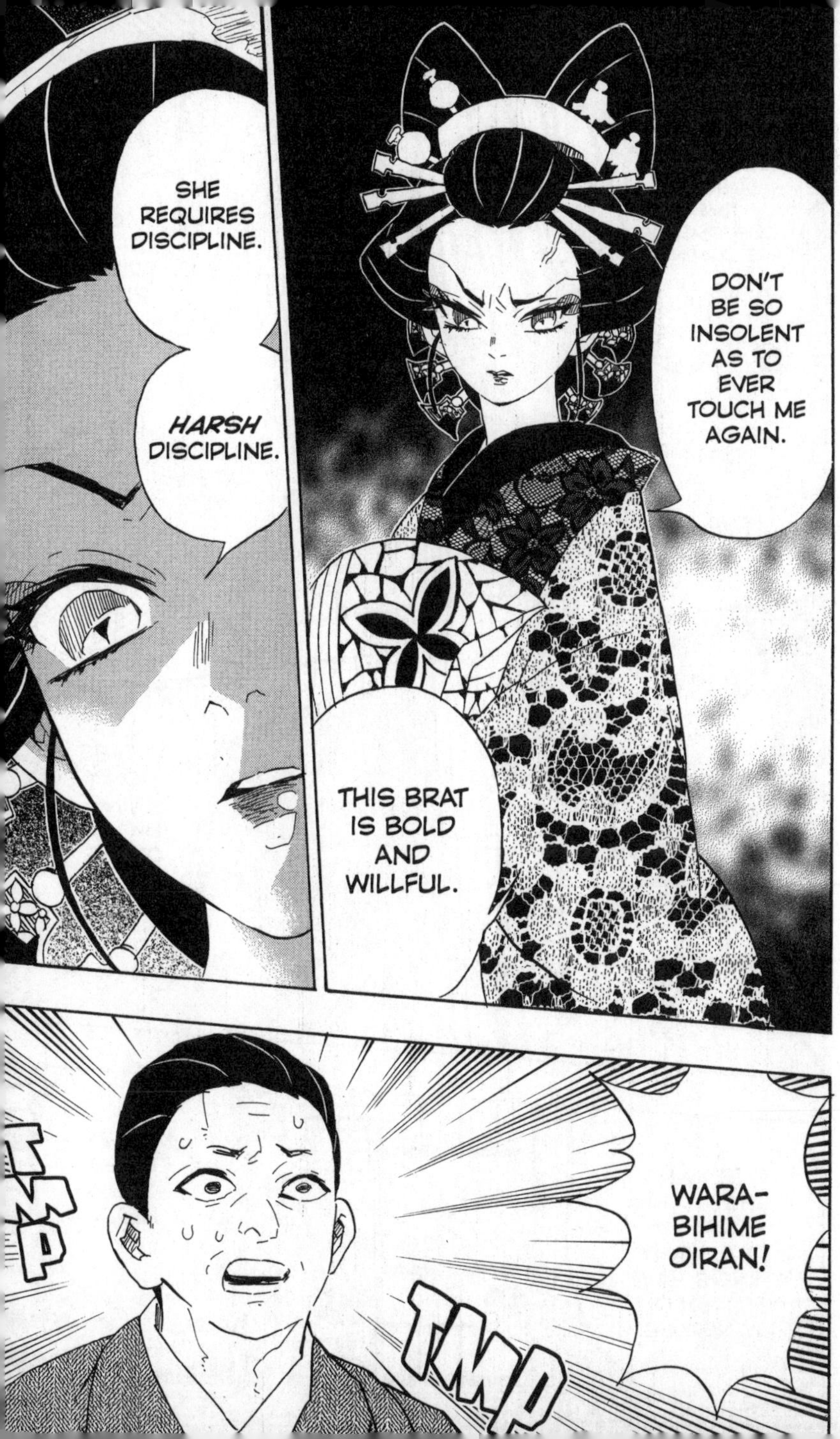
DON'T BE SO INSOLENT AS TO EVER TOUCH ME AGAIN.
THIS BRAT IS BOLD AND WILLFUL.
SHE REQUIRES DISCIPLINE.
HARSH DISCIPLINE.
WARA-BIHIME OIRAN!
TMP
TMP

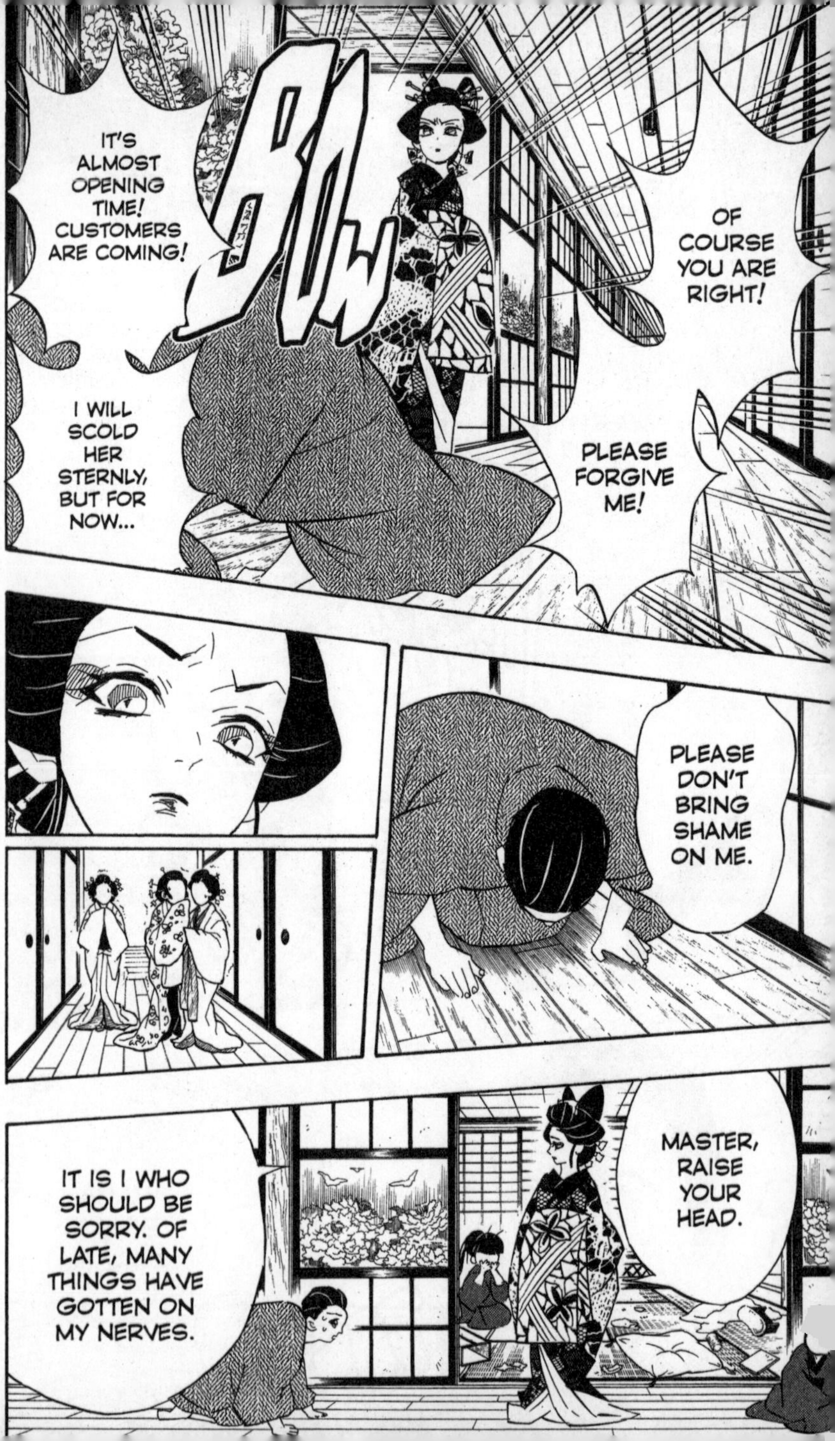
OF COURSE YOU ARE RIGHT!
PLEASE FORGIVE ME!
BOW
IT'S ALMOST OPENING TIME! CUSTOMERS ARE COMING!
I WILL SCOLD HER STERNLY, BUT FOR NOW...
PLEASE DON'T BRING SHAME ON ME.
MASTER, RAISE YOUR HEAD.
IT IS I WHO SHOULD BE SORRY. OF LATE, MANY THINGS HAVE GOTTEN ON MY NERVES.

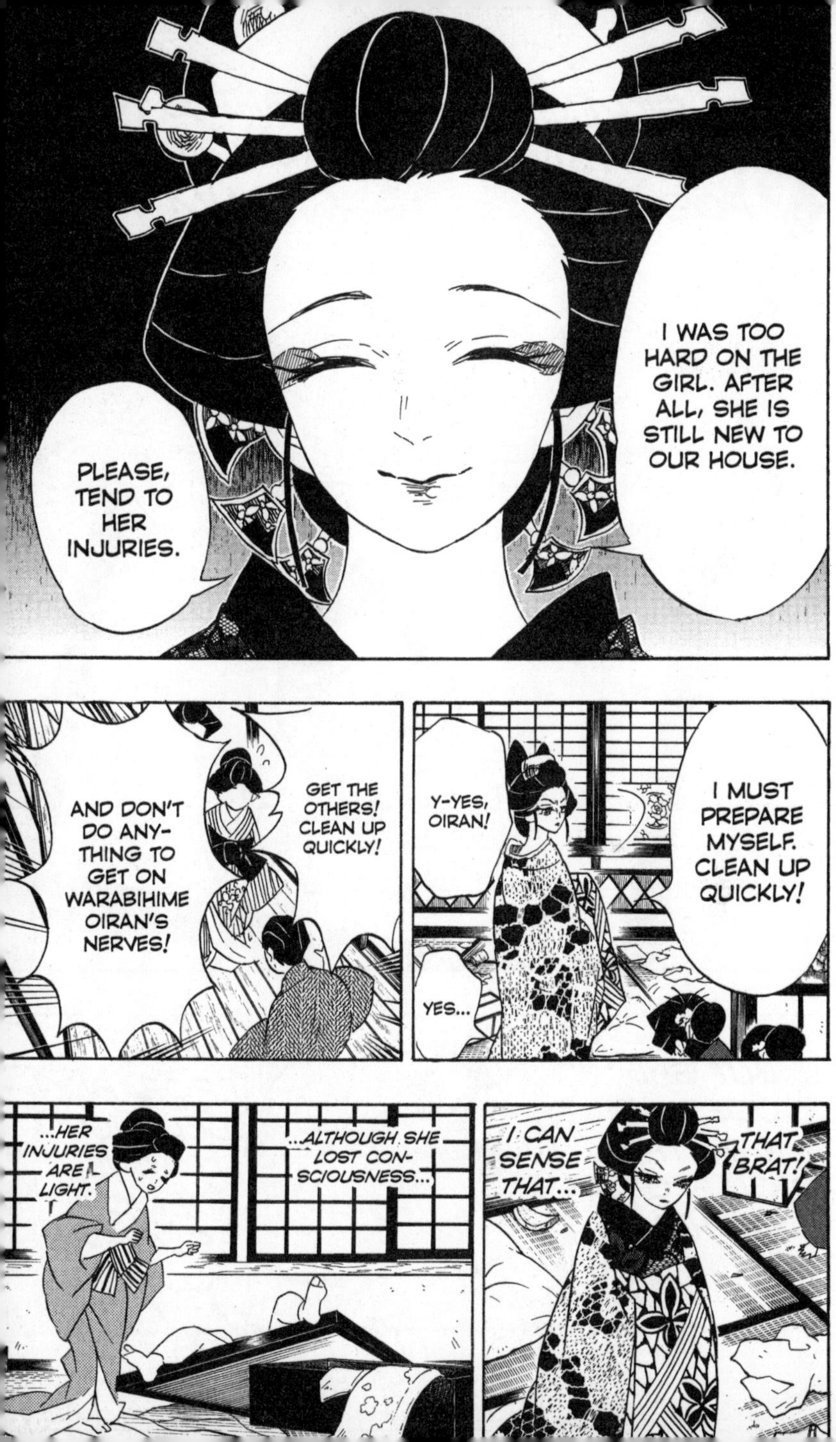
I WAS TOO HARD ON THE GIRL. AFTER ALL, SHE IS STILL NEW TO OUR HOUSE.
PLEASE, TEND TO HER INJURIES.
I MUST PREPARE MYSELF. CLEAN UP QUICKLY!
Y-YES, OIRAN!
YES...
GET THE OTHERS! CLEAN UP QUICKLY!
AND DON'T DO ANY-THING TO GET ON WARABIHIME OIRAN'S NERVES!
THAT BRAT!
I CAN SENSE THAT...
...ALTHOUGH SHE LOST CON-SCIOUSNESS...
...HER INJURIES ARE LIGHT.

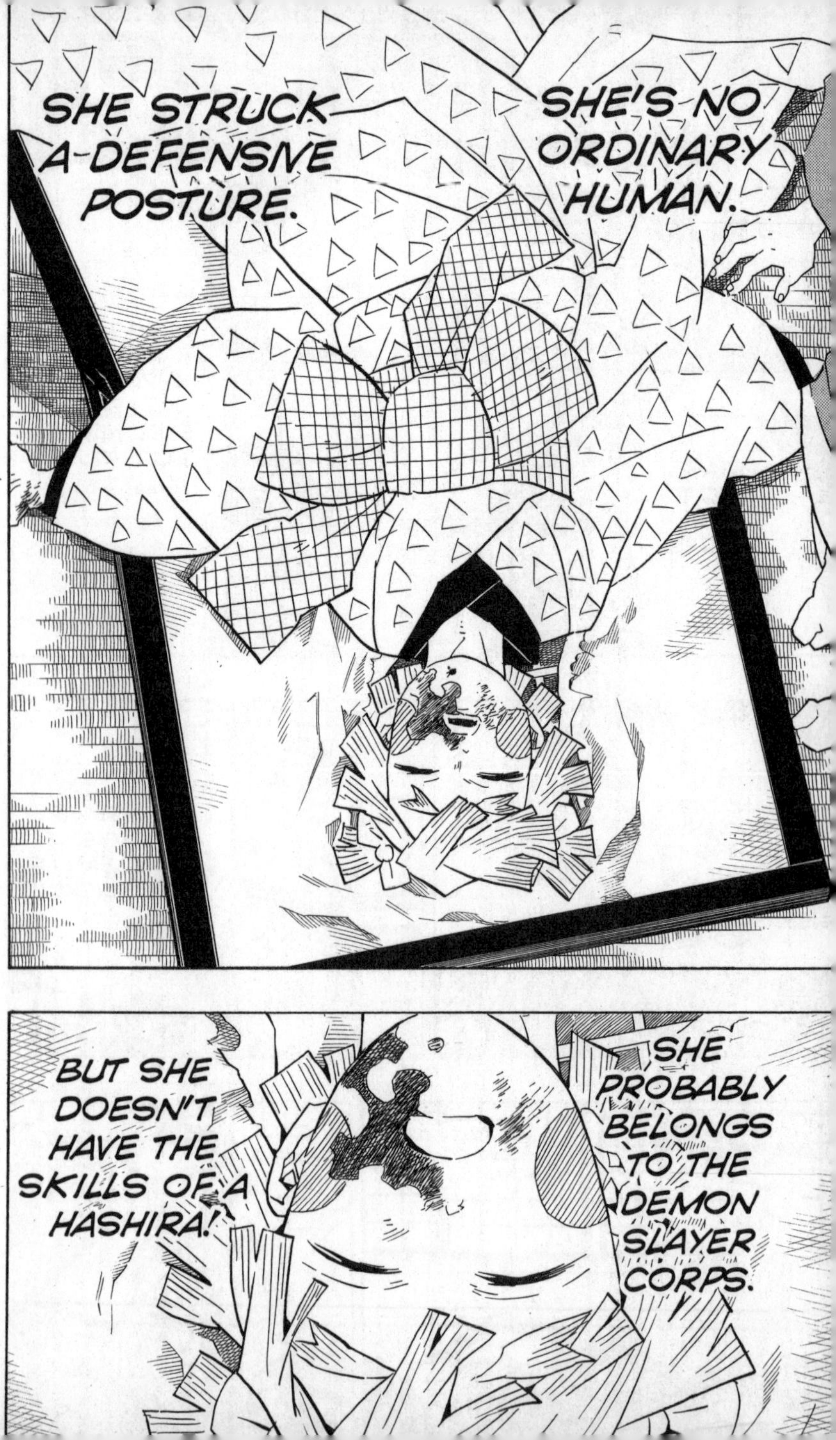
SHE'S NO ORDINARY HUMAN.
SHE STRUCK A DEFENSIVE POSTURE.
SHE PROBABLY BELONGS TO THE DEMON SLAYER CORPS.
BUT SHE DOESN'T HAVE THE SKILLS OF A HASHIRA!

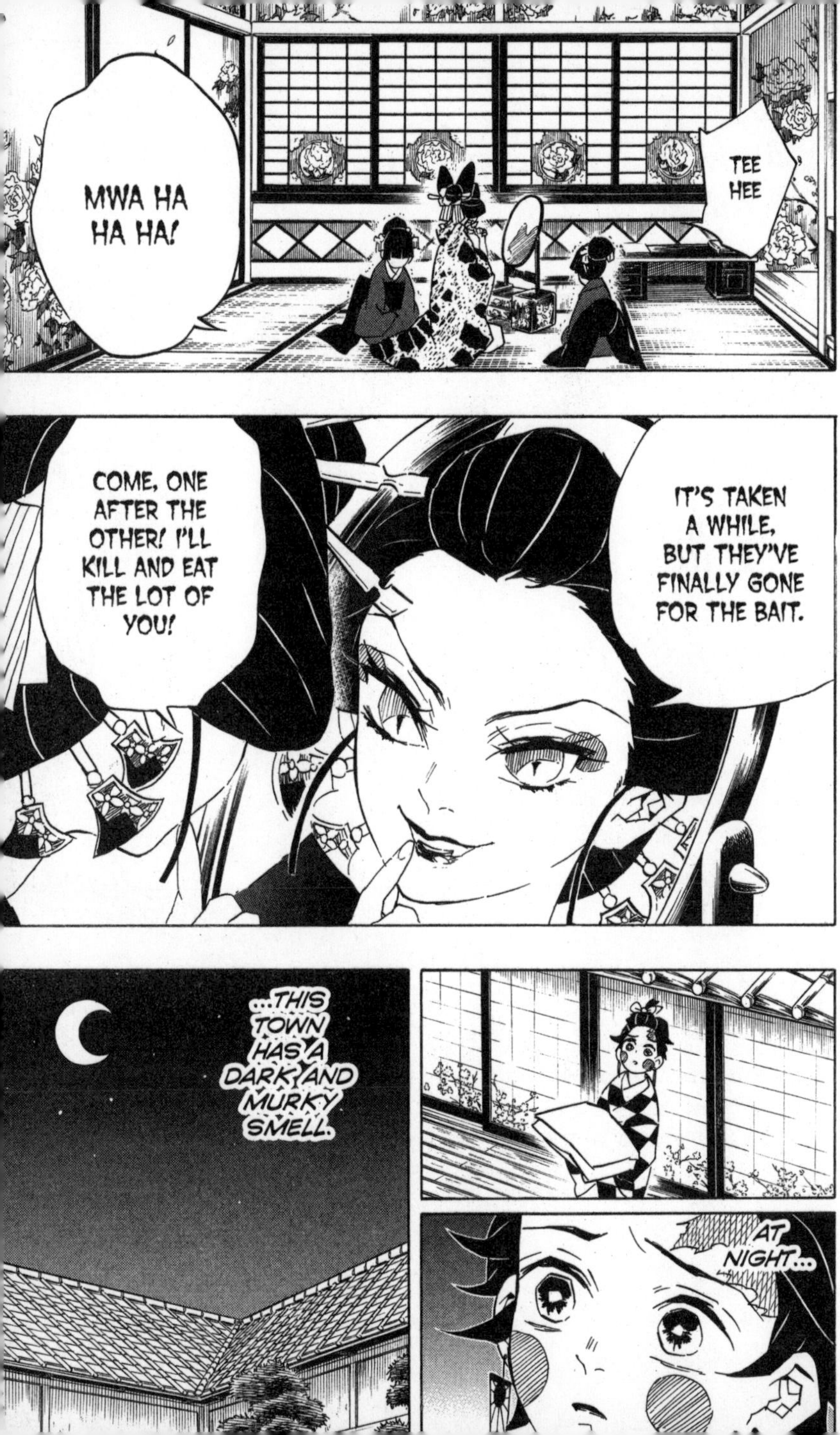
TEE HEE
MWA HA HA HA!
IT'S TAKEN A WHILE, BUT THEY'VE FINALLY GONE FOR THE BAIT.
COME, ONE AFTER THE OTHER! I'LL KILL AND EAT THE LOT OF YOU!
AT NIGHT...
...THIS TOWN HAS A DARK AND MURKY SMELL.

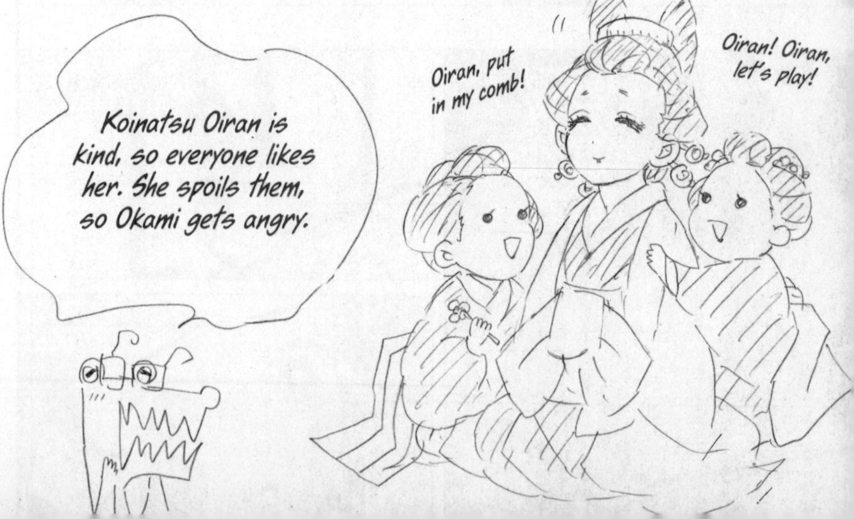
Oiran! Oiran, let's play!
Oiran, put in my comb!
Koinatsu Oiran is kind, so everyone likes her. She spoils them, so Okami gets angry.

CHAPTER 75: VARIOUS FEELINGS

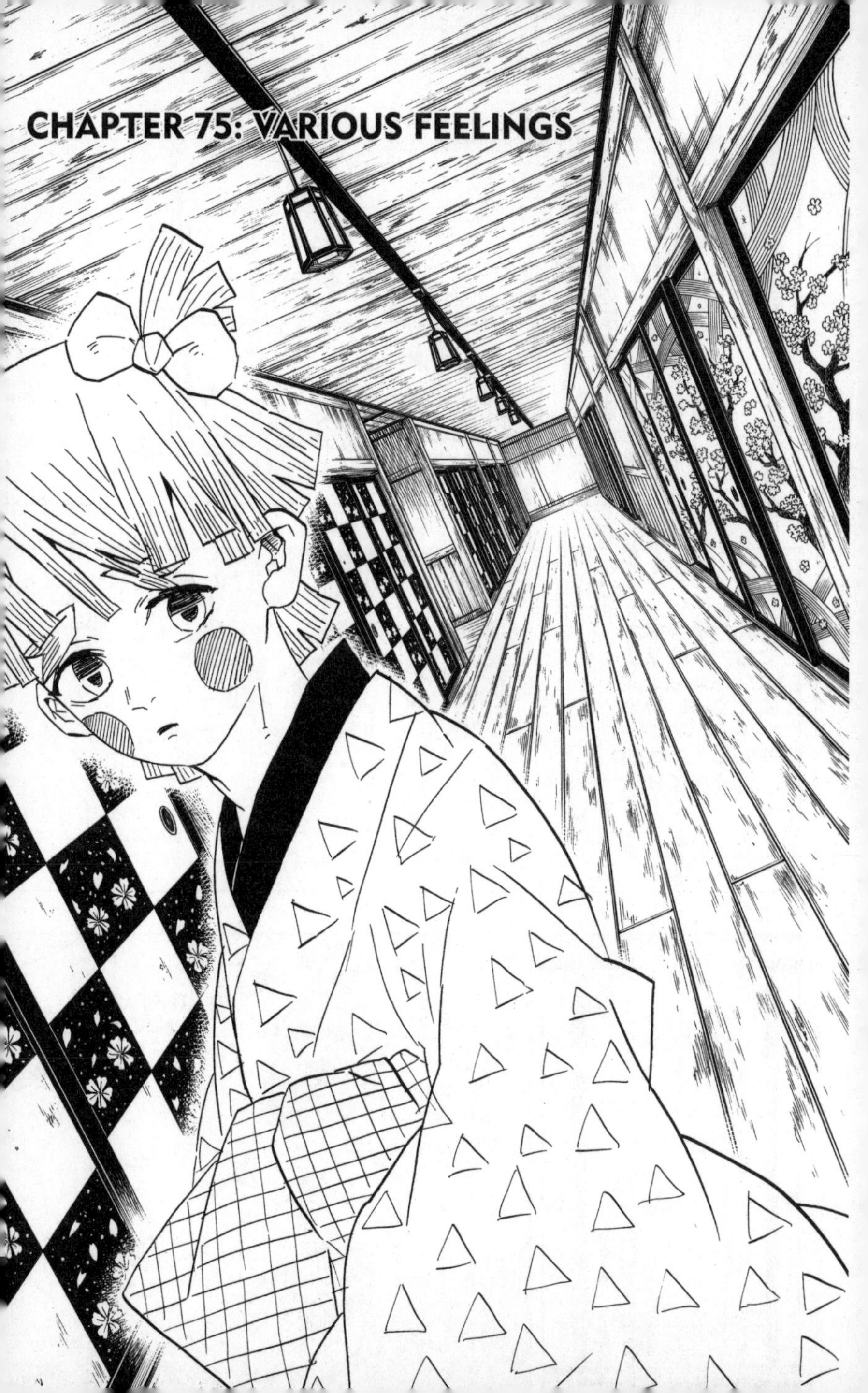

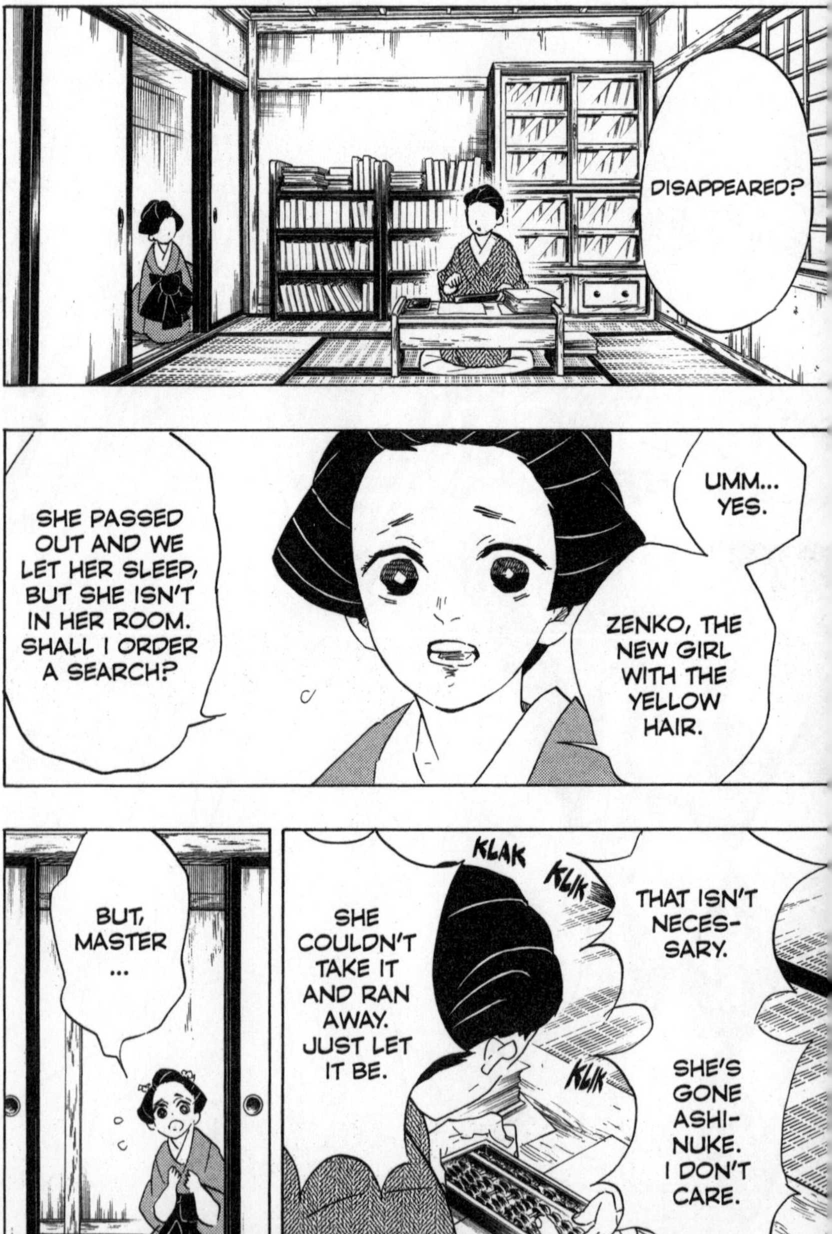
DISAPPEARED?
UMM... YES.
ZENKO, THE NEW GIRL WITH THE YELLOW HAIR.
SHE PASSED OUT AND WE LET HER SLEEP, BUT SHE ISN'T IN HER ROOM. SHALL I ORDER A SEARCH?
KLAK
KLIK
THAT ISN'T NECES-SARY.
KLIK
SHE'S GONE ASHI-NUKE. I DON'T CARE.
SHE COULDN'T TAKE IT AND RAN AWAY. JUST LET IT BE.
BUT, MASTER ...

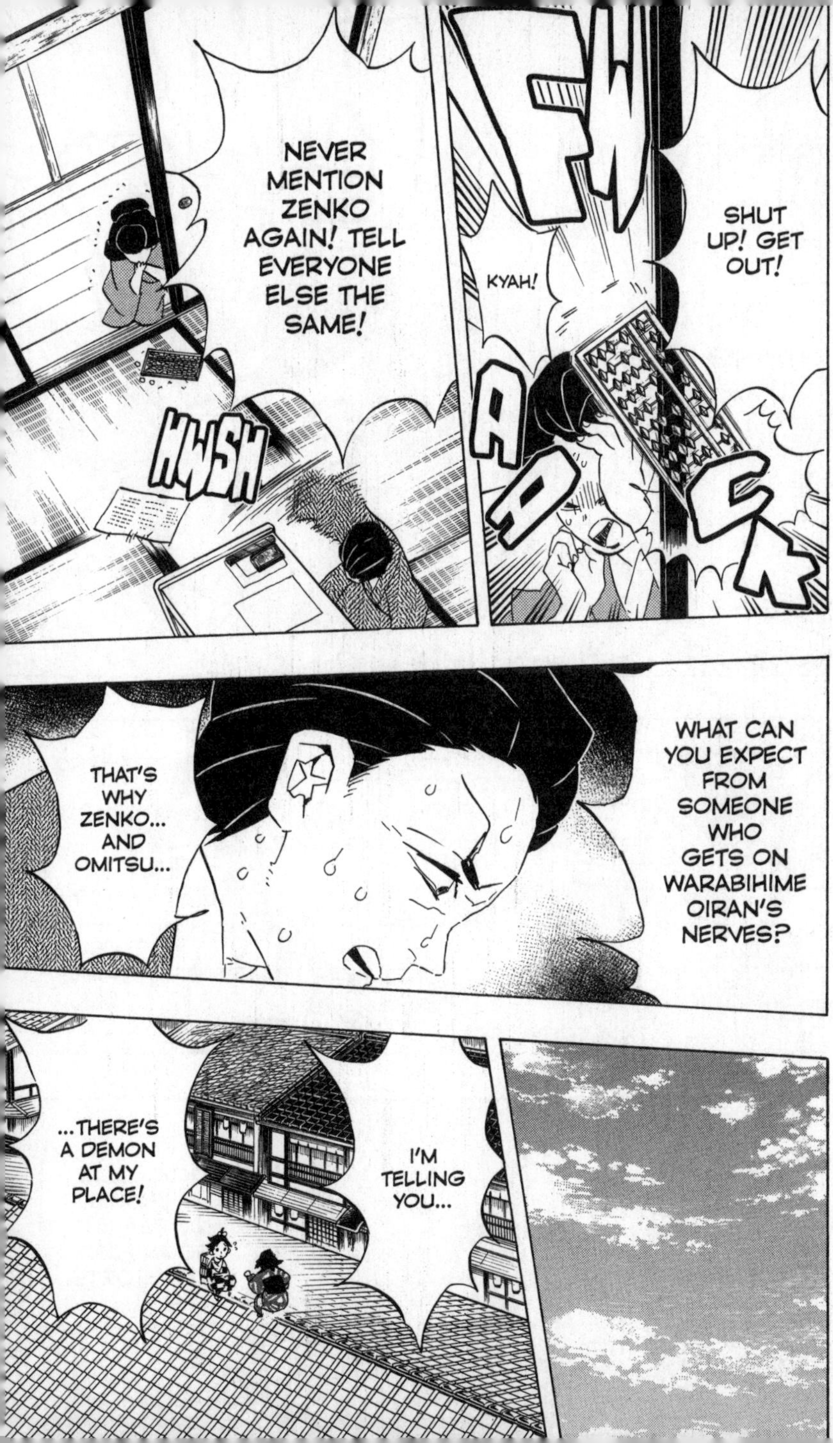
SHUT UP! GET OUT!
KYAH!
NEVER MENTION ZENKO AGAIN! TELL EVERYONE ELSE THE SAME!
HWSH
WHAT CAN YOU EXPECT FROM SOMEONE WHO GETS ON WARABIHIME OIRAN'S NERVES?
THAT'S WHY ZENKO... AND OMITSU...
I'M TELLING YOU...
...THERE'S A DEMON AT MY PLACE!

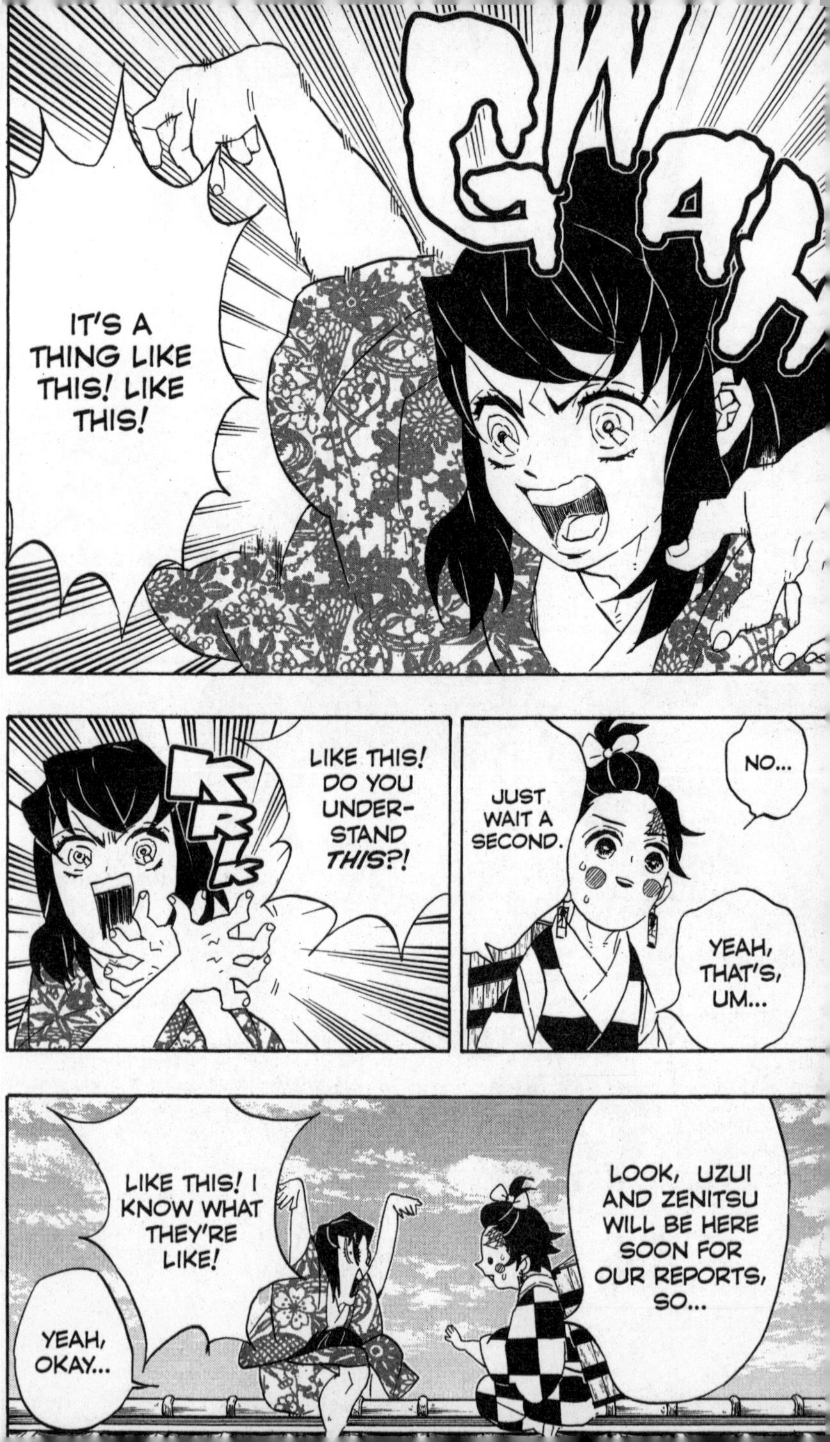
GWAH
IT'S A THING LIKE THIS! LIKE THIS!
NO...
JUST WAIT A SECOND.
YEAH, THAT'S, UM...
LIKE THIS! DO YOU UNDER-STAND *THIS*?!
KRK
LOOK, UZUI AND ZENITSU WILL BE HERE SOON FOR OUR REPORTS, SO...
LIKE THIS! I KNOW WHAT THEY'RE LIKE!
YEAH, OKAY...

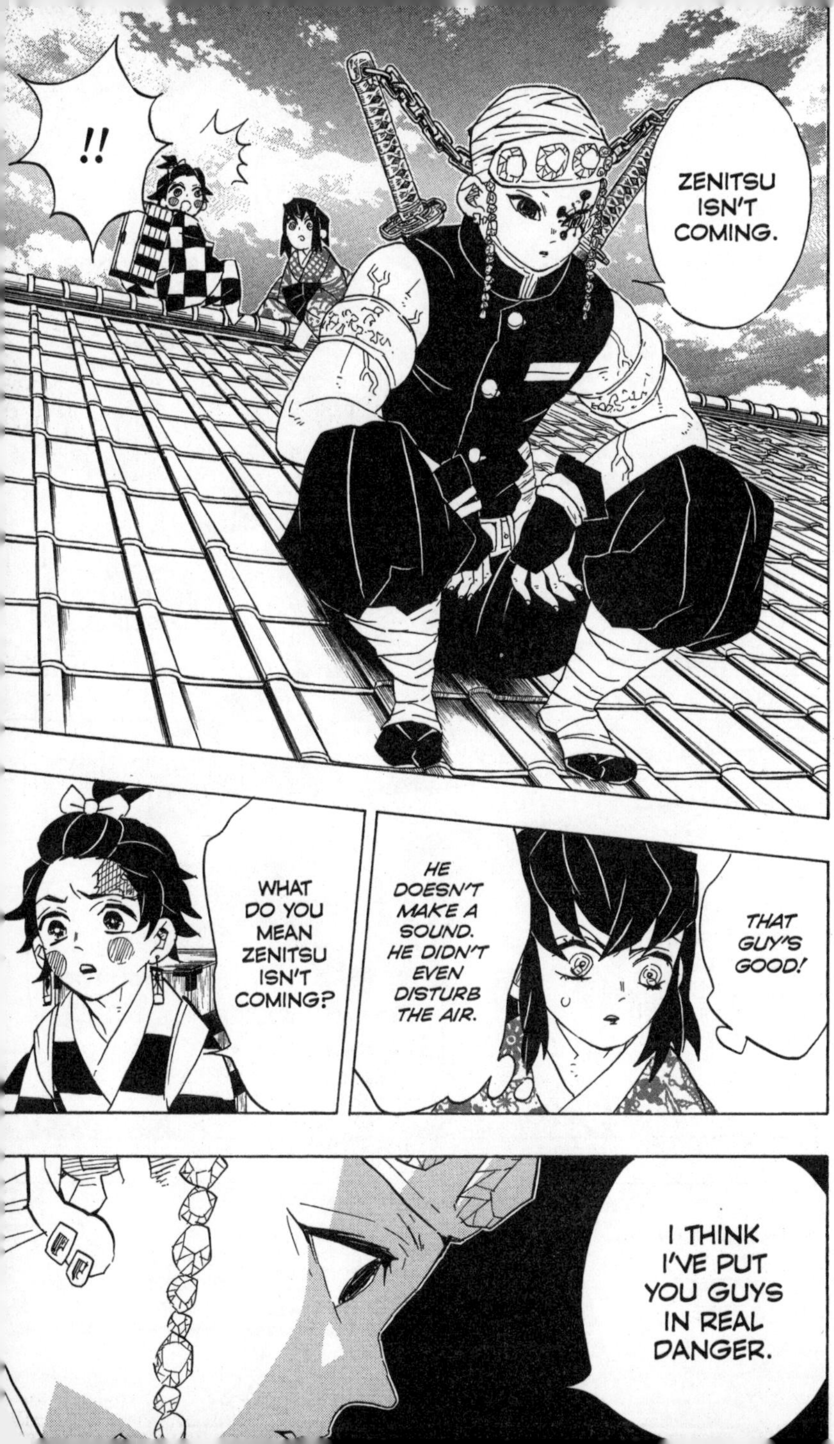
ZENITSU ISN'T COMING.
!!
THAT GUY'S GOOD!
HE DOESN'T MAKE A SOUND. HE DIDN'T EVEN DISTURB THE AIR.
WHAT DO YOU MEAN ZENITSU ISN'T COMING?
I THINK I'VE PUT YOU GUYS IN REAL DANGER.

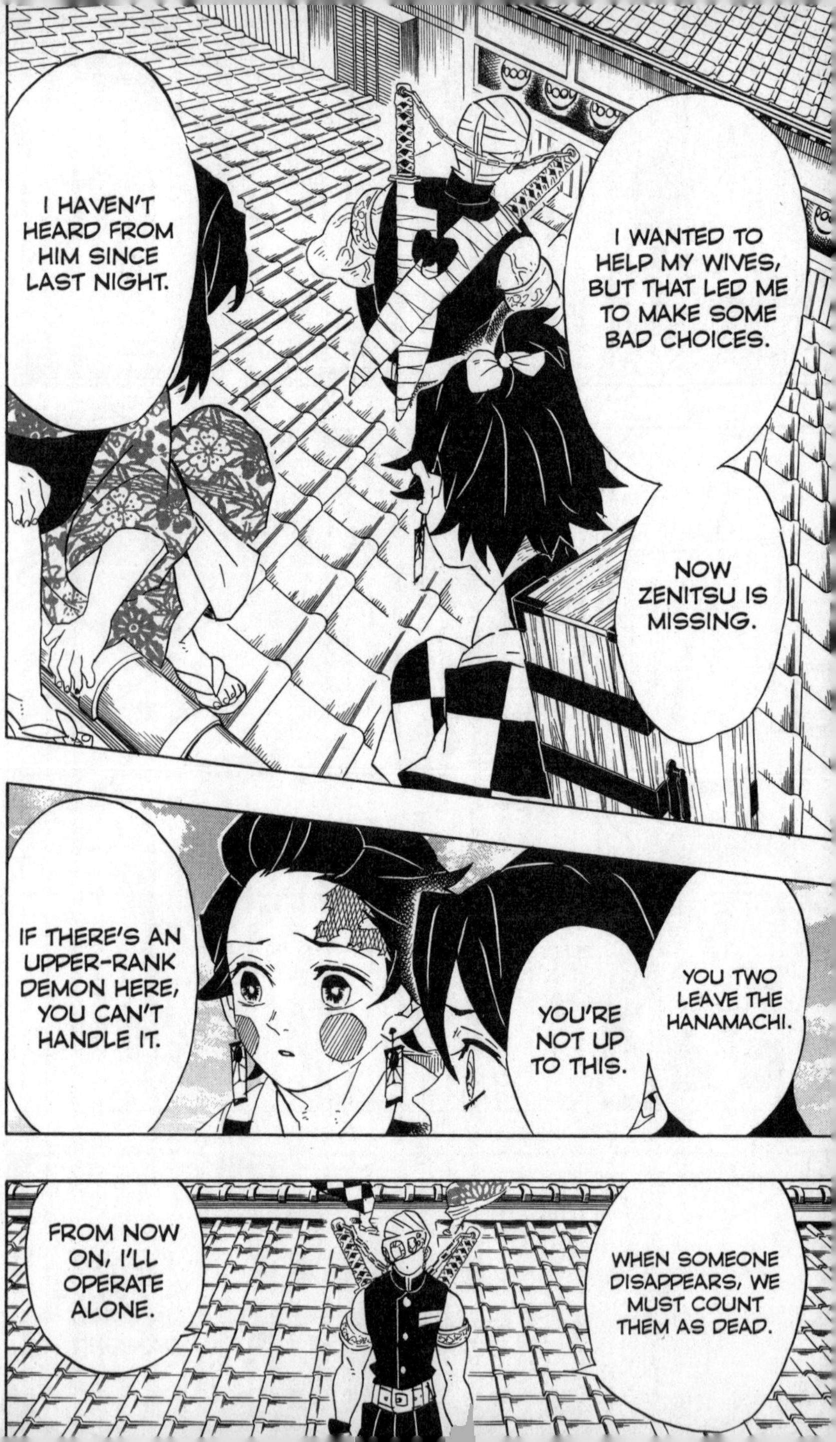
I WANTED TO HELP MY WIVES, BUT THAT LED ME TO MAKE SOME BAD CHOICES.
NOW ZENITSU IS MISSING.
I HAVEN'T HEARD FROM HIM SINCE LAST NIGHT.
YOU TWO LEAVE THE HANAMACHI.
YOU'RE NOT UP TO THIS.
IF THERE'S AN UPPER-RANK DEMON HERE, YOU CAN'T HANDLE IT.
WHEN SOMEONE DISAPPEARS, WE MUST COUNT THEM AS DEAD.
FROM NOW ON, I'LL OPERATE ALONE.

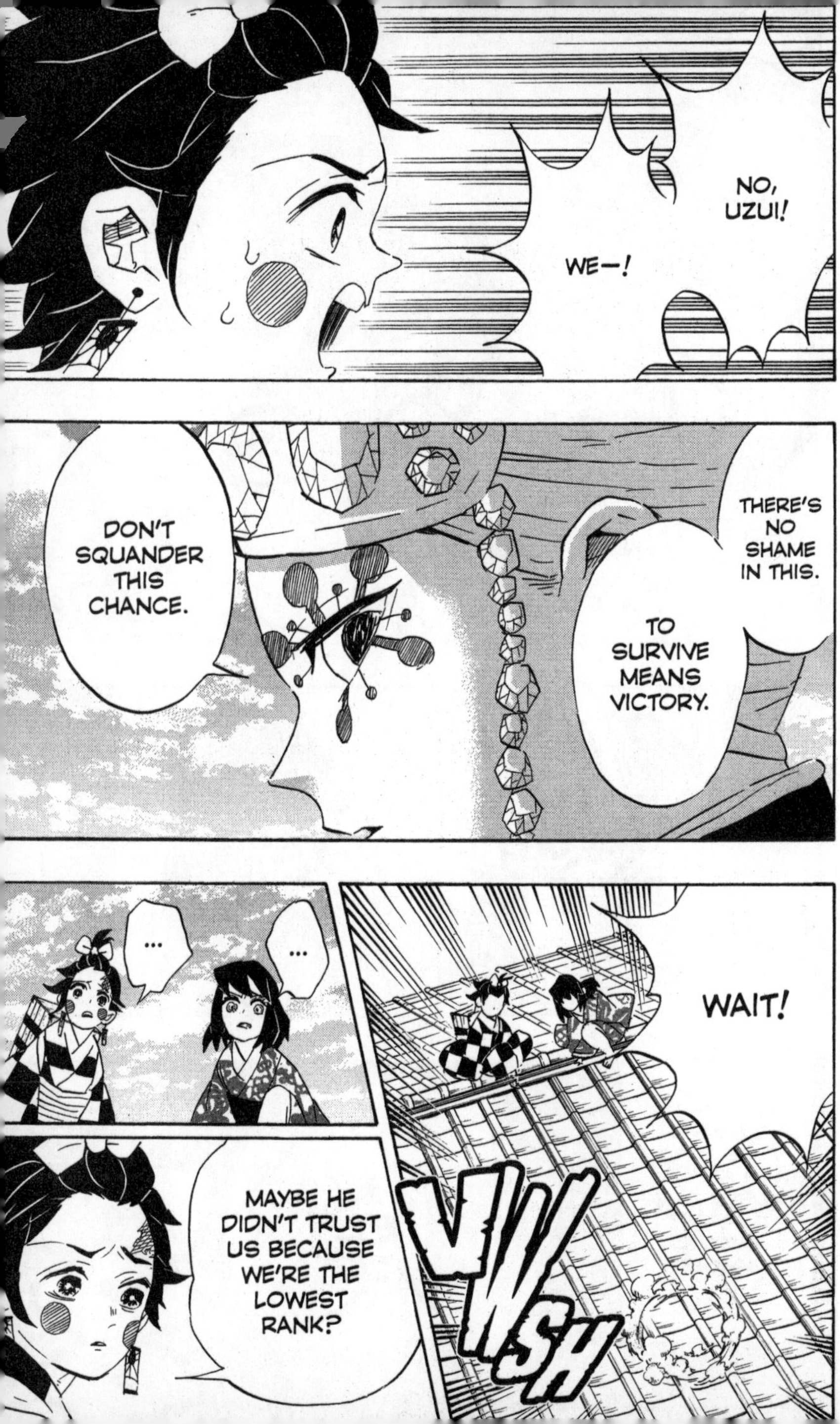
NO, UZUI!
WE—!
THERE'S NO SHAME IN THIS.
TO SURVIVE MEANS VICTORY.
DON'T SQUANDER THIS CHANCE.
WAIT!
VWSH
...
...
MAYBE HE DIDN'T TRUST US BECAUSE WE'RE THE LOWEST RANK?

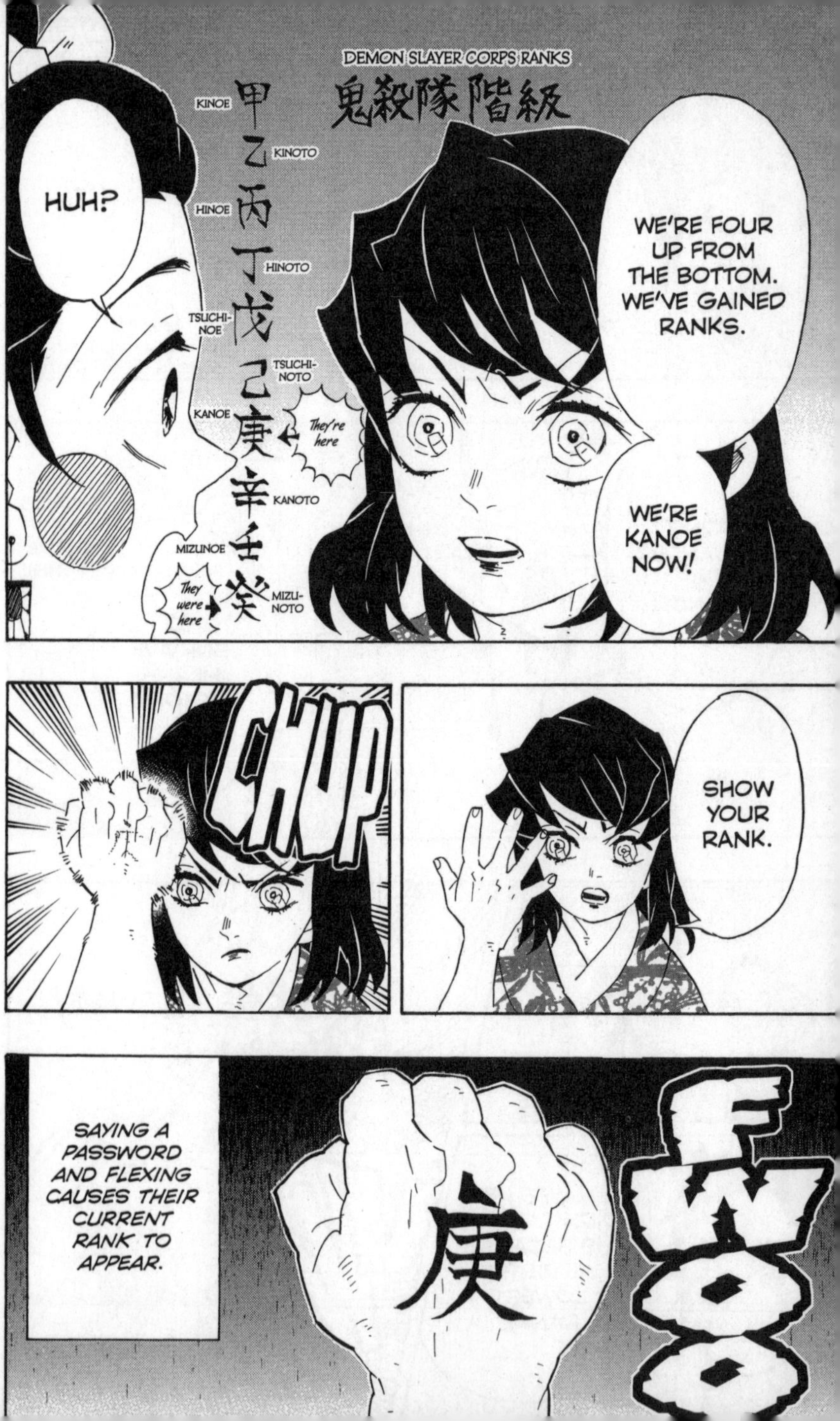
WE'RE FOUR UP FROM THE BOTTOM. WE'VE GAINED RANKS.
WE'RE KANOE NOW!
DEMON SLAYER CORPS RANKS
鬼殺隊階級
甲 KINOE
乙 KINOTO
丙 HINOE
丁 HINOTO
戊 TSUCHI-NOE
己 TSUCHI-NOTO
庚 KANOE
They're here
辛 KANOTO
壬 MIZUNOE
癸 MIZU-NOTO
They were here
HUH?
SHOW YOUR RANK.
CHUP
FWOO
庚
SAYING A PASSWORD AND FLEXING CAUSES THEIR CURRENT RANK TO APPEAR.

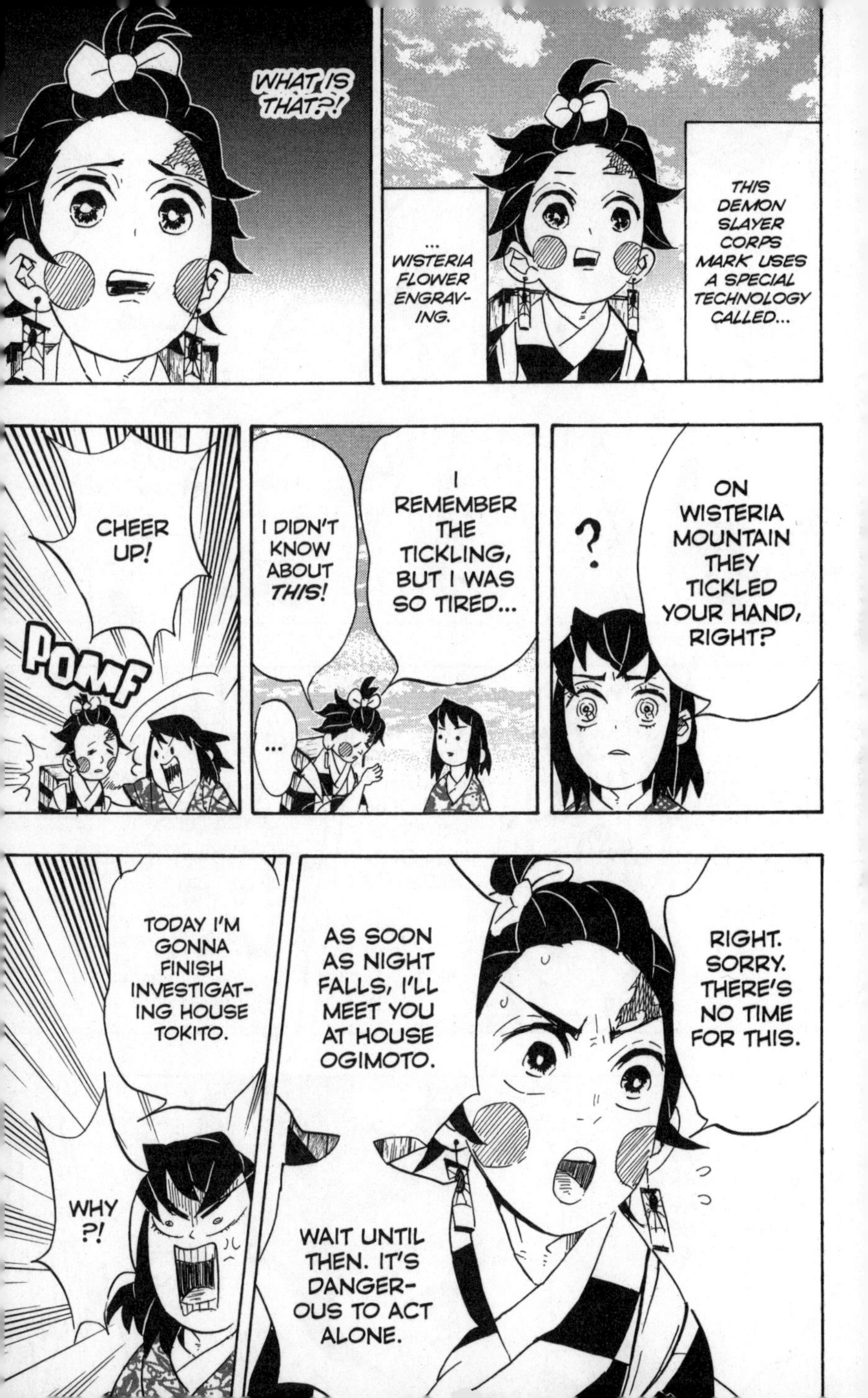
THIS DEMON SLAYER CORPS MARK USES A SPECIAL TECHNOLOGY CALLED...
... WISTERIA FLOWER ENGRAVING.
WHAT IS THAT?!
ON WISTERIA MOUNTAIN THEY TICKLED YOUR HAND, RIGHT?
?
I REMEMBER THE TICKLING, BUT I WAS SO TIRED...
I DIDN'T KNOW ABOUT THIS!
...
CHEER UP!
POMF
RIGHT. SORRY. THERE'S NO TIME FOR THIS.
AS SOON AS NIGHT FALLS, I'LL MEET YOU AT HOUSE OGIMOTO.
WAIT UNTIL THEN. IT'S DANGEROUS TO ACT ALONE.
TODAY I'M GONNA FINISH INVESTIGATING HOUSE TOKITO.
WHY?!

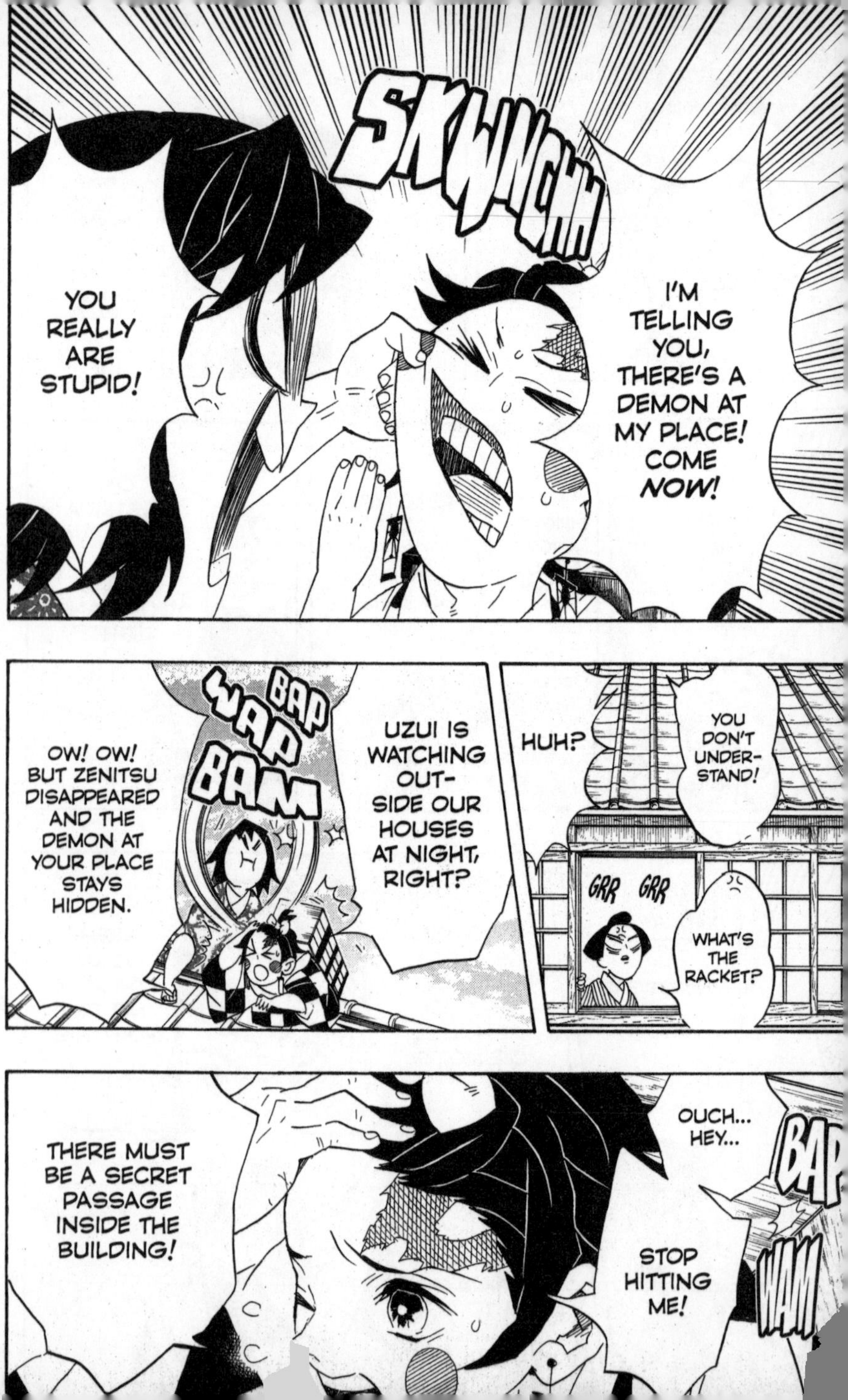
SKWNCHH
I'M TELLING YOU, THERE'S A DEMON AT MY PLACE! COME NOW!
YOU REALLY ARE STUPID!
YOU DON'T UNDER-STAND!
HUH?
GRR GRR
WHAT'S THE RACKET?
UZUI IS WATCHING OUT-SIDE OUR HOUSES AT NIGHT, RIGHT?
BAP WAP BAM
OW! OW! BUT ZENITSU DISAPPEARED AND THE DEMON AT YOUR PLACE STAYS HIDDEN.
BAP
OUCH... HEY...
WAM
STOP HITTING ME!
THERE MUST BE A SECRET PASSAGE INSIDE THE BUILDING!

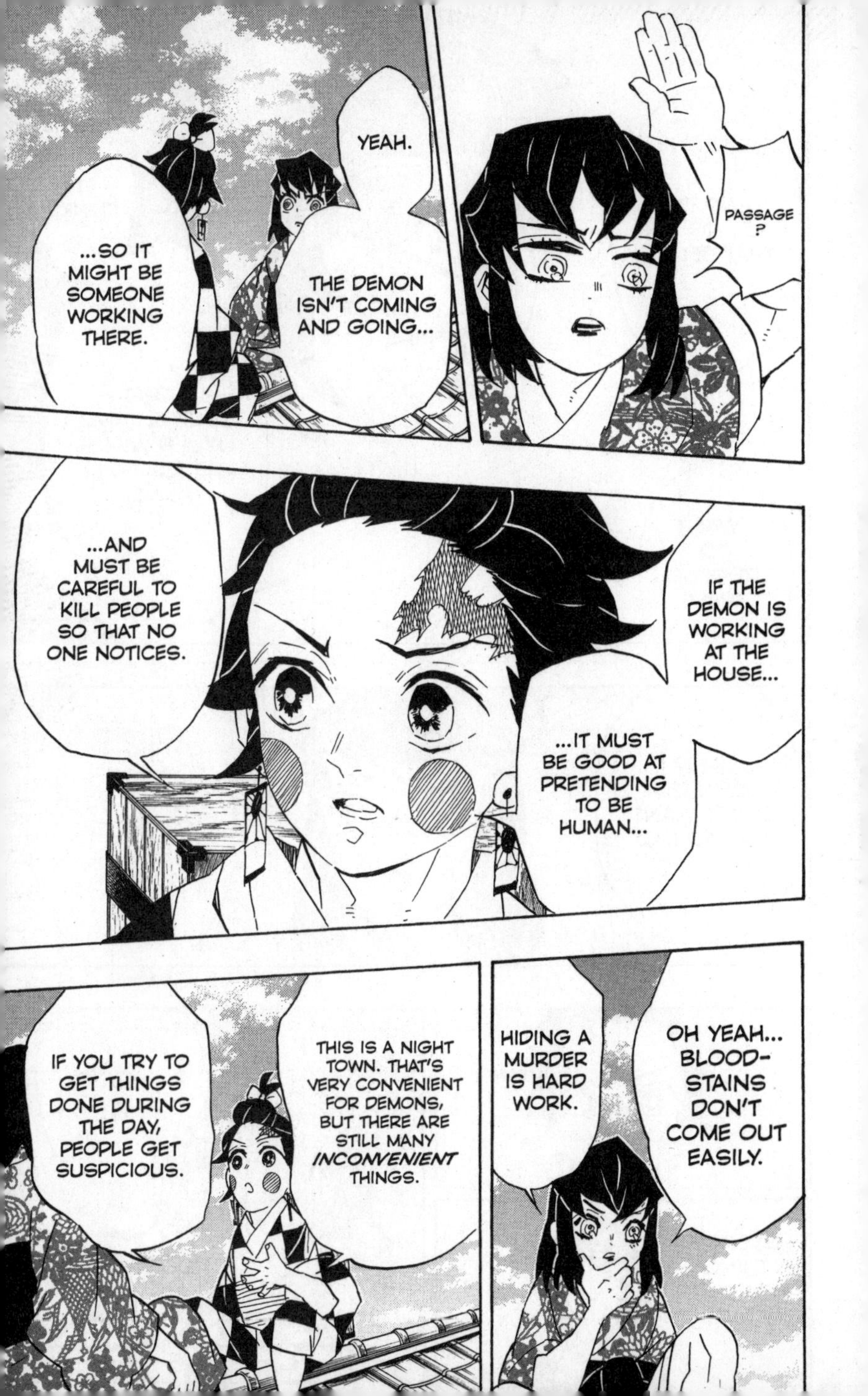
PASSAGE?
YEAH.
THE DEMON ISN'T COMING AND GOING...
...SO IT MIGHT BE SOMEONE WORKING THERE.
IF THE DEMON IS WORKING AT THE HOUSE...
...IT MUST BE GOOD AT PRETENDING TO BE HUMAN...
...AND MUST BE CAREFUL TO KILL PEOPLE SO THAT NO ONE NOTICES.
OH YEAH... BLOOD-STAINS DON'T COME OUT EASILY.
HIDING A MURDER IS HARD WORK.
THIS IS A NIGHT TOWN. THAT'S VERY CONVENIENT FOR DEMONS, BUT THERE ARE STILL MANY *INCONVENIENT* THINGS.
IF YOU TRY TO GET THINGS DONE DURING THE DAY, PEOPLE GET SUSPICIOUS.

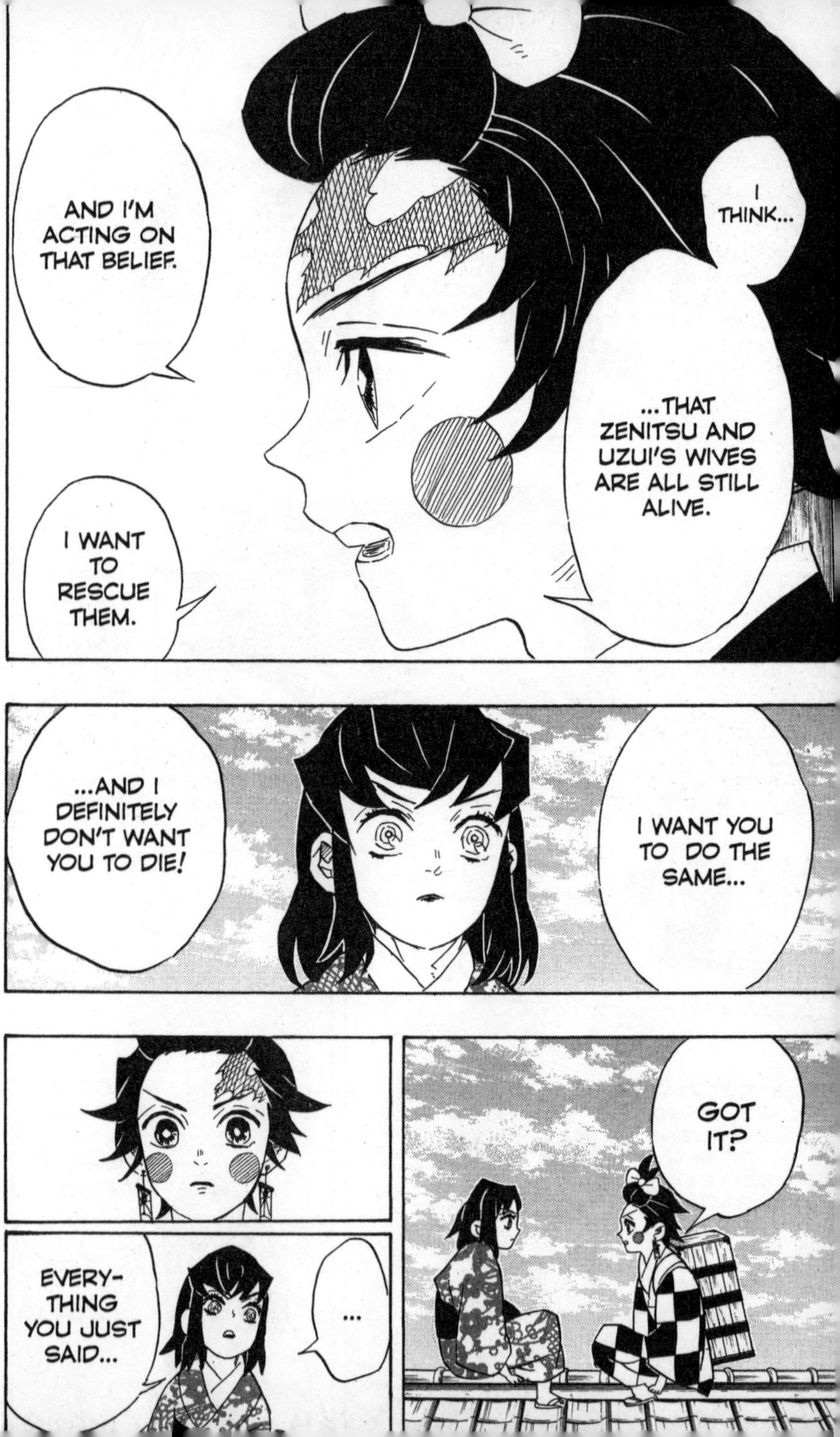
I THINK...
...THAT ZENITSU AND UZUI'S WIVES ARE ALL STILL ALIVE.
AND I'M ACTING ON THAT BELIEF.
I WANT TO RESCUE THEM.
I WANT YOU TO DO THE SAME...
...AND I DEFINITELY DON'T WANT YOU TO DIE!
GOT IT?
...
EVERY-THING YOU JUST SAID...

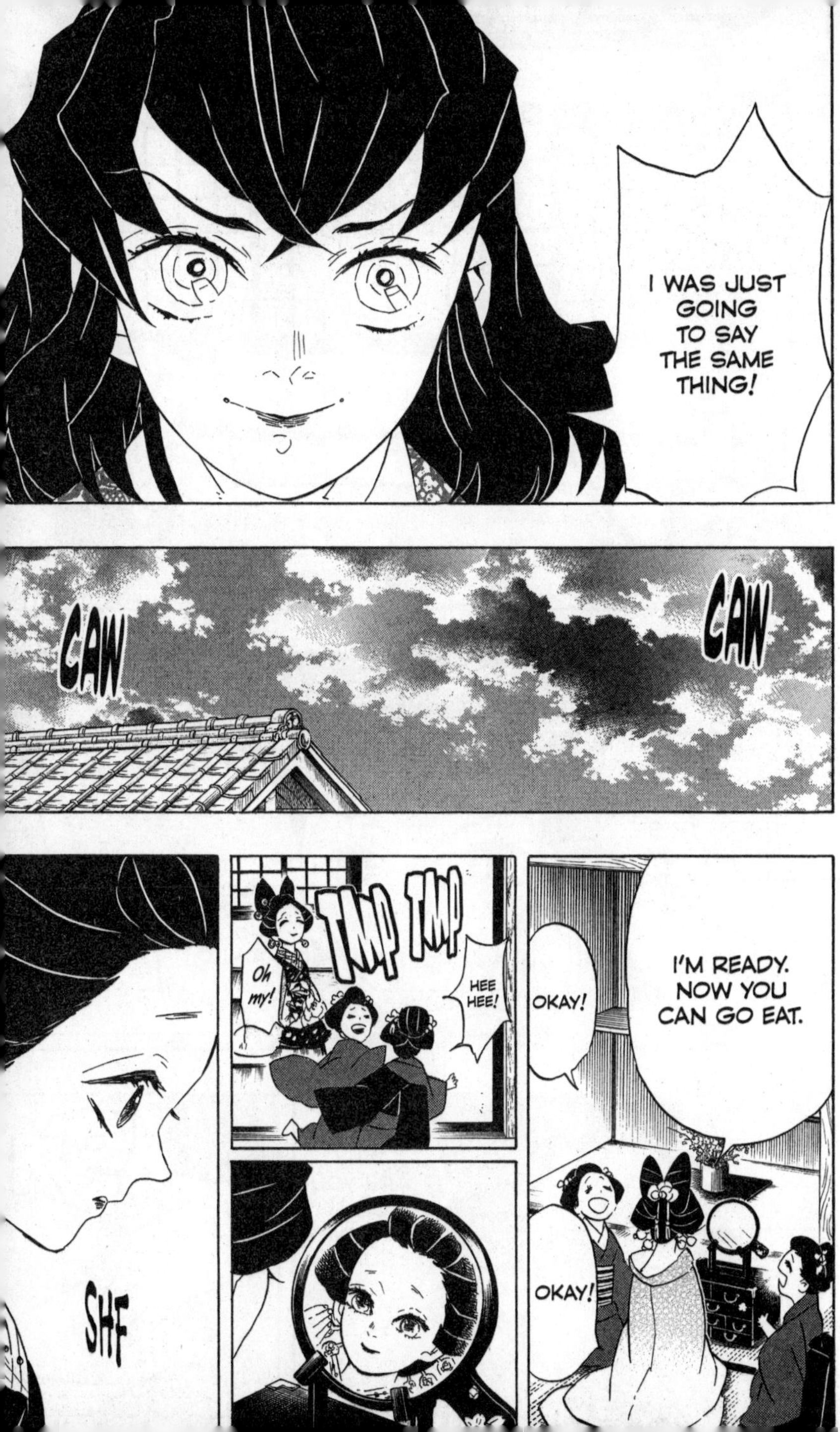
I WAS JUST GOING TO SAY THE SAME THING!
CAW
CAW
I'M READY. NOW YOU CAN GO EAT.
OKAY!
OKAY!
TMP TMP
HEE HEE!
Oh my!
SHF

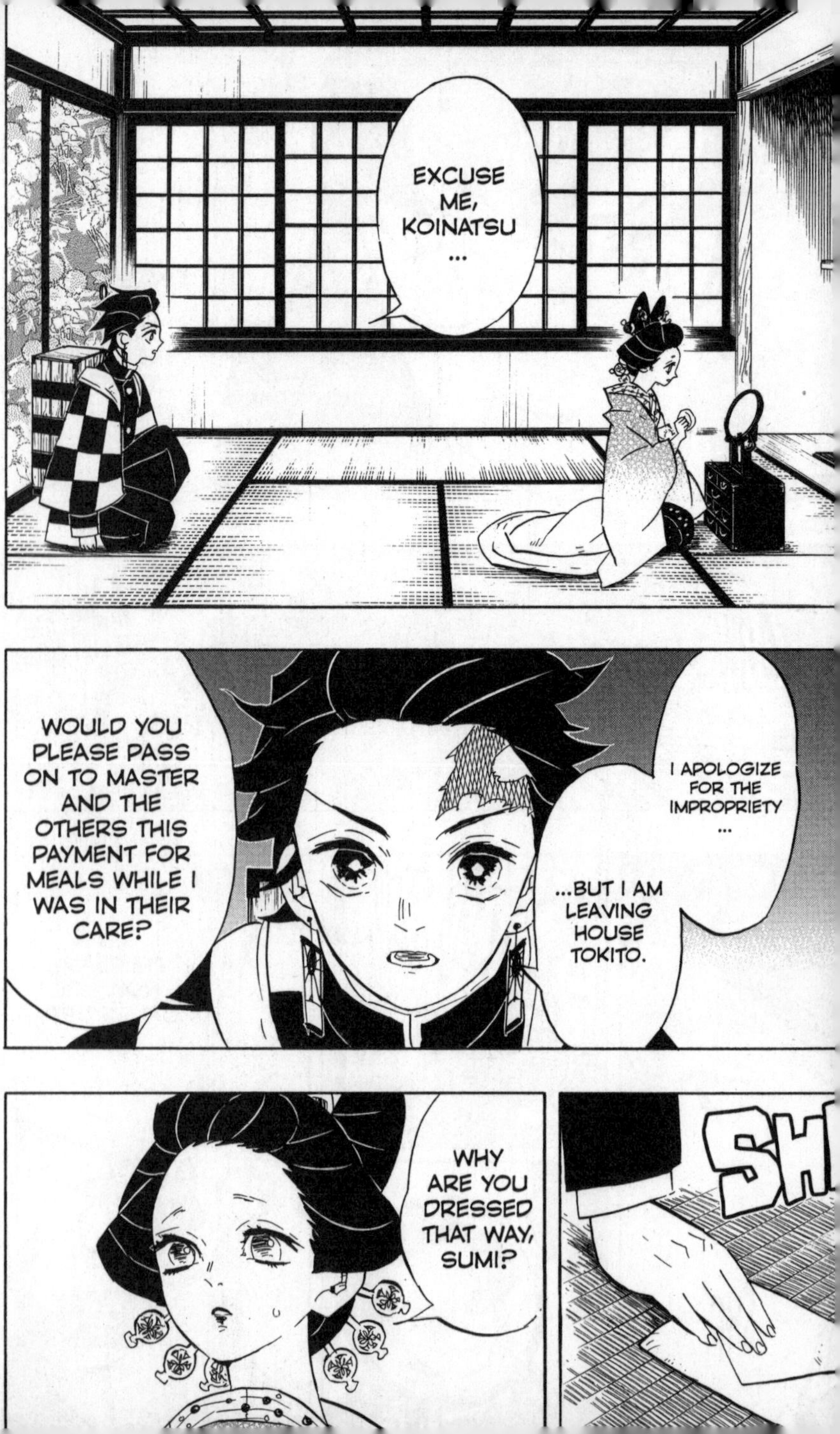
EXCUSE ME, KOINATSU...
I APOLOGIZE FOR THE IMPROPRIETY...
...BUT I AM LEAVING HOUSE TOKITO.
WOULD YOU PLEASE PASS ON TO MASTER AND THE OTHERS THIS PAYMENT FOR MEALS WHILE I WAS IN THEIR CARE?
WHY ARE YOU DRESSED THAT WAY, SUMI?

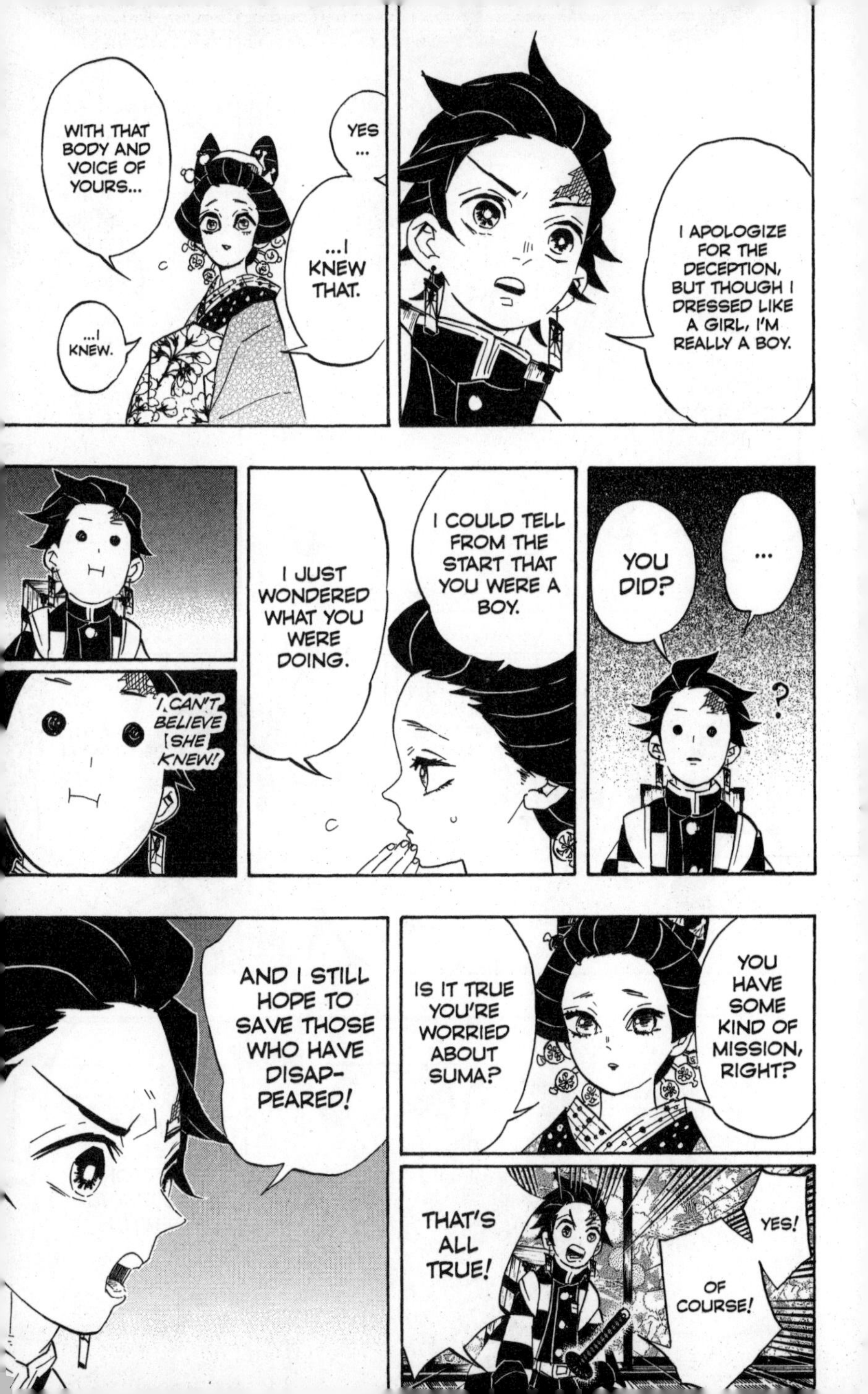
I APOLOGIZE FOR THE DECEPTION, BUT THOUGH I DRESSED LIKE A GIRL, I'M REALLY A BOY.
YES ...
...I KNEW THAT.
WITH THAT BODY AND VOICE OF YOURS...
...I KNEW.
...
YOU DID?
I COULD TELL FROM THE START THAT YOU WERE A BOY.
I JUST WONDERED WHAT YOU WERE DOING.
I CAN'T BELIEVE SHE KNEW!
YOU HAVE SOME KIND OF MISSION, RIGHT?
IS IT TRUE YOU'RE WORRIED ABOUT SUMA?
YES!
OF COURSE!
THAT'S ALL TRUE!
AND I STILL HOPE TO SAVE THOSE WHO HAVE DISAP-PEARED!

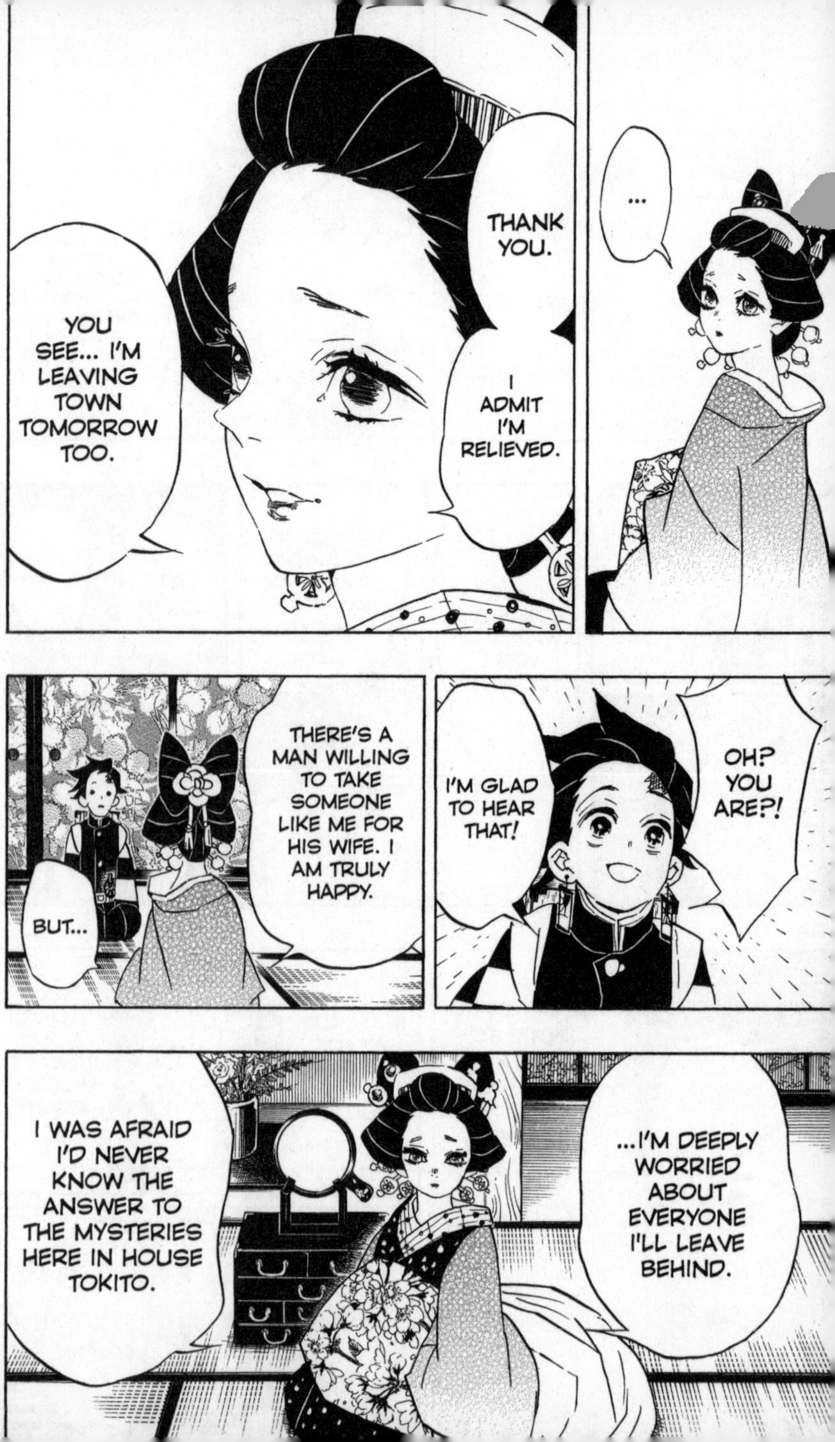
...
THANK YOU.
I ADMIT I'M RELIEVED.
YOU SEE... I'M LEAVING TOWN TOMORROW TOO.
OH? YOU ARE?!
I'M GLAD TO HEAR THAT!
THERE'S A MAN WILLING TO TAKE SOMEONE LIKE ME FOR HIS WIFE. I AM TRULY HAPPY.
BUT...
...I'M DEEPLY WORRIED ABOUT EVERYONE I'LL LEAVE BEHIND.
I WAS AFRAID I'D NEVER KNOW THE ANSWER TO THE MYSTERIES HERE IN HOUSE TOKITO.

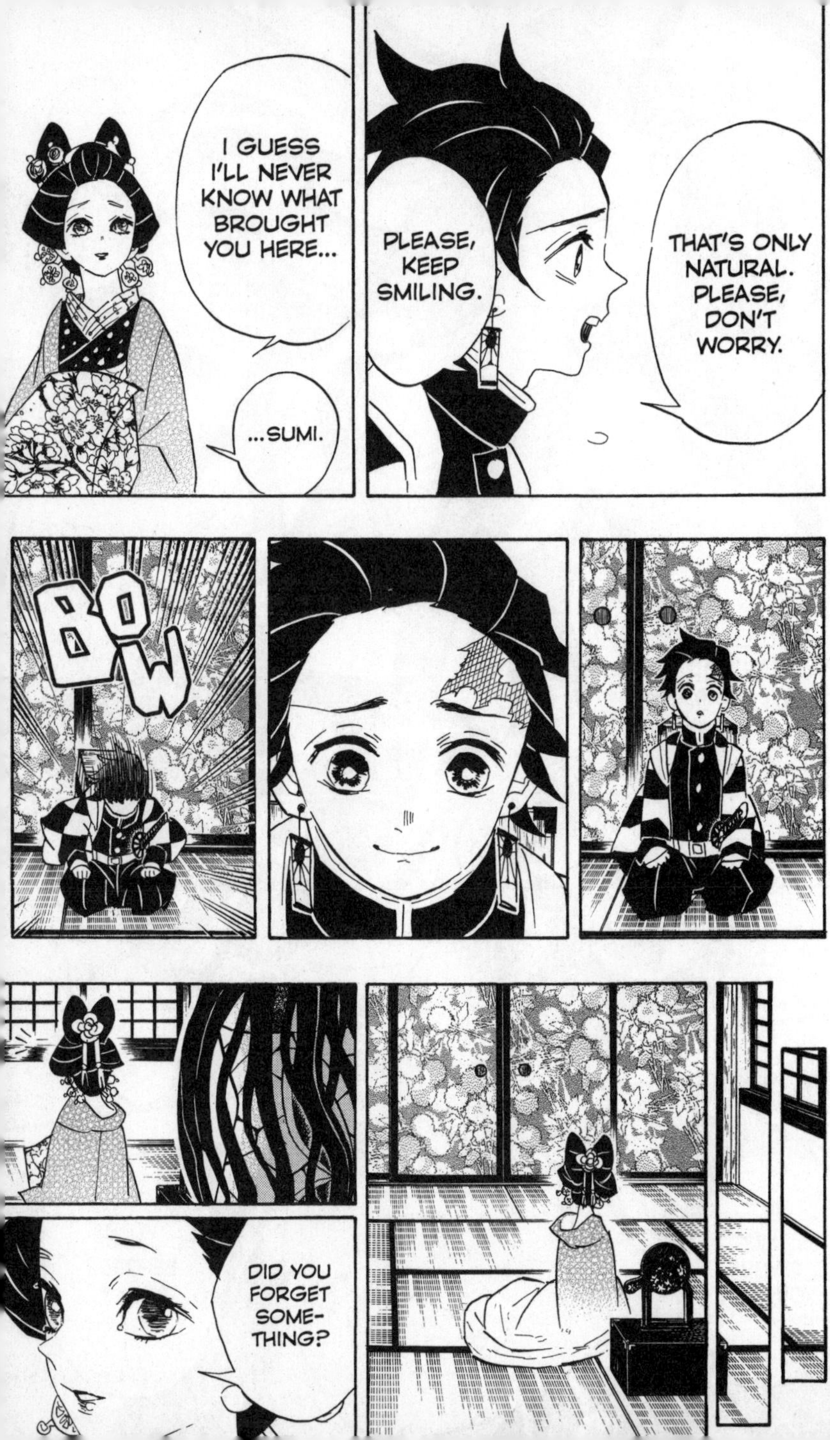
THAT'S ONLY NATURAL. PLEASE, DON'T WORRY.
PLEASE, KEEP SMILING.
I GUESS I'LL NEVER KNOW WHAT BROUGHT YOU HERE...
...SUMI.
BOW
DID YOU FORGET SOME-THING?

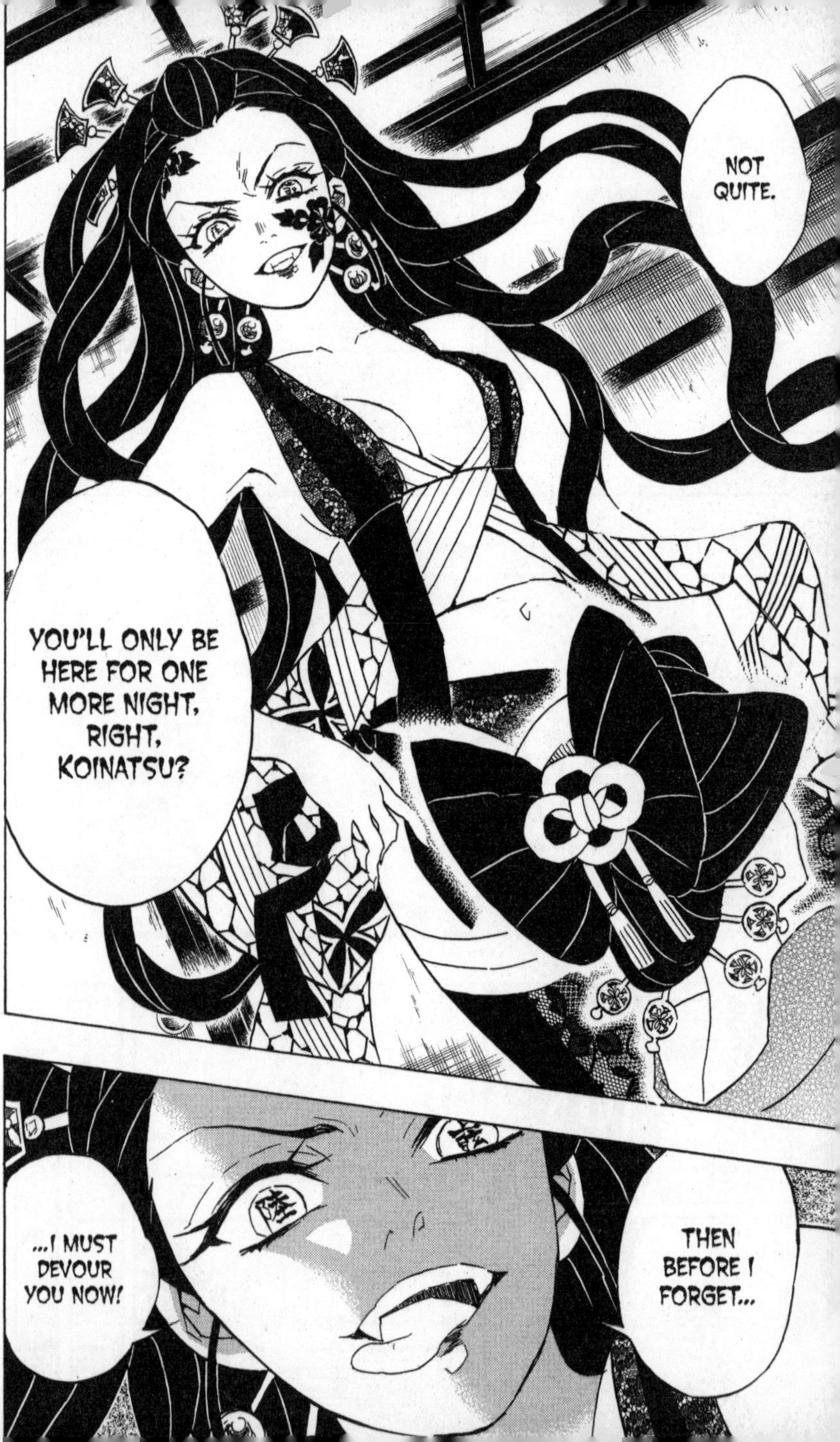
NOT QUITE.
YOU'LL ONLY BE HERE FOR ONE MORE NIGHT, RIGHT, KOINATSU?
THEN BEFORE I FORGET...
...I MUST DEVOUR YOU NOW!

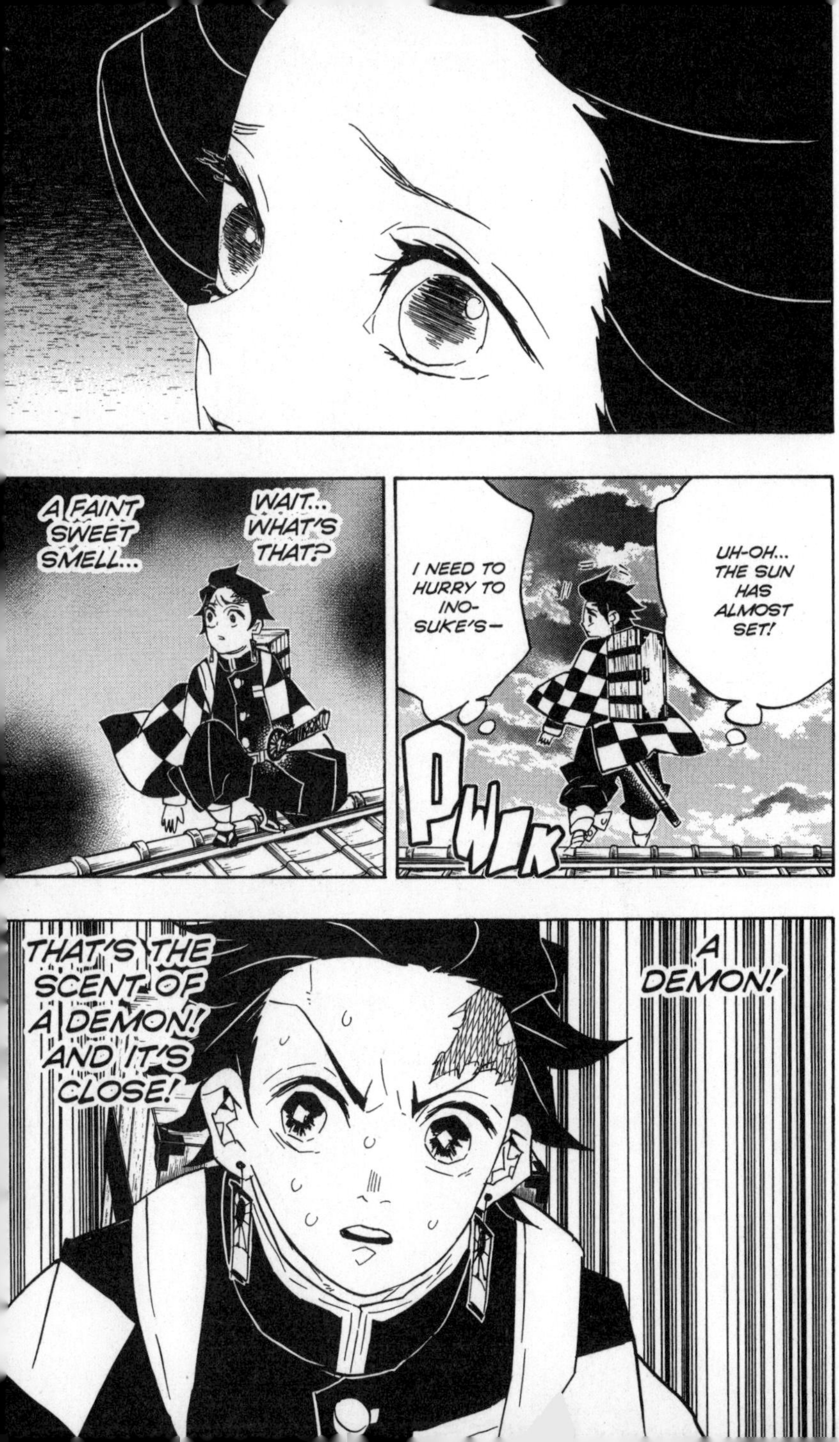
UH-OH... THE SUN HAS ALMOST SET!
I NEED TO HURRY TO INO-SUKE'S—
PWIK
WAIT... WHAT'S THAT?
A FAINT SWEET SMELL...
A DEMON!
THAT'S THE SCENT OF A DEMON! AND IT'S CLOSE!

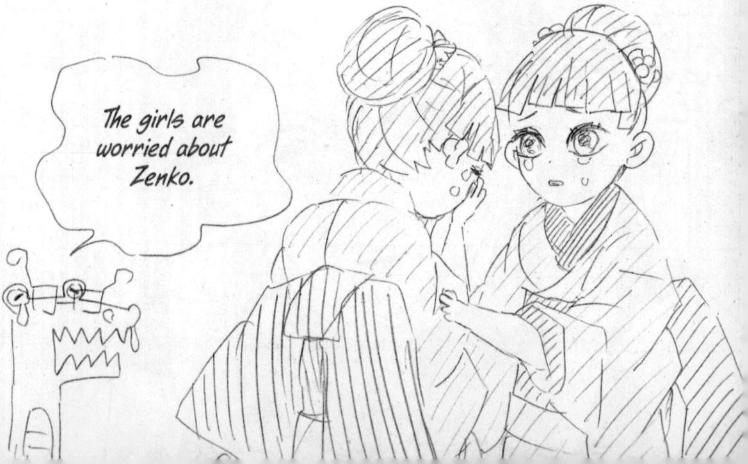
The girls are worried about Zenko.

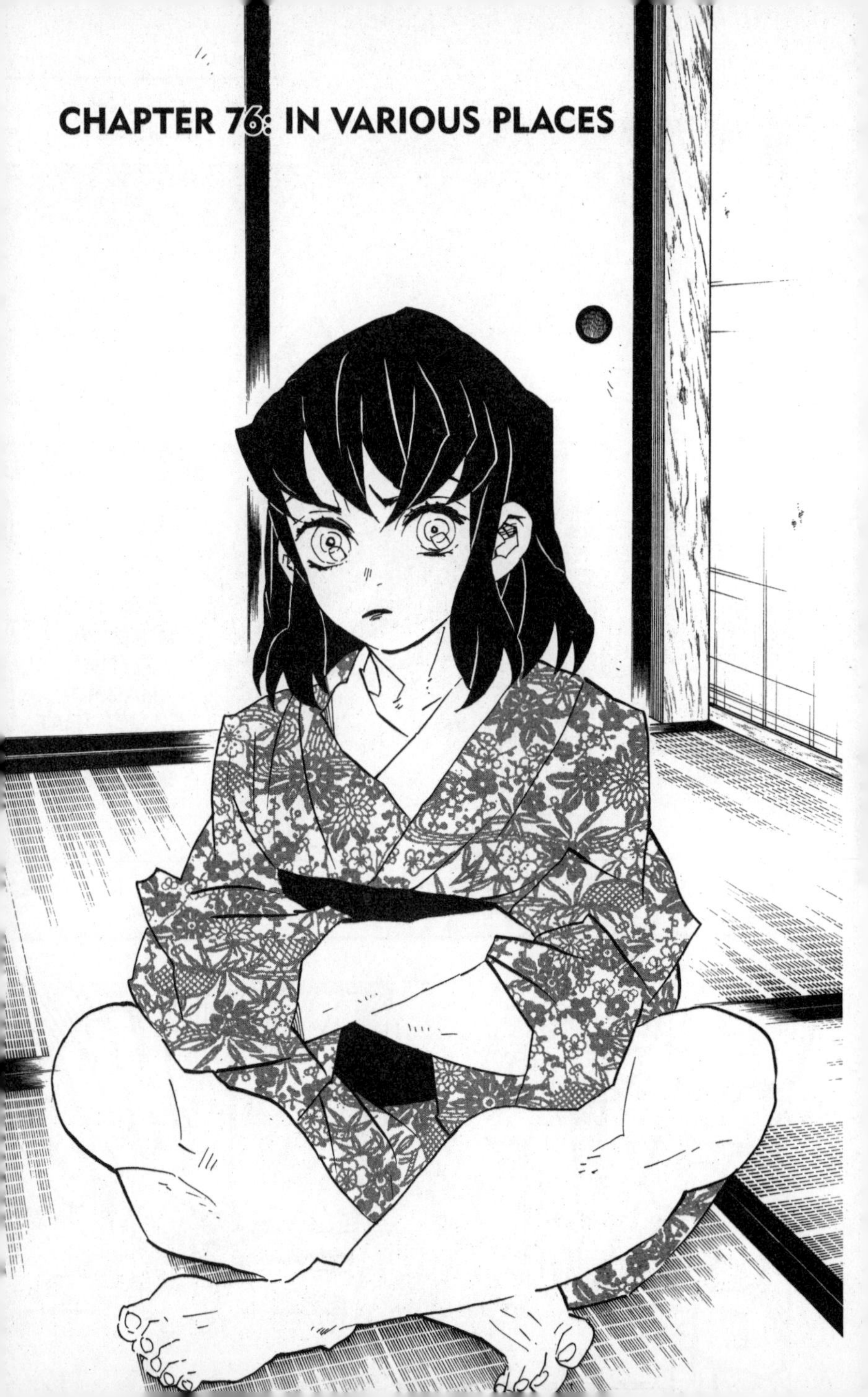
CHAPTER 76: IN VARIOUS PLACES

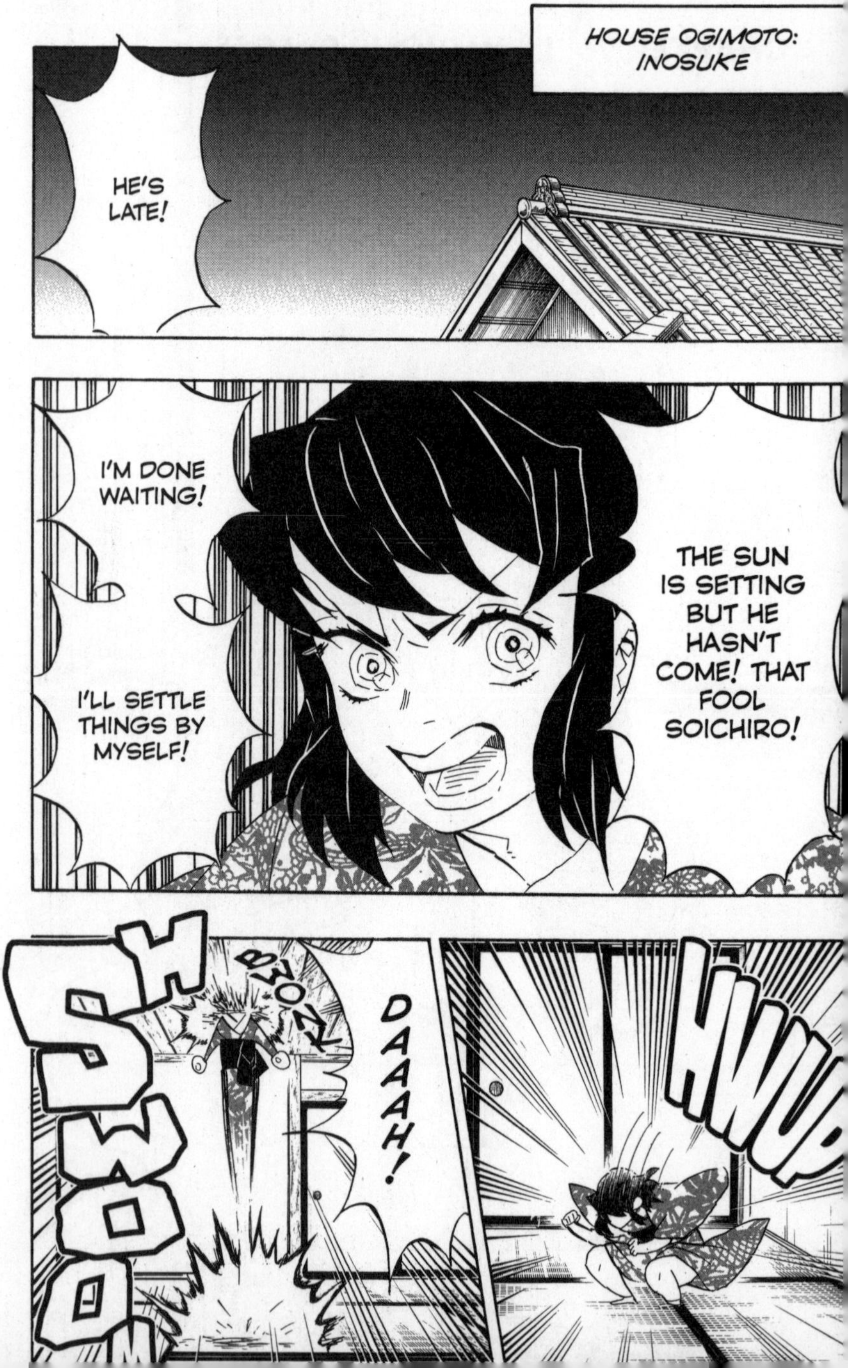
HOUSE OGIMOTO: INOSUKE
HE'S LATE!
THE SUN IS SETTING BUT HE HASN'T COME! THAT FOOL SOICHIRO!
I'M DONE WAITING!
I'LL SETTLE THINGS BY MYSELF!
HWUP
DAAAAH!
BWONK
DOOSH

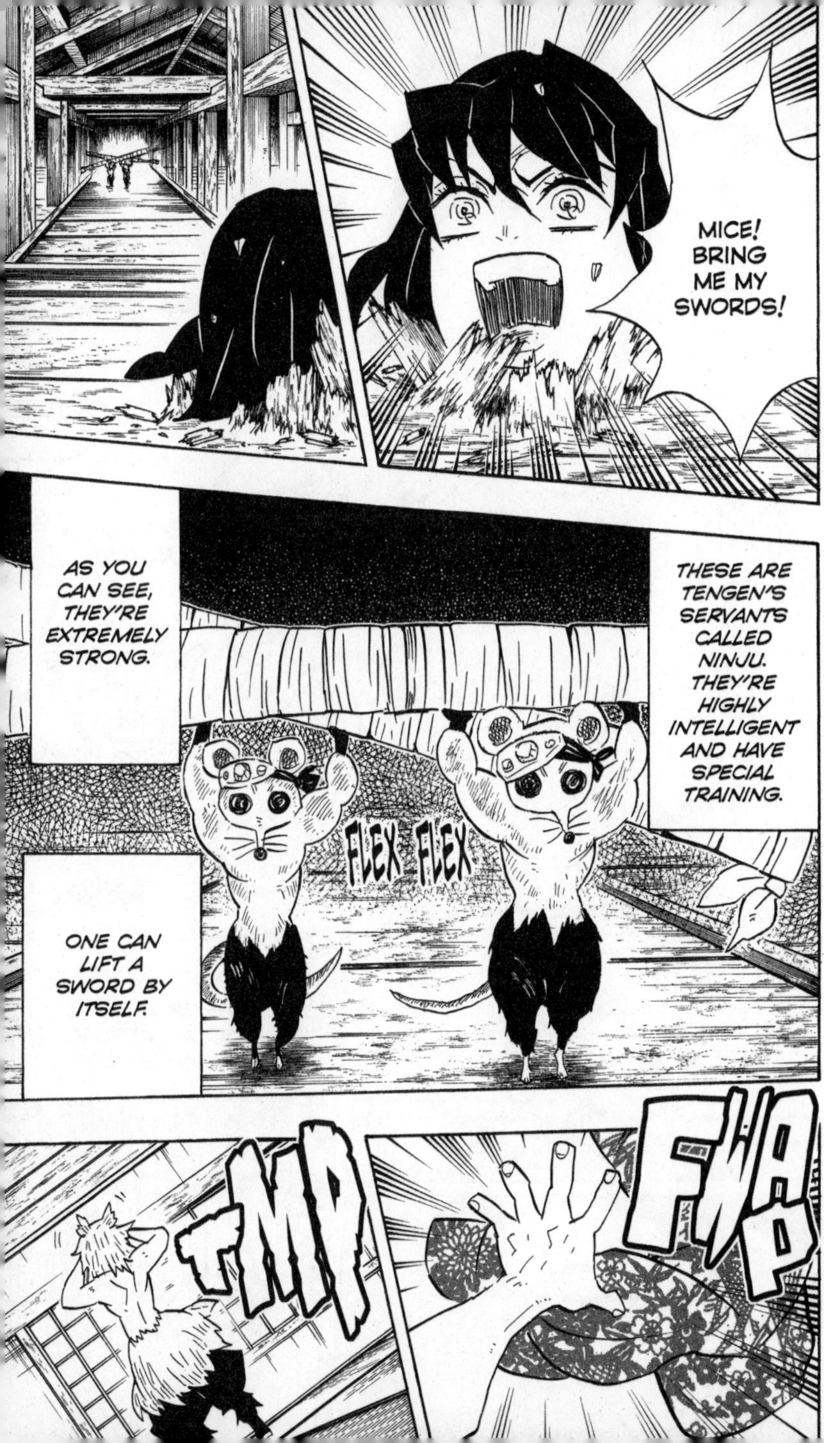
MICE! BRING ME MY SWORDS!
THESE ARE TENGEN'S SERVANTS CALLED NINJU. THEY'RE HIGHLY INTELLIGENT AND HAVE SPECIAL TRAINING.
AS YOU CAN SEE, THEY'RE EXTREMELY STRONG.
FLEX FLEX
ONE CAN LIFT A SWORD BY ITSELF.
FWAP
TMP

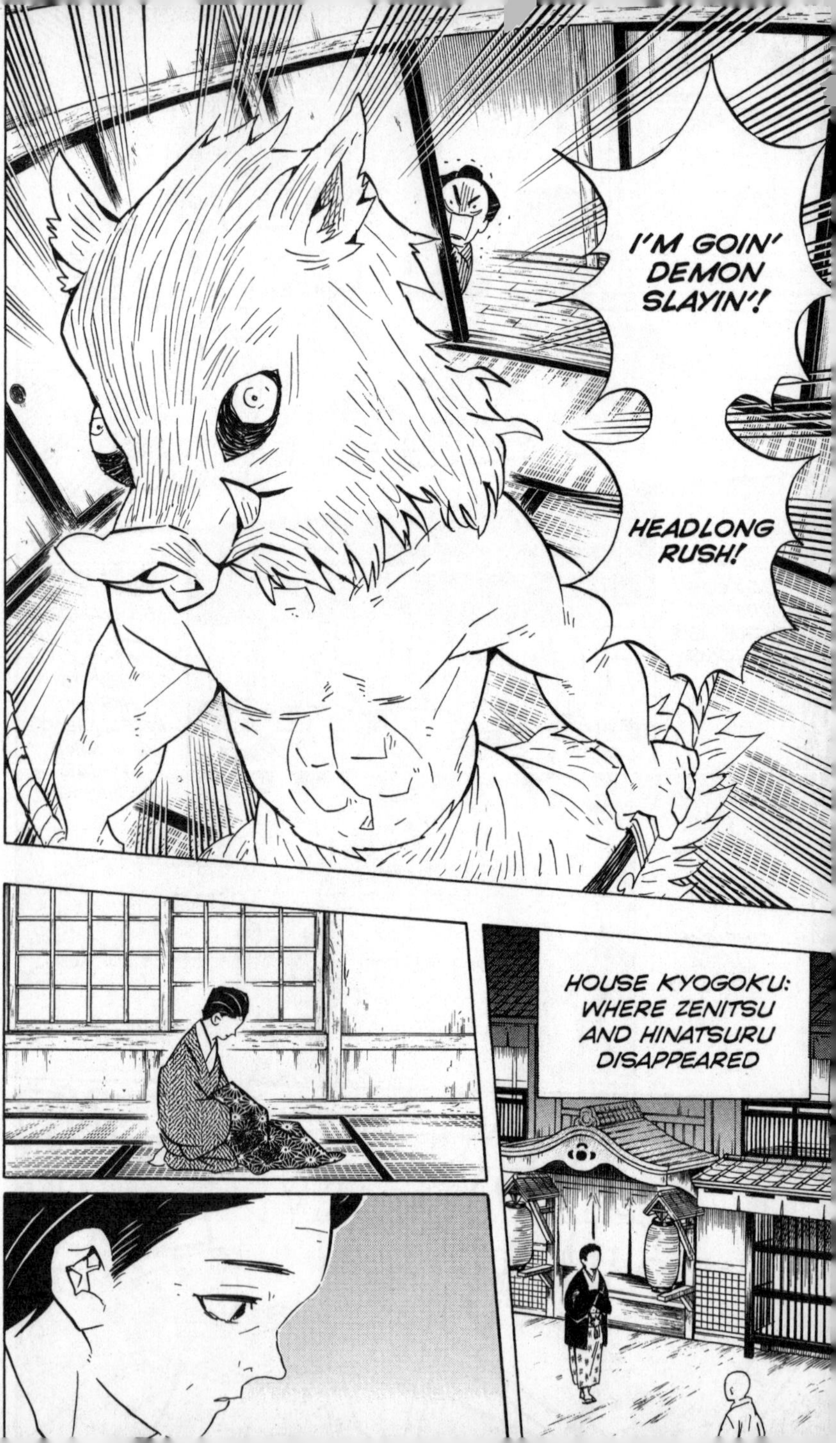
I'M GOIN' DEMON SLAYIN'!
HEADLONG RUSH!
HOUSE KYOGOKU: WHERE ZENITSU AND HINATSURU DISAPPEARED

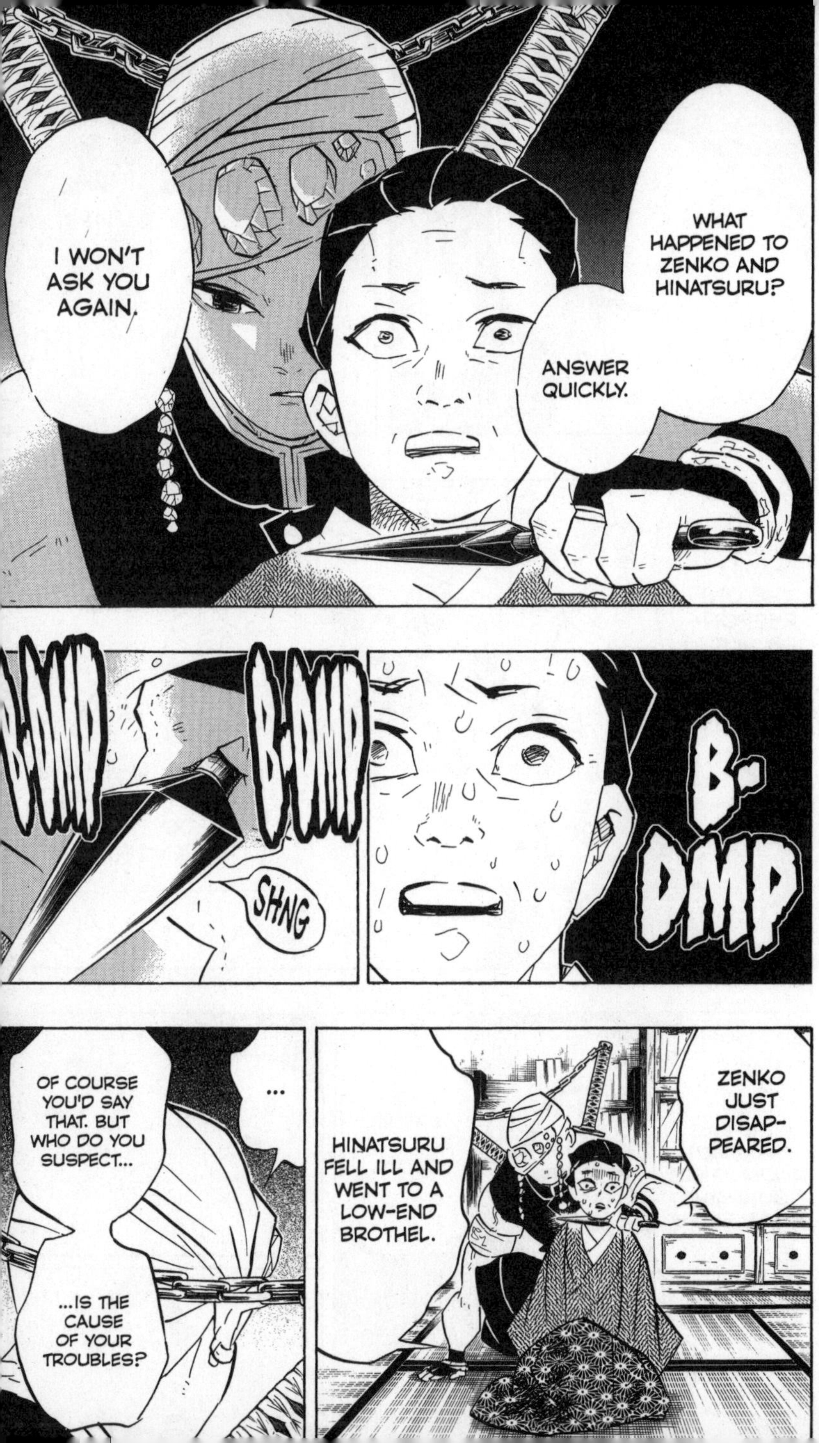

WHAT HAPPENED TO ZENKO AND HINATSURU?
ANSWER QUICKLY.
I WON'T ASK YOU AGAIN.
B-DMP
B-DMP
B-DMP
SHNG
ZENKO JUST DISAP-PEARED.
HINATSURU FELL ILL AND WENT TO A LOW-END BROTHEL.
...
OF COURSE YOU'D SAY THAT. BUT WHO DO YOU SUSPECT...
...IS THE CAUSE OF YOUR TROUBLES?

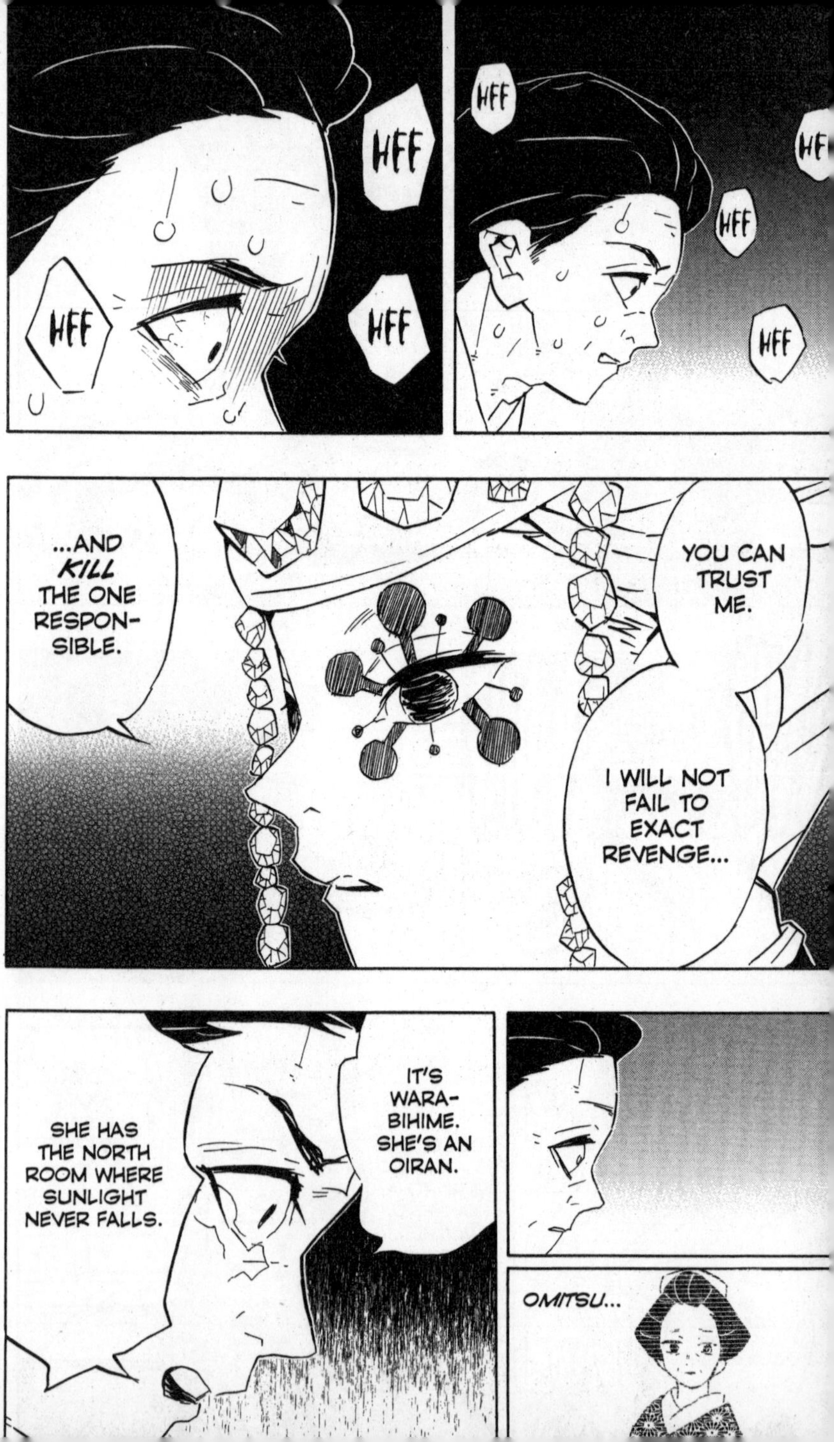
HFF
HFF
HFF
HFF
HFF
HFF
HFF
HFF
YOU CAN TRUST ME.
I WILL NOT FAIL TO EXACT REVENGE...
...AND *KILL* THE ONE RESPONSIBLE.
OMITSU...
IT'S WARABIHIME. SHE'S AN OIRAN.
SHE HAS THE NORTH ROOM WHERE SUNLIGHT NEVER FALLS.

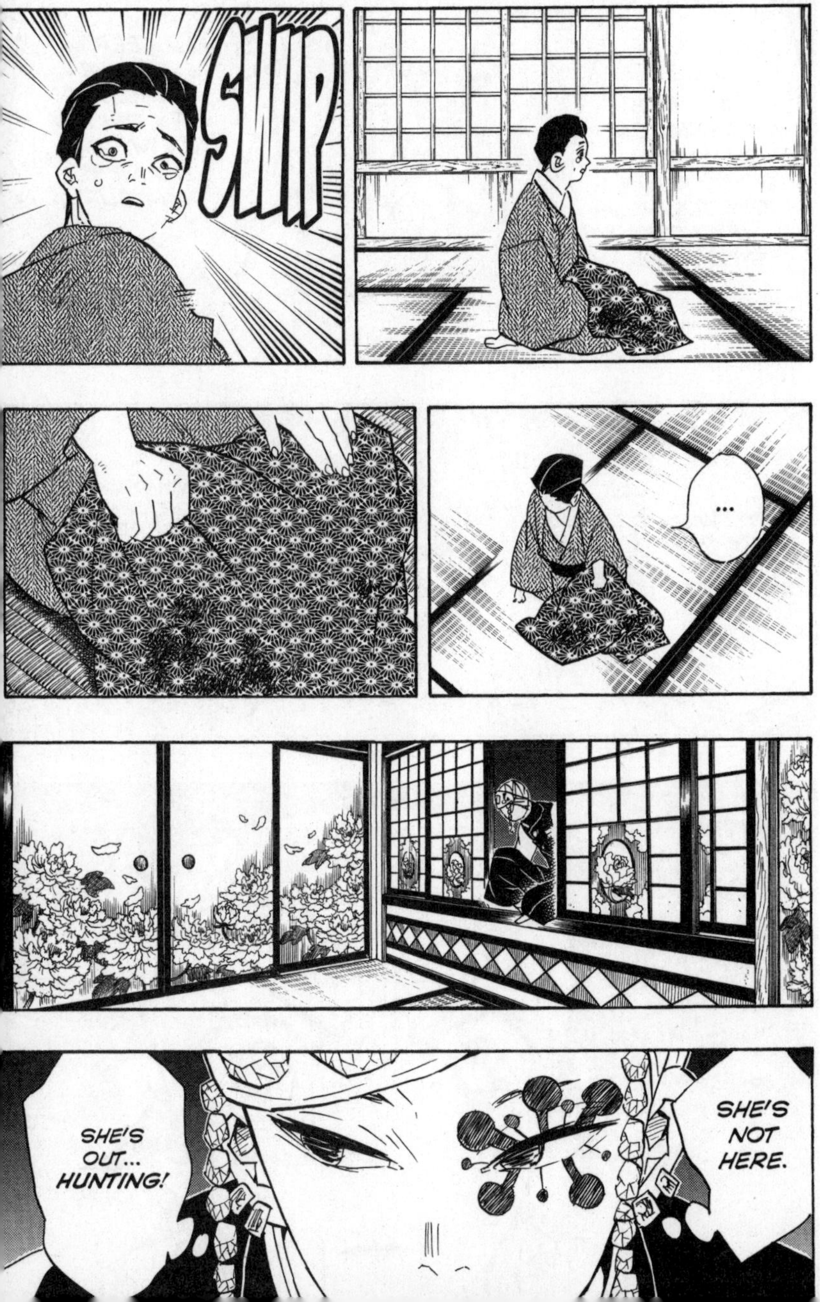
SWIP
...
SHE'S NOT HERE.
SHE'S OUT... HUNTING!

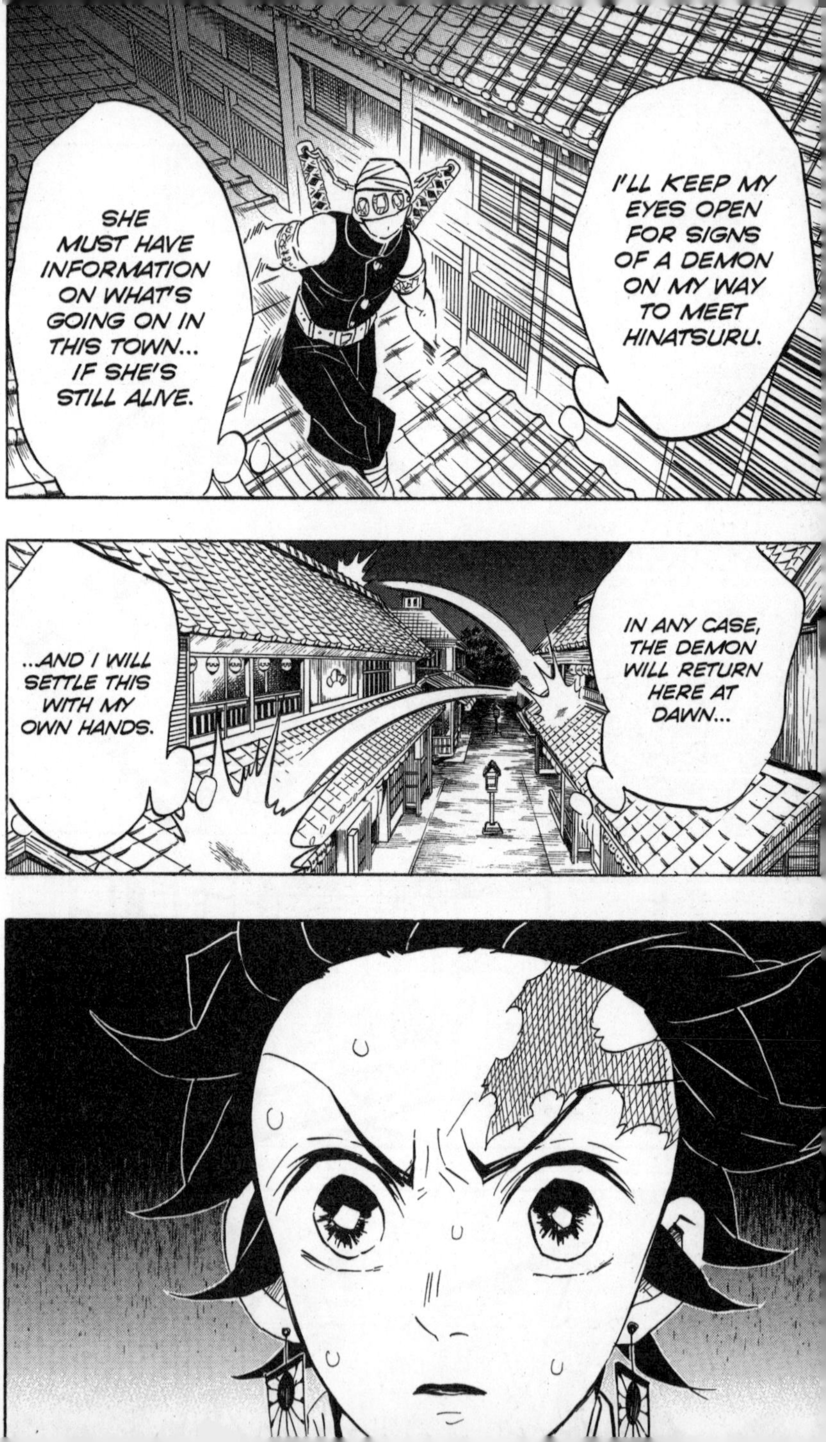
I'LL KEEP MY EYES OPEN FOR SIGNS OF A DEMON ON MY WAY TO MEET HINATSURU.
SHE MUST HAVE INFORMATION ON WHAT'S GOING ON IN THIS TOWN... IF SHE'S STILL ALIVE.
IN ANY CASE, THE DEMON WILL RETURN HERE AT DAWN...
...AND I WILL SETTLE THIS WITH MY OWN HANDS.

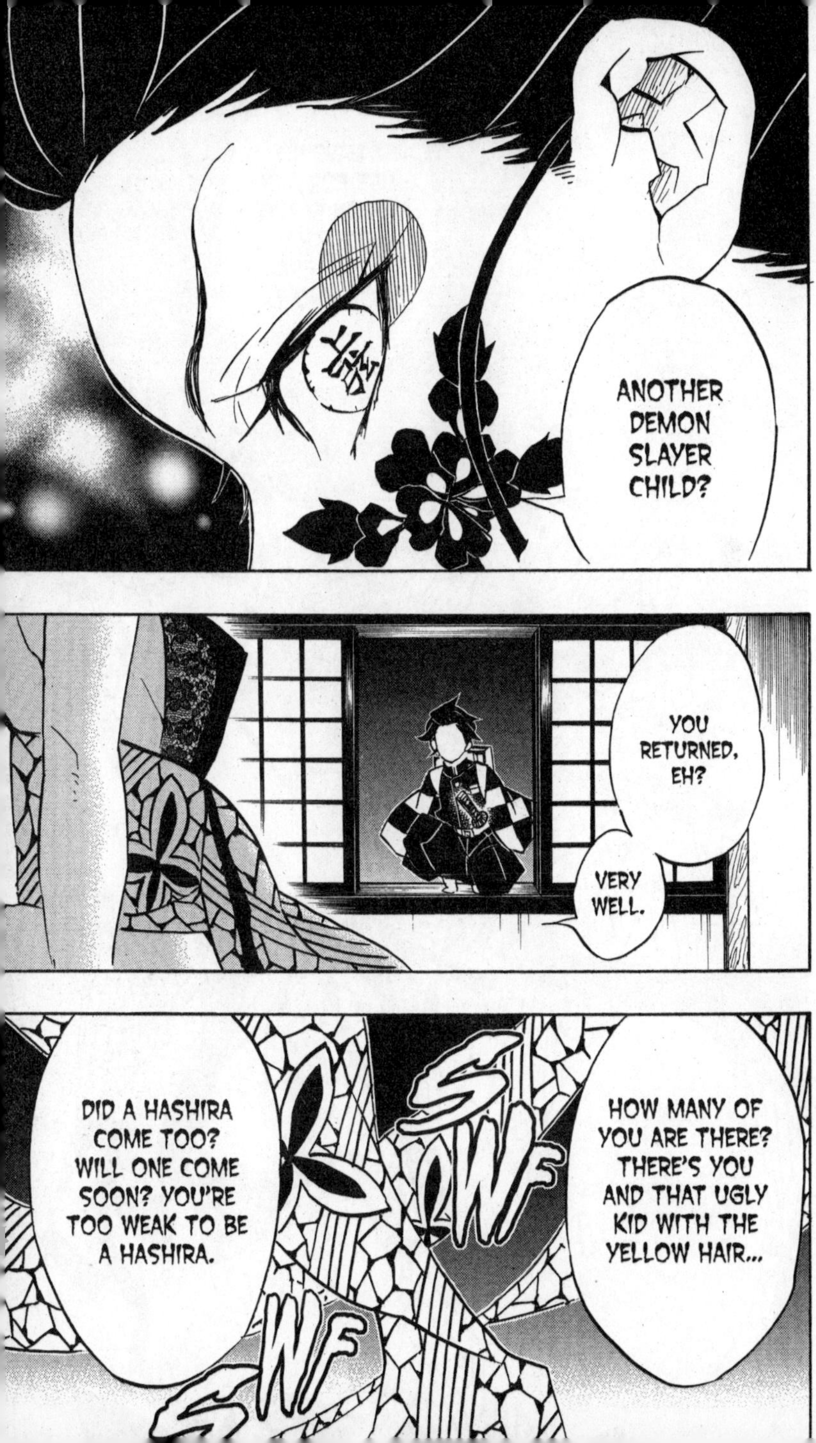
ANOTHER DEMON SLAYER CHILD?
YOU RETURNED, EH?
VERY WELL.
HOW MANY OF YOU ARE THERE? THERE'S YOU AND THAT UGLY KID WITH THE YELLOW HAIR...
SWF
DID A HASHIRA COME TOO? WILL ONE COME SOON? YOU'RE TOO WEAK TO BE A HASHIRA.
SWF

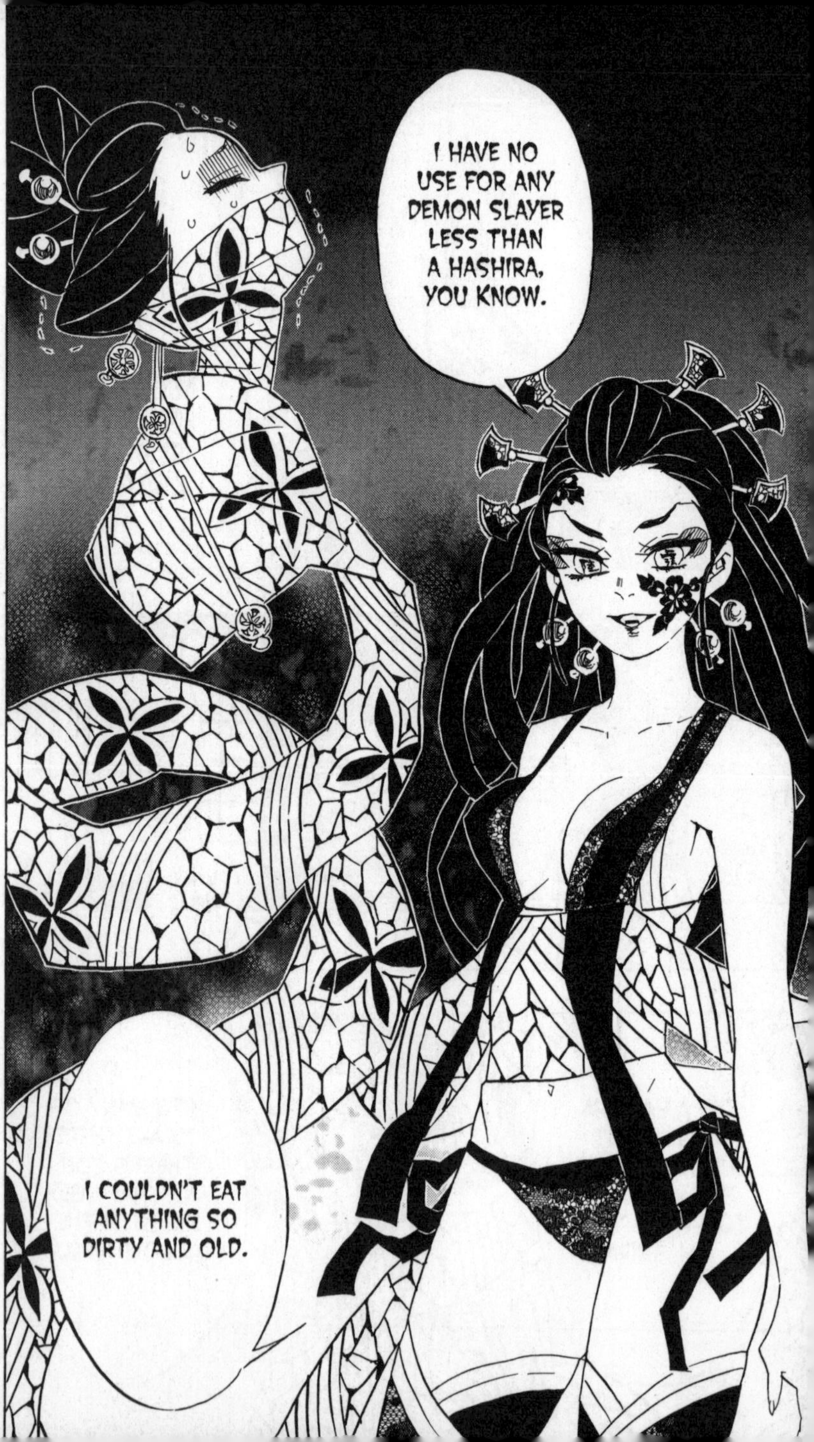
I HAVE NO USE FOR ANY DEMON SLAYER LESS THAN A HASHIRA, YOU KNOW.
I COULDN'T EAT ANYTHING SO DIRTY AND OLD.

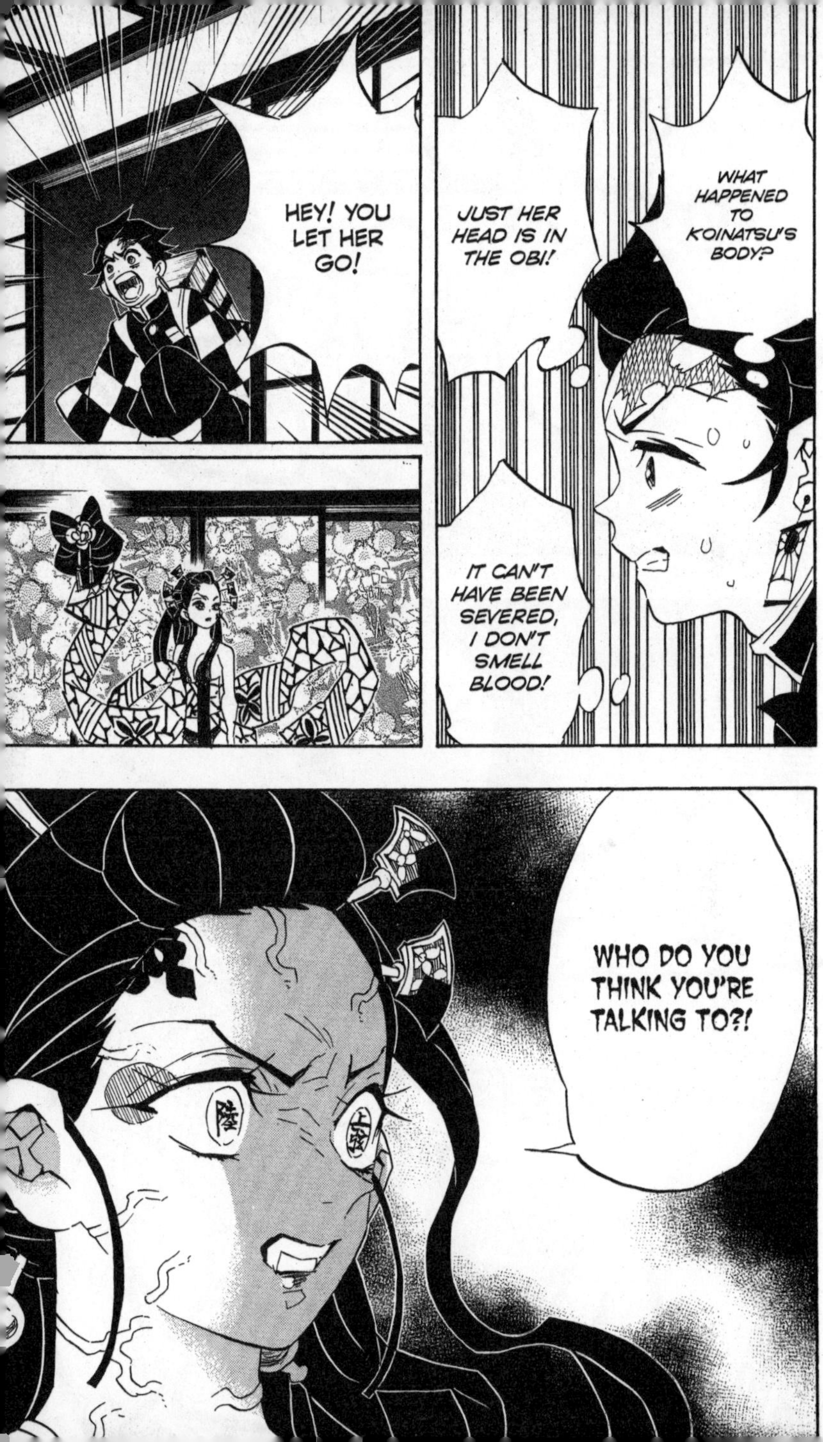
WHAT HAPPENED TO KOINATSU'S BODY?
JUST HER HEAD IS IN THE OBI!
IT CAN'T HAVE BEEN SEVERED, I DON'T SMELL BLOOD!
HEY! YOU LET HER GO!
WHO DO YOU THINK YOU'RE TALKING TO?!

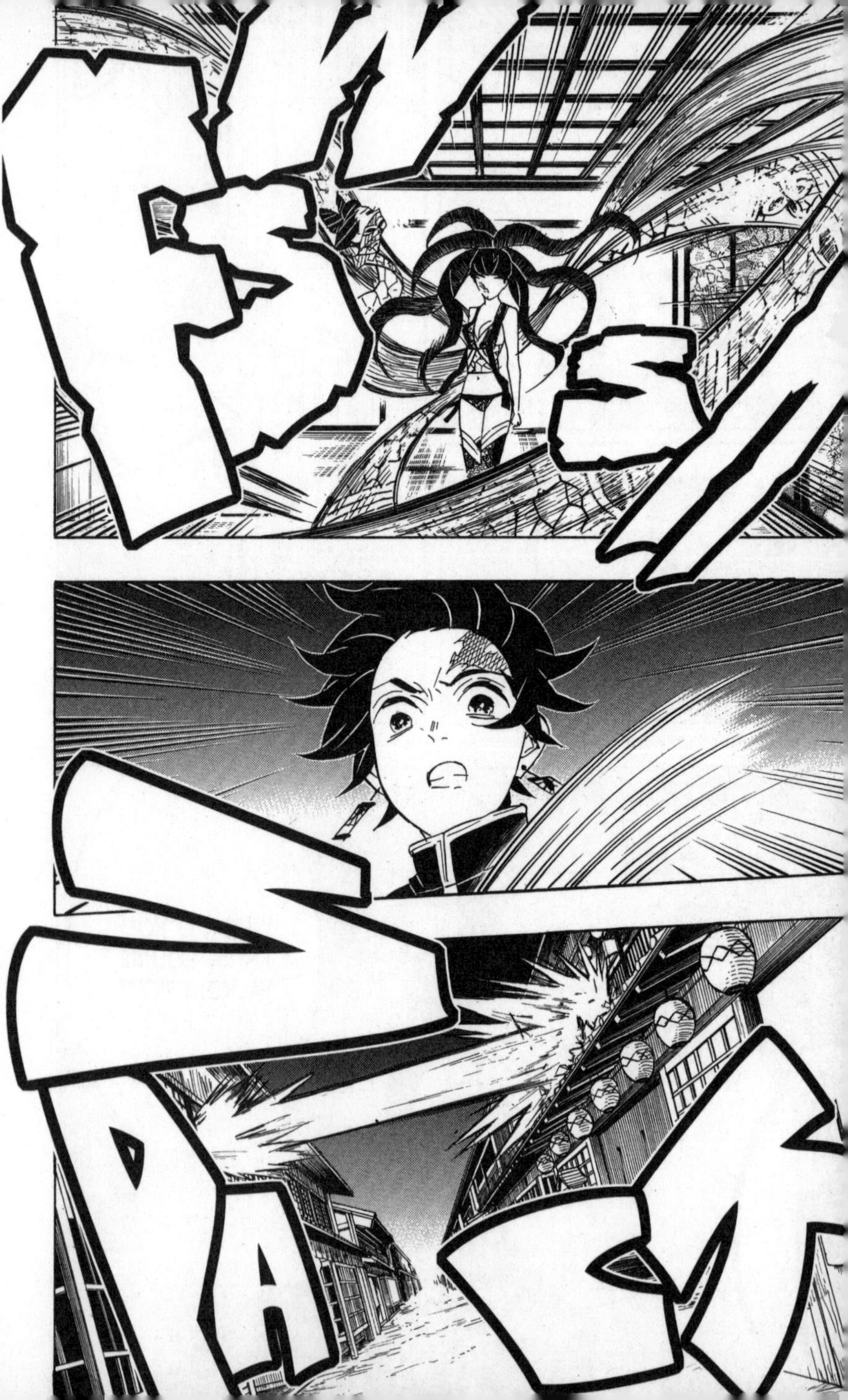

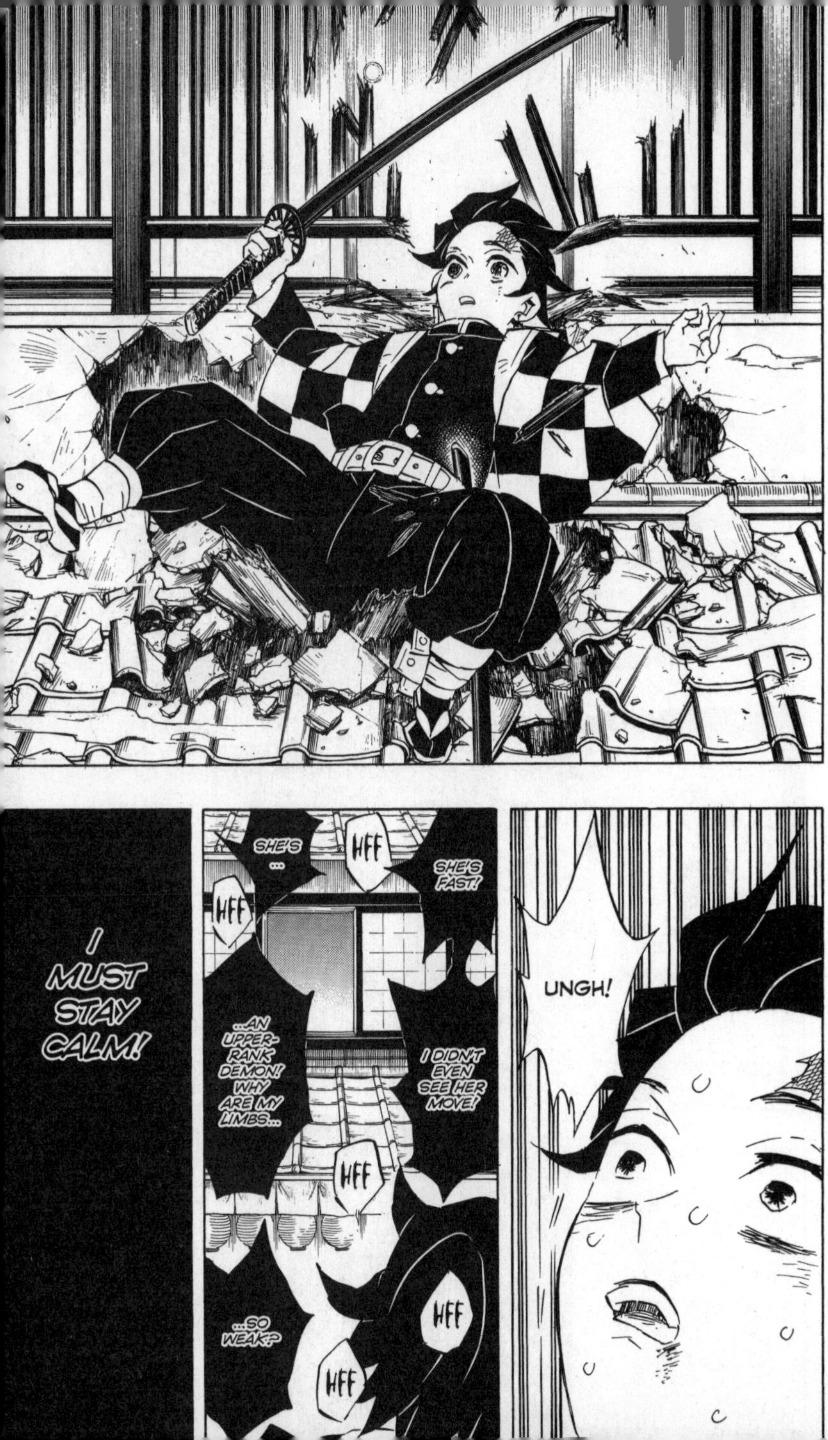
UNGH!
SHE'S FAST!
HFF
SHE'S ...
HFF
I DIDN'T EVEN SEE HER MOVE!
...AN UPPER-RANK DEMON! WHY ARE MY LIMBS...
HFF
HFF
...SO WEAK?
HFF
I MUST STAY CALM!

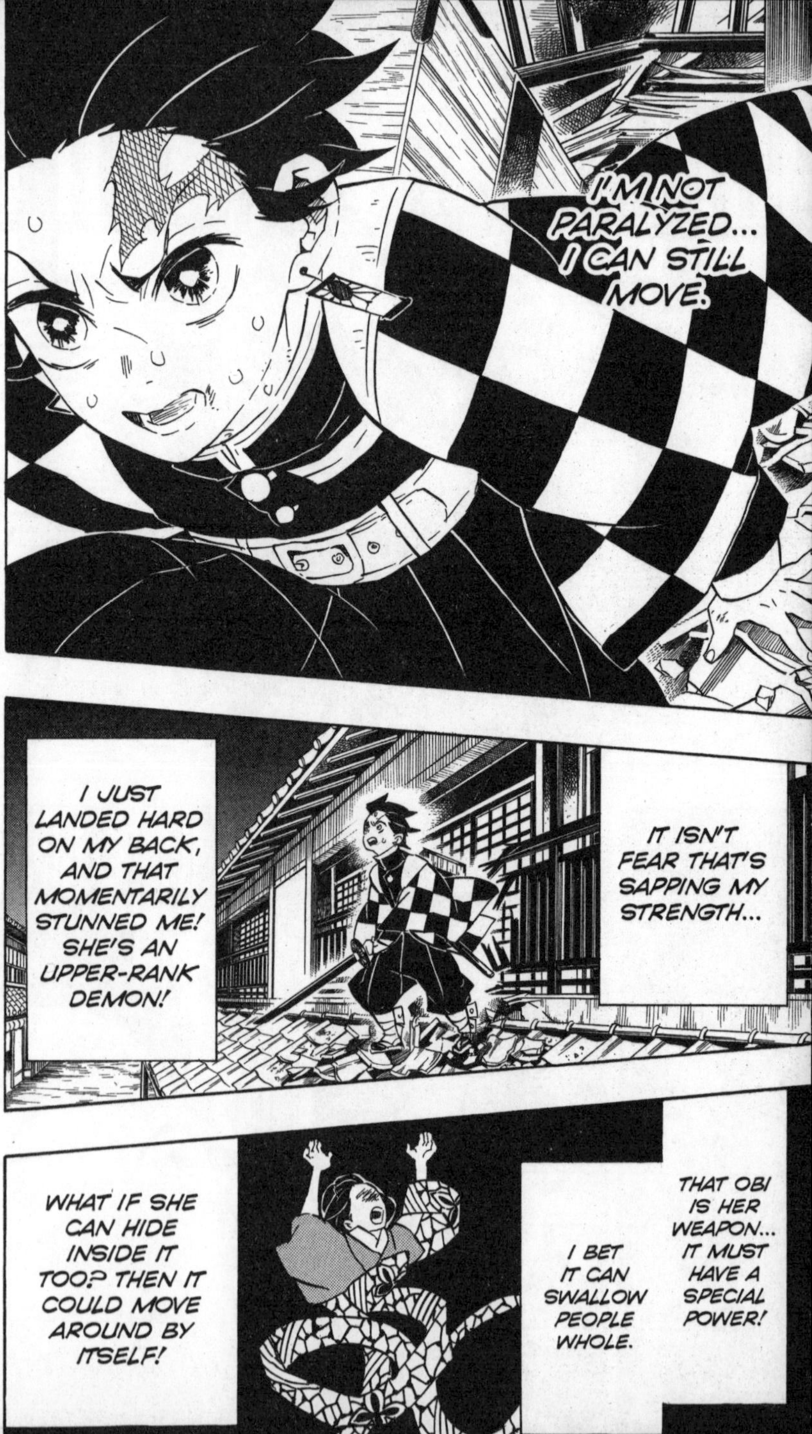
I'M NOT PARALYZED... I CAN STILL MOVE.
IT ISN'T FEAR THAT'S SAPPING MY STRENGTH...
I JUST LANDED HARD ON MY BACK, AND THAT MOMENTARILY STUNNED ME! SHE'S AN UPPER-RANK DEMON!
THAT OBI IS HER WEAPON... IT MUST HAVE A SPECIAL POWER!
I BET IT CAN SWALLOW PEOPLE WHOLE.
WHAT IF SHE CAN HIDE INSIDE IT TOO? THEN IT COULD MOVE AROUND BY ITSELF!

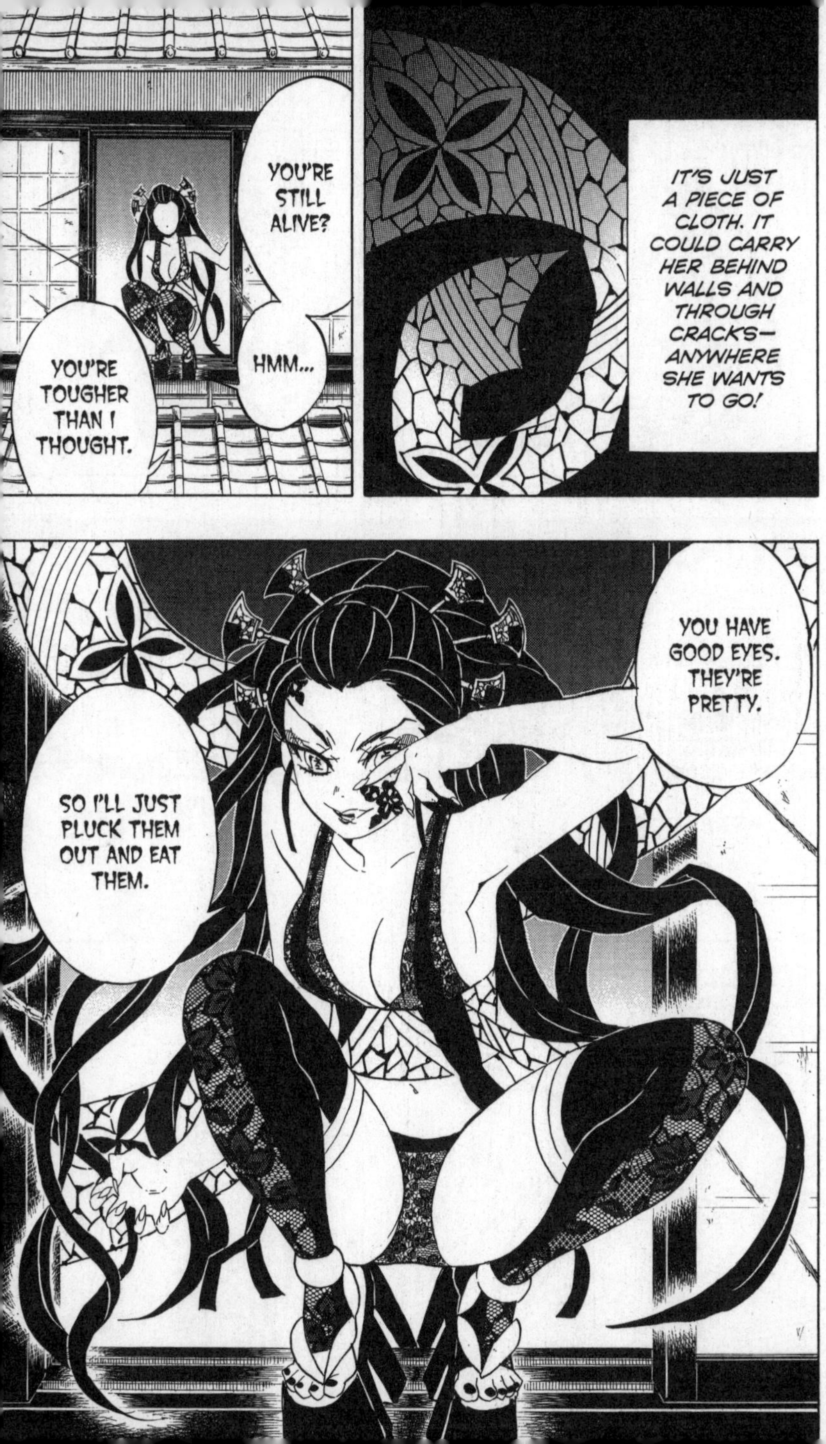
IT'S JUST A PIECE OF CLOTH. IT COULD CARRY HER BEHIND WALLS AND THROUGH CRACKS—ANYWHERE SHE WANTS TO GO!
YOU'RE STILL ALIVE?
HMM...
YOU'RE TOUGHER THAN I THOUGHT.
YOU HAVE GOOD EYES. THEY'RE PRETTY.
SO I'LL JUST PLUCK THEM OUT AND EAT THEM.

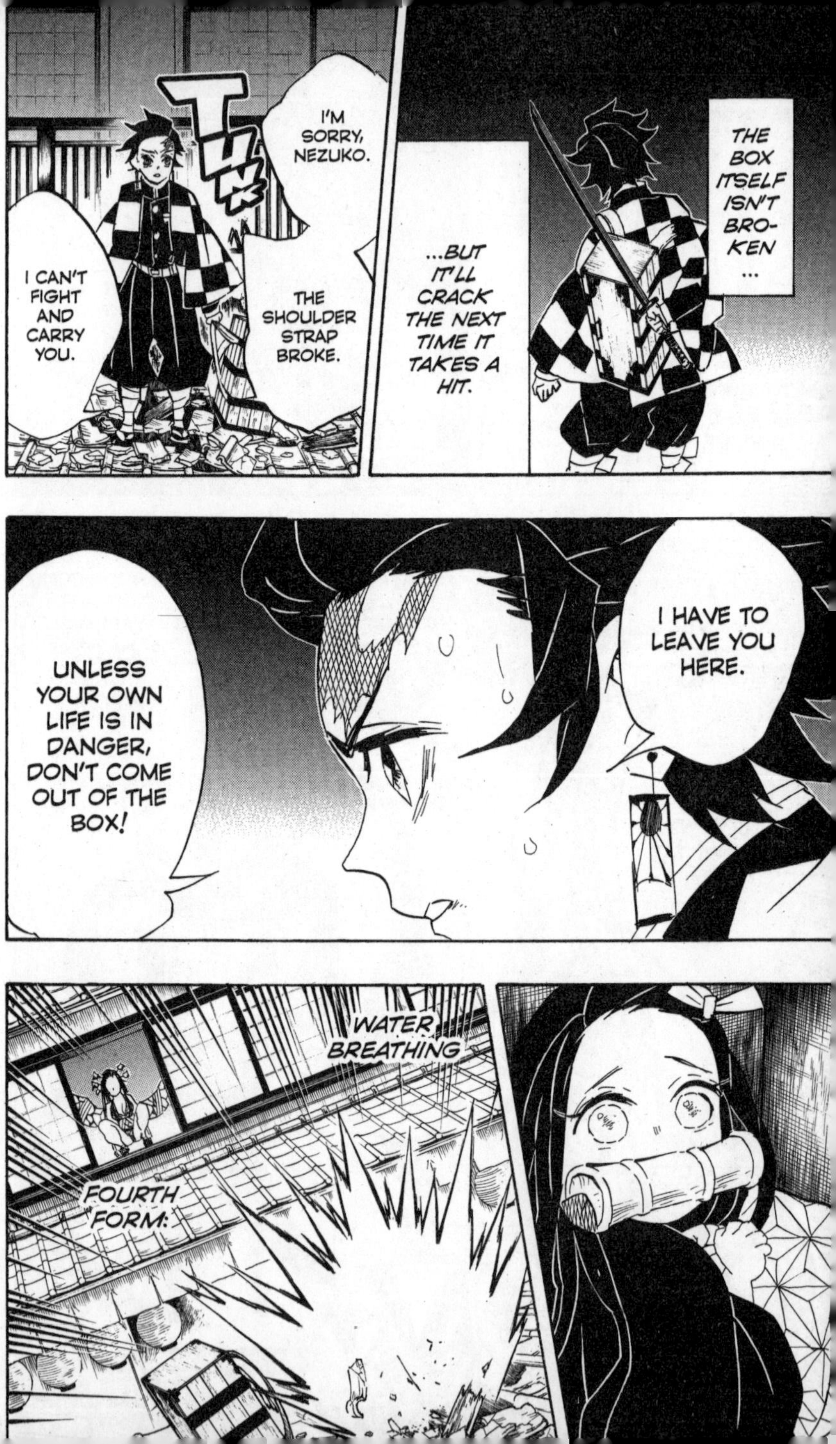
THE BOX ITSELF ISN'T BRO-KEN...
...BUT IT'LL CRACK THE NEXT TIME IT TAKES A HIT.
TUNK
I'M SORRY, NEZUKO.
THE SHOULDER STRAP BROKE.
I CAN'T FIGHT AND CARRY YOU.
I HAVE TO LEAVE YOU HERE.
UNLESS YOUR OWN LIFE IS IN DANGER, DON'T COME OUT OF THE BOX!
WATER BREATHING
FOURTH FORM:

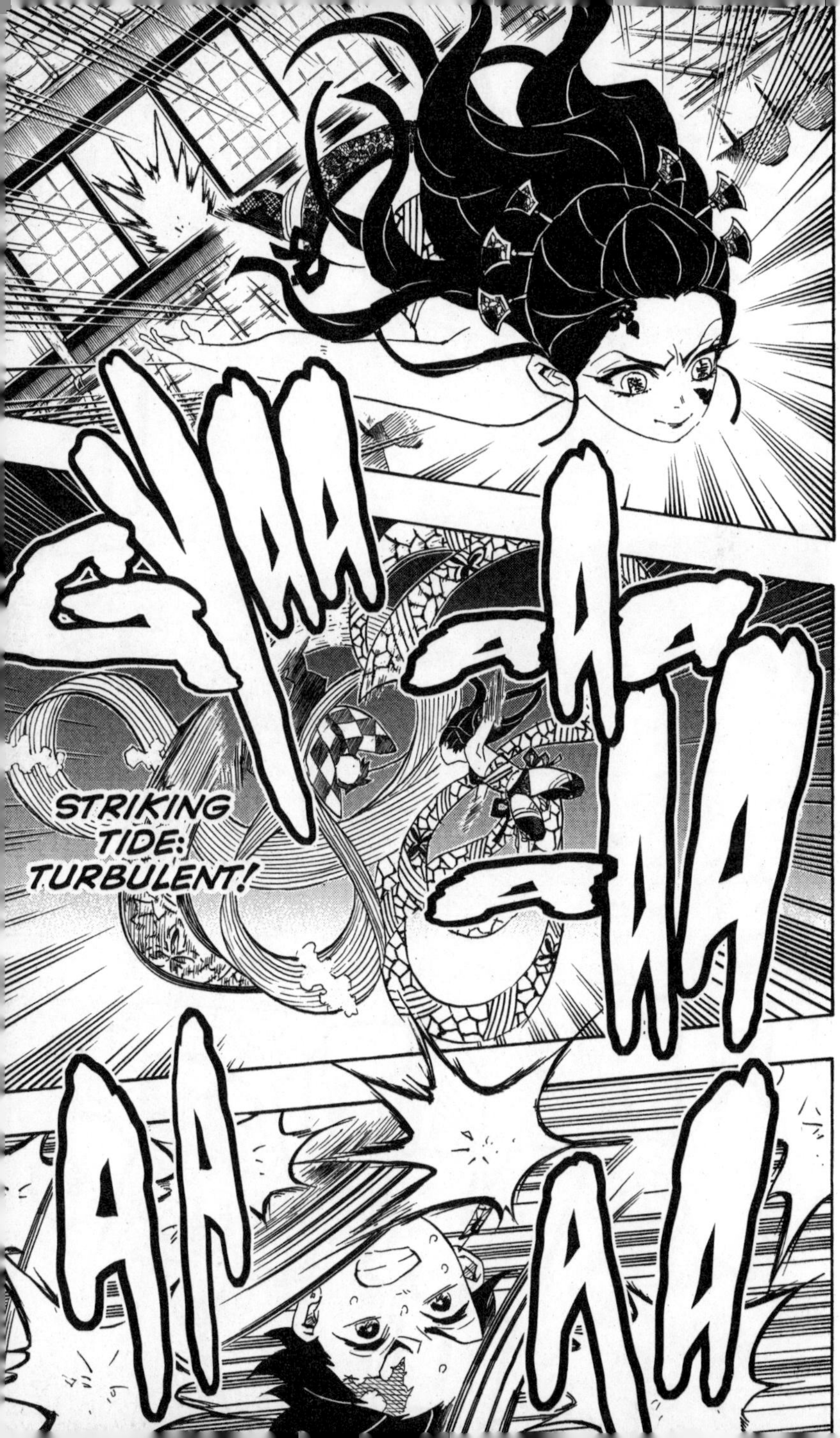
STRIKING TIDE: TURBULENT!

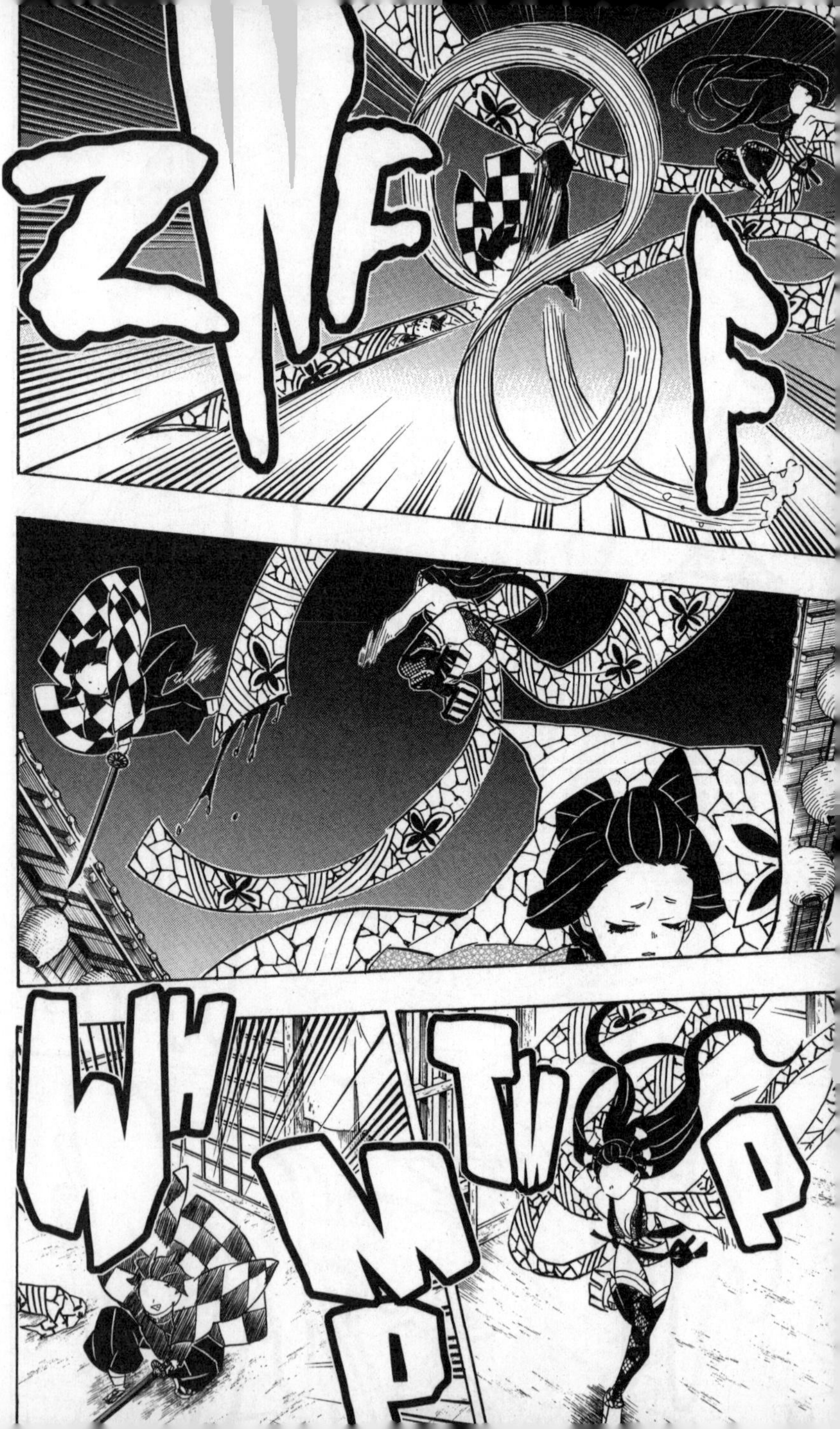

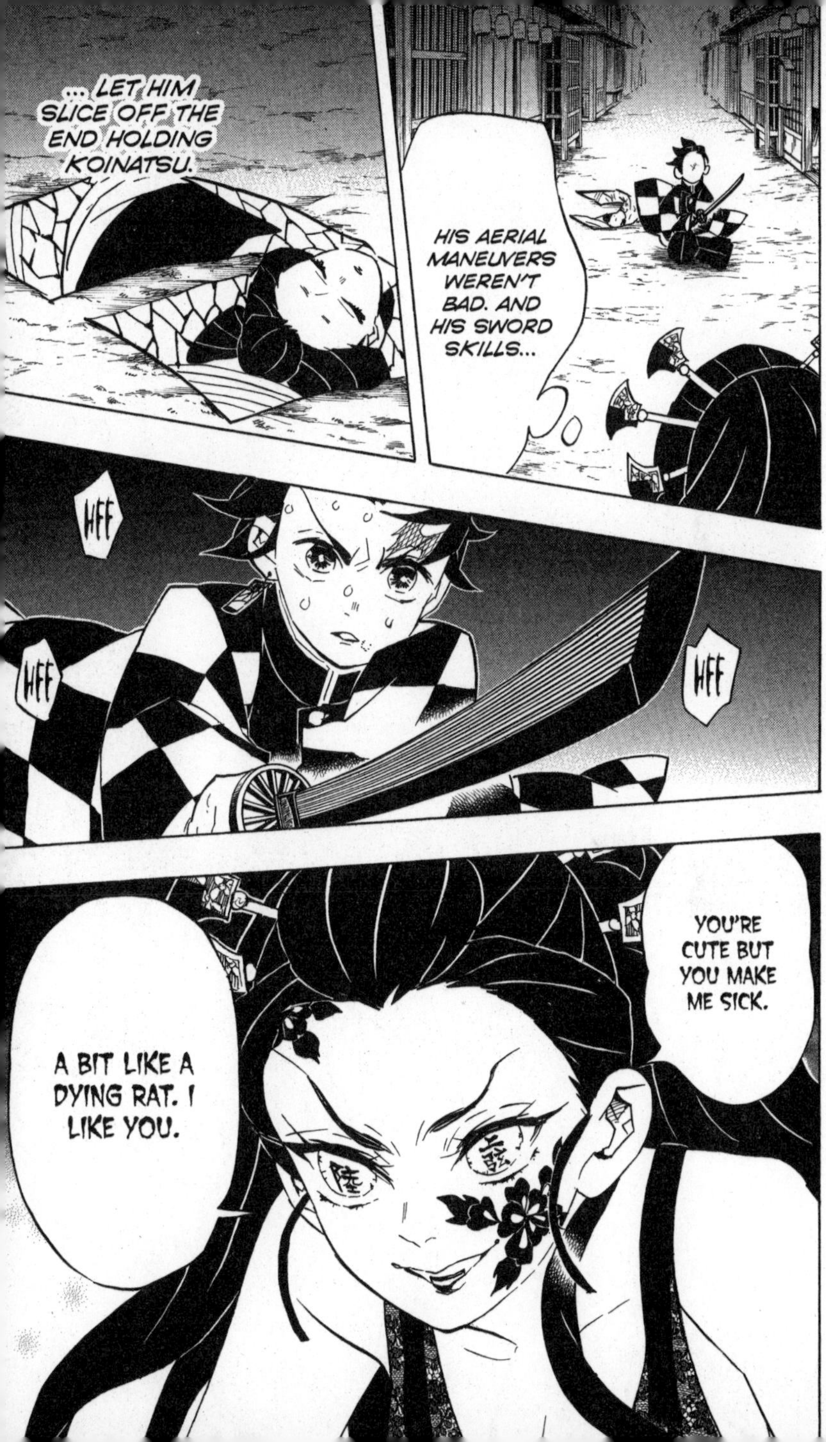
HIS AERIAL MANEUVERS WEREN'T BAD. AND HIS SWORD SKILLS...
... LET HIM SLICE OFF THE END HOLDING KOINATSU.
HFF
HFF
HFF
YOU'RE CUTE BUT YOU MAKE ME SICK.
A BIT LIKE A DYING RAT. I LIKE YOU.

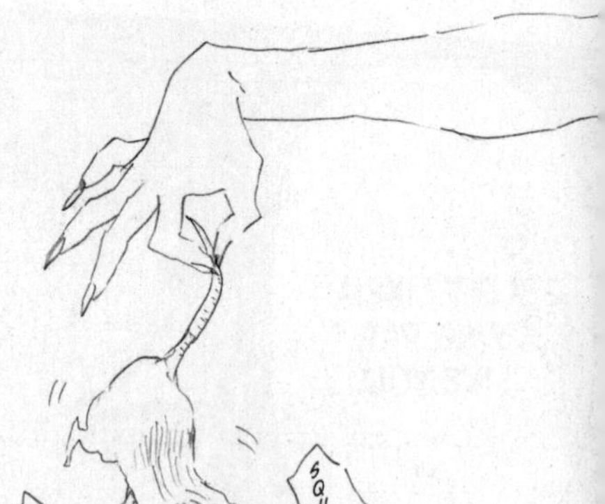
SQUEEK
SQUEEK

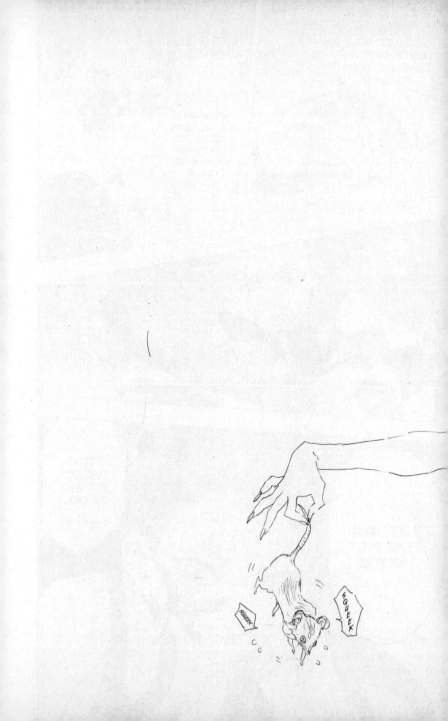

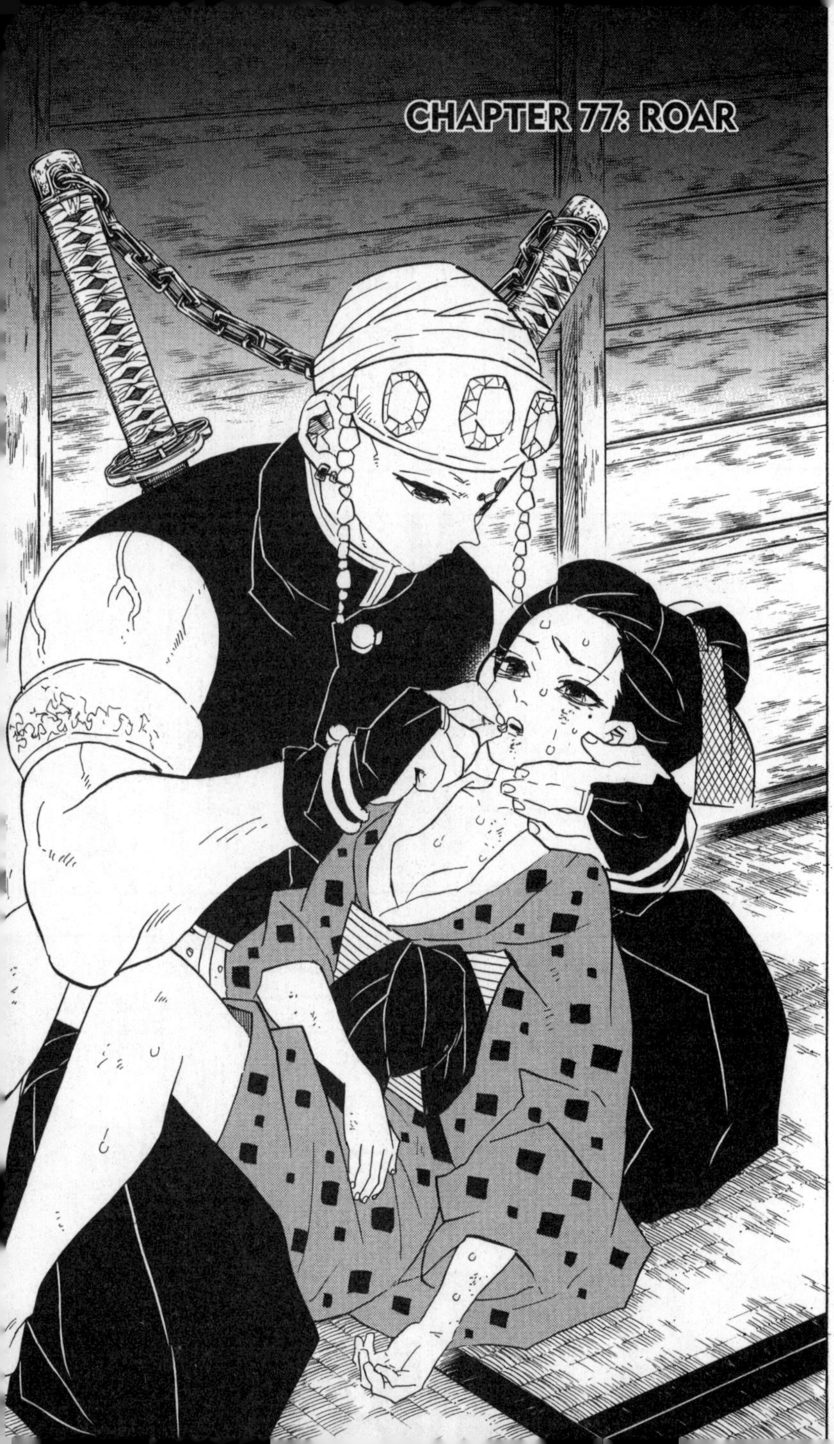
CHAPTER 77: ROAR

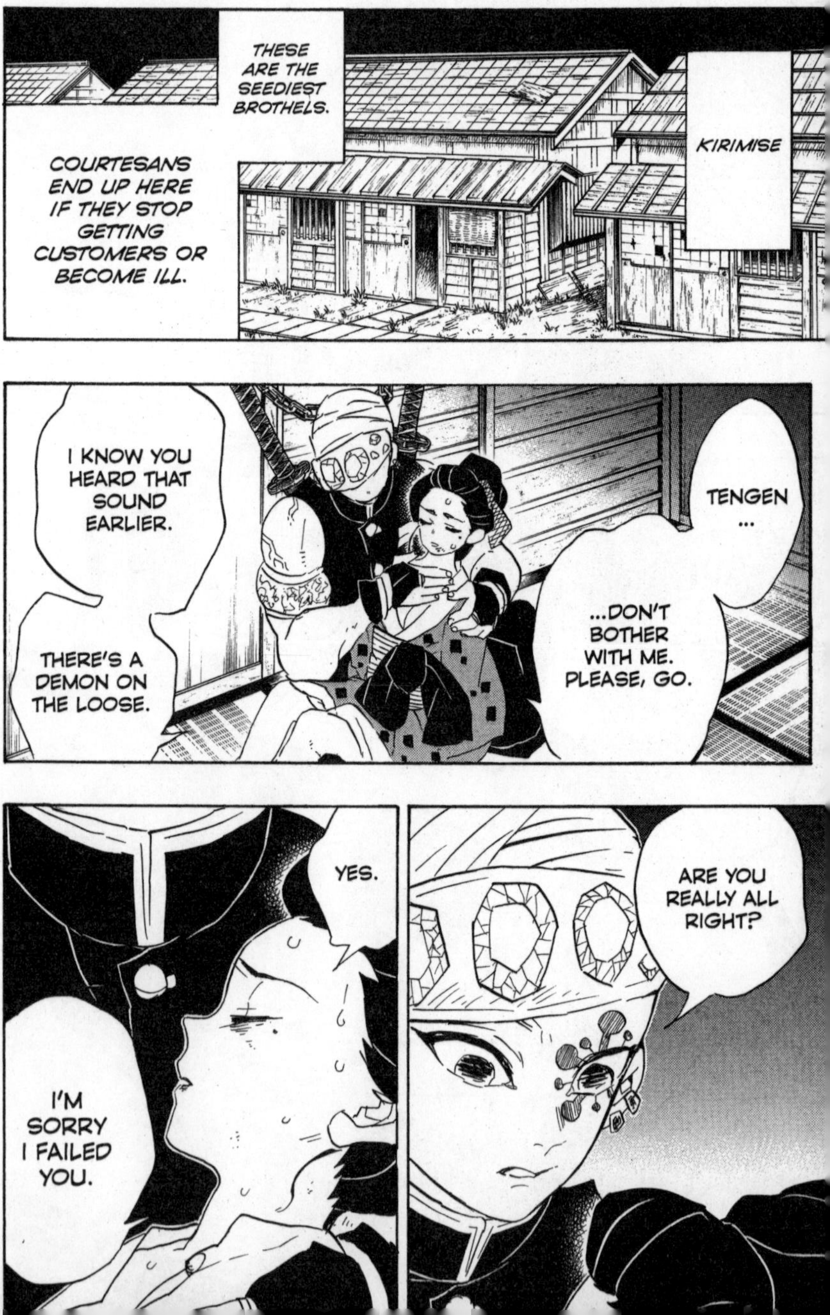
KIRIMISE
THESE ARE THE SEEDIEST BROTHELS.
COURTESANS END UP HERE IF THEY STOP GETTING CUSTOMERS OR BECOME ILL.
TENGEN ...
...DON'T BOTHER WITH ME. PLEASE, GO.
I KNOW YOU HEARD THAT SOUND EARLIER.
THERE'S A DEMON ON THE LOOSE.
ARE YOU REALLY ALL RIGHT?
YES.
I'M SORRY I FAILED YOU.

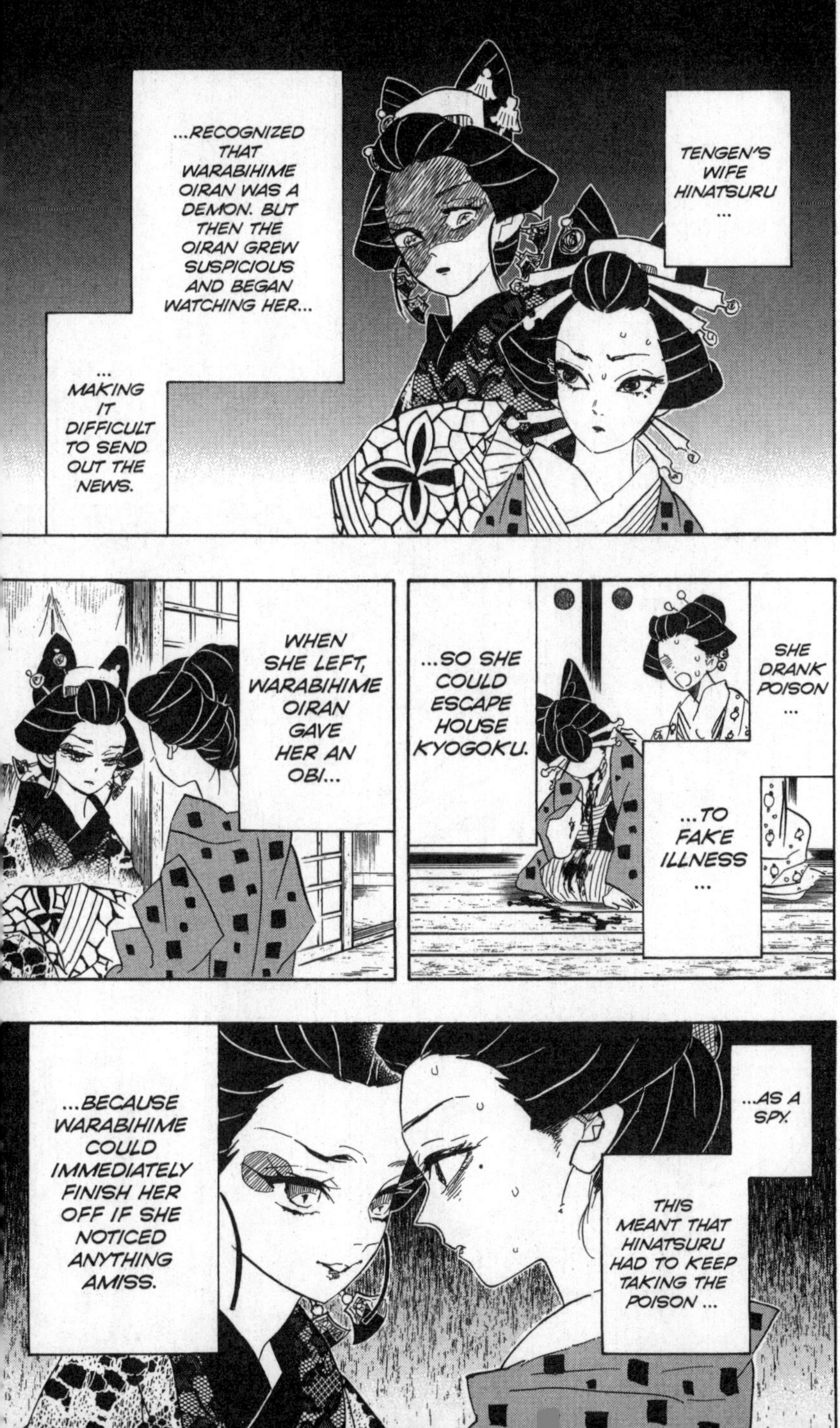
TENGEN'S WIFE HINATSURU ...
...RECOGNIZED THAT WARABIHIME OIRAN WAS A DEMON. BUT THEN THE OIRAN GREW SUSPICIOUS AND BEGAN WATCHING HER...
... MAKING IT DIFFICULT TO SEND OUT THE NEWS.
SHE DRANK POISON ...
...TO FAKE ILLNESS ...
...SO SHE COULD ESCAPE HOUSE KYOGOKU.
WHEN SHE LEFT, WARABIHIME OIRAN GAVE HER AN OBI...
...AS A SPY.
THIS MEANT THAT HINATSURU HAD TO KEEP TAKING THE POISON ...
...BECAUSE WARABIHIME COULD IMMEDIATELY FINISH HER OFF IF SHE NOTICED ANYTHING AMISS.

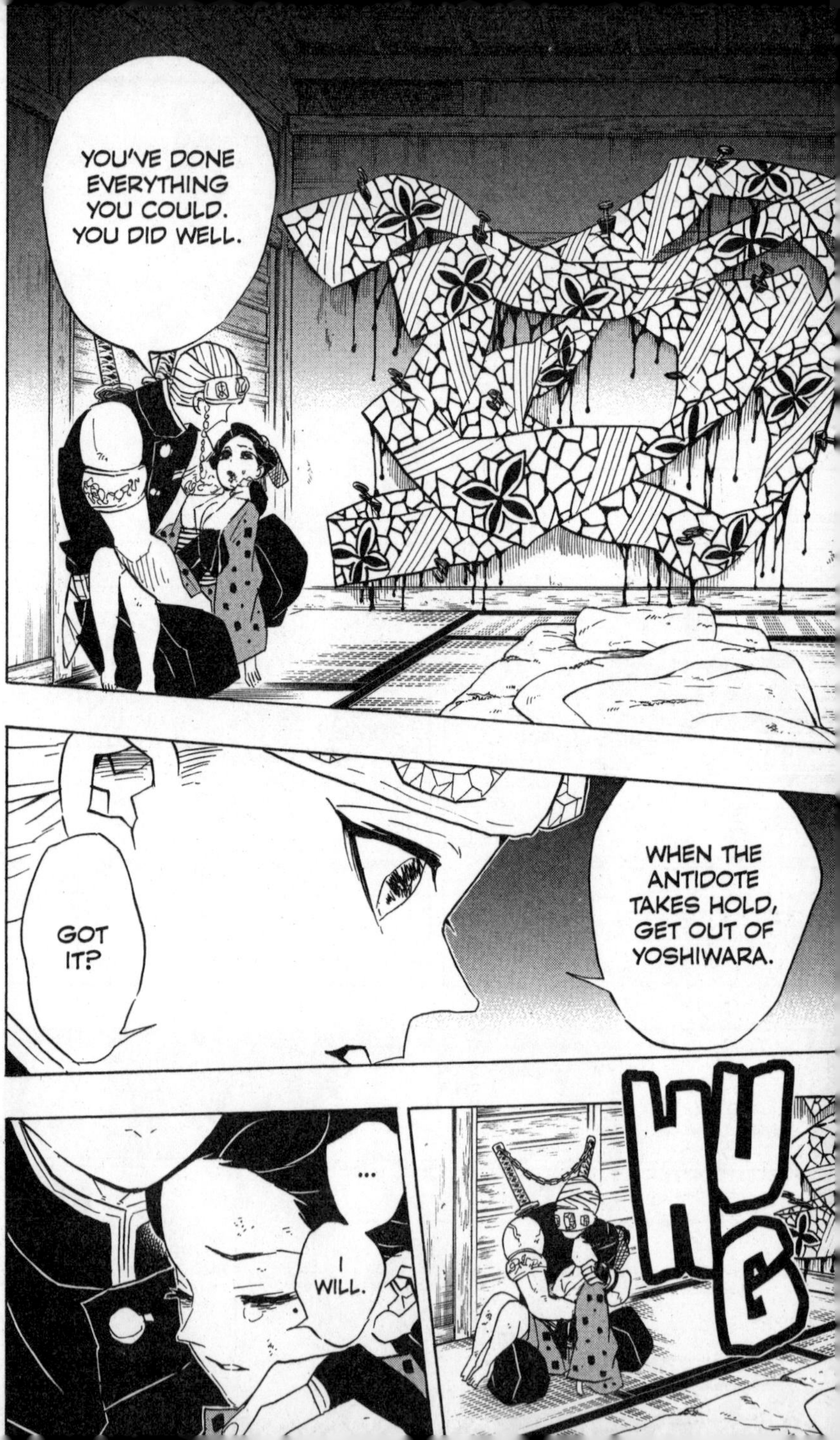
YOU'VE DONE EVERYTHING YOU COULD. YOU DID WELL.
WHEN THE ANTIDOTE TAKES HOLD, GET OUT OF YOSHIWARA.
GOT IT?
HUG
...
I WILL.

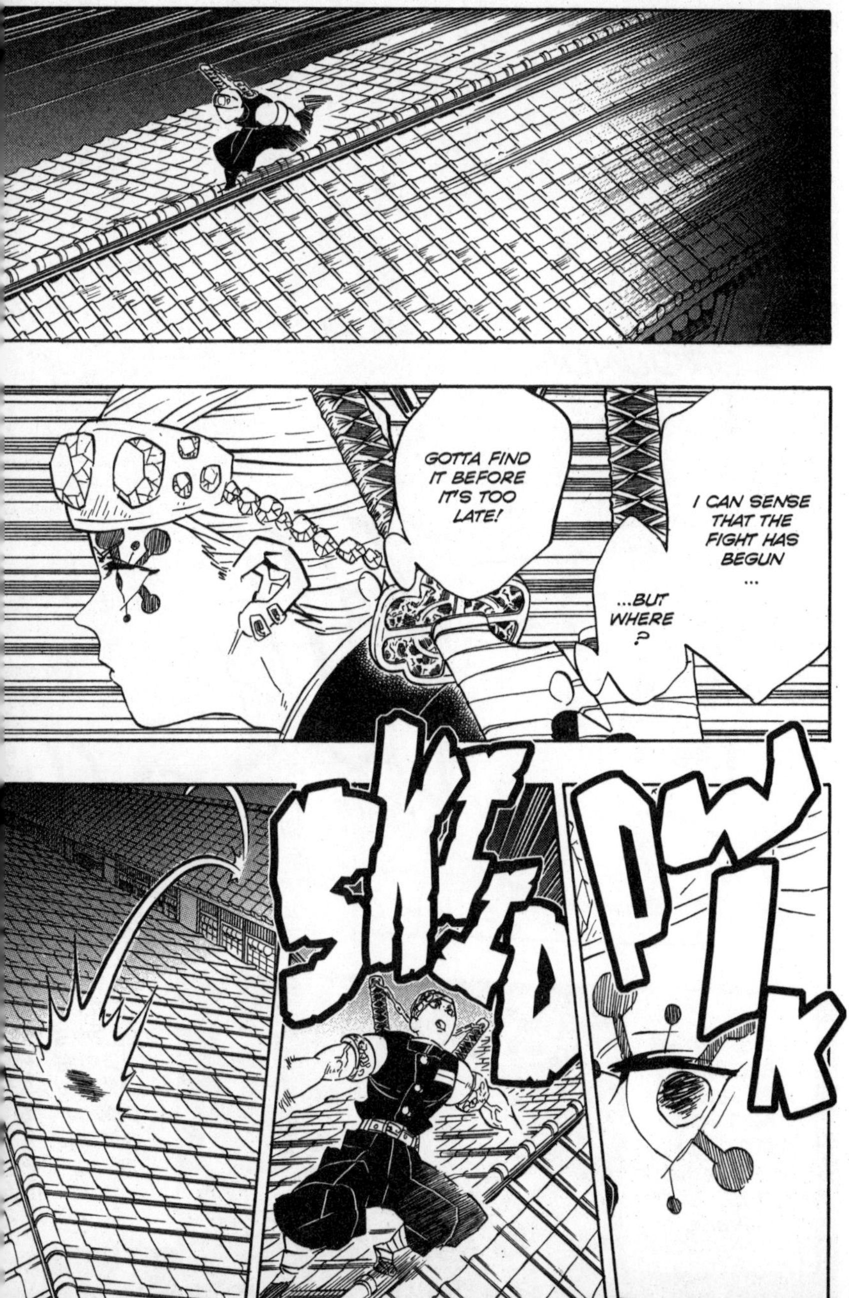
I CAN SENSE THAT THE FIGHT HAS BEGUN ...
...BUT WHERE?
GOTTA FIND IT BEFORE IT'S TOO LATE!
SKID

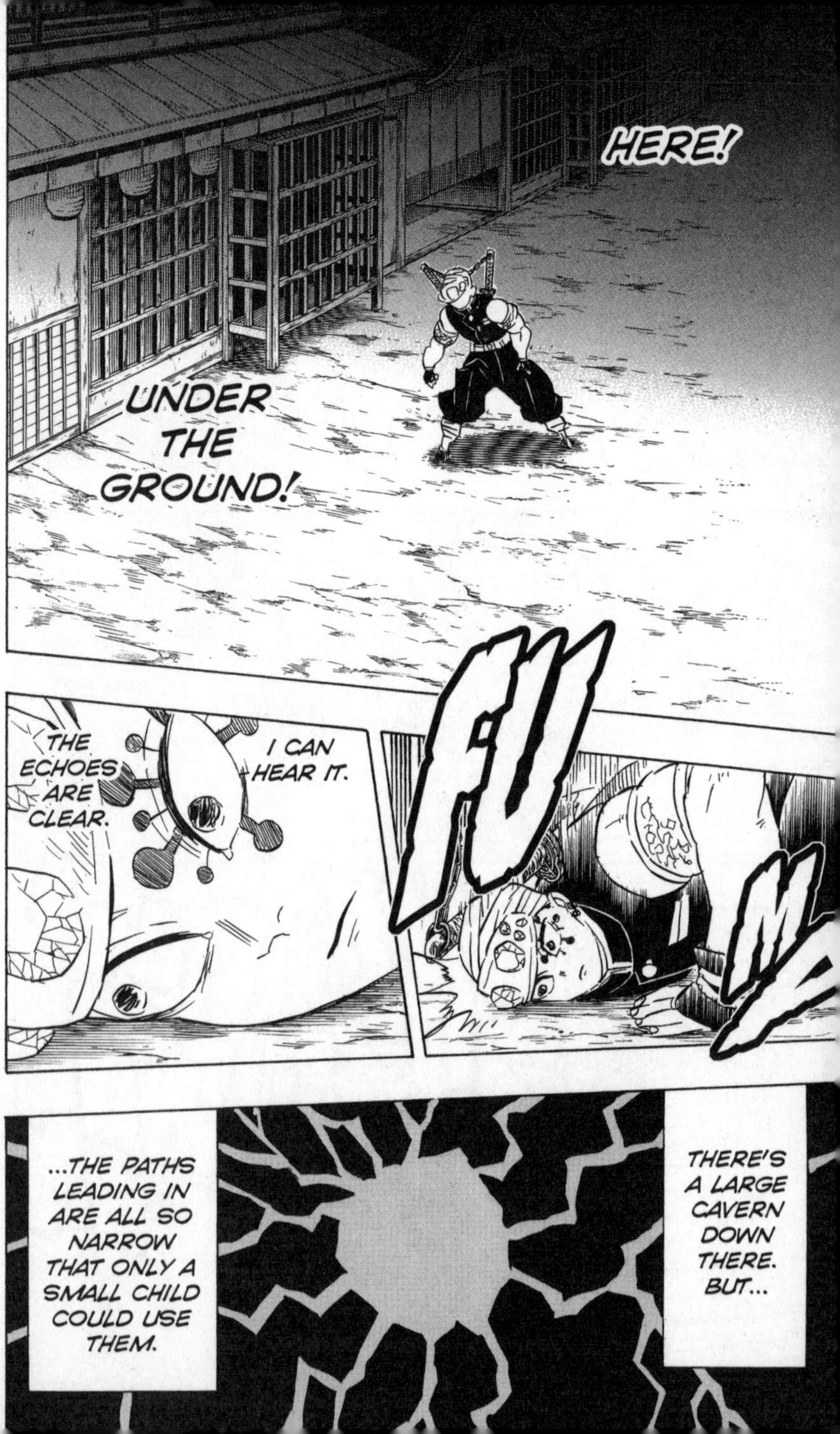
HERE!
UNDER THE GROUND!
FUM
I CAN HEAR IT.
THE ECHOES ARE CLEAR.
THERE'S A LARGE CAVERN DOWN THERE. BUT...
...THE PATHS LEADING IN ARE ALL SO NARROW THAT ONLY A SMALL CHILD COULD USE THEM.

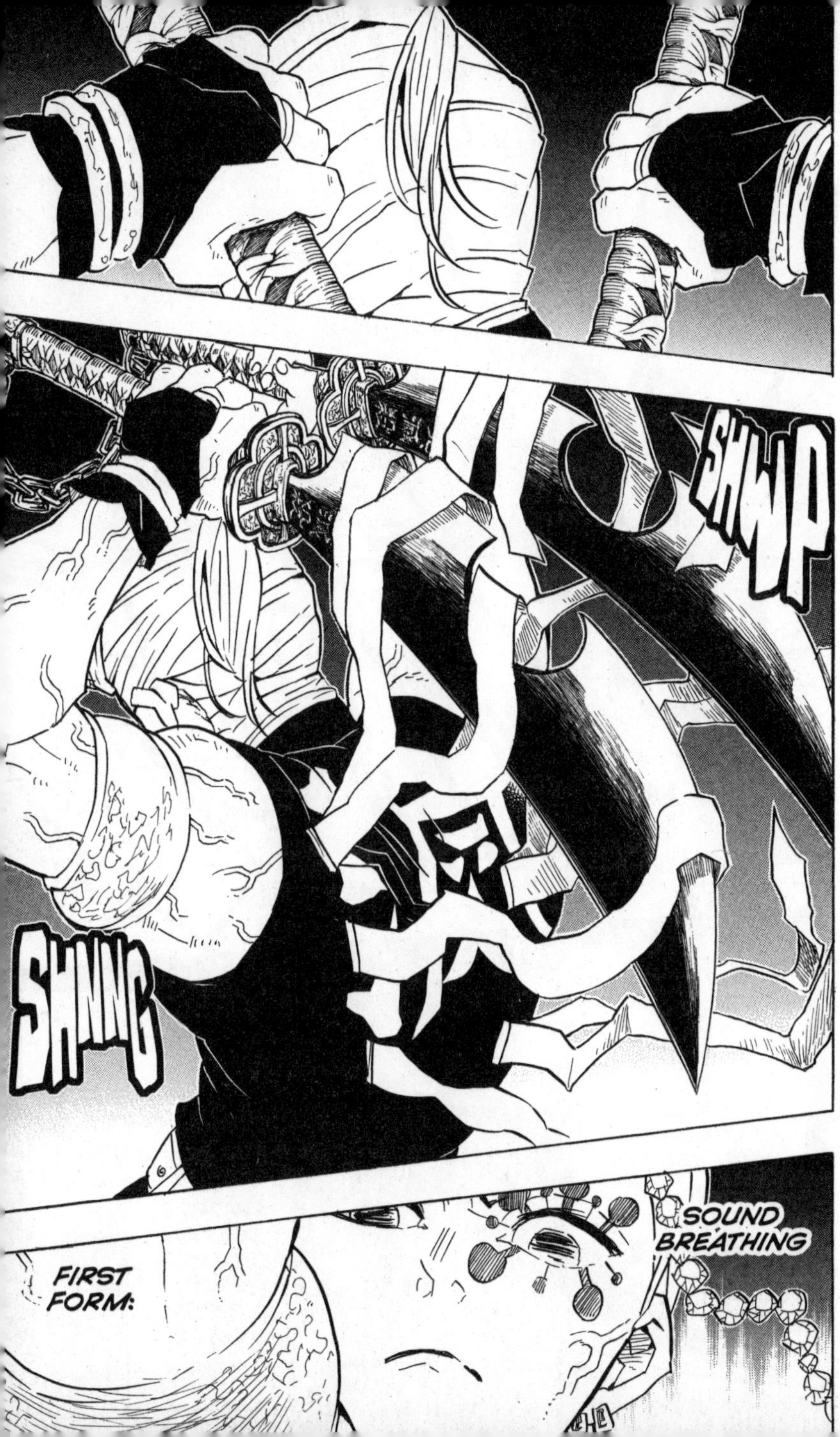
SHWP
SHING
SOUND BREATHING
FIRST FORM:

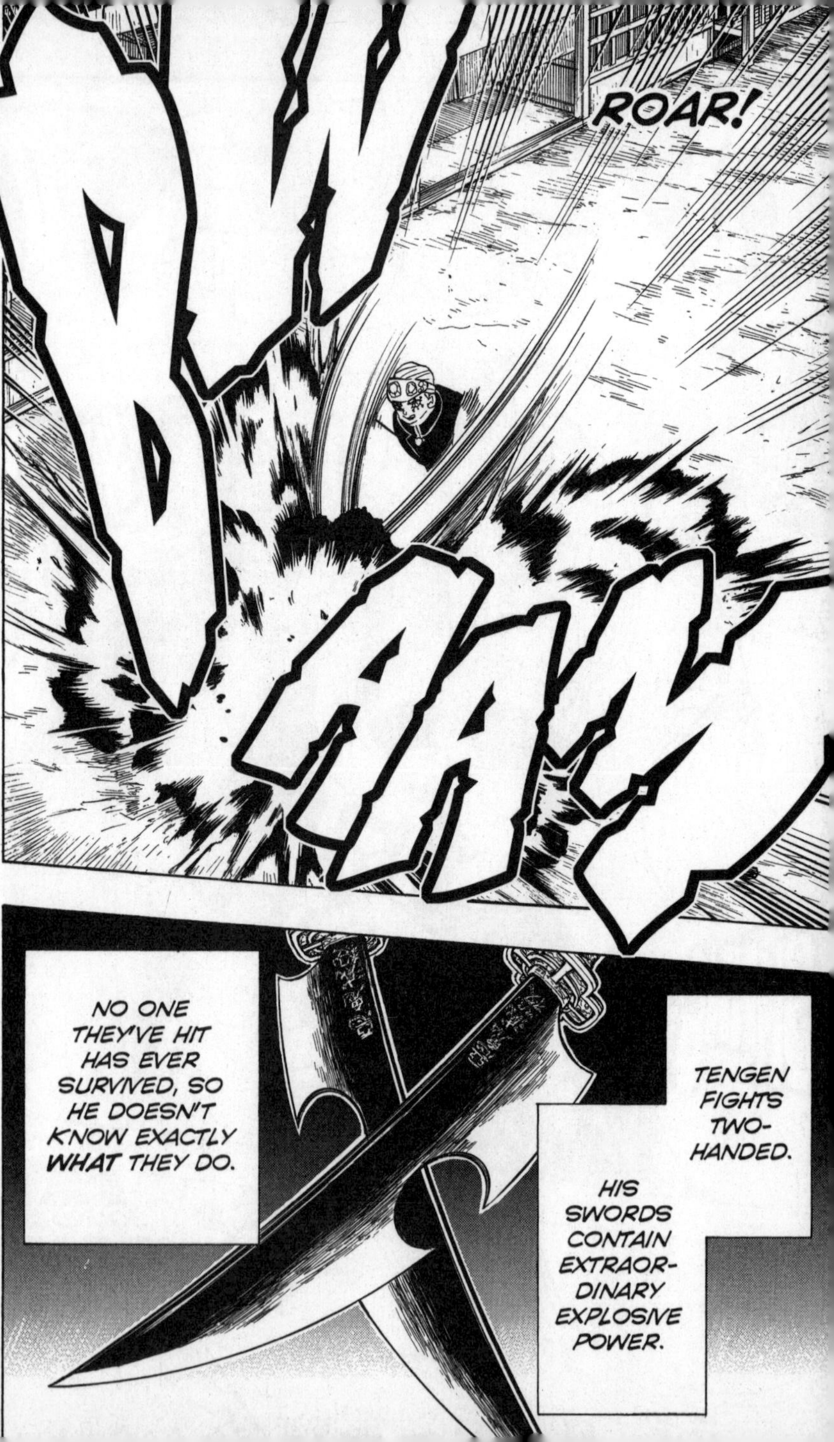
ROAR!
TENGEN FIGHTS TWO-HANDED.
HIS SWORDS CONTAIN EXTRAOR-DINARY EXPLOSIVE POWER.
NO ONE THEY'VE HIT HAS EVER SURVIVED, SO HE DOESN'T KNOW EXACTLY **WHAT** THEY DO.

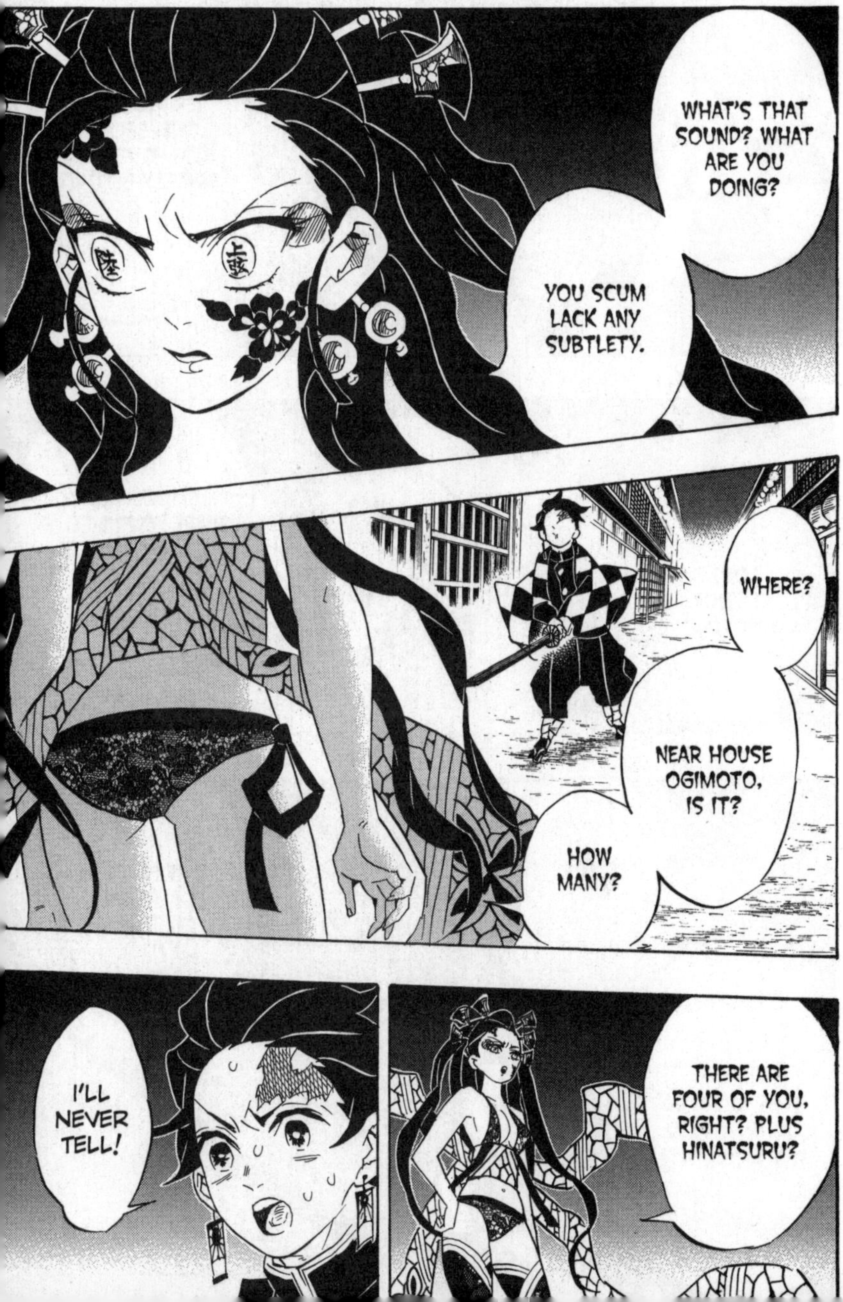
WHAT'S THAT SOUND? WHAT ARE YOU DOING?
YOU SCUM LACK ANY SUBTLETY.
WHERE?
NEAR HOUSE OGIMOTO, IS IT?
HOW MANY?
THERE ARE FOUR OF YOU, RIGHT? PLUS HINATSURU?
I'LL NEVER TELL!

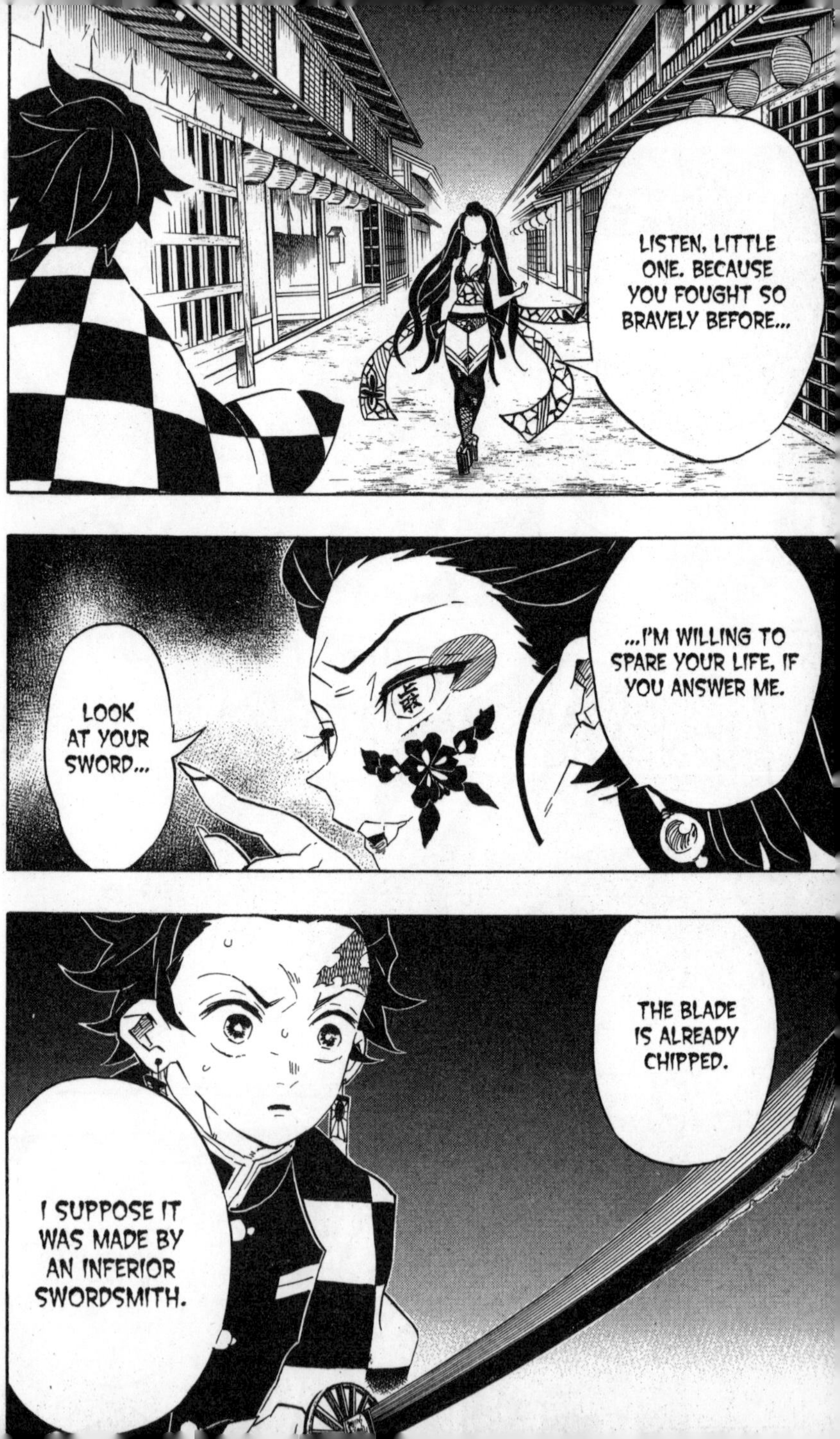
LISTEN, LITTLE ONE. BECAUSE YOU FOUGHT SO BRAVELY BEFORE...
...I'M WILLING TO SPARE YOUR LIFE, IF YOU ANSWER ME.
LOOK AT YOUR SWORD...
THE BLADE IS ALREADY CHIPPED.
I SUPPOSE IT WAS MADE BY AN INFERIOR SWORDSMITH.

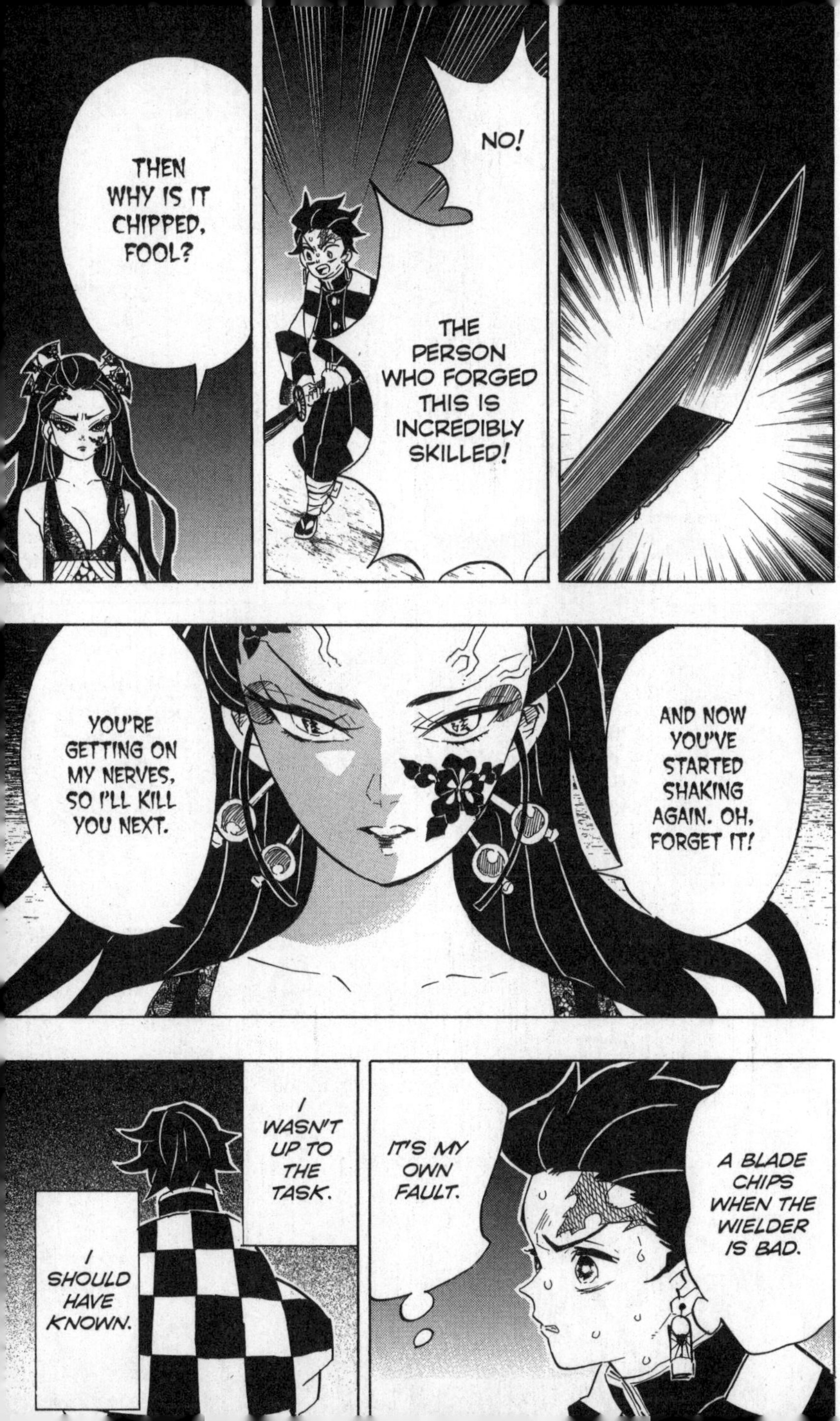
NO!
THE PERSON WHO FORGED THIS IS INCREDIBLY SKILLED!
THEN WHY IS IT CHIPPED, FOOL?
AND NOW YOU'VE STARTED SHAKING AGAIN. OH, FORGET IT!
YOU'RE GETTING ON MY NERVES, SO I'LL KILL YOU NEXT.
A BLADE CHIPS WHEN THE WIELDER IS BAD.
IT'S MY OWN FAULT.
I WASN'T UP TO THE TASK.
I SHOULD HAVE KNOWN.

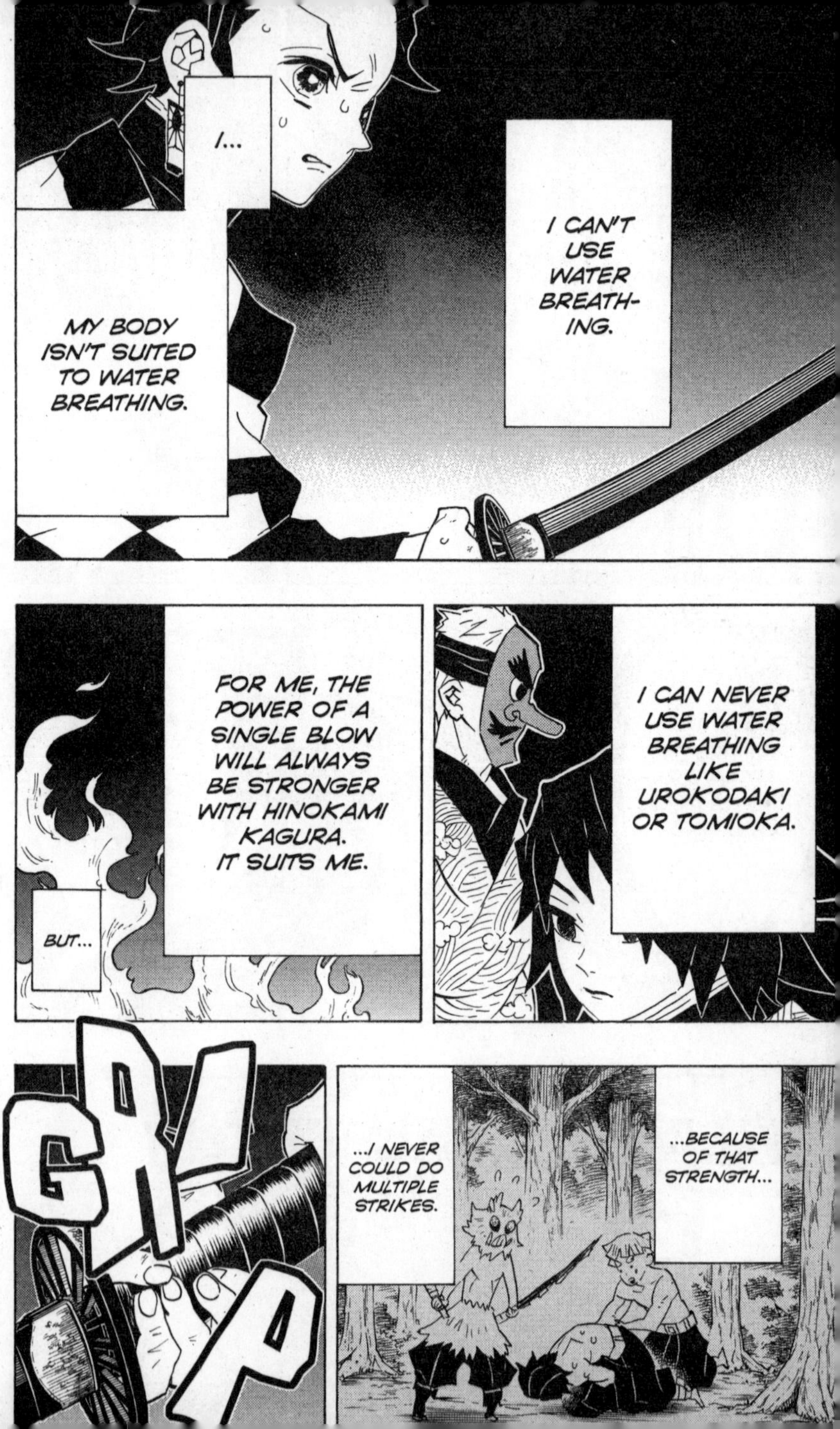
I...
I CAN'T USE WATER BREATH-ING.
MY BODY ISN'T SUITED TO WATER BREATHING.
I CAN NEVER USE WATER BREATHING LIKE UROKODAKI OR TOMIOKA.
FOR ME, THE POWER OF A SINGLE BLOW WILL ALWAYS BE STRONGER WITH HINOKAMI KAGURA. IT SUITS ME.
BUT...
...BECAUSE OF THAT STRENGTH...
...I NEVER COULD DO MULTIPLE STRIKES.
GRIP

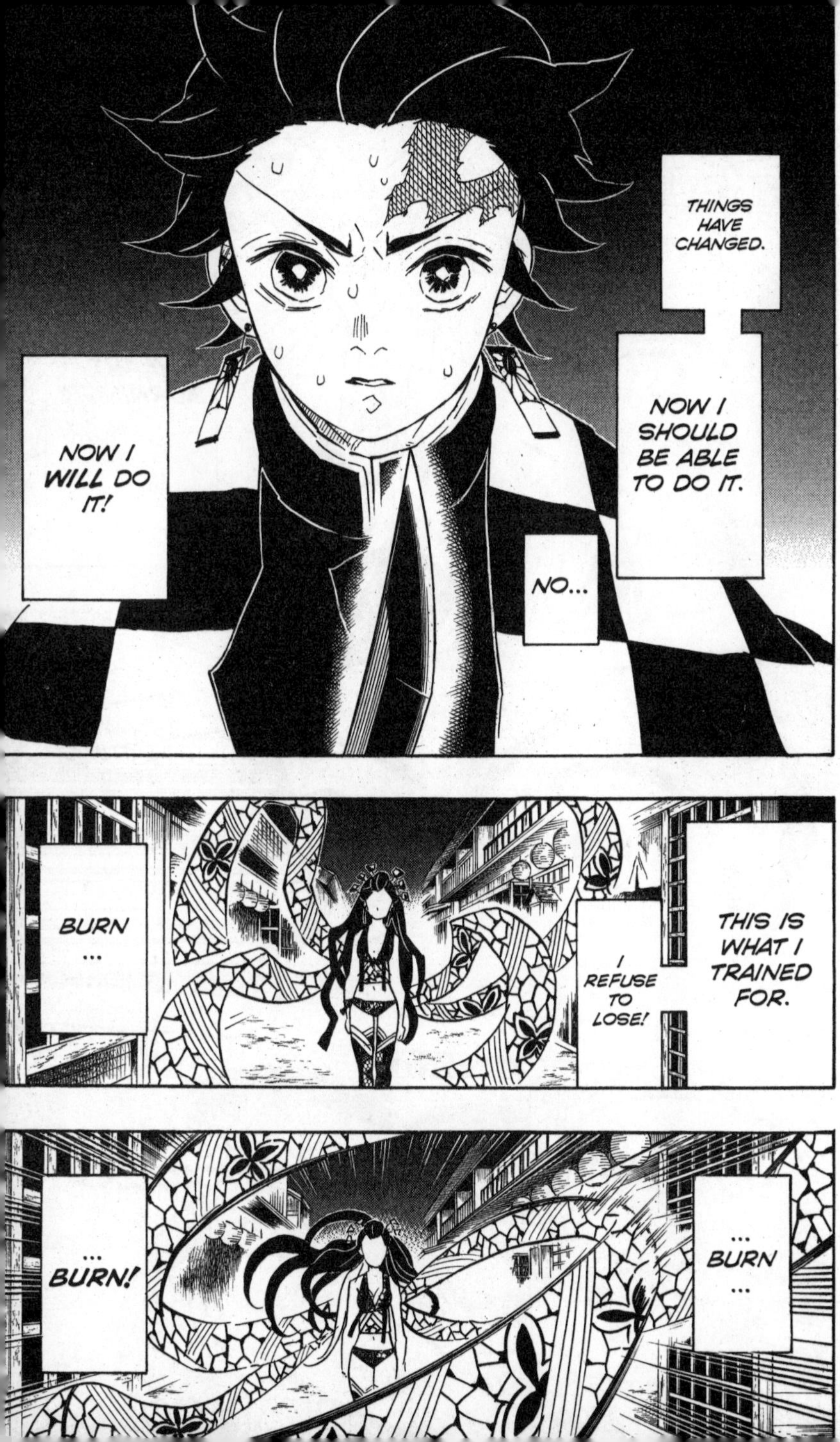
THINGS HAVE CHANGED.
NOW I SHOULD BE ABLE TO DO IT.
NO...
NOW I WILL DO IT!
THIS IS WHAT I TRAINED FOR.
I REFUSE TO LOSE!
BURN ...
... BURN ...
... BURN!

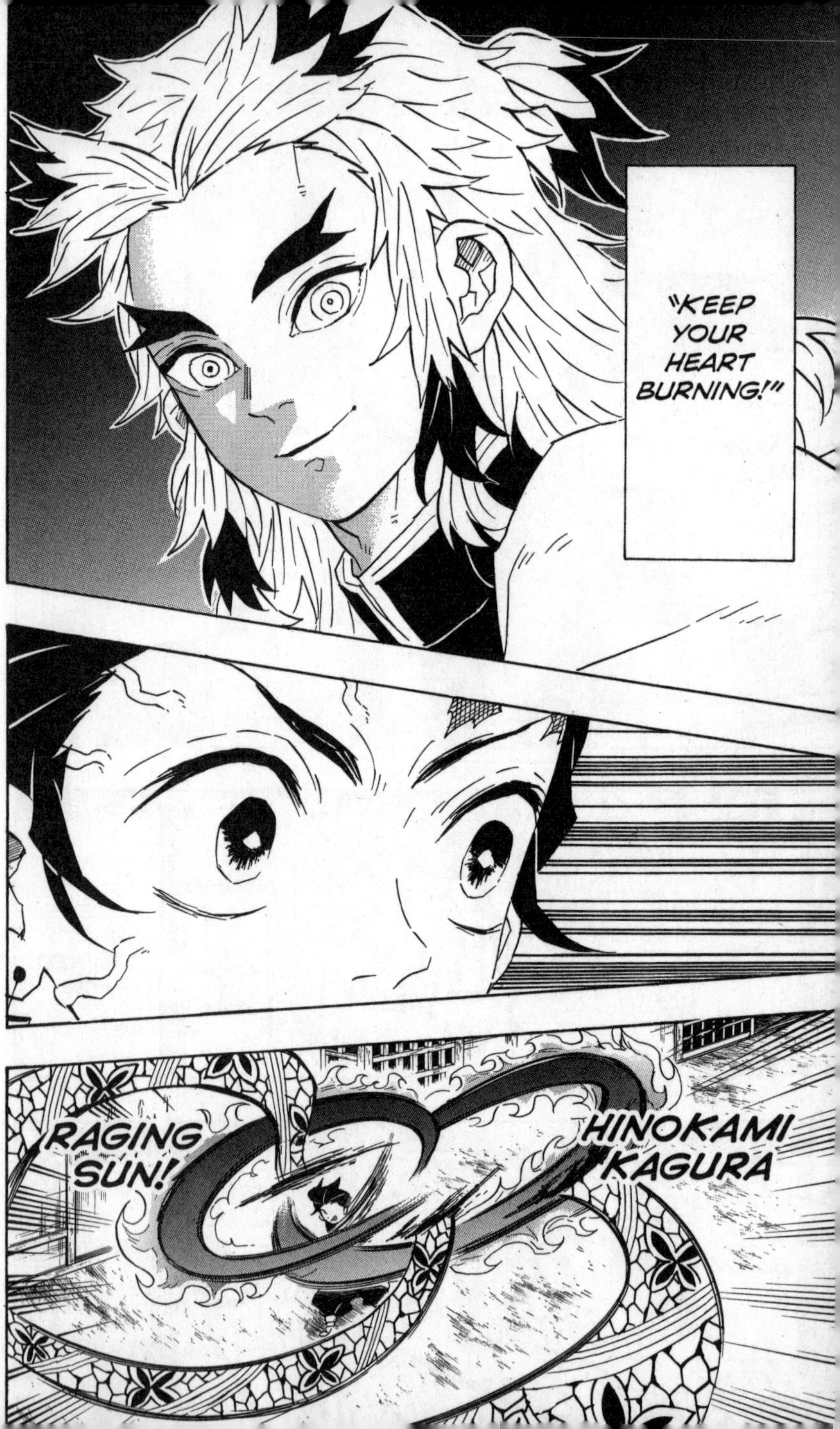
"KEEP YOUR HEART BURNING!"
HINOKAMI KAGURA
RAGING SUN!

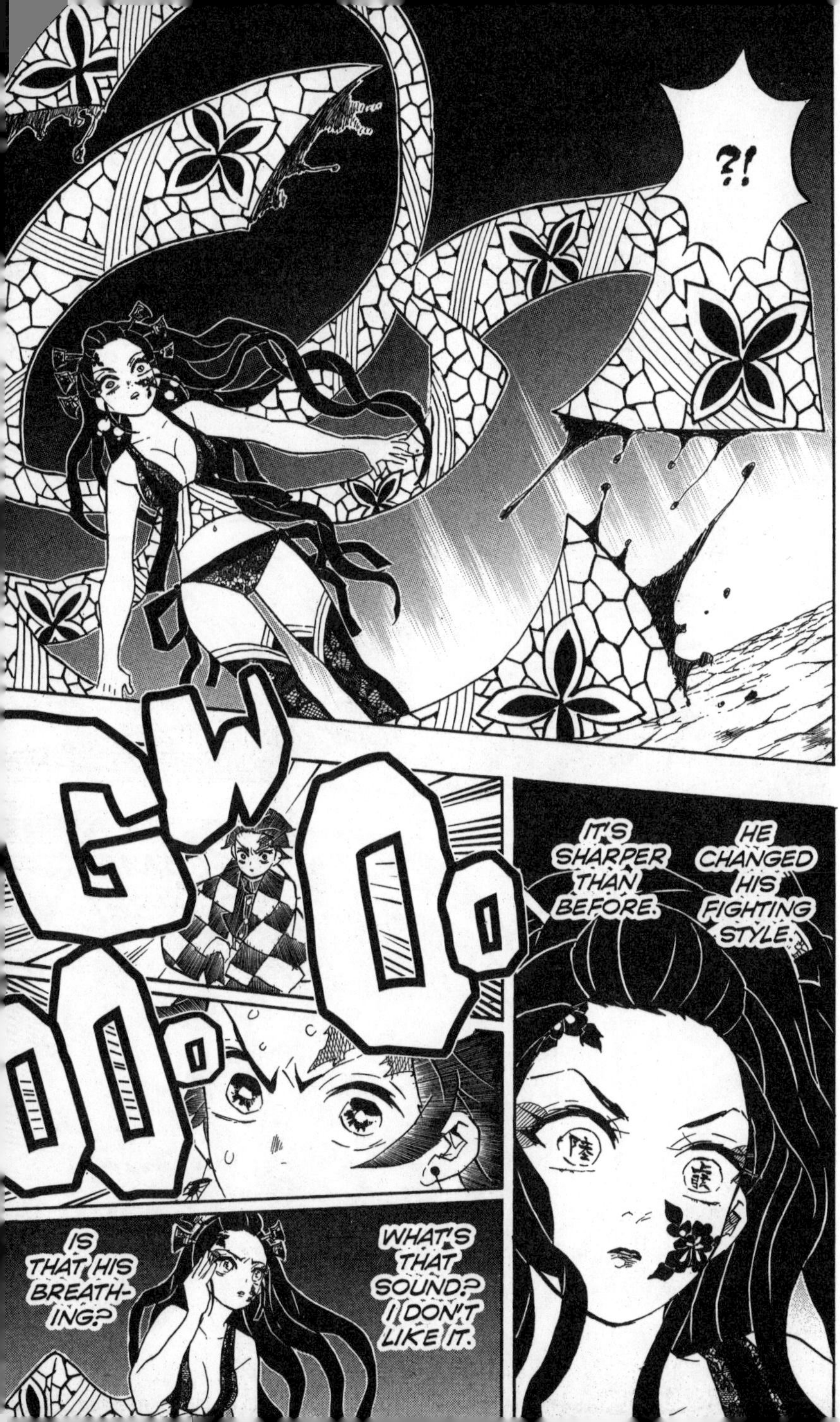
?!
HE CHANGED HIS FIGHTING STYLE.
IT'S SHARPER THAN BEFORE.
GWOOOO
WHAT'S THAT SOUND? I DON'T LIKE IT.
IS THAT HIS BREATH-ING?

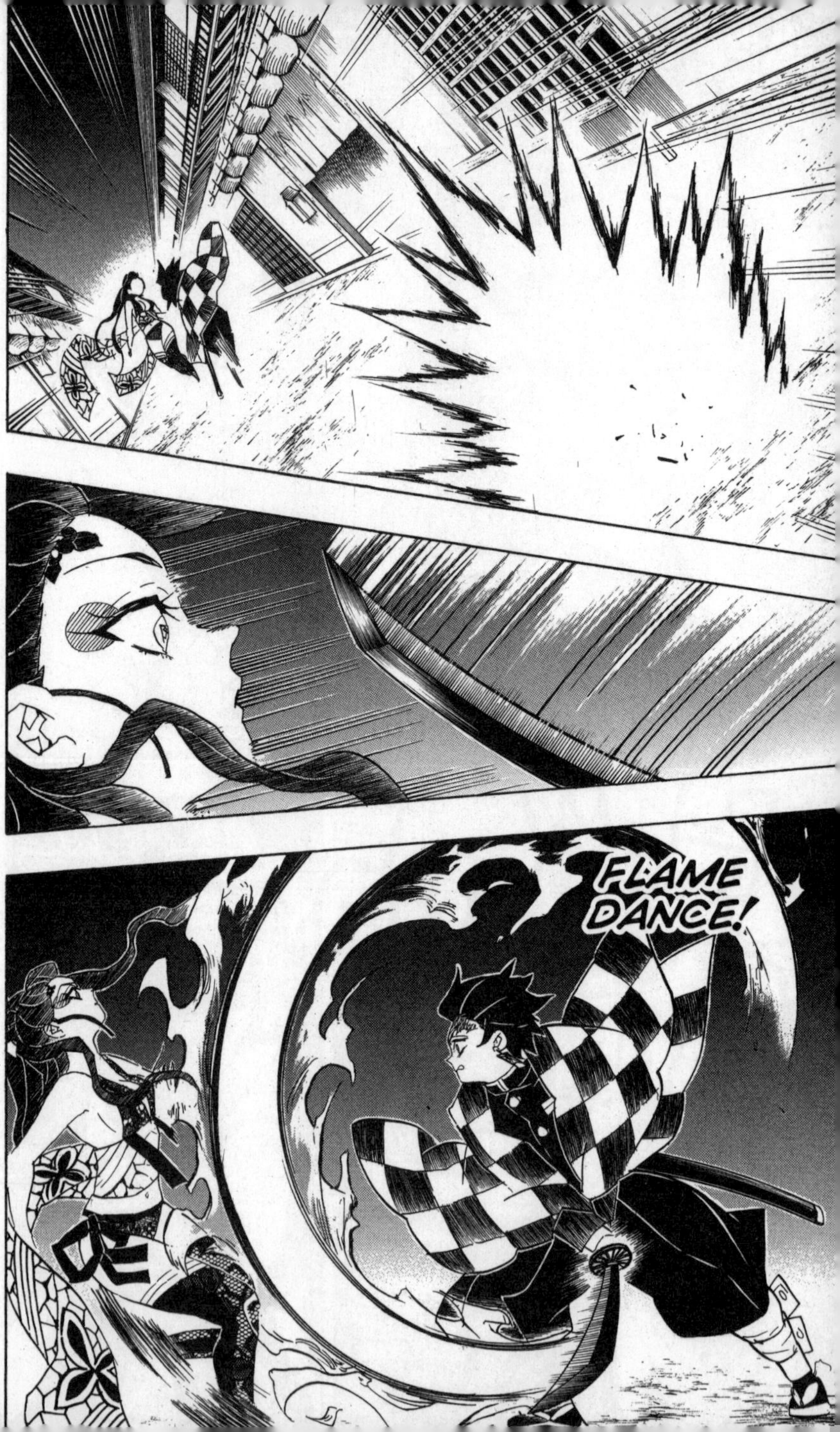
FLAME DANCE!

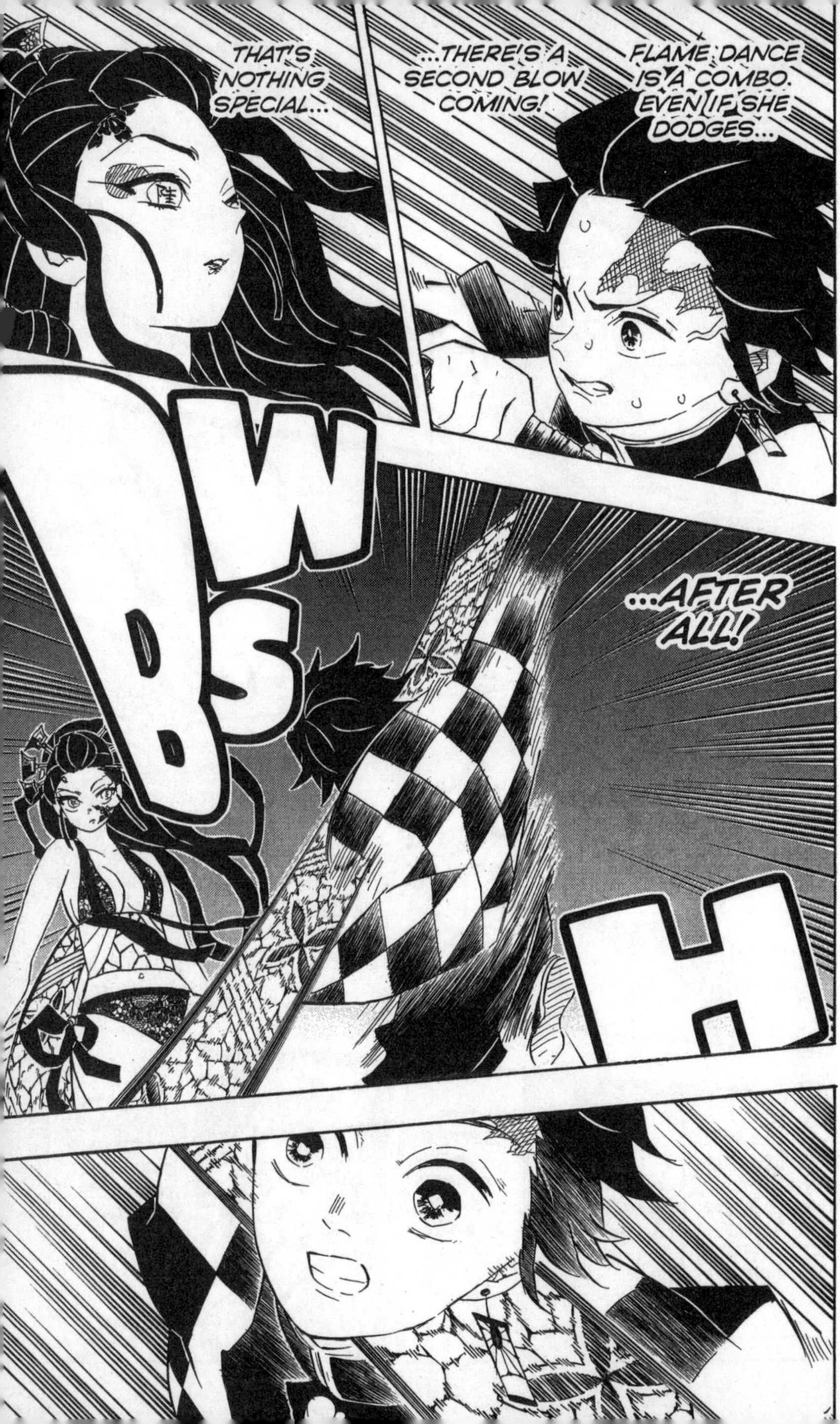
FLAME DANCE IS A COMBO. EVEN IF SHE DODGES...
...THERE'S A SECOND BLOW COMING!
THAT'S NOTHING SPECIAL...
...AFTER ALL!

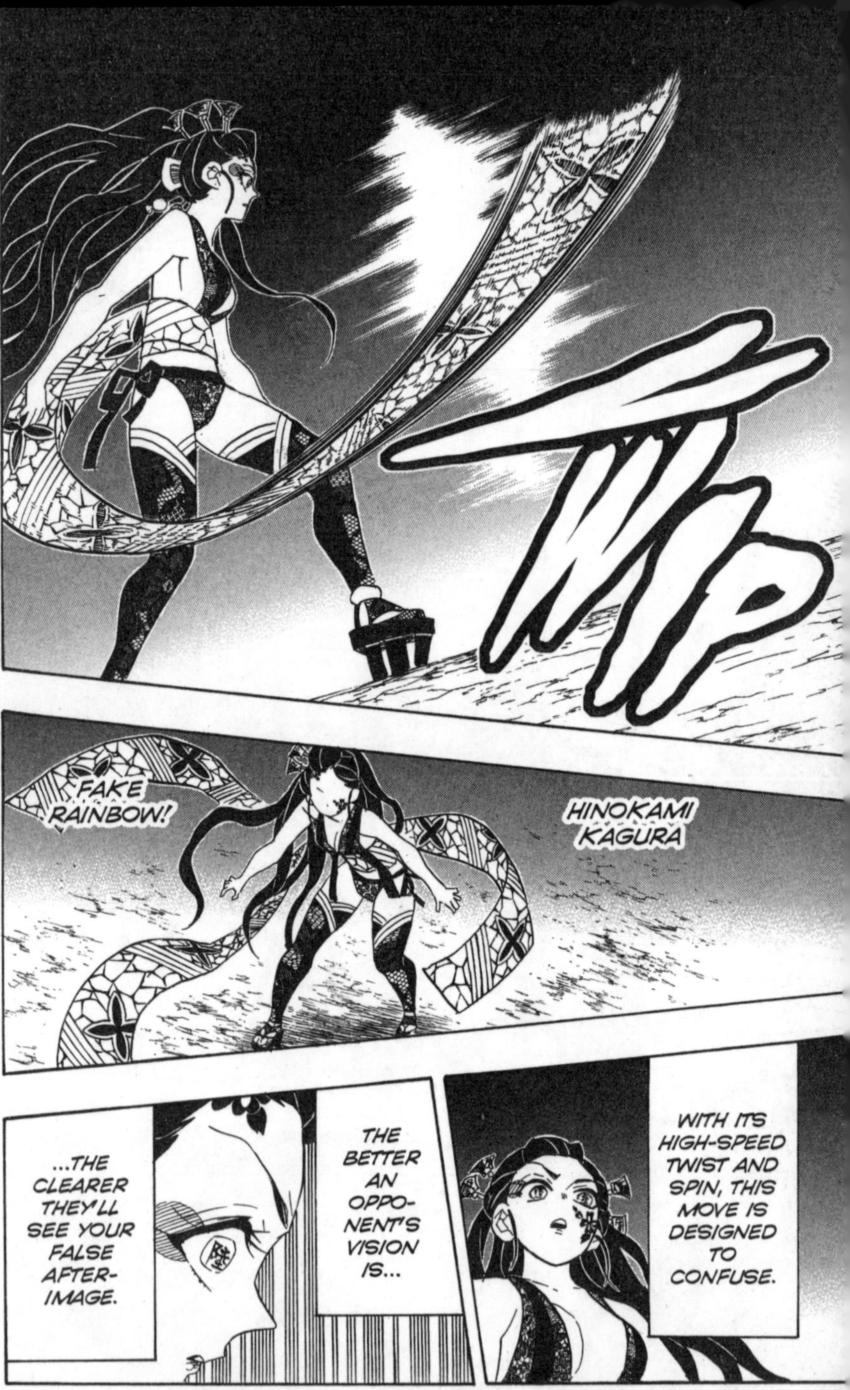
WHIP
HINOKAMI KAGURA
FAKE RAINBOW!
WITH ITS HIGH-SPEED TWIST AND SPIN, THIS MOVE IS DESIGNED TO CONFUSE.
THE BETTER AN OPPO-NENT'S VISION IS...
...THE CLEARER THEY'LL SEE YOUR FALSE AFTER-IMAGE.

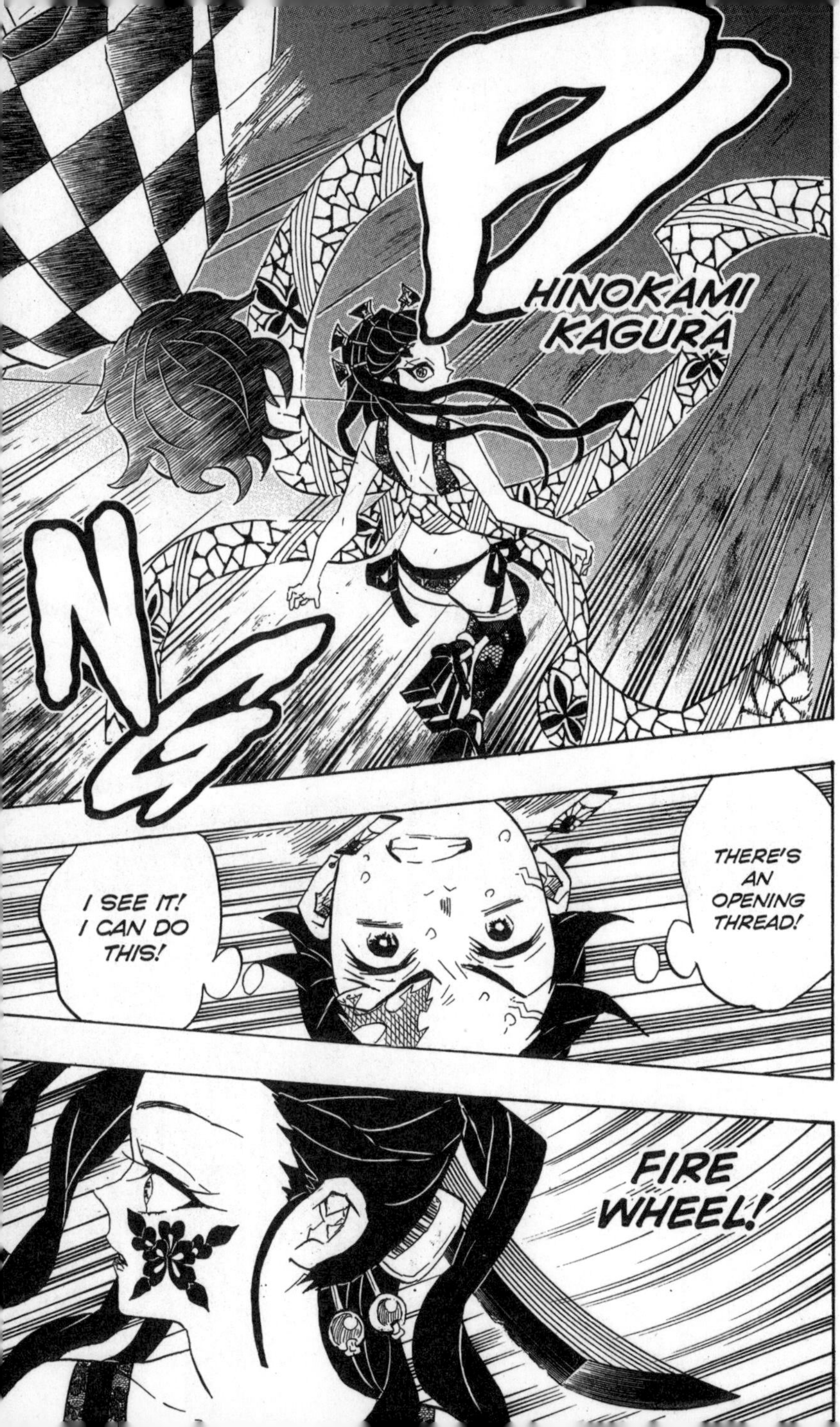
HINOKAMI KAGURA
THERE'S AN OPENING THREAD!
I SEE IT! I CAN DO THIS!
FIRE WHEEL!

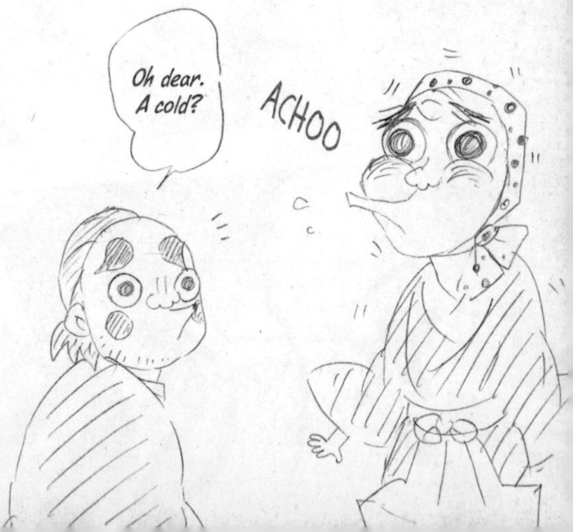
ACHOO
Oh dear. A cold?

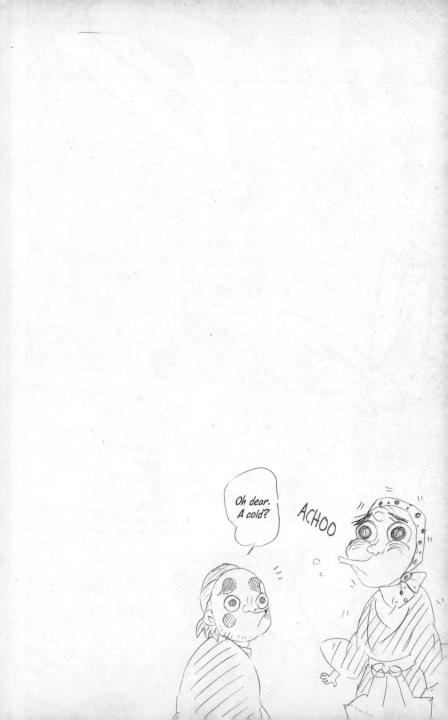

CHAPTER 78: WRIGGLY

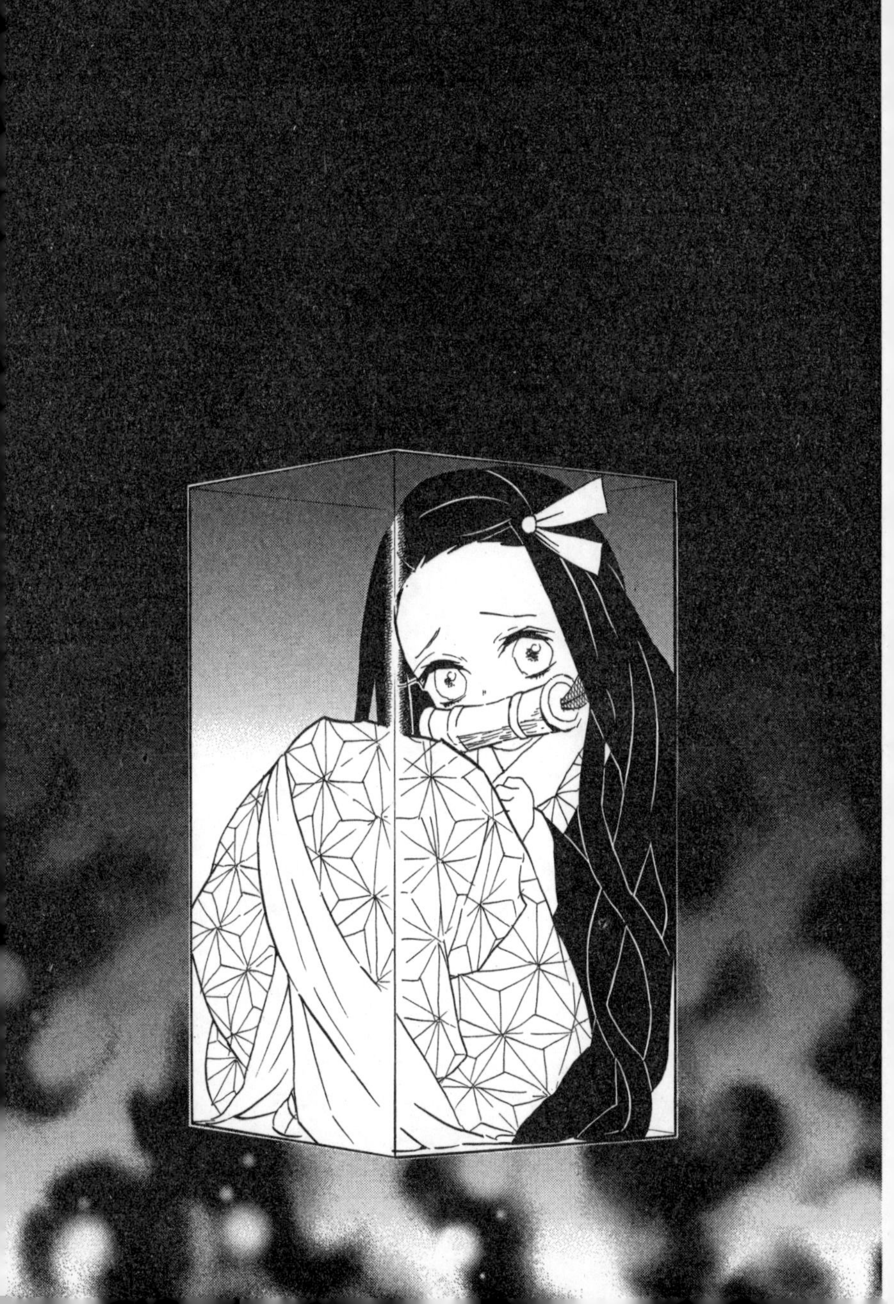

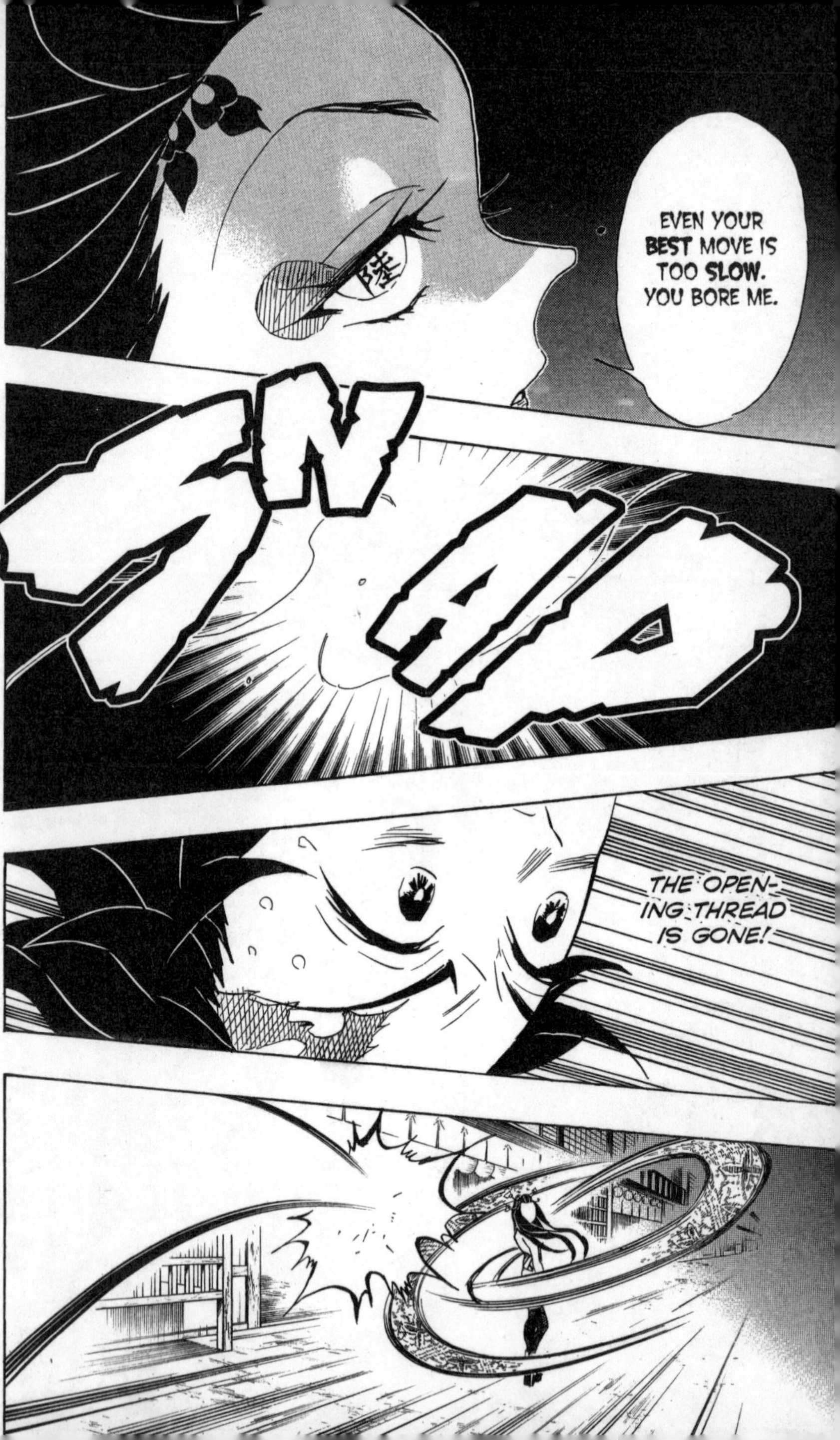
EVEN YOUR BEST MOVE IS TOO SLOW. YOU BORE ME.
SNAP
THE OPEN-ING THREAD IS GONE!

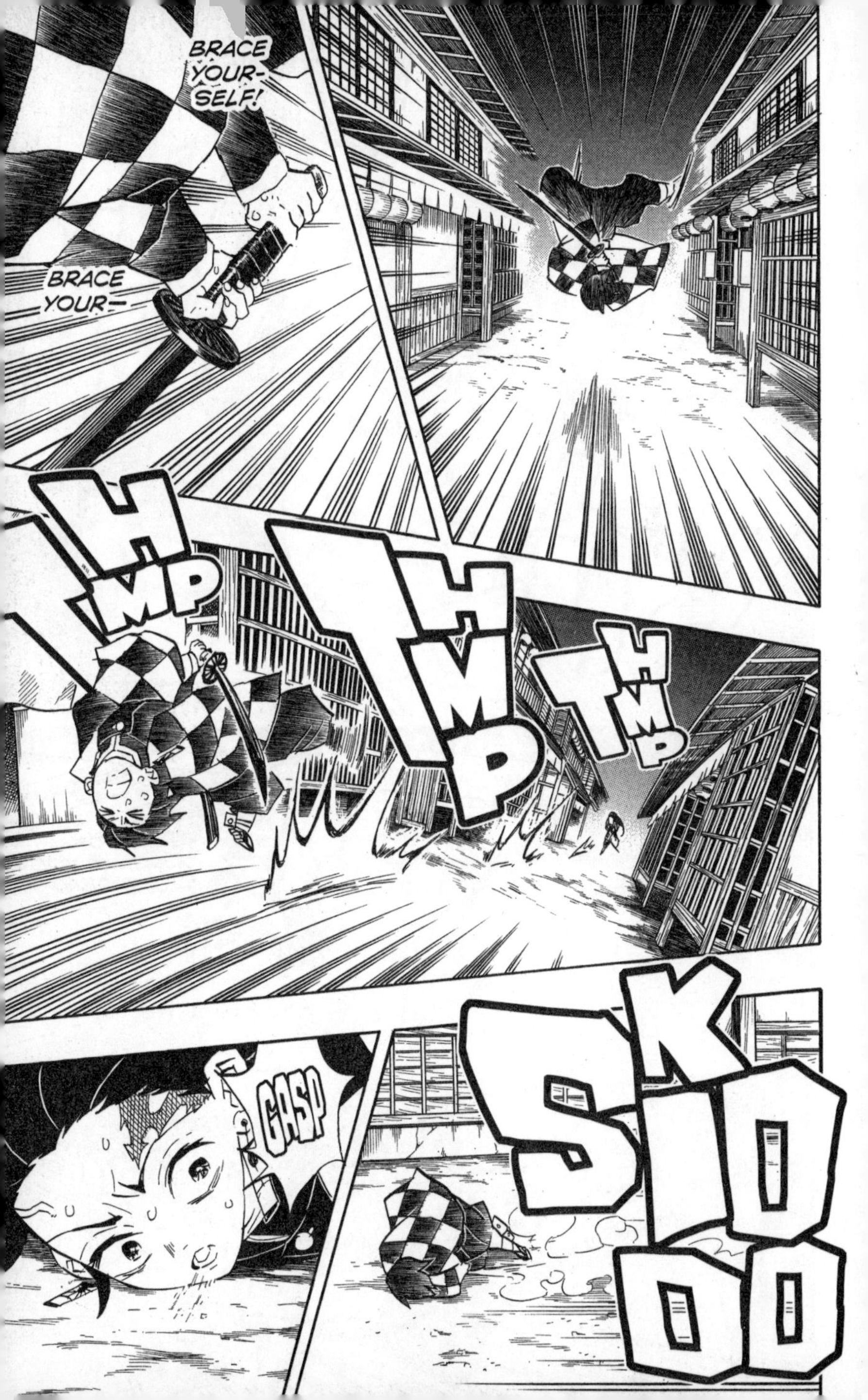
BRACE YOUR-SELF!
BRACE YOUR—
THUMP
THUMP
THUMP
SKIDDD
GASP

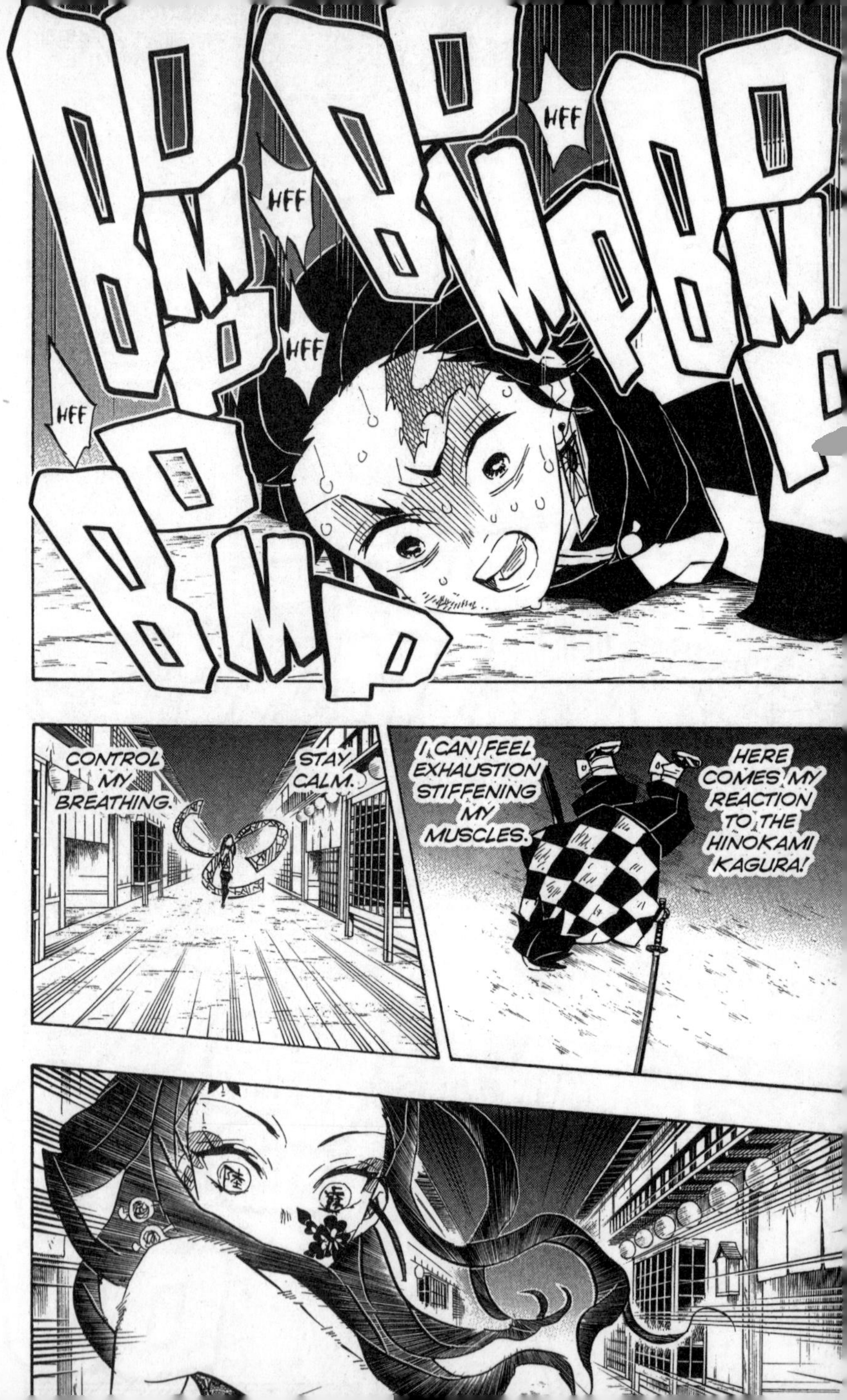
HFF
HFF
HFF
HFF
HERE COMES MY REACTION TO THE HINOKAMI KAGURA!
I CAN FEEL EXHAUSTION STIFFENING MY MUSCLES.
STAY CALM.
CONTROL MY BREATHING.

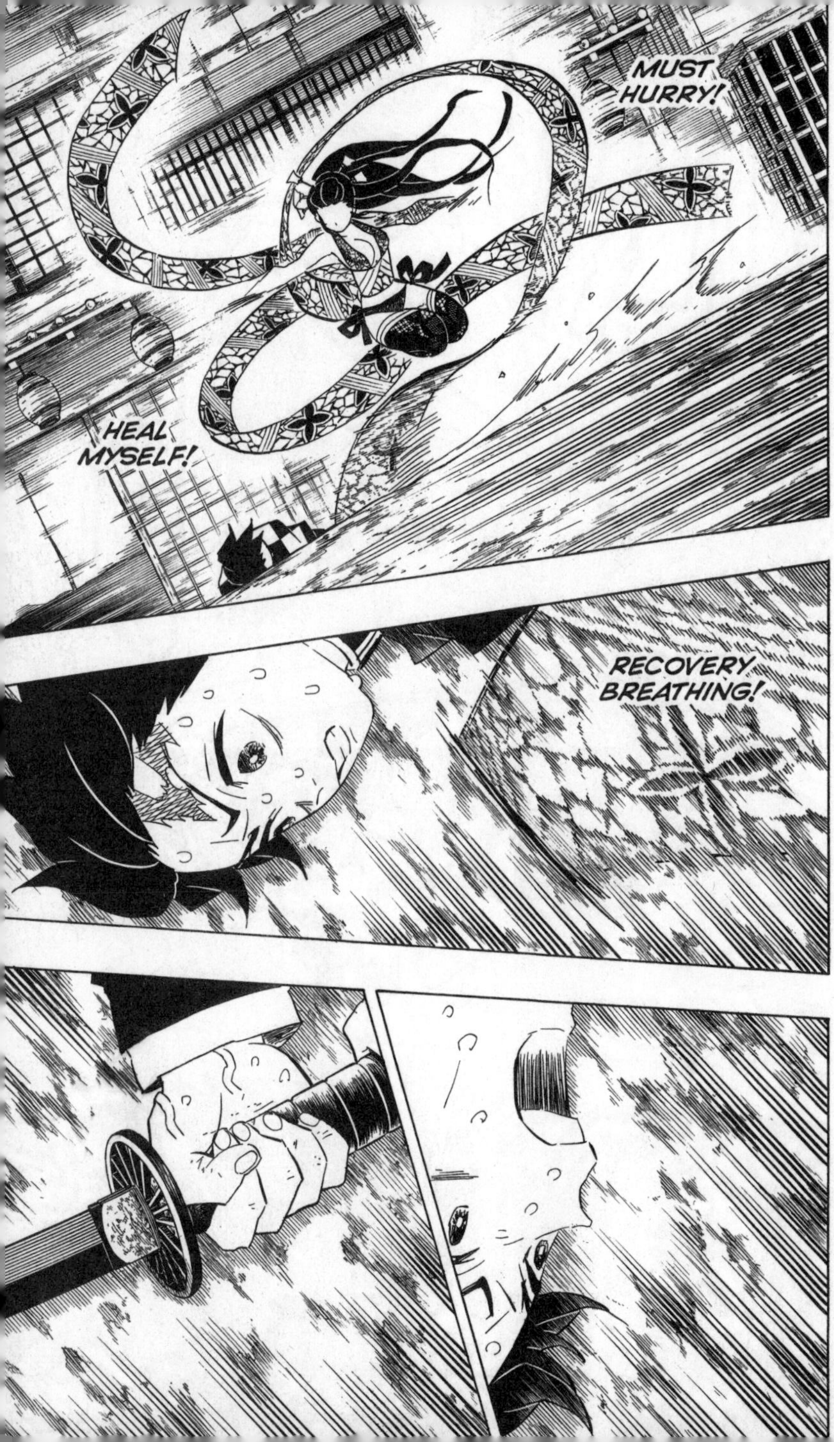
MUST HURRY!
HEAL MYSELF!
RECOVERY BREATHING!

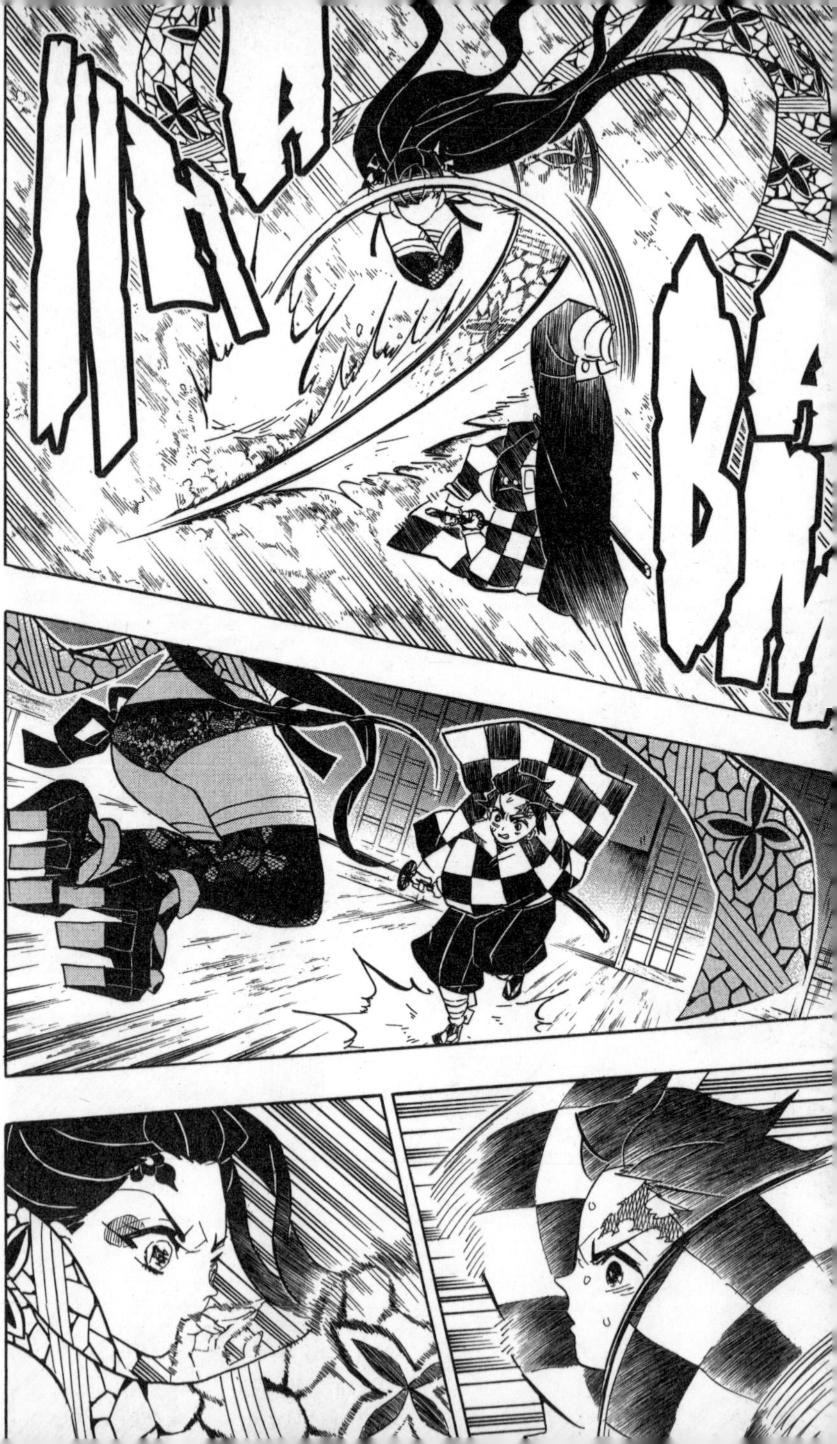

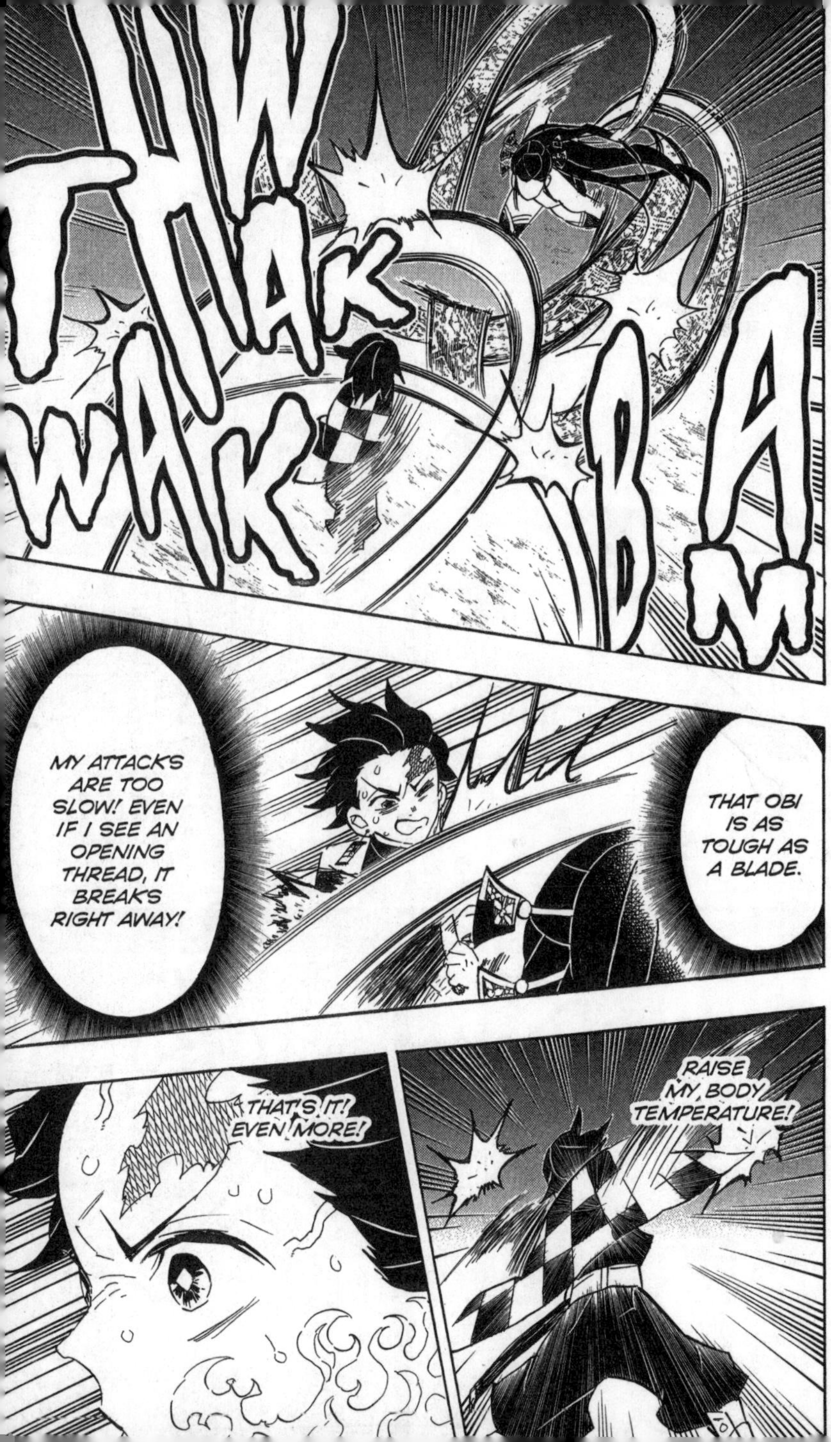
BAM
THWAK
WAK
THAT OBI IS AS TOUGH AS A BLADE.
MY ATTACKS ARE TOO SLOW! EVEN IF I SEE AN OPENING THREAD, IT BREAKS RIGHT AWAY!
RAISE MY BODY TEMPERATURE!
THAT'S IT! EVEN MORE!

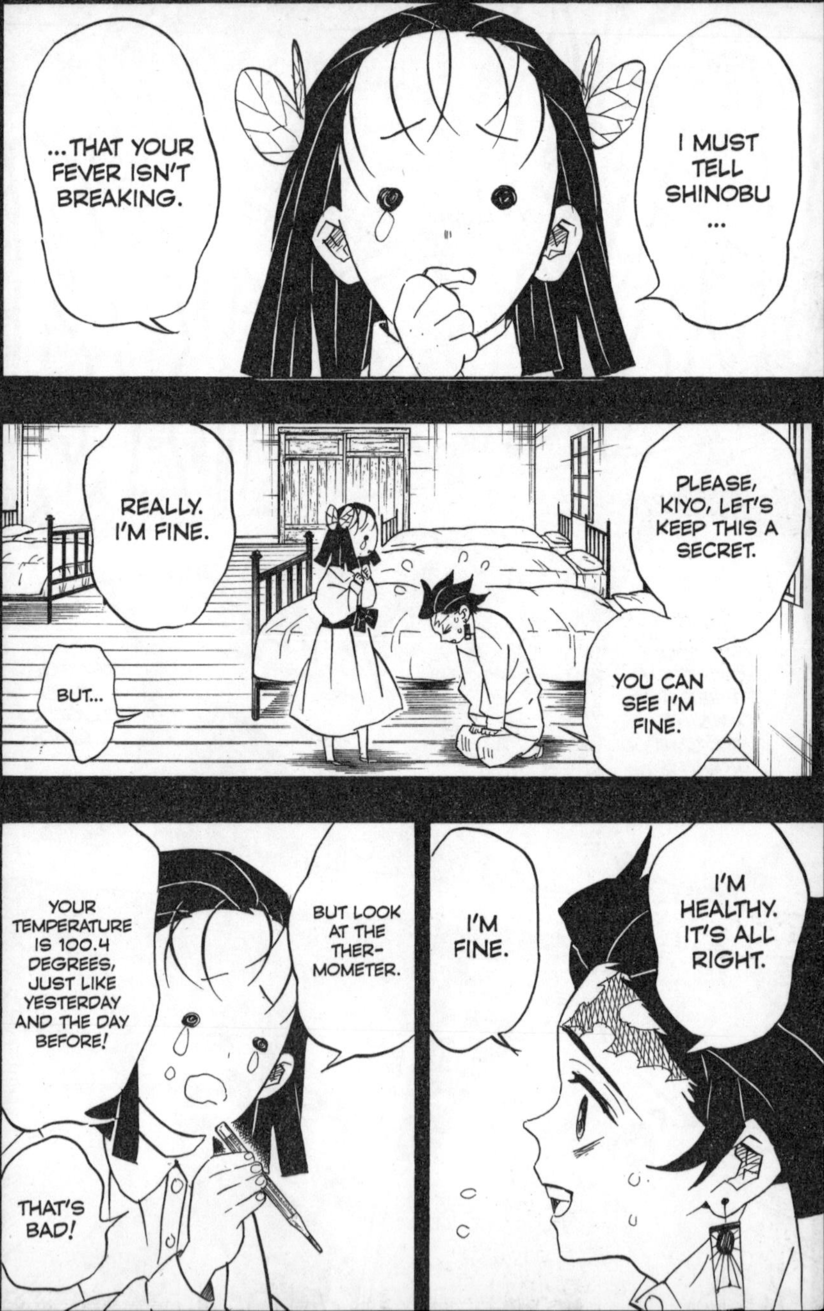
I MUST TELL SHINOBU ...
...THAT YOUR FEVER ISN'T BREAKING.
PLEASE, KIYO, LET'S KEEP THIS A SECRET.
YOU CAN SEE I'M FINE.
REALLY. I'M FINE.
BUT...
I'M HEALTHY. IT'S ALL RIGHT.
I'M FINE.
BUT LOOK AT THE THER-MOMETER.
YOUR TEMPERATURE IS 100.4 DEGREES, JUST LIKE YESTERDAY AND THE DAY BEFORE!
THAT'S BAD!

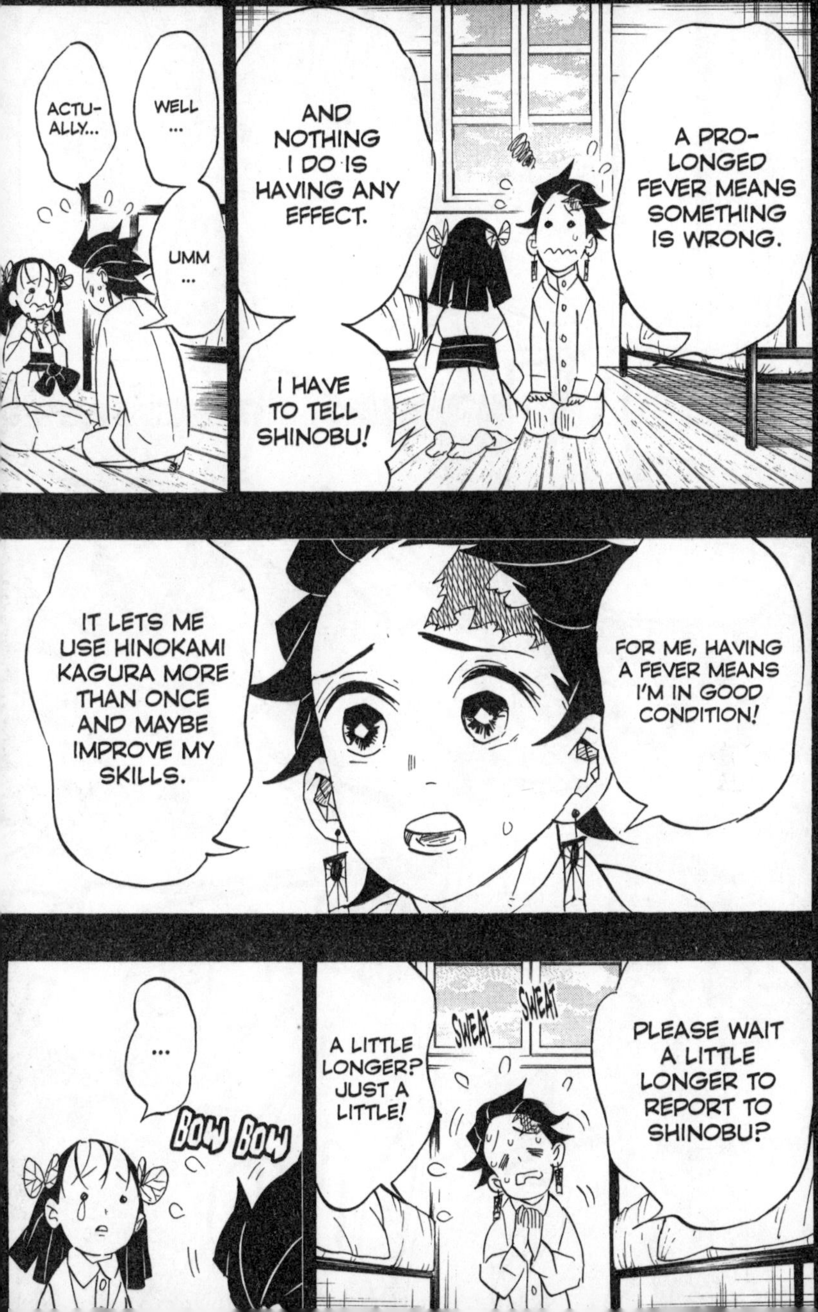
A PRO-LONGED FEVER MEANS SOMETHING IS WRONG.
AND NOTHING I DO IS HAVING ANY EFFECT.
I HAVE TO TELL SHINOBU!
WELL ...
ACTU-ALLY...
UMM ...
FOR ME, HAVING A FEVER MEANS I'M IN GOOD CONDITION!
IT LETS ME USE HINOKAMI KAGURA MORE THAN ONCE AND MAYBE IMPROVE MY SKILLS.
PLEASE WAIT A LITTLE LONGER TO REPORT TO SHINOBU?
SWEAT
SWEAT
A LITTLE LONGER? JUST A LITTLE!
...
BOW BOW

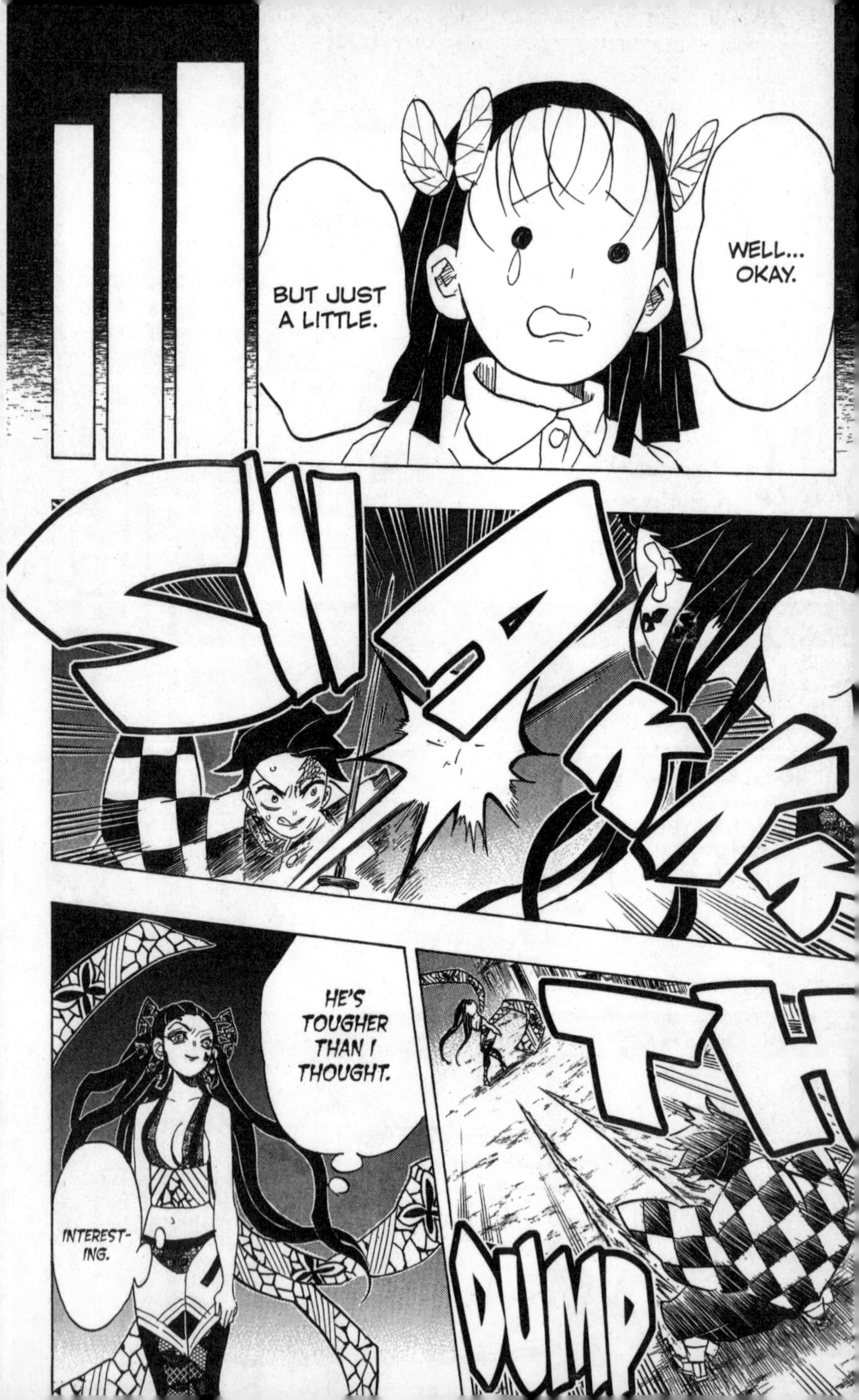
WELL... OKAY.
BUT JUST A LITTLE.
DUMP
HE'S TOUGHER THAN I THOUGHT.
INTERESTING.

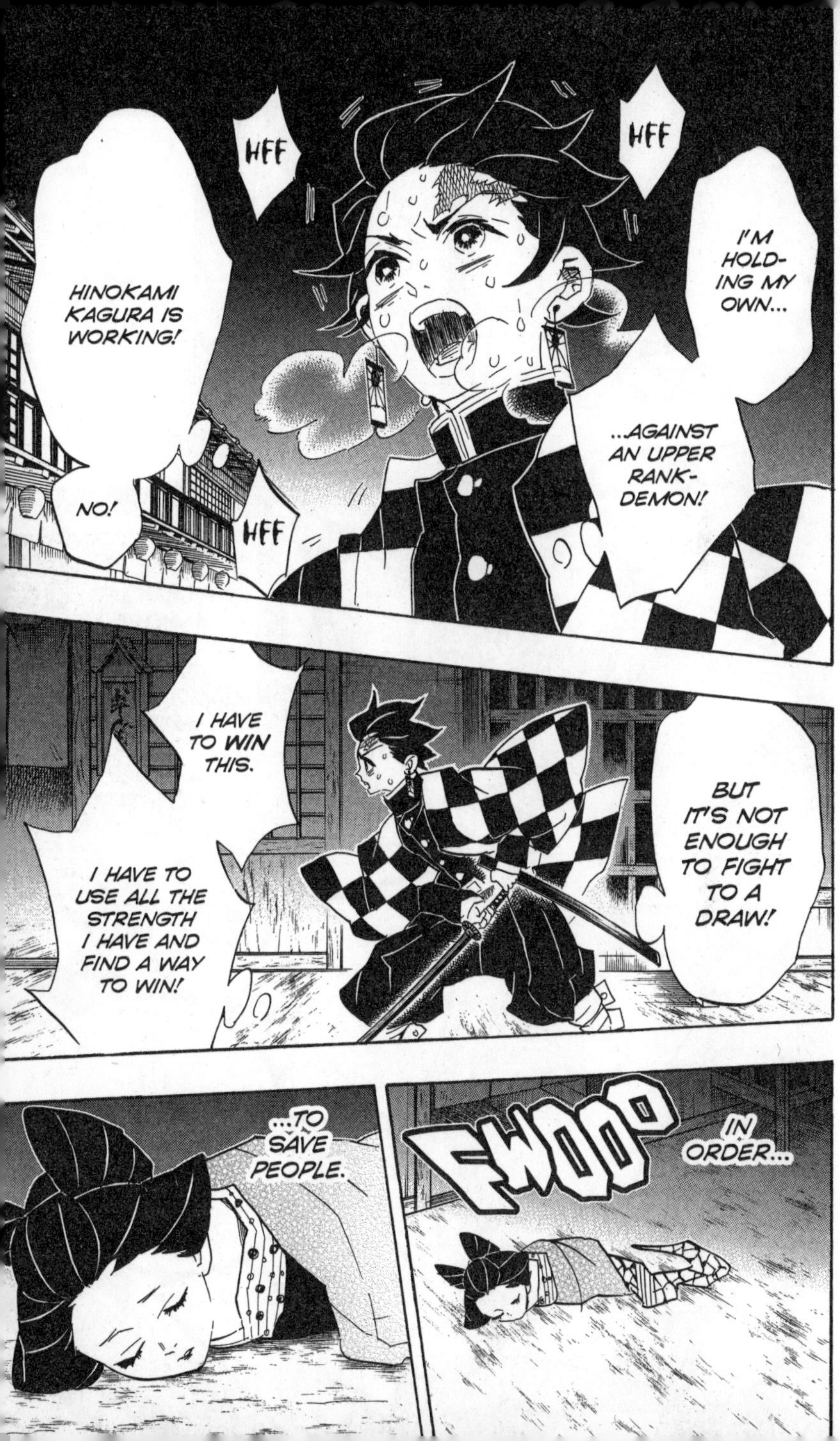
HFF
I'M HOLDING MY OWN...
...AGAINST AN UPPER RANK-DEMON!
HFF
HINOKAMI KAGURA IS WORKING!
NO!
HFF
BUT IT'S NOT ENOUGH TO FIGHT TO A DRAW!
I HAVE TO WIN THIS.
I HAVE TO USE ALL THE STRENGTH I HAVE AND FIND A WAY TO WIN!
IN ORDER...
FWOOP
...TO SAVE PEOPLE.

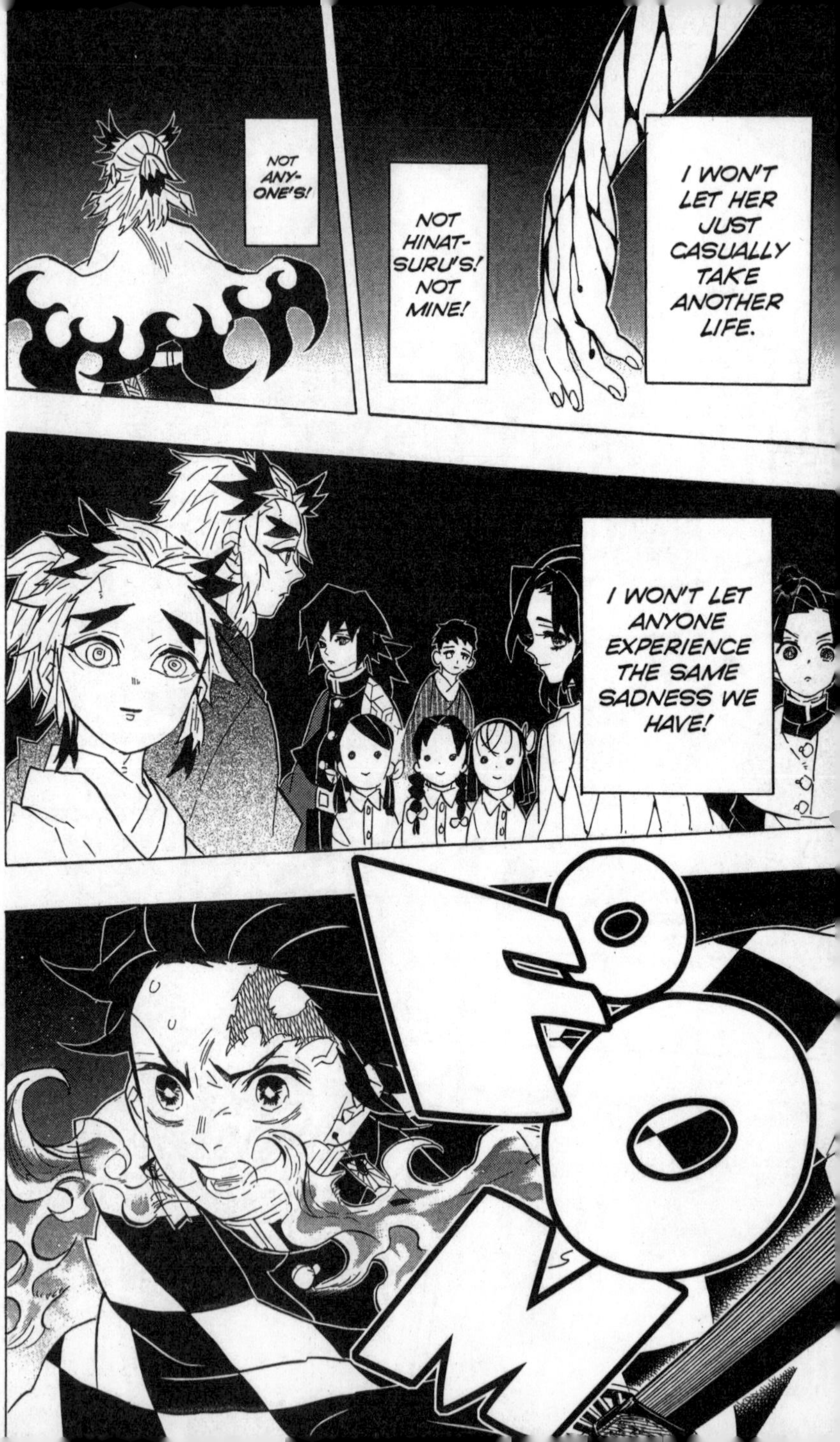
I WON'T LET HER JUST CASUALLY TAKE ANOTHER LIFE.
NOT HINAT-SURU'S! NOT MINE!
NOT ANY-ONE'S!
I WON'T LET ANYONE EXPERIENCE THE SAME SADNESS WE HAVE!

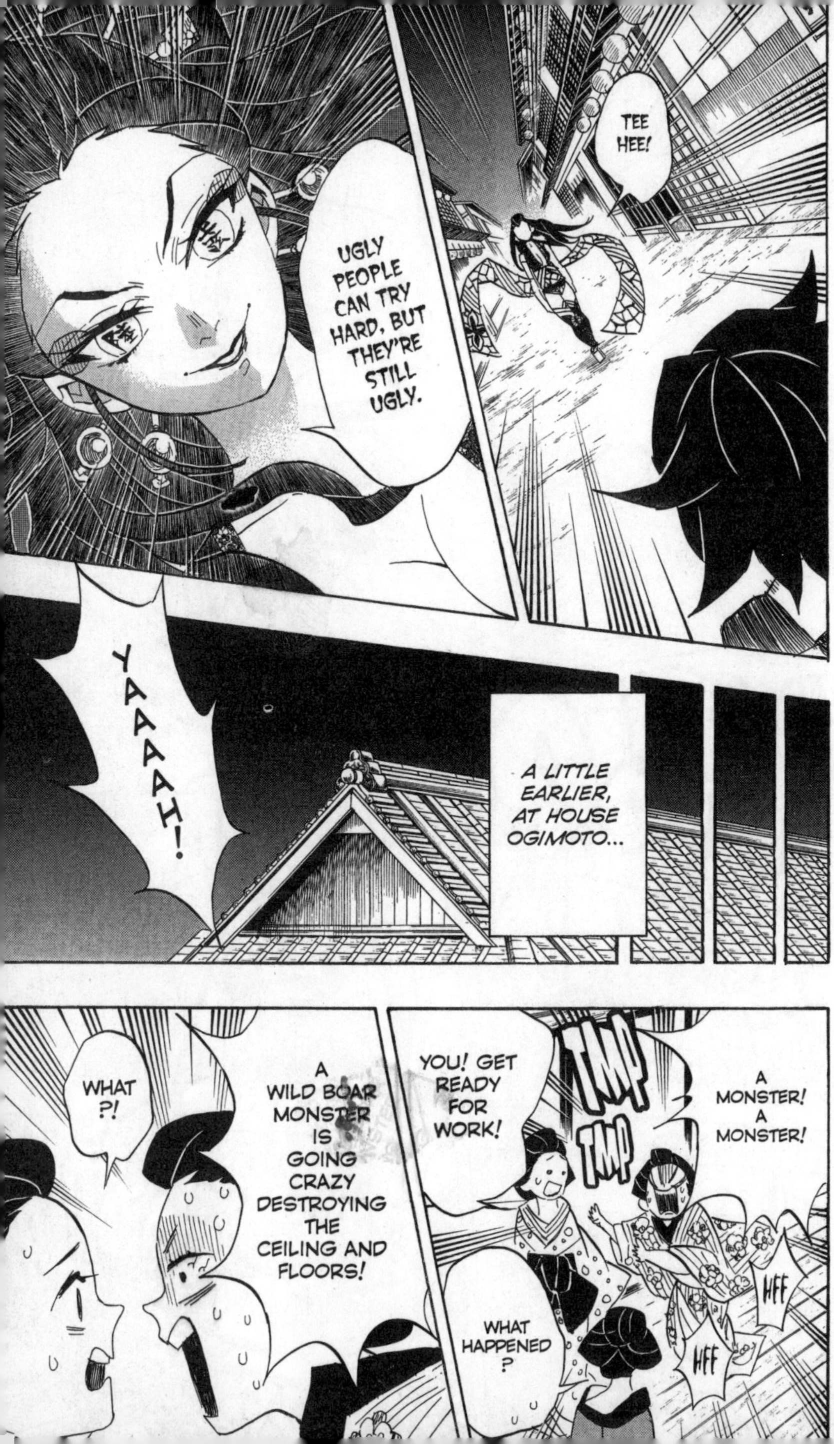
TEE HEE!
UGLY PEOPLE CAN TRY HARD, BUT THEY'RE STILL UGLY.
A LITTLE EARLIER, AT HOUSE OGIMOTO...
YAAAAAH!
A MONSTER! A MONSTER!
TMP
TMP
YOU! GET READY FOR WORK!
HFF
HFF
WHAT HAPPENED?
A WILD BOAR MONSTER IS GOING CRAZY DESTROYING THE CEILING AND FLOORS!
WHAT?!

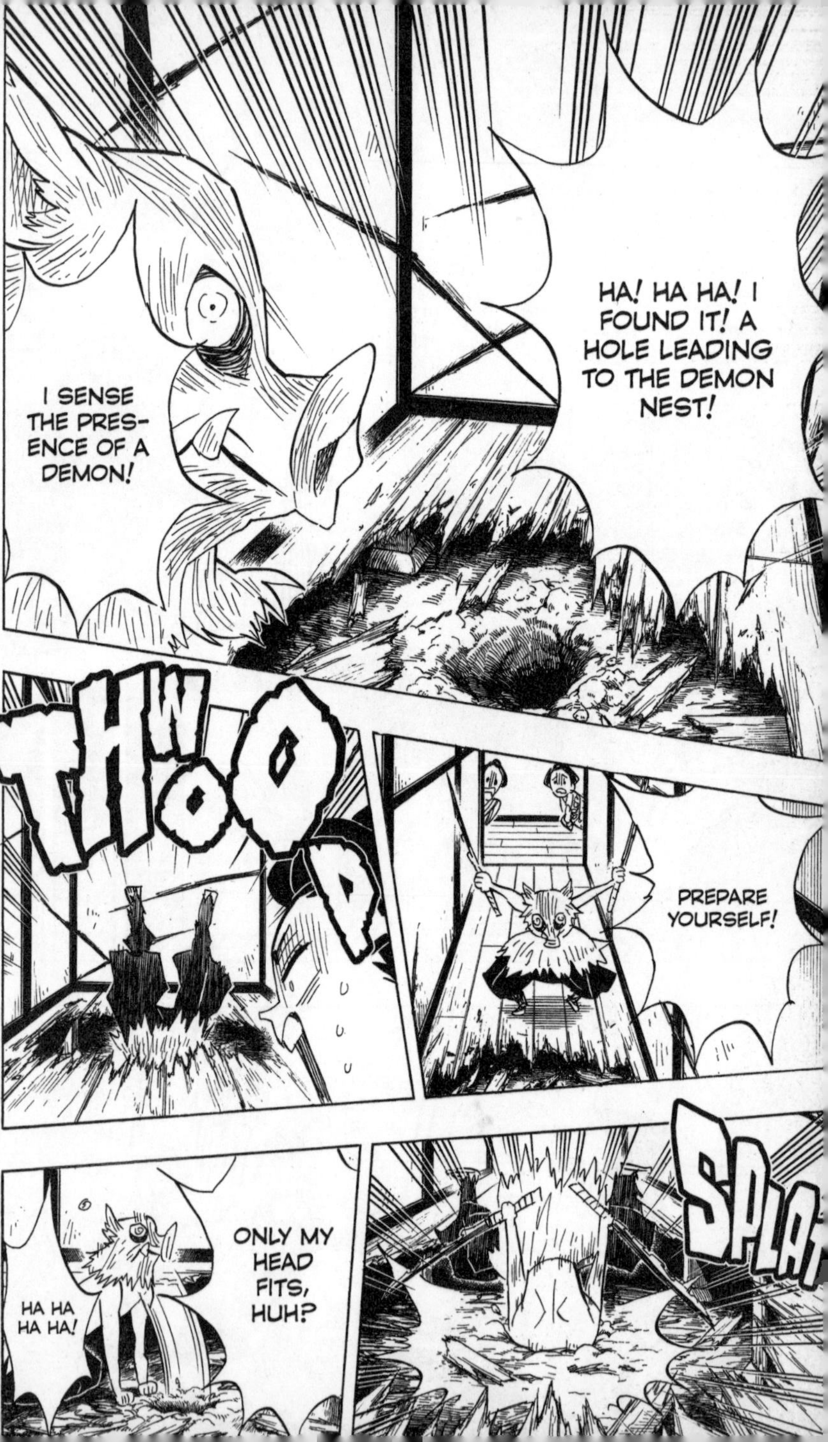
HA! HA HA! I FOUND IT! A HOLE LEADING TO THE DEMON NEST!
I SENSE THE PRESENCE OF A DEMON!
PREPARE YOURSELF!
THWOOP
SPLAT
ONLY MY HEAD FITS, HUH?
HA HA HA HA!

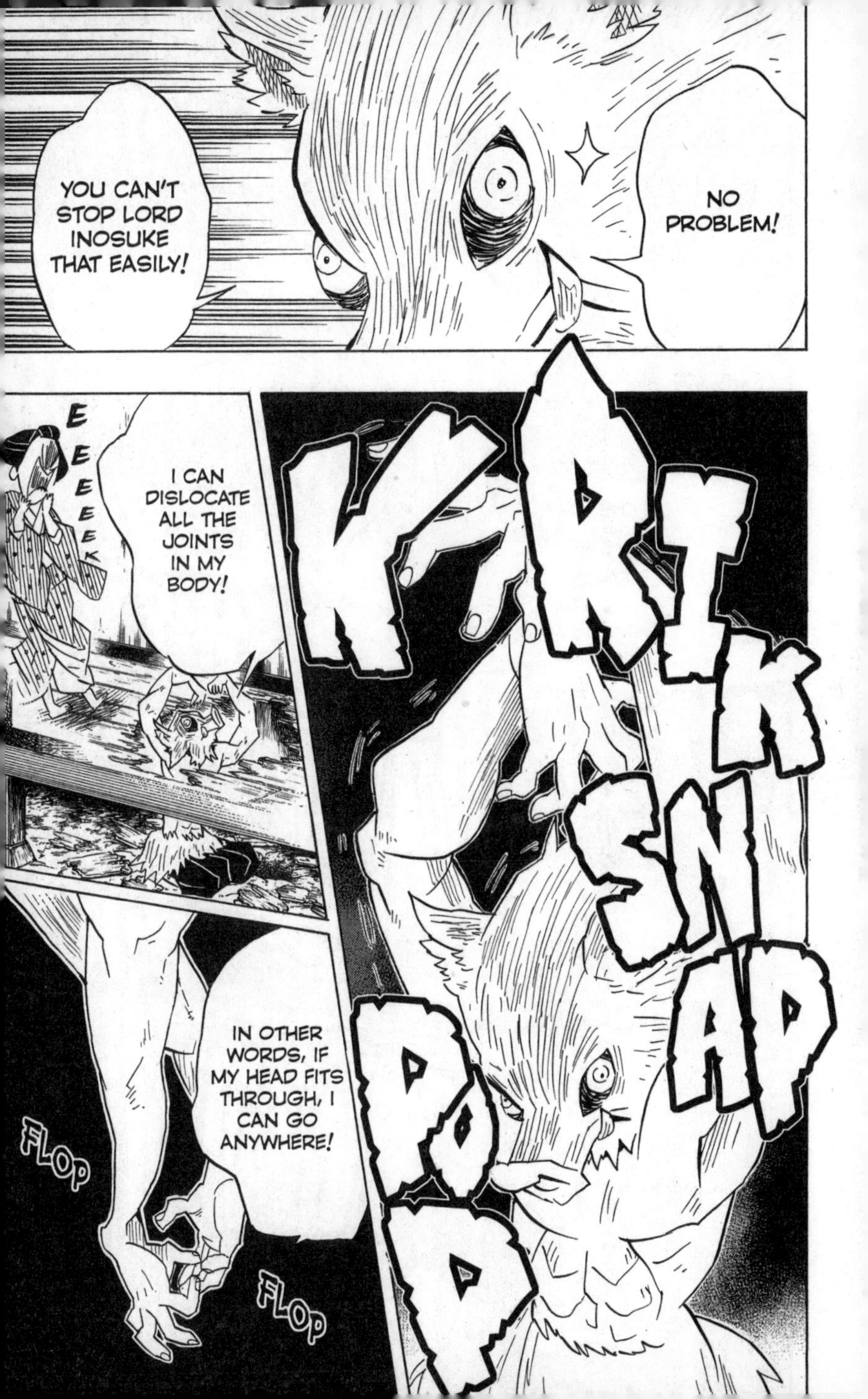
NO PROBLEM!
YOU CAN'T STOP LORD INOSUKE THAT EASILY!
KRIK
SNAP
POP
I CAN DISLOCATE ALL THE JOINTS IN MY BODY!
EEEEEEK
IN OTHER WORDS, IF MY HEAD FITS THROUGH, I CAN GO ANYWHERE!
FLOP
FLOP

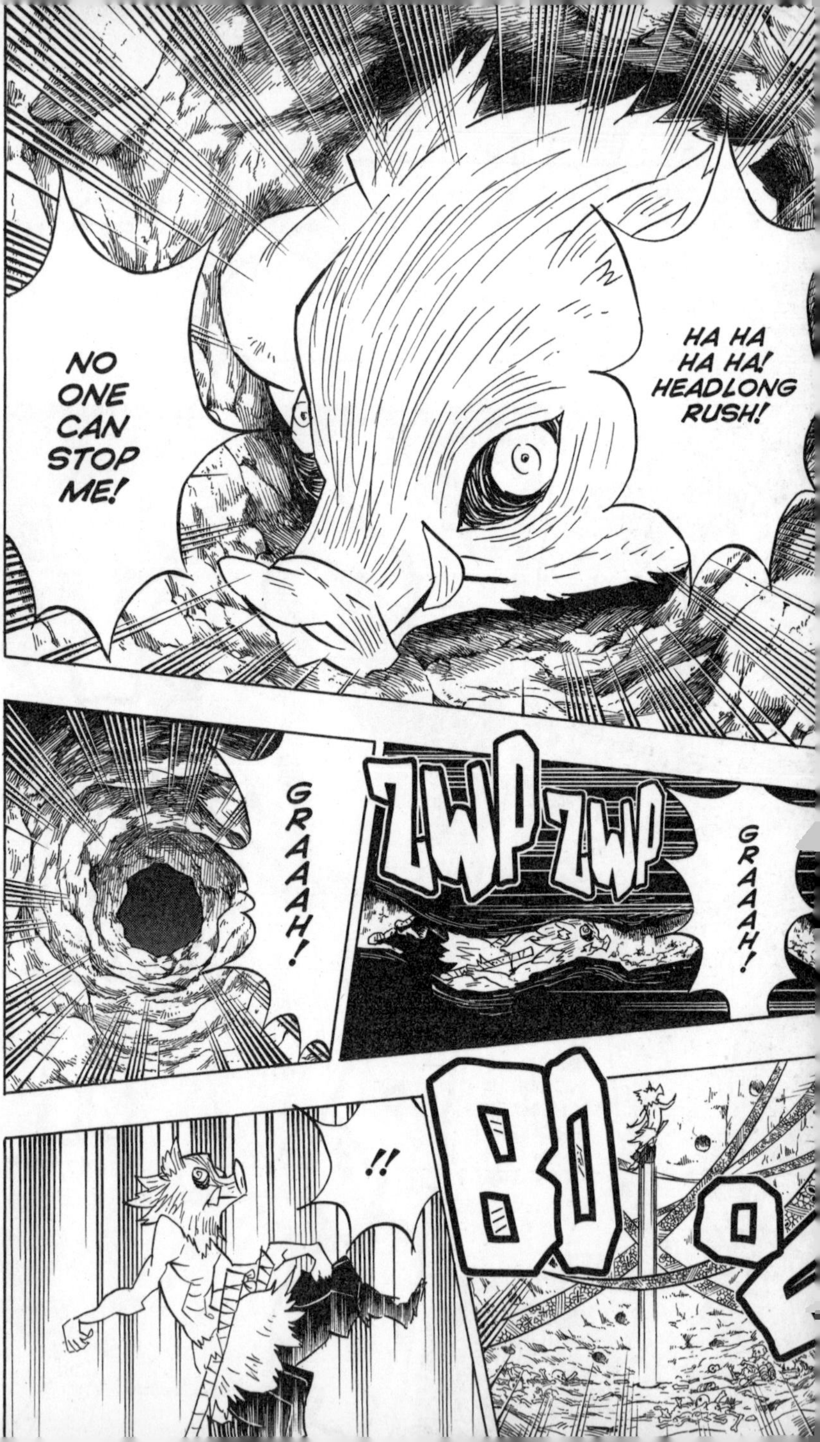
HA HA HA HA! HEADLONG RUSH!
NO ONE CAN STOP ME!
GRAAAH!
ZWP ZWP
GRAAAH!
!!

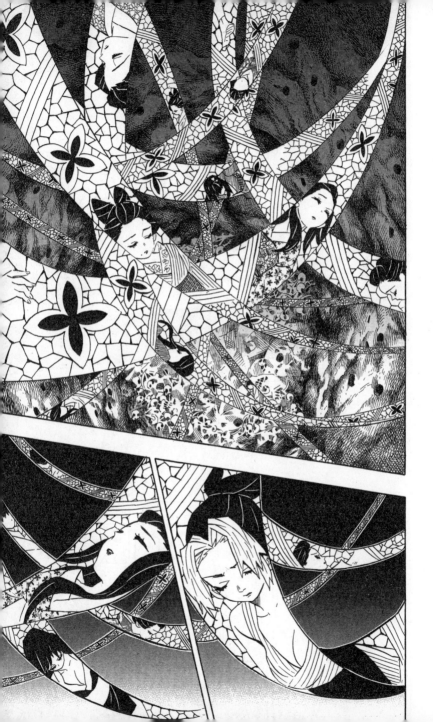

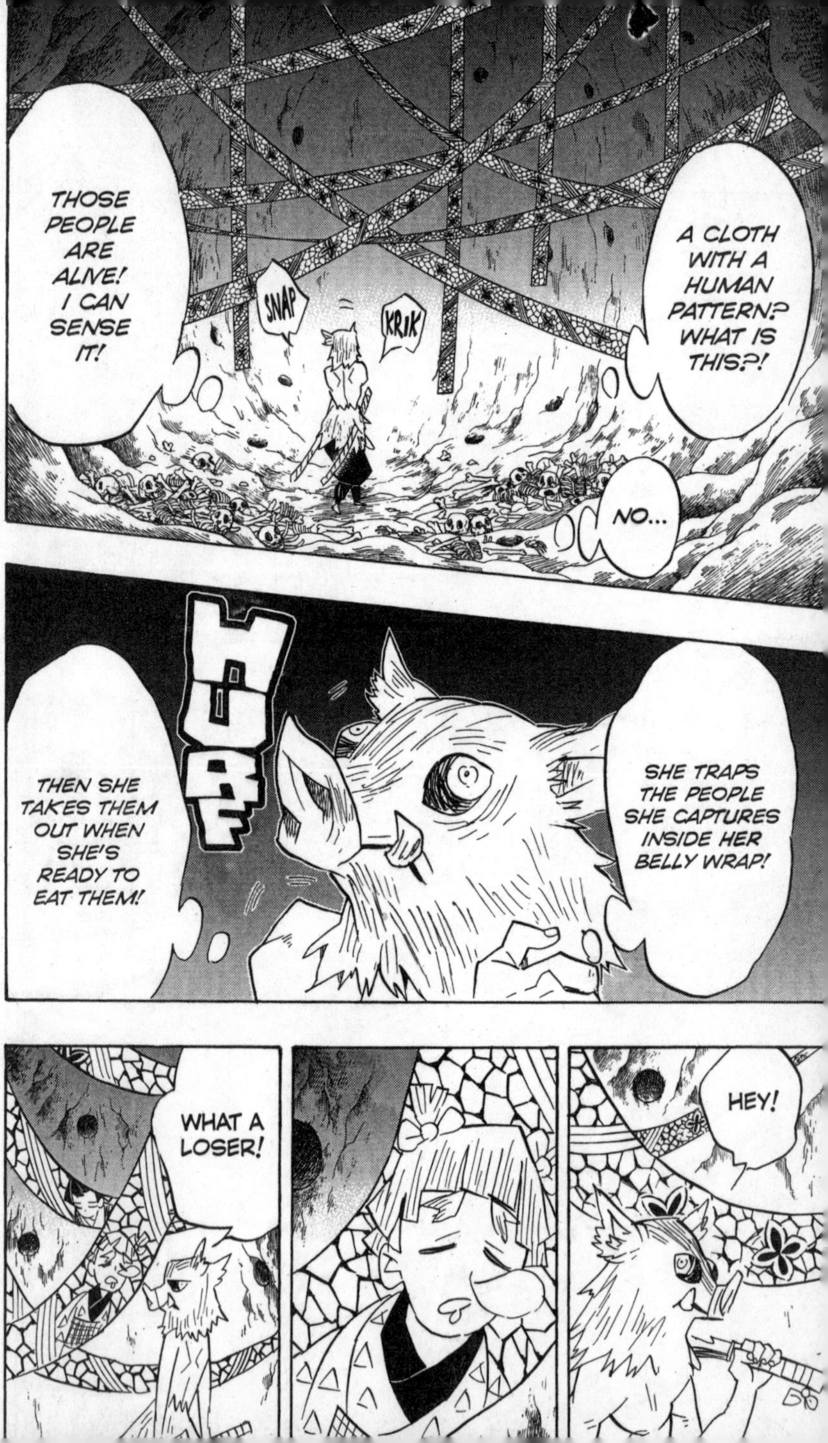
A CLOTH WITH A HUMAN PATTERN? WHAT IS THIS?!
NO...
KRIK
SNAP
THOSE PEOPLE ARE ALIVE! I CAN SENSE IT!
SHE TRAPS THE PEOPLE SHE CAPTURES INSIDE HER BELLY WRAP!
THEN SHE TAKES THEM OUT WHEN SHE'S READY TO EAT THEM!
HEY!
WHAT A LOSER!

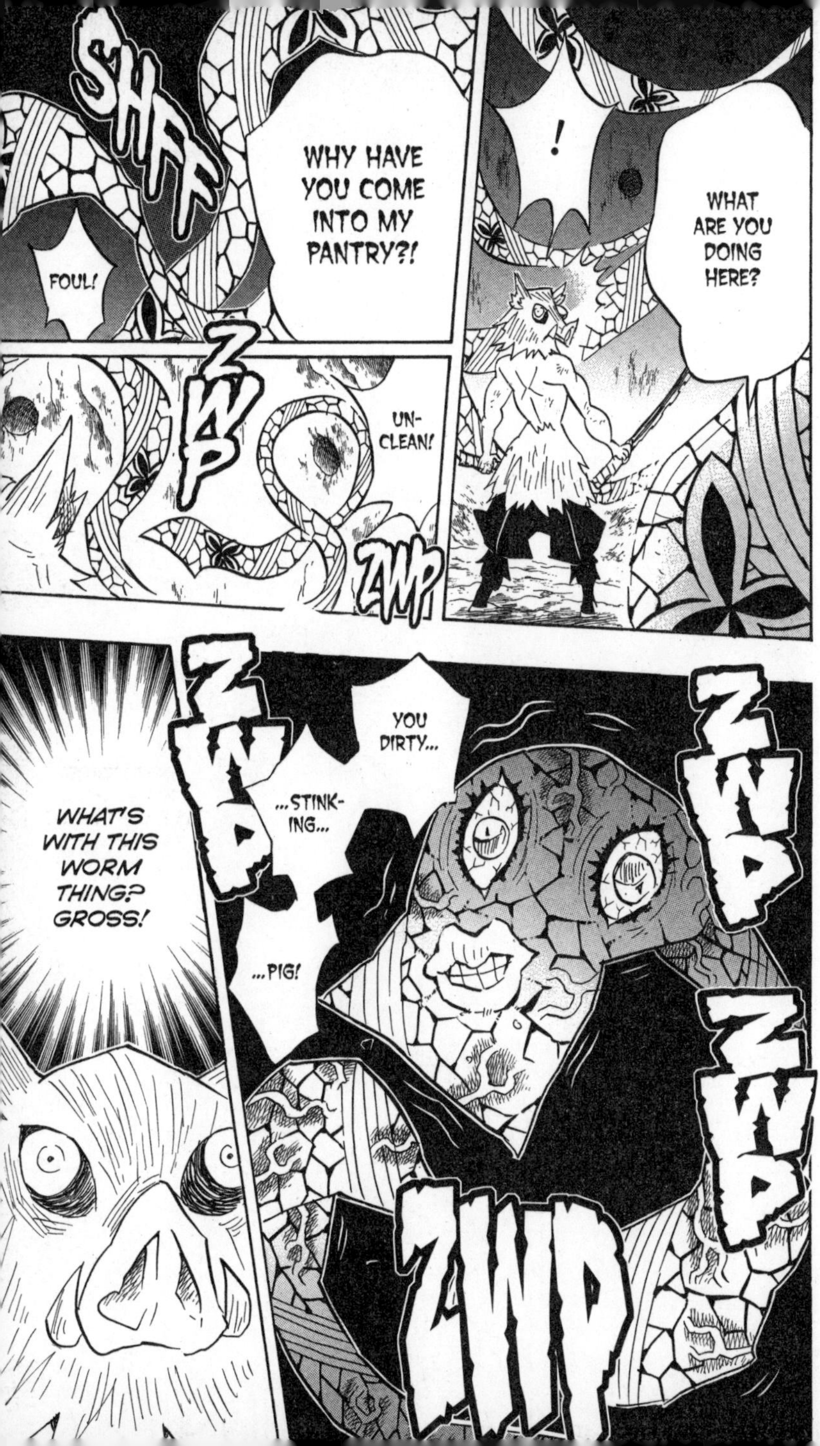
!
WHAT ARE YOU DOING HERE?
WHY HAVE YOU COME INTO MY PANTRY?!
SHFF
FOUL!
ZWP
UN-CLEAN!
ZWP
ZWP
ZWP
YOU DIRTY...
...STINK-ING...
...PIG!
ZWP
ZWP
WHAT'S WITH THIS WORM THING? GROSS!

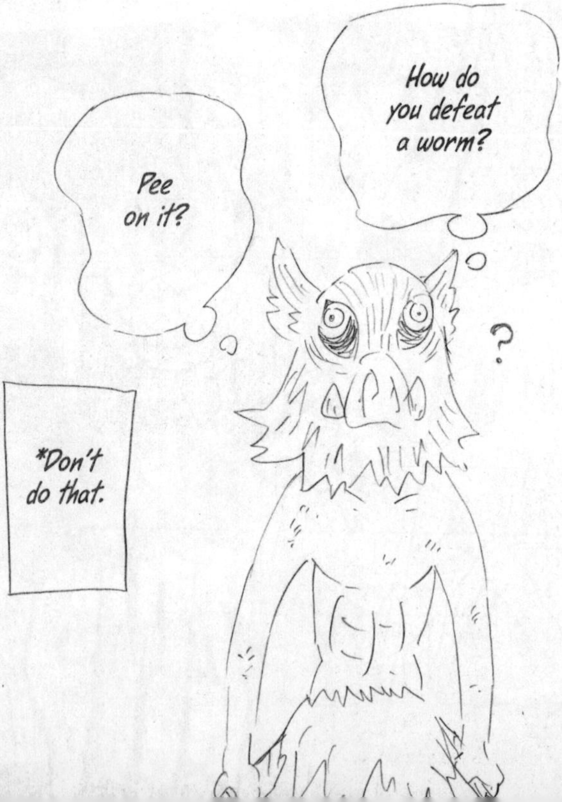
How do you defeat a worm?
Pee on it?
*Don't do that.

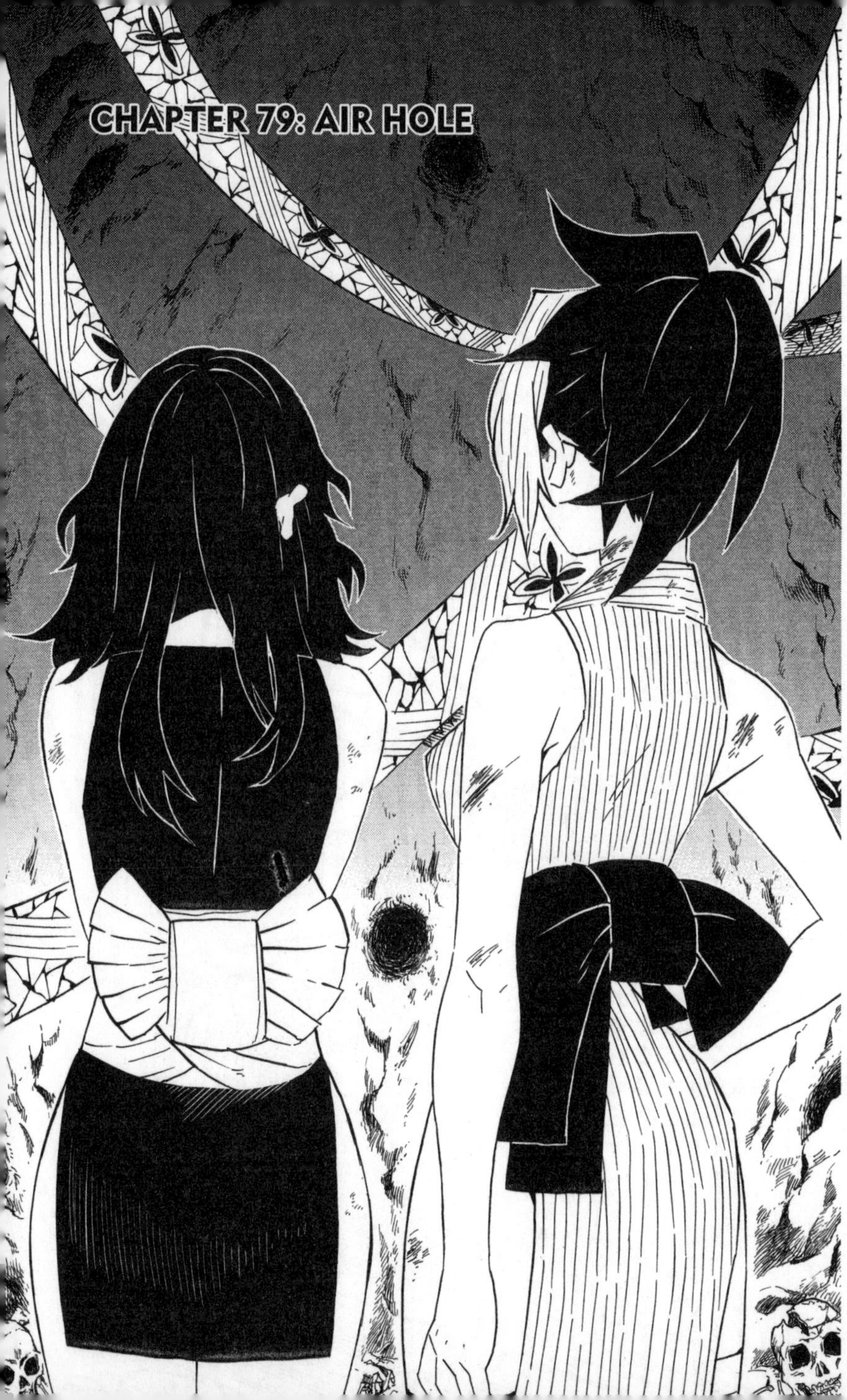
CHAPTER 79: AIR HOLE

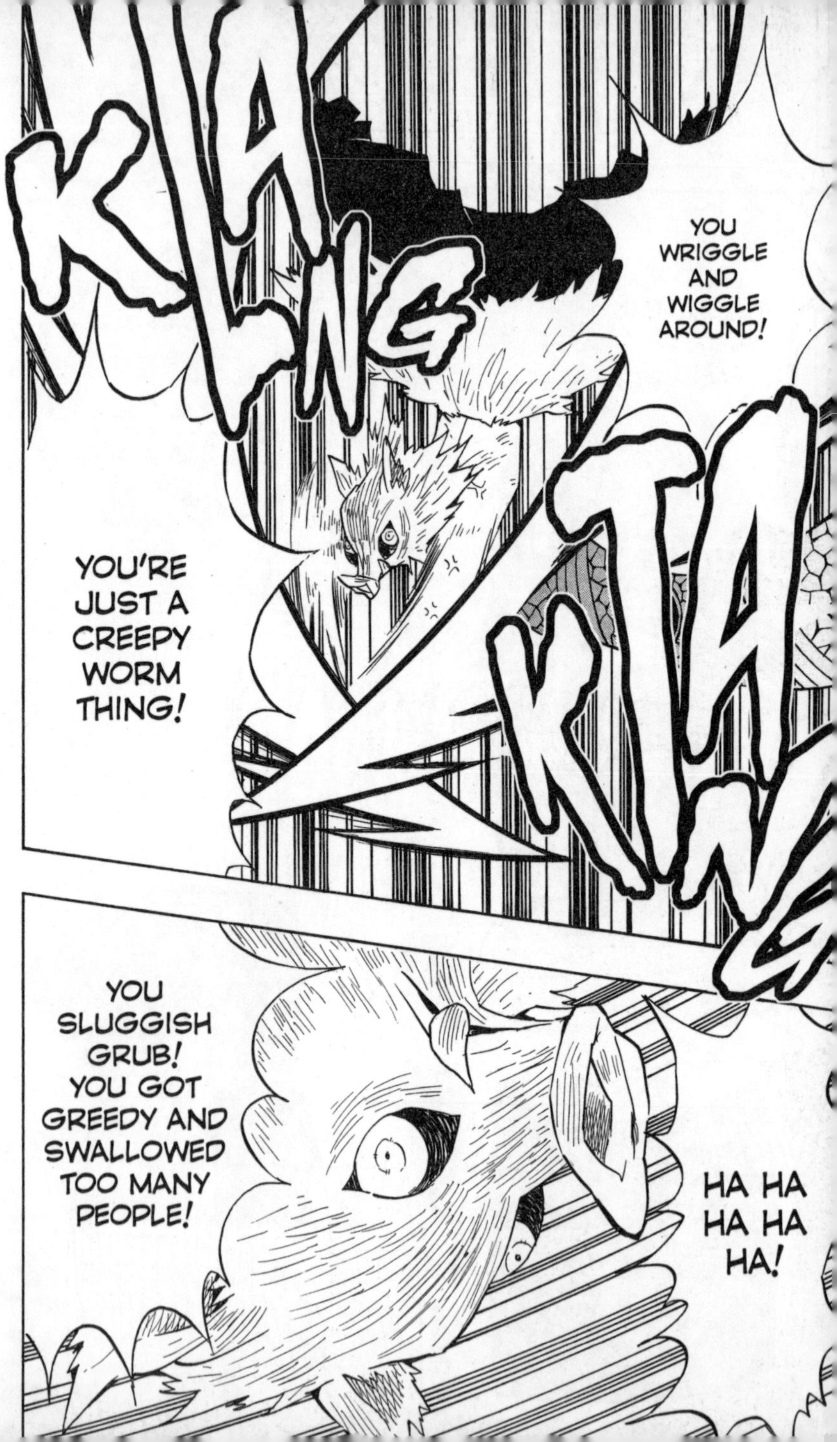
YOU WRIGGLE AND WIGGLE AROUND!
KLANG
KLANG
YOU'RE JUST A CREEPY WORM THING!
HA HA HA HA HA!
YOU SLUGGISH GRUB! YOU GOT GREEDY AND SWALLOWED TOO MANY PEOPLE!

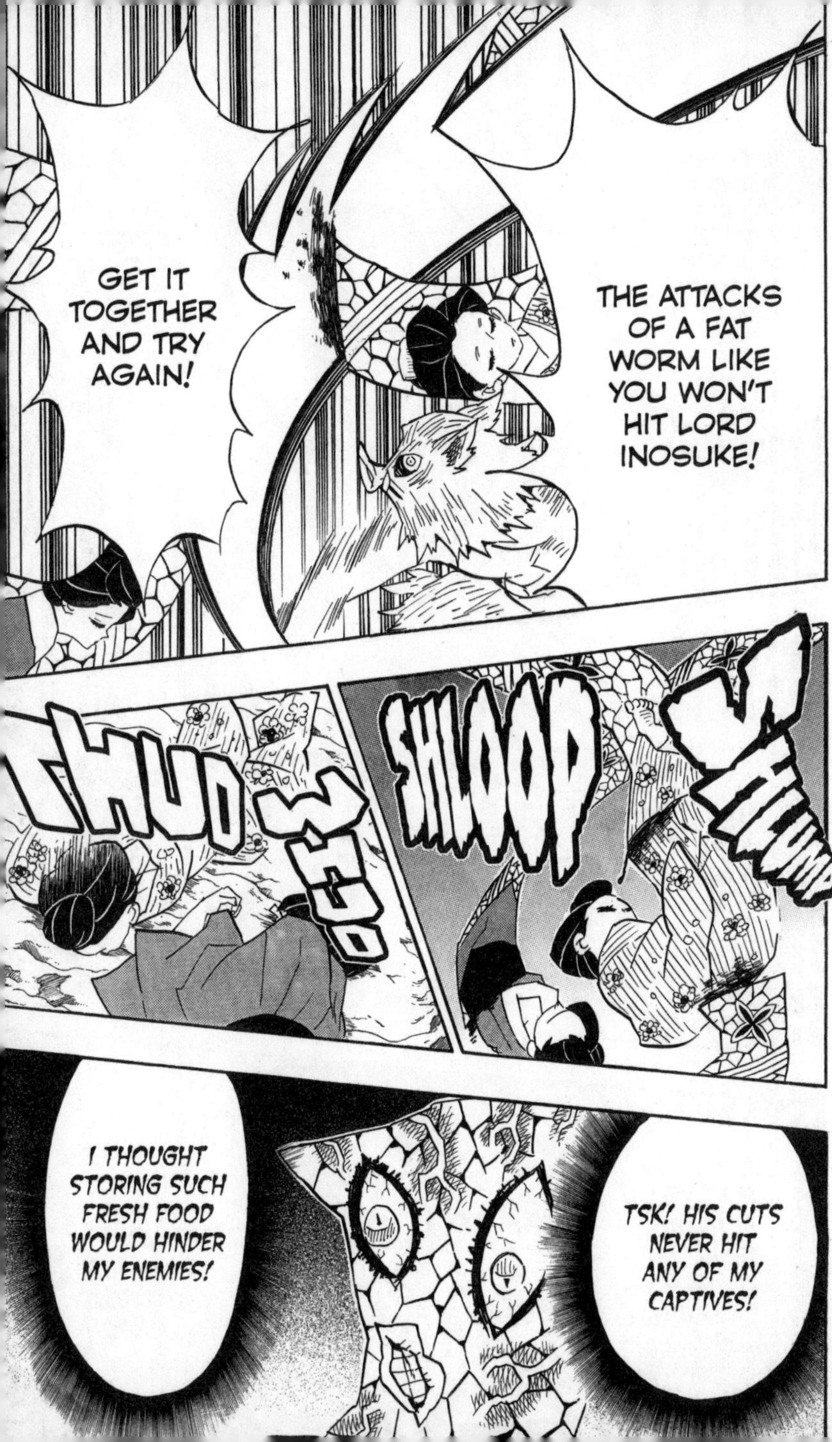
THE ATTACKS OF A FAT WORM LIKE YOU WON'T HIT LORD INOSUKE!
GET IT TOGETHER AND TRY AGAIN!
SHWUMP
SHLOOP
TSK! HIS CUTS NEVER HIT ANY OF MY CAPTIVES!
I THOUGHT STORING SUCH FRESH FOOD WOULD HINDER MY ENEMIES!

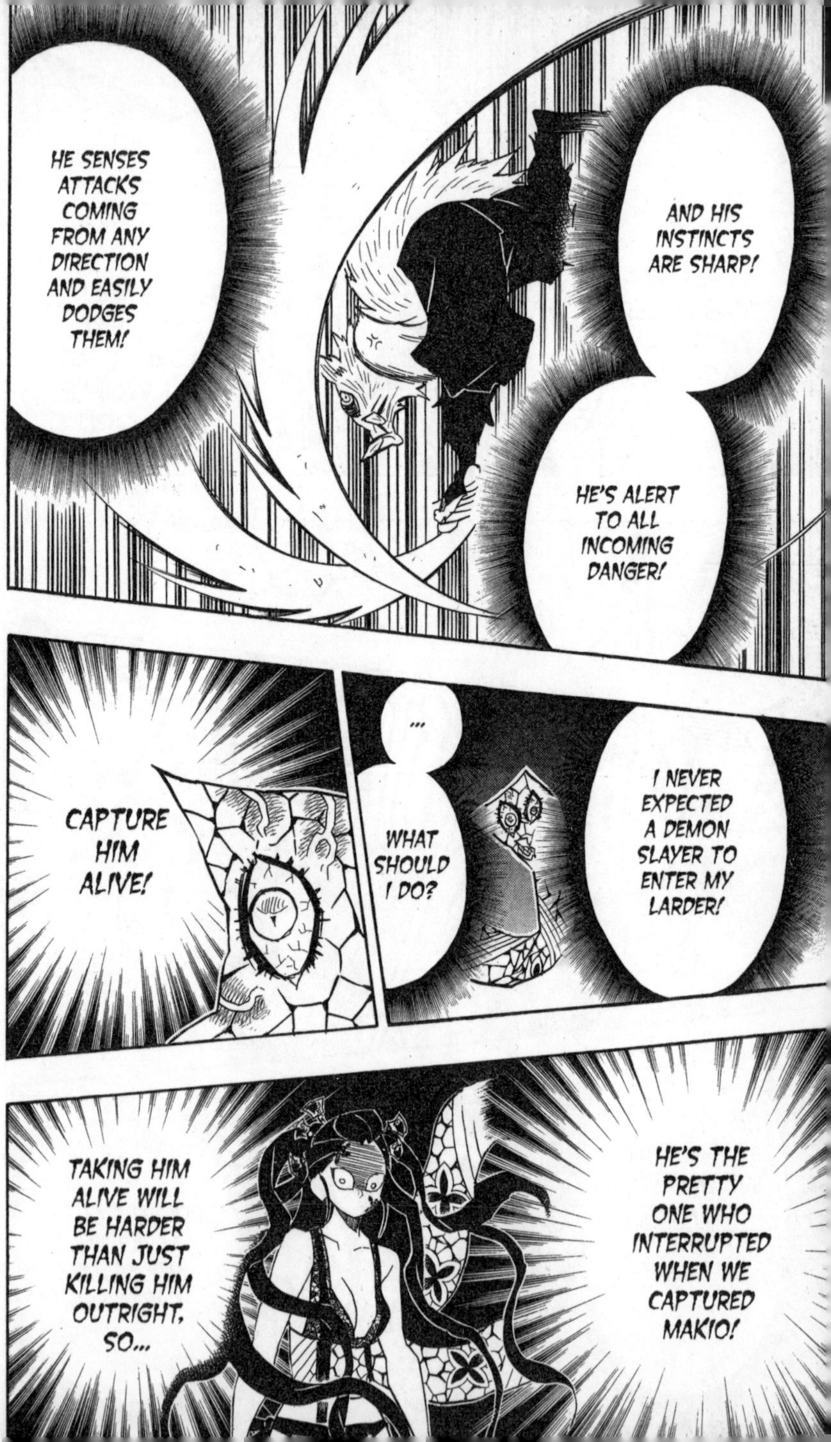
AND HIS INSTINCTS ARE SHARP!
HE'S ALERT TO ALL INCOMING DANGER!
HE SENSES ATTACKS COMING FROM ANY DIRECTION AND EASILY DODGES THEM!
I NEVER EXPECTED A DEMON SLAYER TO ENTER MY LARDER!
...
WHAT SHOULD I DO?
CAPTURE HIM ALIVE!
HE'S THE PRETTY ONE WHO INTERRUPTED WHEN WE CAPTURED MAKIO!
TAKING HIM ALIVE WILL BE HARDER THAN JUST KILLING HIM OUTRIGHT, SO...

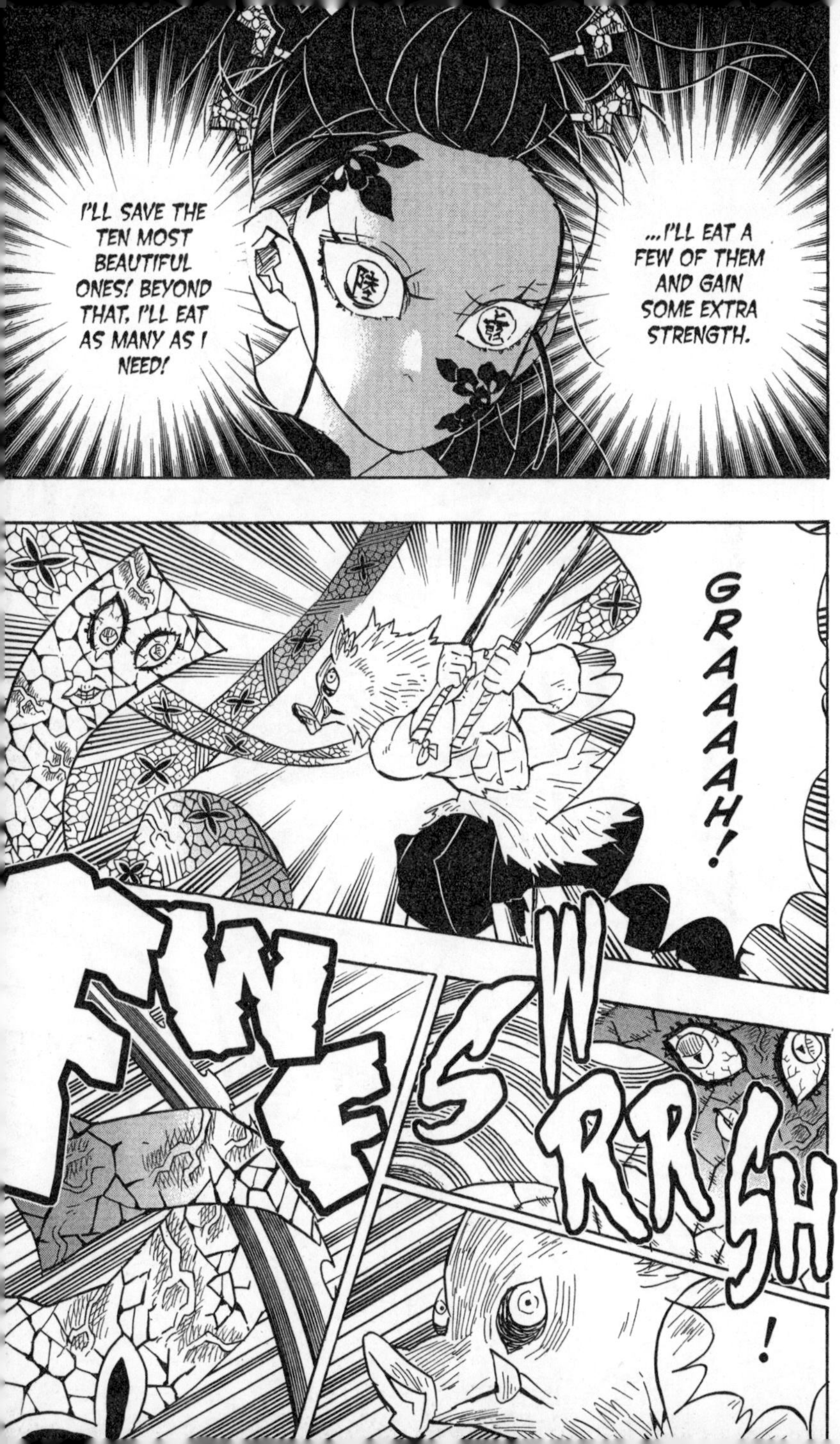
...I'LL EAT A FEW OF THEM AND GAIN SOME EXTRA STRENGTH.
I'LL SAVE THE TEN MOST BEAUTIFUL ONES! BEYOND THAT, I'LL EAT AS MANY AS I NEED!
GRAAAAAH!
SWRRSH!

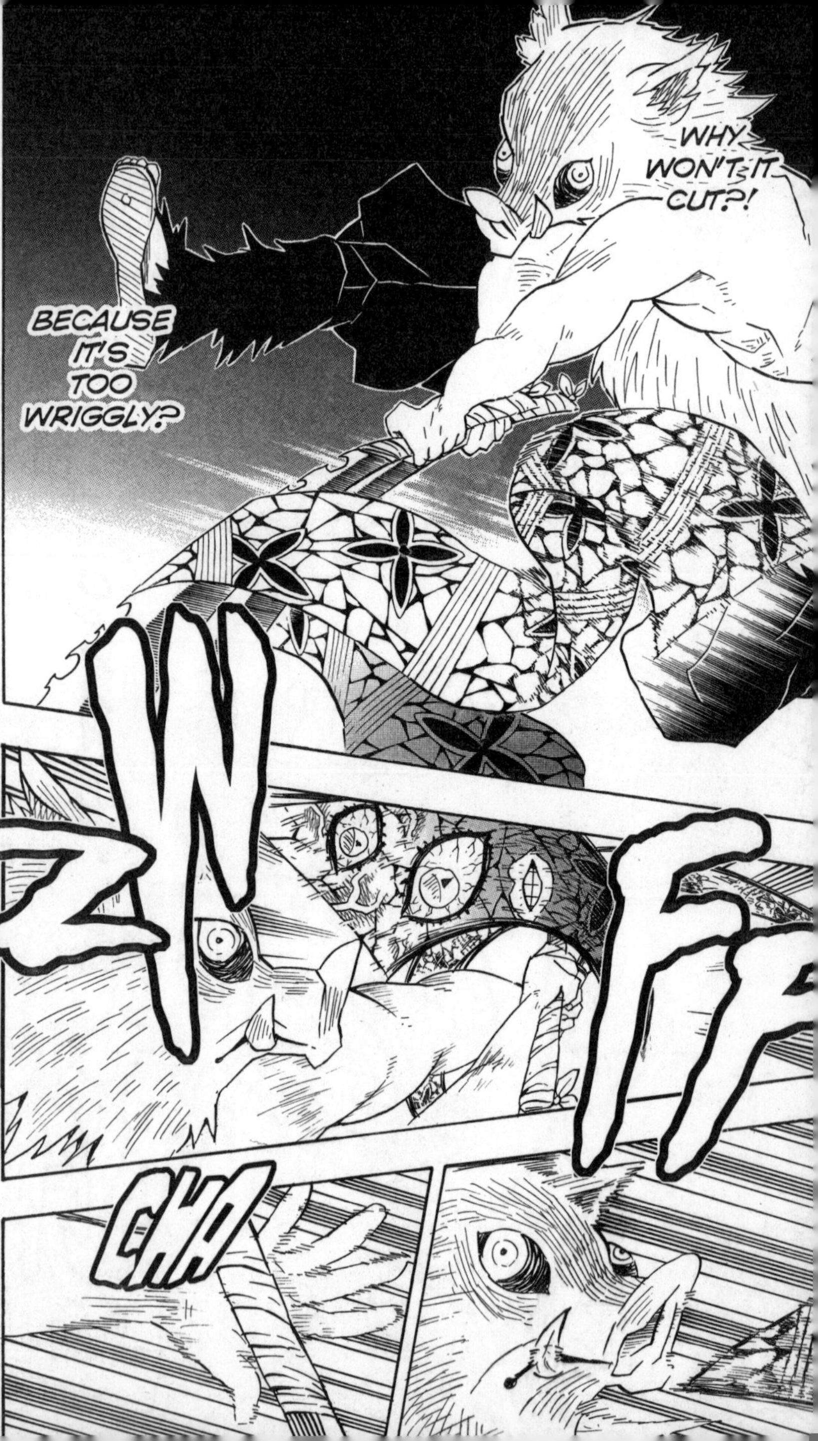
WHY WON'T IT CUT?!
BECAUSE IT'S TOO WRIGGLY?
CHA

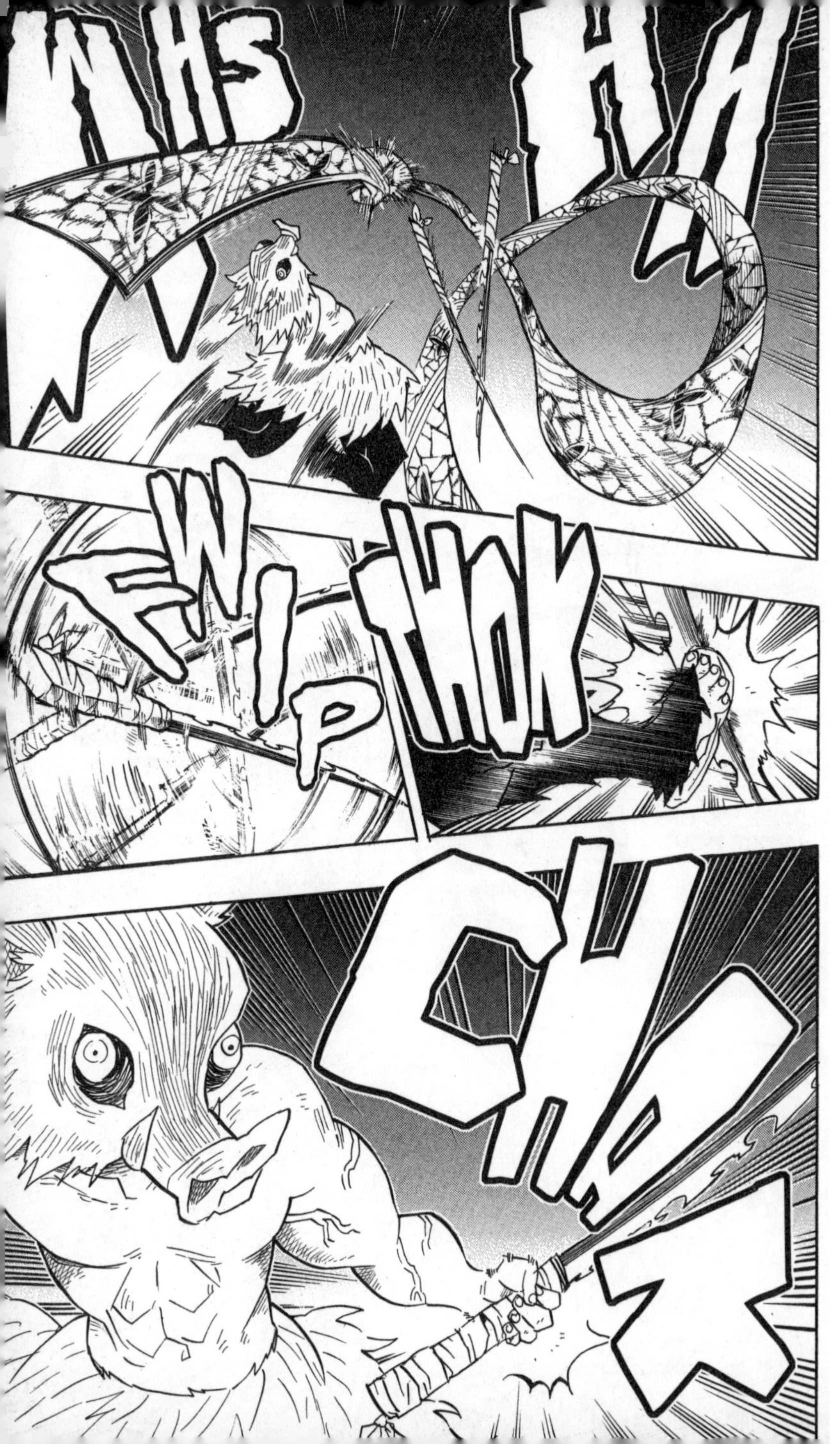
WHS
HA
THOK
FWIP
CHAK

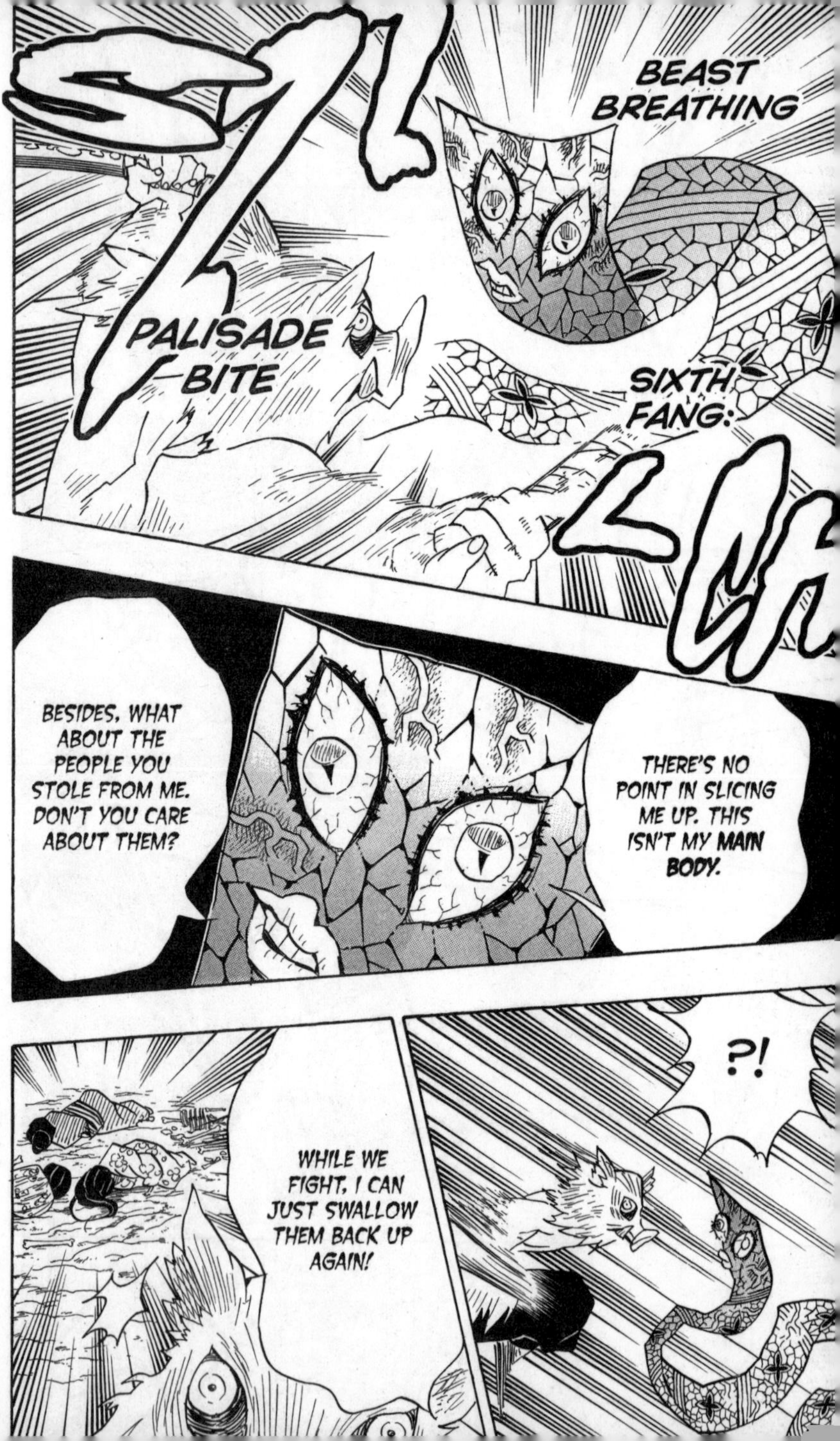
BEAST BREATHING
SIXTH FANG:
PALISADE BITE
THERE'S NO POINT IN SLICING ME UP. THIS ISN'T MY **MAIN BODY.**
BESIDES, WHAT ABOUT THE PEOPLE YOU STOLE FROM ME. DON'T YOU CARE ABOUT THEM?
?!
WHILE WE FIGHT, I CAN JUST SWALLOW THEM BACK UP AGAIN!

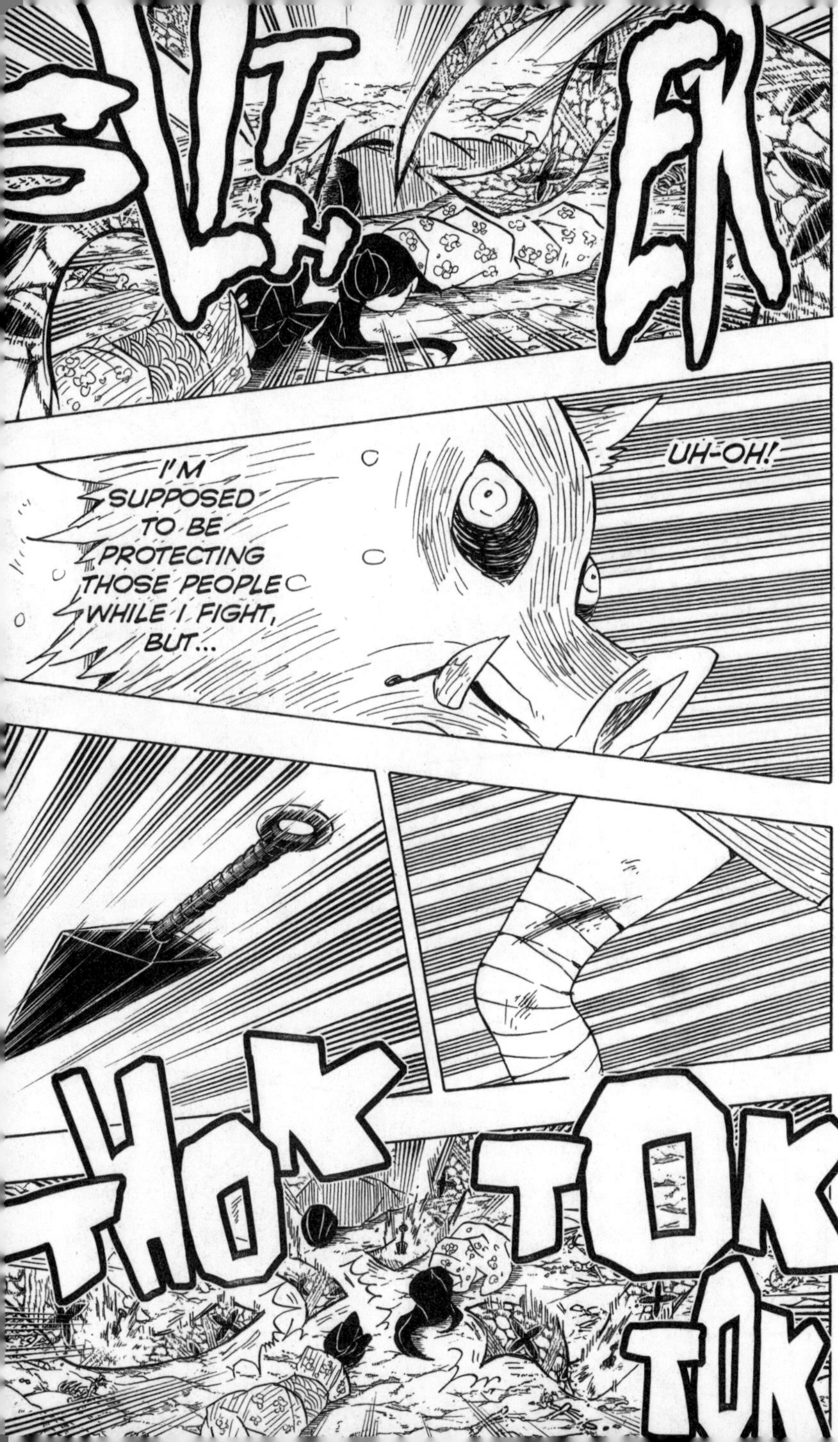
UH-OH!
I'M SUPPOSED TO BE PROTECTING THOSE PEOPLE WHILE I FIGHT, BUT...
TOK
THOK
TOK

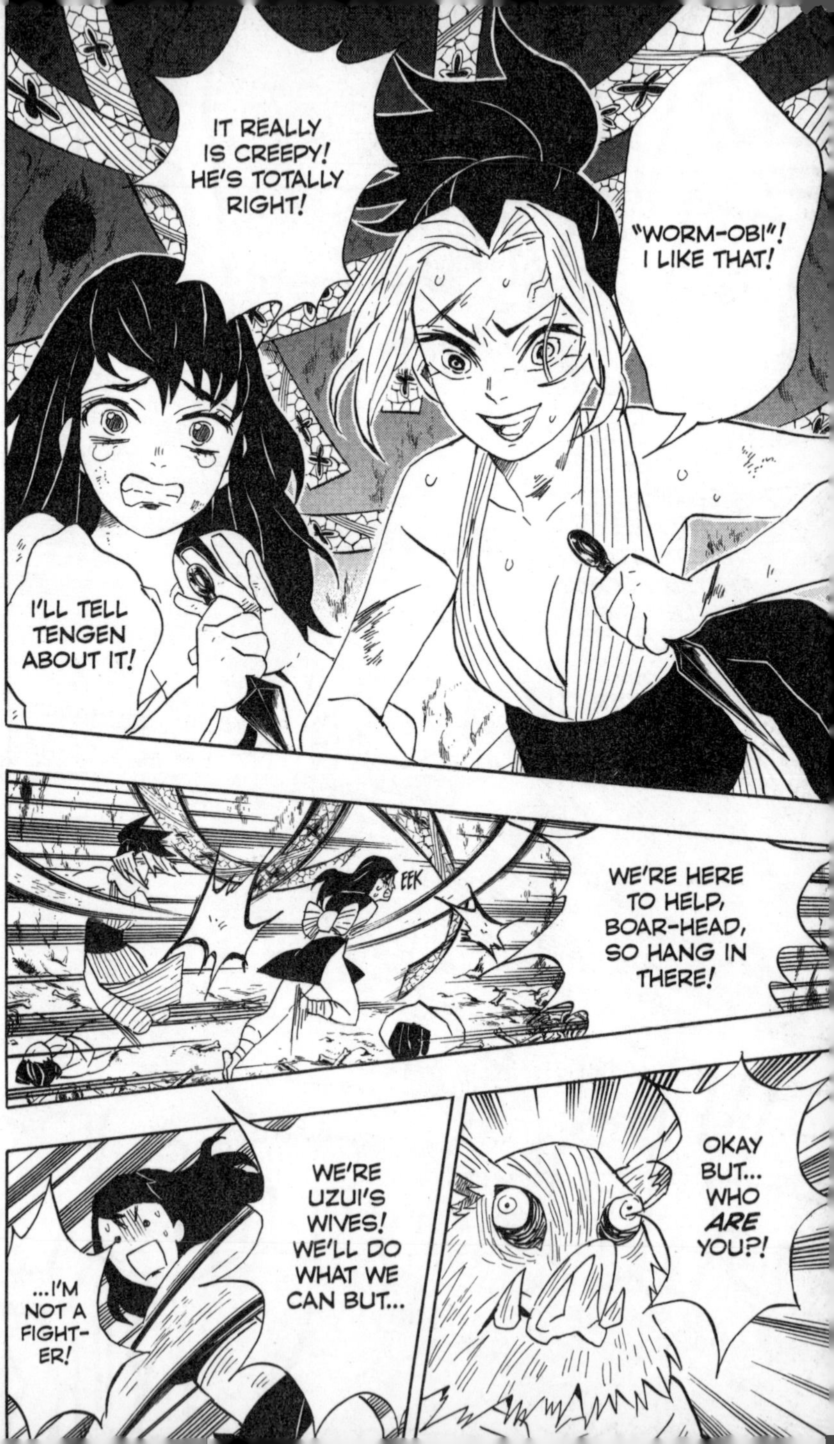
"WORM-OBI"! I LIKE THAT!
IT REALLY IS CREEPY! HE'S TOTALLY RIGHT!
I'LL TELL TENGEN ABOUT IT!
WE'RE HERE TO HELP, BOAR-HEAD, SO HANG IN THERE!
EEK
OKAY BUT... WHO *ARE* YOU?!
WE'RE UZUI'S WIVES! WE'LL DO WHAT WE CAN BUT...
...I'M NOT A FIGHT-ER!

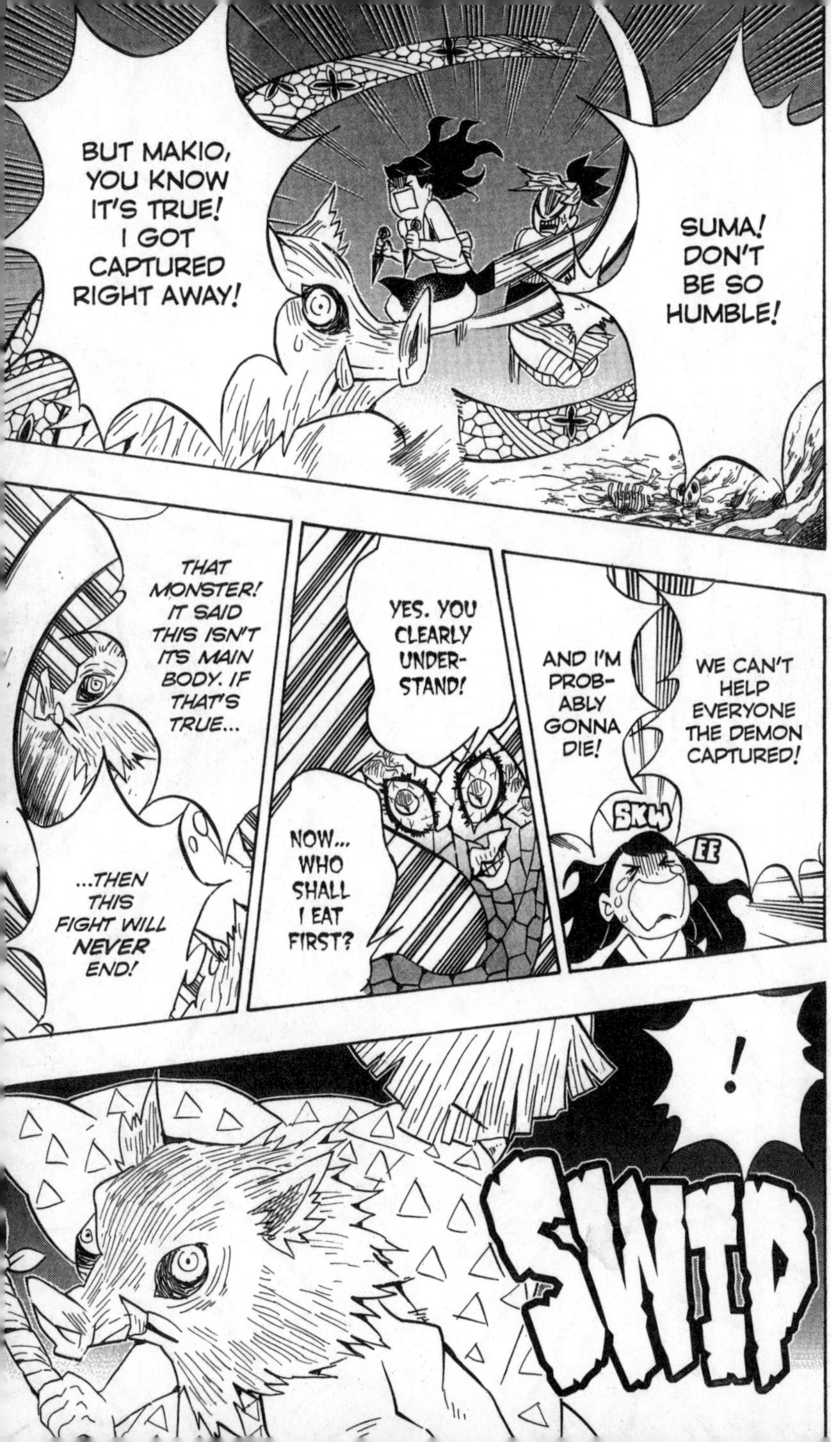
SUMA! DON'T BE SO HUMBLE!
BUT MAKIO, YOU KNOW IT'S TRUE! I GOT CAPTURED RIGHT AWAY!
WE CAN'T HELP EVERYONE THE DEMON CAPTURED!
AND I'M PROB-ABLY GONNA DIE!
SKWEE
YES. YOU CLEARLY UNDER-STAND!
NOW... WHO SHALL I EAT FIRST?
THAT MONSTER! IT SAID THIS ISN'T ITS MAIN BODY. IF THAT'S TRUE...
...THEN THIS FIGHT WILL NEVER END!
!
SNIP

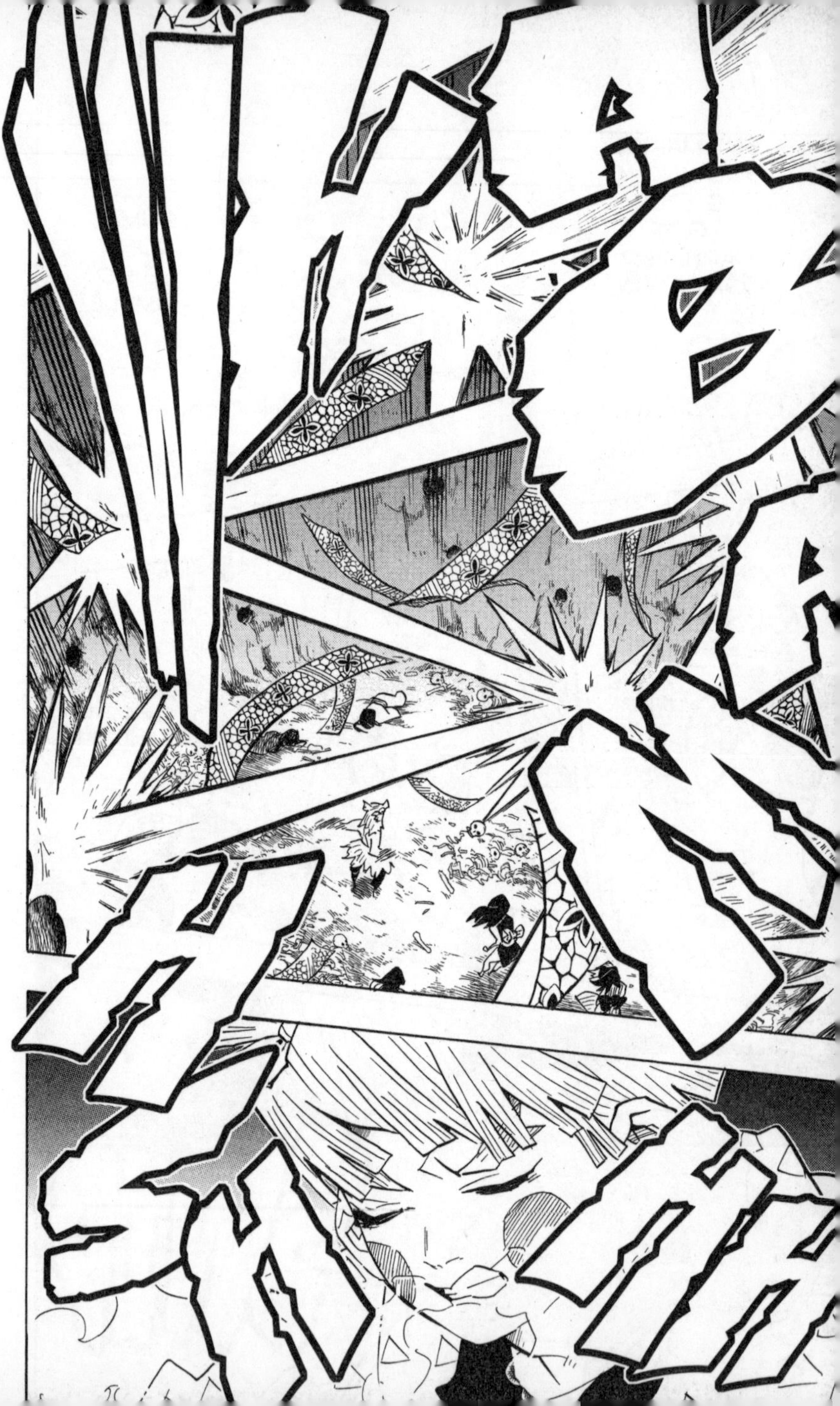

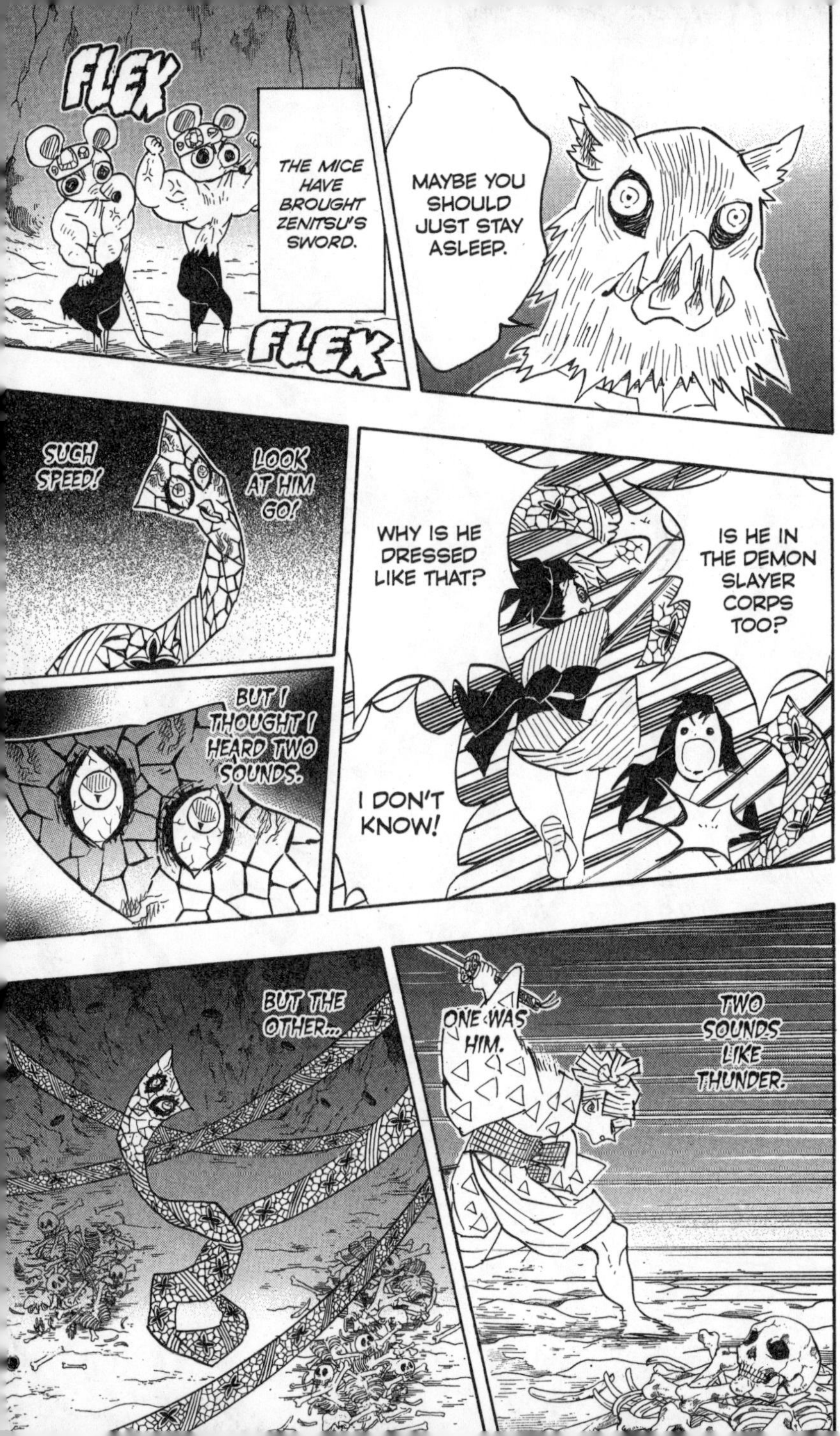
MAYBE YOU SHOULD JUST STAY ASLEEP.
FLEX
THE MICE HAVE BROUGHT ZENITSU'S SWORD.
FLEX
IS HE IN THE DEMON SLAYER CORPS TOO?
WHY IS HE DRESSED LIKE THAT?
I DON'T KNOW!
LOOK AT HIM GO!
SUCH SPEED!
BUT I THOUGHT I HEARD TWO SOUNDS.
TWO SOUNDS LIKE THUNDER.
ONE WAS HIM.
BUT THE OTHER...

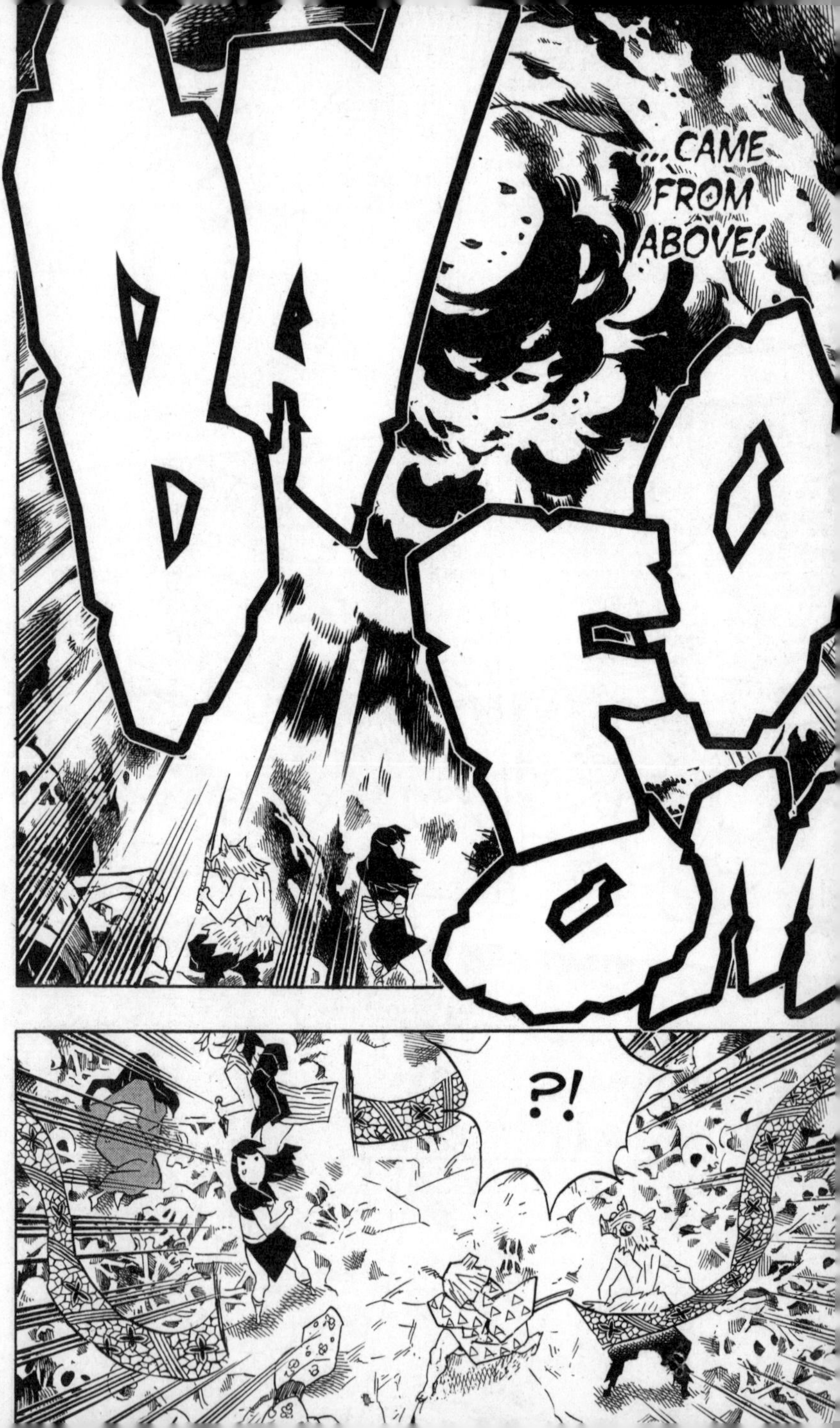
...CAME FROM ABOVE!
?!

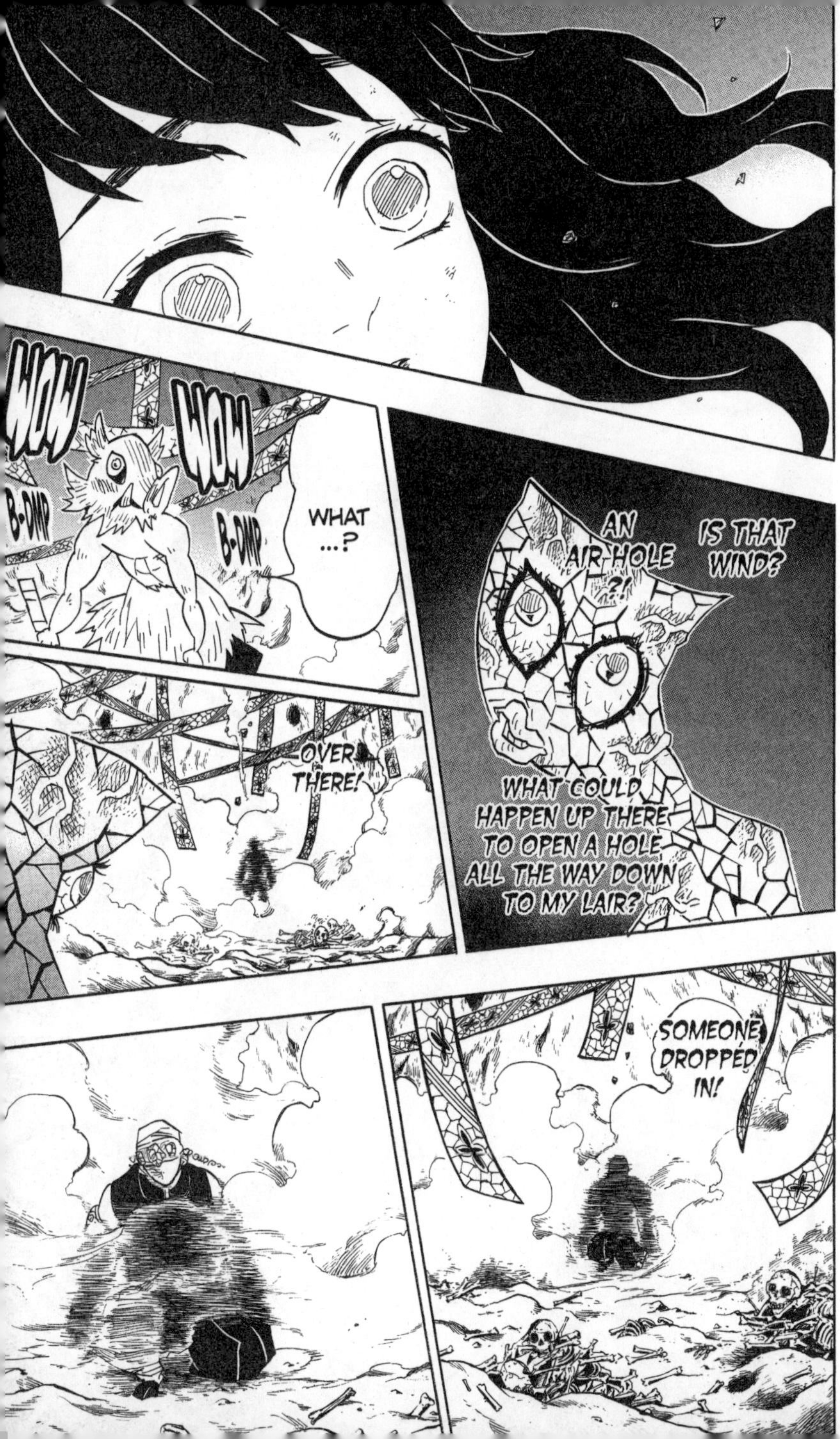
IS THAT WIND?
AN AIR HOLE ?!
WHAT COULD HAPPEN UP THERE TO OPEN A HOLE ALL THE WAY DOWN TO MY LAIR?
WHAT ...?
WOW
B-DMP
WOW
B-DMP
OVER THERE!
SOMEONE DROPPED IN!

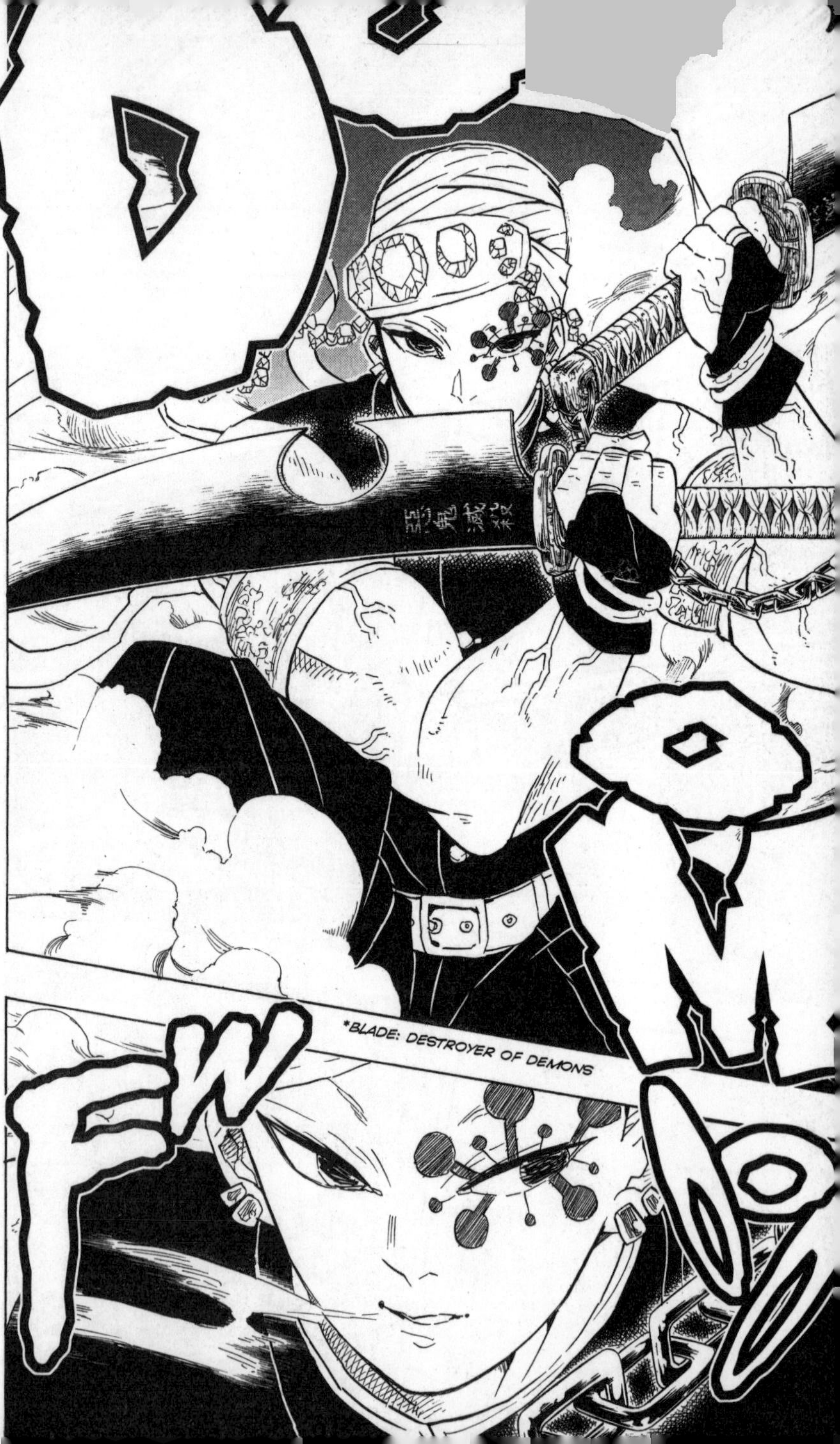
*BLADE: DESTROYER OF DEMONS

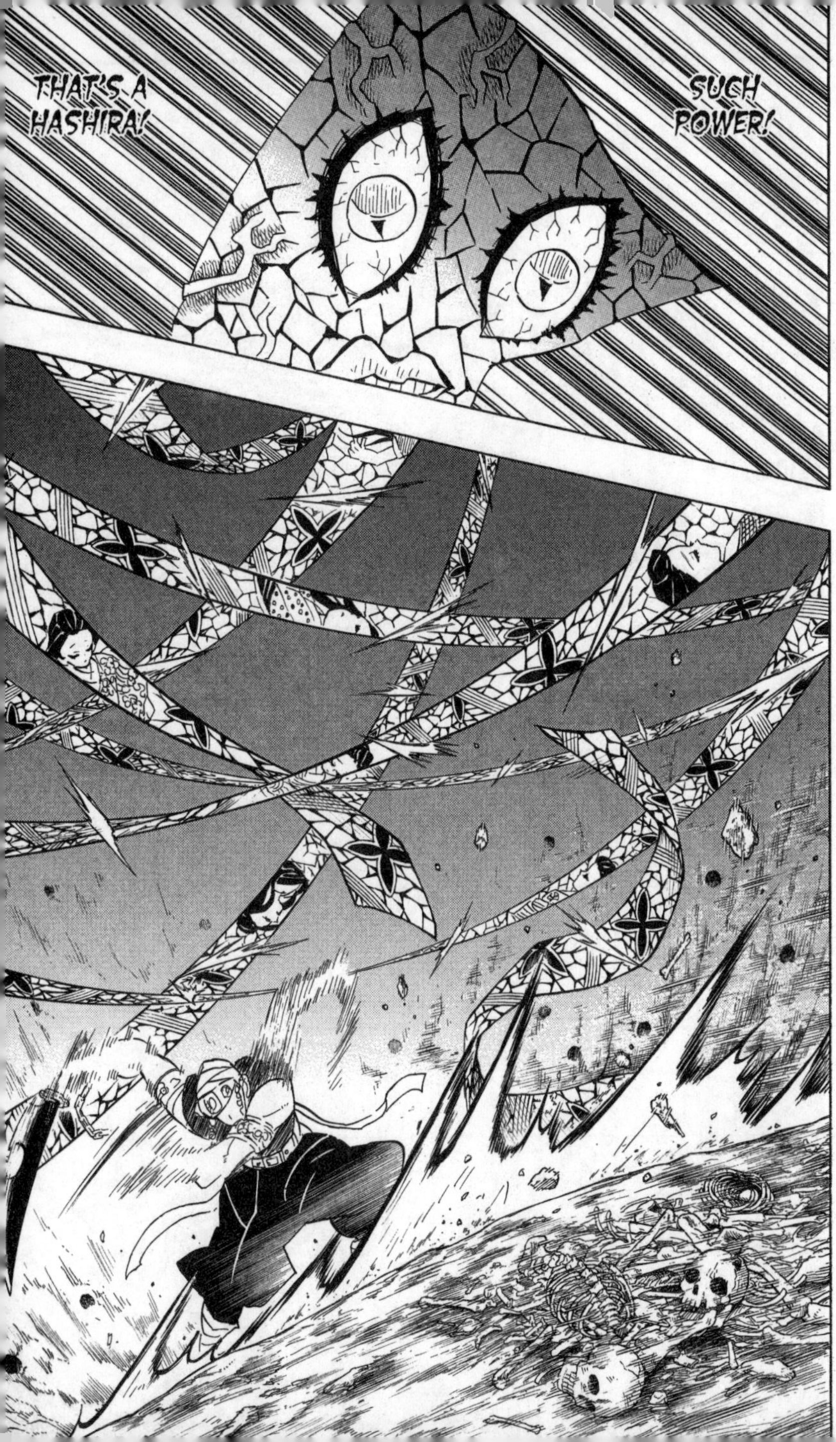
SUCH POWER!
THAT'S A HASHIRA!

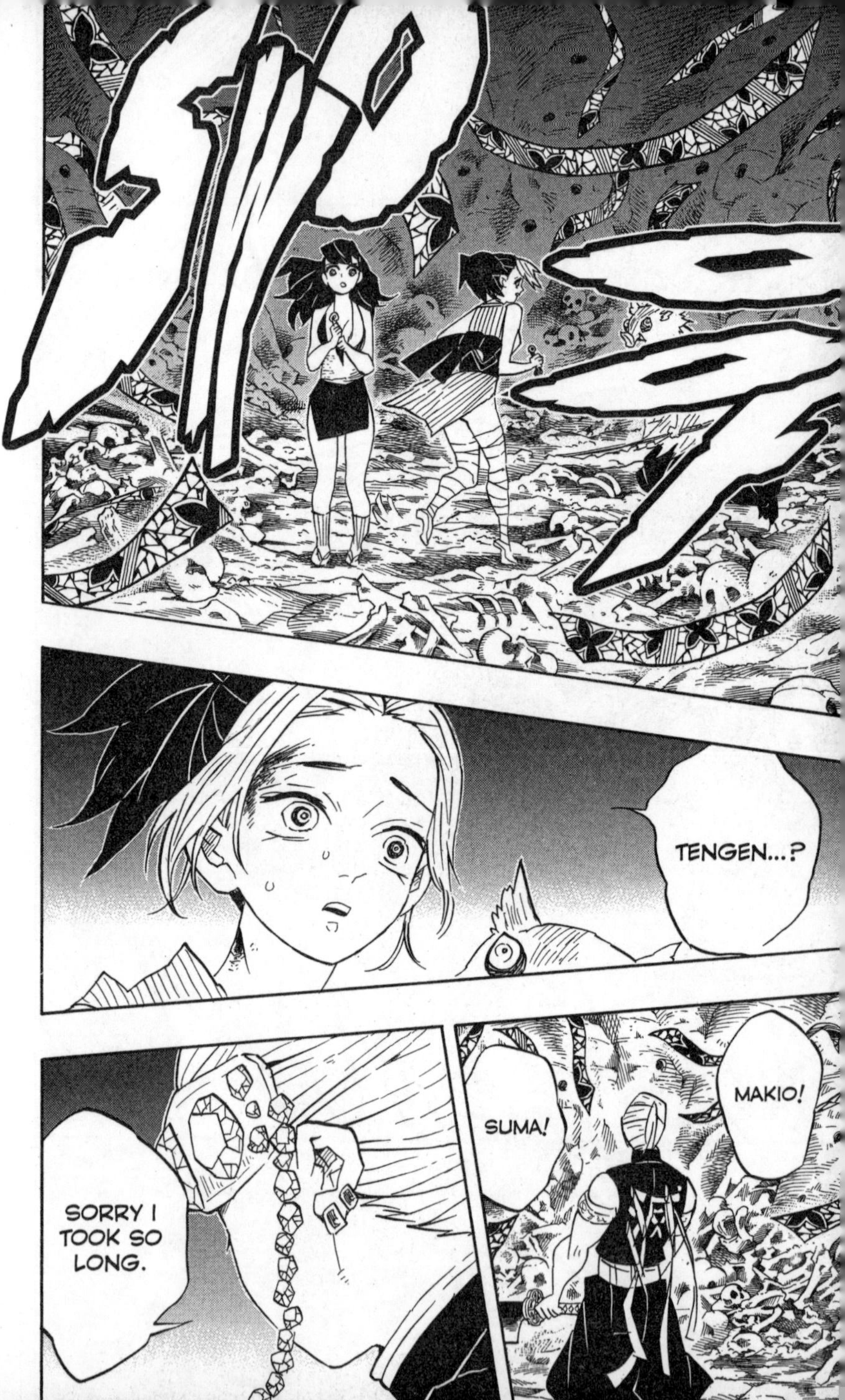
TENGEN...?
MAKIO!
SUMA!
SORRY I TOOK SO LONG.

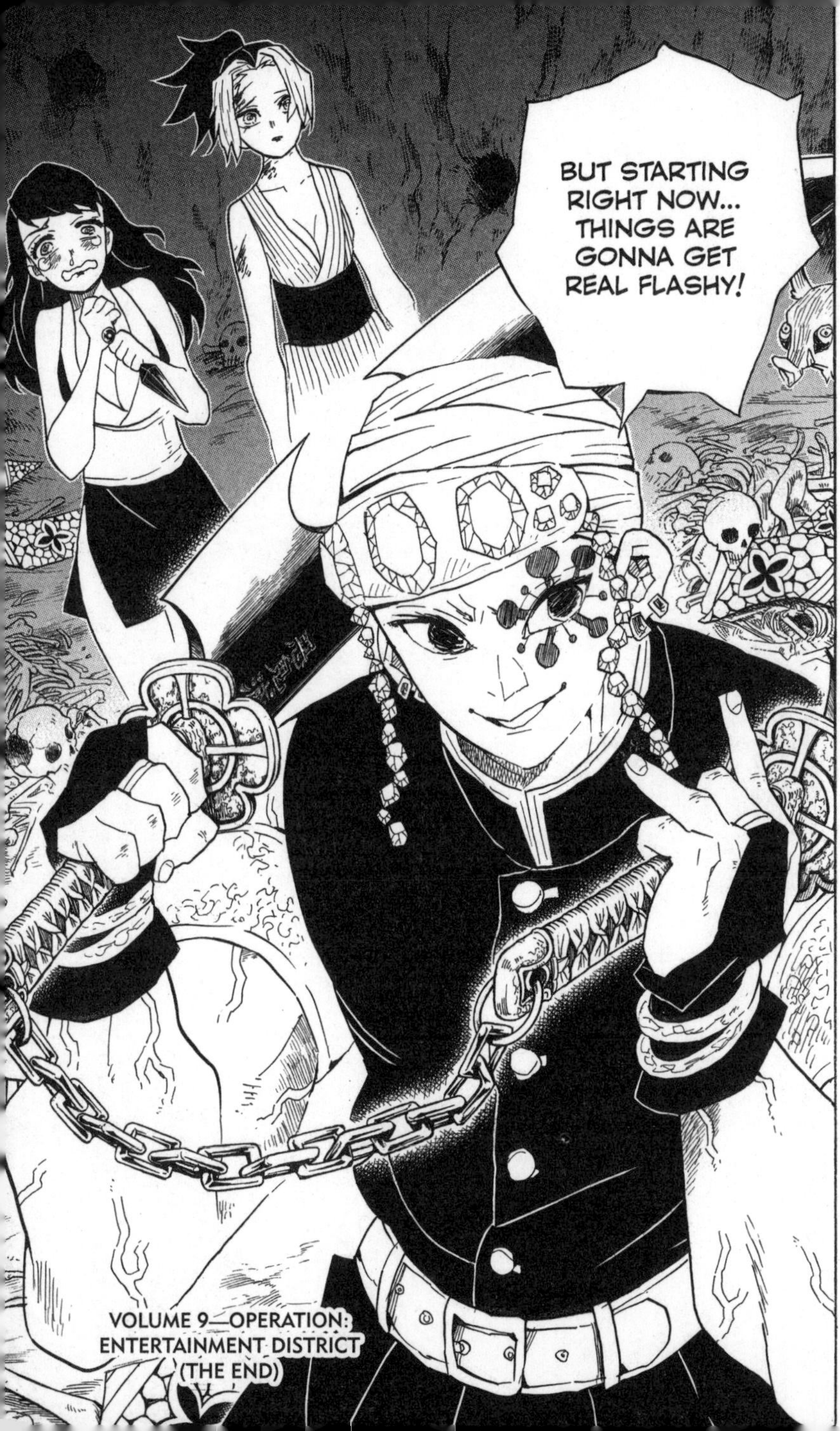
BUT STARTING RIGHT NOW... THINGS ARE GONNA GET REAL FLASHY!
VOLUME 9—OPERATION: ENTERTAINMENT DISTRICT (THE END)

Junior High and High School ☆ Kimetsu Academy Story

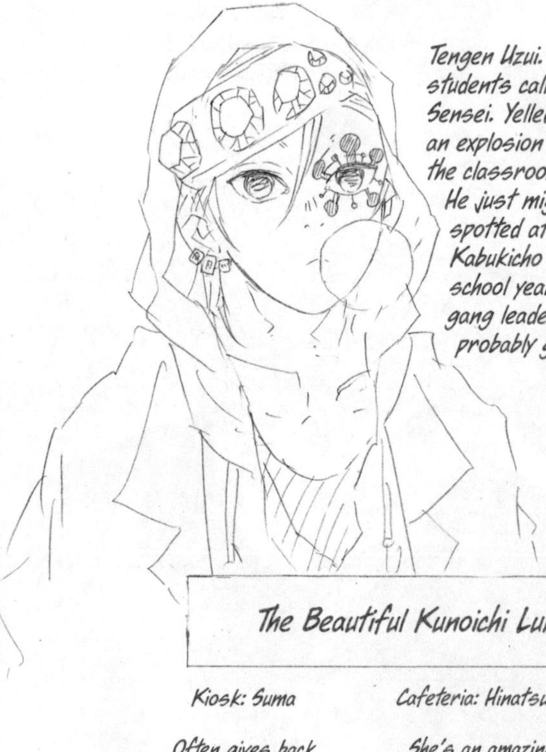

Tengen Uzui. Art teacher. The students call him Gangsta Sensei. Yelled out that art is an explosion and then blew up the classroom with dynamite. He just might have been spotted at a fight in Kabukicho during his high school years. He was a gang leader, so he's probably good in a fight.

The Beautiful Kunoichi Lunch Ladies

Kiosk: Suma

Often gives back the wrong change.

Cafeteria: Hinatsuru

She's an amazing cook. People say she has a golden palate.

Cafeteria: Makio

Speaks loudly. Works fast. Has a quick temper.

*Kunoichi is a nickname the boy students gave them.

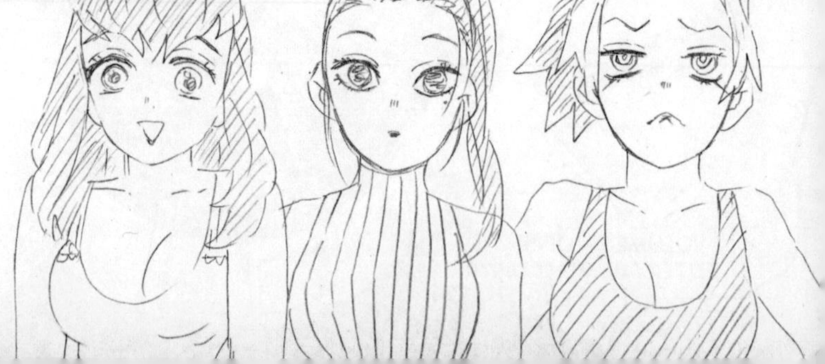

Tamio Enmu. A big train geek. He keeps doing weird things that sometimes cause the trains to run late. He's been arrested six times. He isn't sorry about inconveniencing people, so other train fans hate him. Actually, everyone hates him. And he has no girlfriend.

Stolen camera →

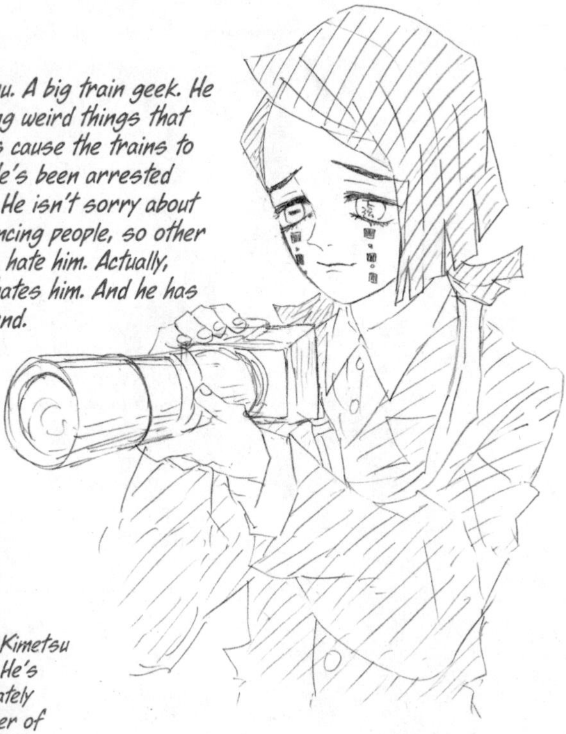

Kimetsu Town

Shinjuro Rengoku
Instructor at the Kimetsu Town kendo dojo. He's been depressed lately because the number of students is decreasing.

Senjuro Rengoku
Year 1, junior high. A boy who seems to be average at everything. Likes to read.

Ruka Rengoku
She teaches a calligraphy class. Her expression is nearly emotionless, so many people are scared of her at first.

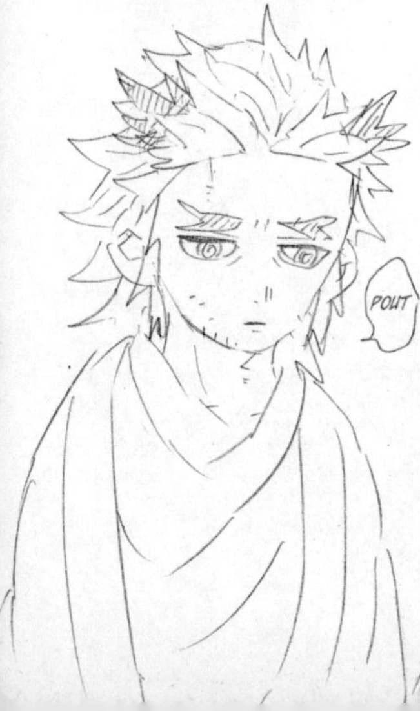

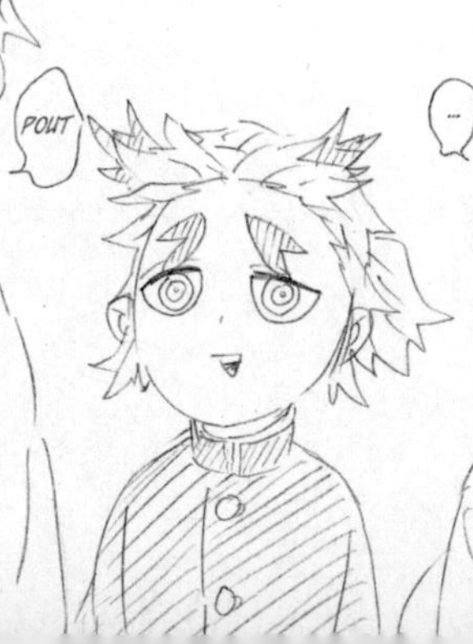
POUT

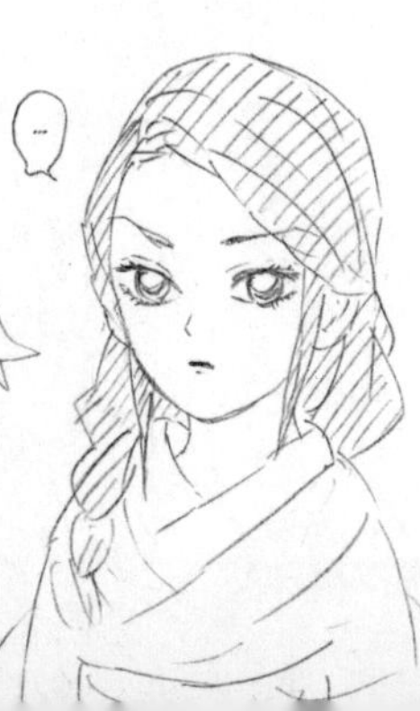
...

Black ✳ Clover

STORY & ART BY YŪKI TABATA

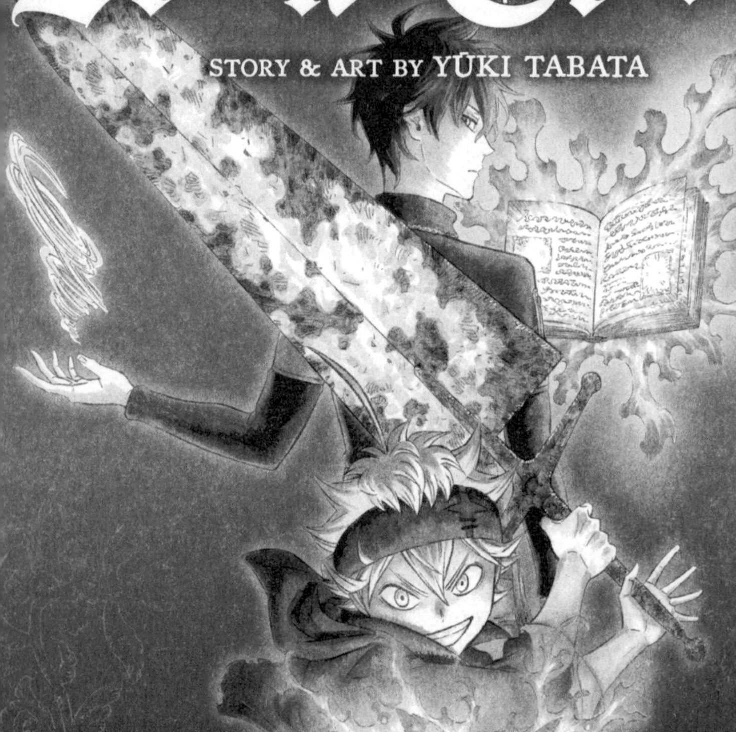

Asta is a young boy who dreams of becoming the greatest mage in the kingdom. Only one problem—he can't use any magic! Luckily for Asta, he receives the incredibly rare five-leaf clover grimoire that gives him the power of anti-magic. Can someone who can't use magic really become the Wizard King? One thing's for sure—Asta will never give up!

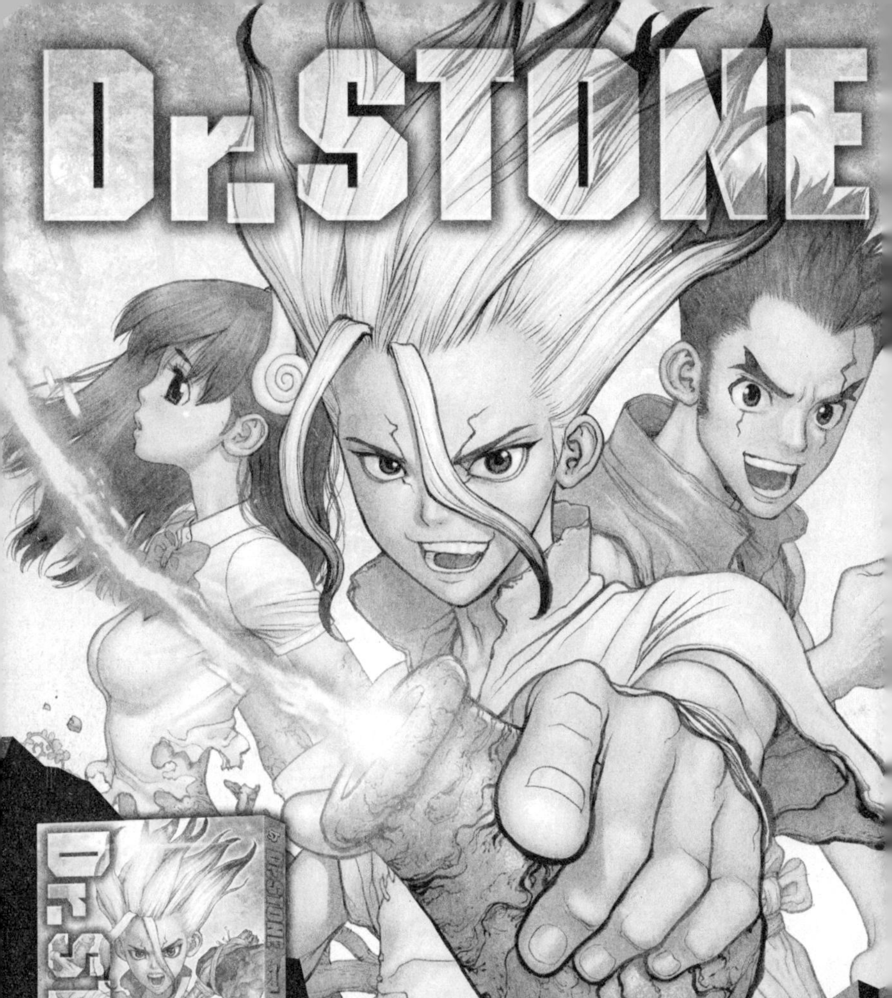

Dr.STONE

STORY BY
RIICHIRO INAGAKI

ART BY
BOICHI

One fateful day, all of humanity turned to stone. Many millennia later, Taiju frees himself from petrification and finds himself surrounded by statues. The situation looks grim—until he runs into his science-loving friend Senku! Together they plan to restart civilization with the power of science!

YOU'RE READING THE
WRONG WAY!

142

DEMON SLAYER: KIMETSU NO YAIBA
reads from right to left, starting in the
upper-right corner. Japanese is read from
right to left, meaning that action, sound
effects and word-balloon order are com-
pletely reversed from English order.